P9-DBQ-775

HISTORICAL ATLAS OF ISLAM

Historical Atlas of Islam

Malise Ruthven
with
Azim Nanji

Harvard University Press
Cambridge, Massachusetts
2004

Printed in Singapore

Library of Congress Cataloging-in-Publication Data

Ruthven, Malise
Historical atlas of Islam / by Malise Ruthven; with Azim Nanji
p. cm
ISBN 0-674-01385-9 (hc : alk. paper)
1. Islamic countries—Historical geography—Maps. 2. Islamic countries—Civilization—Maps. 3. Islam—History—Maps. 4. Civilization, Islamic—Maps. I. Nanji, Azim. II. Title

G1786.S1R9 2004
911'.1767—dc22 2003055208

CONTENTS

Introduction

Since September 11th, 2001, barely a day passes without stories about Islam—the religion of about one-fifth of humanity—appearing in the media. The terrorists, who hijacked four American airliners and flew them into the World Trade Center in New York and the Pentagon near Washington, killed more than three thousand people. This unleashed a "War on Terrorism" by the United States and its allies, leading to the removal of two Muslim governments, one in Afghanistan and the other in Iraq. It raised the profile of Islam throughout the world as a subject for analysis and discussion. The debates, in newspaper columns and broadcasting studios, in cafes, bars, and homes, have been heated and passionate. Questions that were previously discussed in the rarified atmosphere of academic conferences or graduate seminars, have entered the mainstream of public consciousness. What is the "law of jihad"? How is it that a "religion of peace" subscribed to by millions of ordinary, decent believers, can become an ideology of hatred for an angry minority? Why has Islam after the fall of communism become so freighted with passionate intensity? Or, to use the title of a best-selling essay by Bernard Lewis, the doyen of Orientalist scholars, "What went wrong?" with Islamic history, with its relationship with itself, and with the modern world?

Such questions are no longer academic, but are arguably of vital concern to most of the peoples living on this planet. Few would deny that Islam, or some variation thereof—whether distorted, perverted, corrupted, or hijacked by extremists—has become a force to be reckoned with, or at least a label attached to a phenomenon with menacing potentialities. Numerous atrocities have been attributed to and claimed by Islamic extremists, both before and since 9/11, causing mayhem and carnage in many of the world's cities and tourist destinations: Nairobi, Dar es Salaam, Mombasa, Riyadh, Casablanca, Bali, Tunisia, Jakarta, Bombay (Mumbhai), and Istanbul. The list grows longer, the casualties mount. The responses of people and their governments are angry and perplexed. The far-reaching consequences of these responses for international peace and security should be enough to convince anyone (and not just the media editors who mold public consciousness to fit their advertisers' priorities) that extreme manifestations of Islam are setting the agenda for argument and action in the twenty-first century.

Muslims living in the West and in the growing areas of the Muslim world that come within the West's electronic footprint understandably resent the negative exposure that comes with the increasing concerns of outsiders. Islam is a religion of peace: the word "Islam," a verbal noun meaning submission

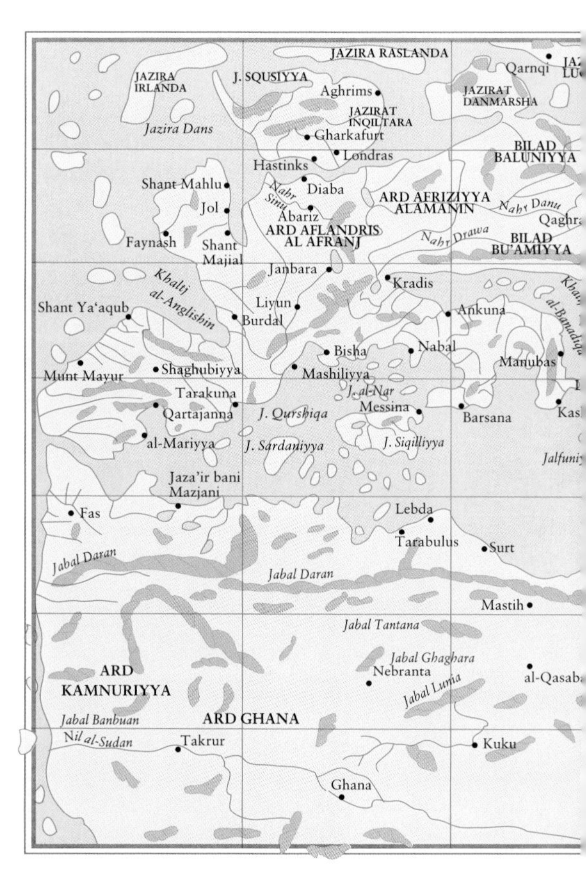

(to God) is etymologically related to the word salam, meaning peace. The standard greeting most Muslims use when joining a gathering or meeting strangers is "as-salaam alaikum"—"Peace be upon you." Westerners who accuse Islam of being a violent religion misunderstand its nature. Attaching the label "Muslim" or "Islamic" to acts of terrorism is grossly unfair. When a right-wing Christian fanatic like Timothy McVeigh blew up a US federal building in Oklahoma City, the worst atrocity committed on American soil before 9/11, no one described him a "Christian" terrorist. In the view of many of Islam's adherents, "Westerners" who have abandoned their own faith, or are blinkered by religious prejudice, do not "understand" Islam. Certain hostile media distort Western viewpoints, prejudicing sentiments and attitudes with Islamophobia—the equivalent of anti-Semitism applied to Muslims instead of Jews. Some scholars, trained in western academies, are accused of viewing Islam through the misshapen lens of Orientalism, a discipline corrupted by its associations with imperialism, when specialist knowledge was placed at the service of power.

This is fraught, contested territory and the writer who ventures into it does so at his or her peril. As with other religious traditions, every generalization about Islam is open to challenge, because for every normative description of Islamic faith, belief, and practice, there exist important variants and considerable diversity. The problem of definition is made more difficult because there is no overarching ecclesiastical institution, no Islamic papacy, with prescriptive power to decree what is and what is not Islamic. (Even protestant churches define their religious positions in contradistinction to Roman Catholicism.)

Being Muslim, like being a Jew, embraces ancestry as well as belief. People described as

The World according to al-Idrisi 549–1154

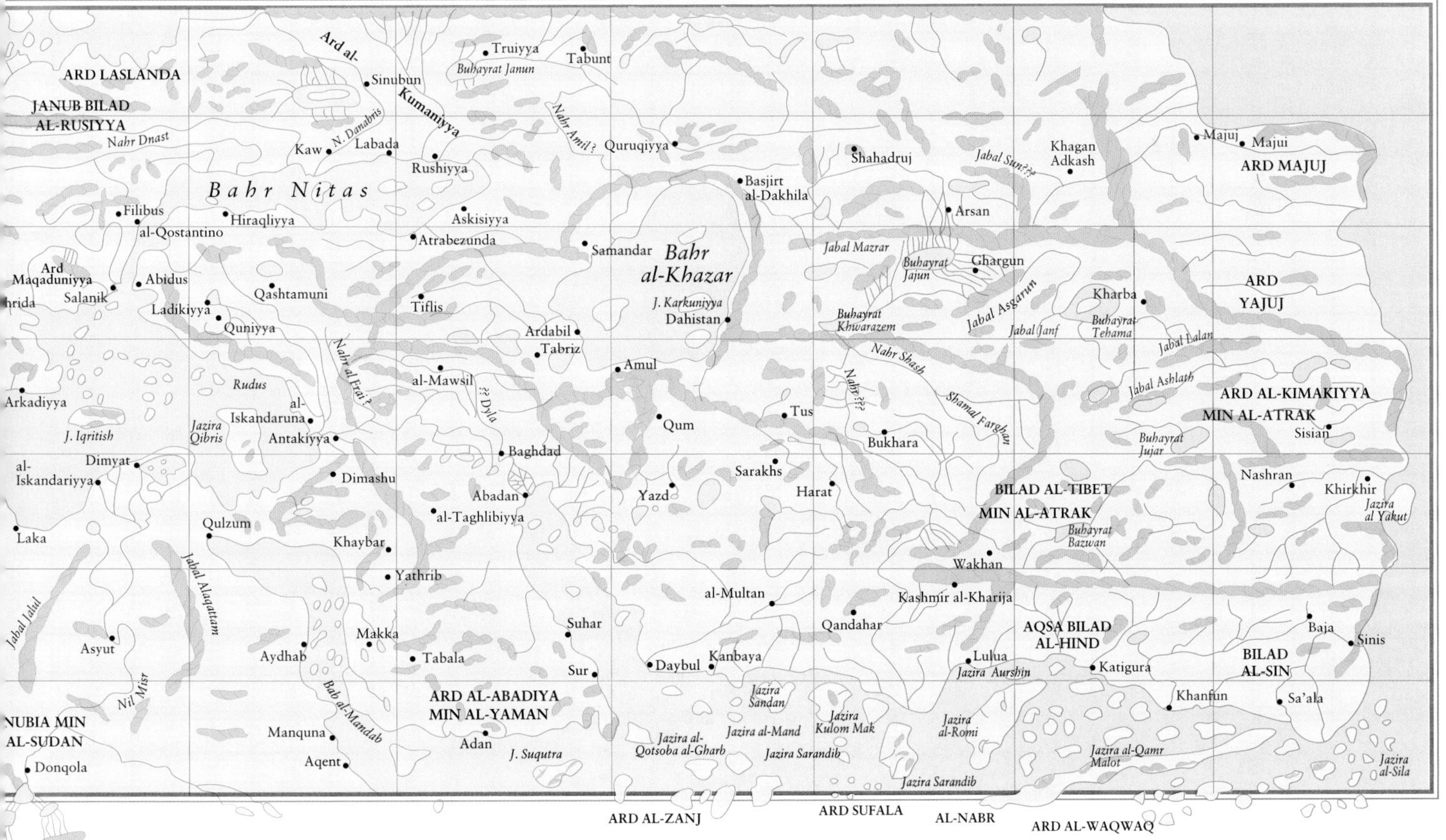

Muslims are religiously observant in different ways. One can be culturally Muslim, as one can be culturally Jewish, without subscribing to a particular set of religious prescriptions or beliefs. It would not be inappropriate to describe many nonreligious Americans and Europeans as "cultural Christians" given the seminal importance played by Christianity in the development of Western culture. The fact that the term is rarely, if ever, used is revealing of western cultural hegemony and its pretensions to universality. The Christian underpinning of Western culture is so taken for granted that no one troubles to make it apparent. At the same time the term "Christian" has been appropriated by protestant fundamentalists who seek to define themselves in contradistinction to secular humanists or religious believers with whose outlook they violently disagree.

Similar problems of definition apply in the Muslim world. Just as there are theological disagreements between Christian churches over all sorts of questions of belief and ritual, within the Islamic fold there are groups who differ from themselves ritualistically or in terms of their respective tradition of interpretation and practice.

Among the major groups in Islam, historically, the two most significant are the Sunni and Shia.

The Shia maintain that, shortly before his death, the prophet Muhammad (c. 570–632), designated Ali, his first cousin and husband of his daughter Fatima, as his successor. They further believe that this succession continued in a line of Imams (spiritual leaders) descendent from Ali and Fatima, each specifically designated by the previous Imam. The larger body of the Shia, the "Twelvers" or Imamis, believe that the last of these leaders who "disappeared" in 873 will reappear as the Mahdi or messiah at some future time.

The Sunnis, on the other hand, maintain that the Prophet had made an indication favoring one of his companions, Abu Bakr (r. 624–632), who was accepted as Caliph or successor by agreement of the main leaders in the community after the death of the Prophet. He, in turn, appointed Umar (r. 634–644), who on his deathbed designated Uthman (r. 644–656), after consultation with leading Muslims. Uthman was succeeded by Ali (r. 656–661), again with the consent of leading Muslims of the time. In the view of the Sunni majority the four caliphs constitute a "rightly guided Caliphate."

Over time the Shia and Sunni both developed distinctive community identities. They are divided into various branches and organized into different movements and tendencies. While these, and other groups, differed with each other and often fought over their differences, the general tenor of relations, in premodern urban societies, tended to be based on mutual coexistence and intellectual debate.

In recent times, however, there has been a tendency for extremist sects and radical groups to anathematize their religious opponents, or to declare those ruling over them to be outside the pale of Islam. This narrow perspective may be contrasted with a growing awareness among the majority of Muslim peoples of the diversity and plurality of interpretations within the Umma.

Currently, the climate of religious intolerance manifested in some parts of the Muslim world has complex origins and may be symptomatic, like the puritan extremism that flourished in Europe in the seventeenth century, of the dislocating effects of economic and social changes. As will become clear from the maps and essays that follow, modernity came to the Muslim world on the wings of colonial power, rather than as a consequence of internally generated transformations. The "best community" decreed by God for "ordering the good and forbidding the evil" has lost the moral, and political, hegemony it held in what was once the most civilized part of the world, outside China. When

Islam was in the ascendant, so was the climate of tolerance it engendered. Muslim scholars and theologians polemicized against each other but were careful not to denounce those who affirmed the shahada—the declaration of faith—and who prayed toward Mecca. As the American scholar, Carl Ernst observes, "In any society in the world today, religious pluralism is a sociological fact. If one group claims authority over all the rest, demanding their allegiance and submission, this will be experienced as the imposition of power through religious rhetoric." [Carl Ernst, *Following Muhammad: Rethinking Islam in the Contemporary World* (London and Chapel Hill, p, 206]

In principle, if not always in practice, a Muslim is one who follows Islam, an Arabic word meaning "submission" or, more precisely, "self-surrender" to the will of God as revealed to the prophet Muhammad. These revelations, delivered orally over the period of Muhammad's active prophetic career from about 610 until his death, are contained in the Koran, the scripture that stands at the foundation of the Islamic religion and the diverse cultural systems that flow from it. A few revisionist scholars working in Western universities have challenged the traditional Islamic account of the Koran's origins, arguing that the text was constructed out of a larger body of oral materials following the Arab conquest of the Fertile Crescent. The great majority of scholars, however, Muslim and non-Muslim, regard the Koran as the written record of the revelations accumulated in the course of Muhammad's career. Unlike the Bible, there are no signs of multiple authorship. In contrast to the New Testament in particular, where the sayings of Jesus have been incorporated into four distinct narratives of his life presumed to have been written by different authors, the Koran contains many allusions to events in the Prophet's life, but does not spell them out in detail. The story of Muhammad's career as Prophet and Statesman (if one can use a rather modern term for the leader of the movement that united the tribes of the Arabian Peninsula) was constructed from a different body of oral materials. Known as Hadith (traditions or reports about the Prophet's behavior), they acquired written form after Muhammad's death.

The Koran is divided into 114 sections known as suras (rows), each of which is composed of varying numbers of verses known as ayas (signs or miracles). Apart from the first sura, the Fatiha, or Opening, a seven-verse invocation used as a prayer in numerous rituals, including daily prayers or salat, the suras are arranged in approximate order of decreasing length, with the shortest at the end and the longest near the beginning. Most standard editions divide the suras into passages revealed in Mecca (which tend to be shorter, and hence located near the end of the book) and those belonging to the period of the Prophet's sojourn in Medina, where he emigrated with his earliest followers to escape persecution in Mecca in 622, the Year One of the Muslim era. Meccan passages, especially the early ones, convey vivid messages about personal accountability, reward and punishment—in heaven and hell—while celebrating the glories and beauty of the natural world as proof of God's creative power and sovereignty. The Medinese passages, while replicating many of the same themes, contain positive teachings on social and legal issues (including rules governing sexual relations and inheritance, and punishments prescribed for certain categories of crime). Such passages, supplemented with material from the Hadith literature came to be the key sources for the development of a legal system knowns as the Sharia. Different scholars of Muslim thoughts added other sources to create a methodology for the future systematization and implementation of the Sharia.

For believing Muslims, the Koran is the direct speech of God, dictated without human editing. Muhammad has been described by some modern Muslim scholars as a passive transmitter of the Divine Word. The Prophet, himself, is supposed to have been ummi (illiterate), although some scholars question this as he was an active and successful merchant. For a majority of Muslims, the Koran, whose text was written down and stabilized during the reign of the third caliph, Uthman (r. 644–656), was "uncreated" and coeternal with God. Hence, for believing Muslims, the Koran occupies the position Christ has for Christians. God reveals himself, not through a person, but through the language contained in a holy text. Other religious traditions, including Buddhism, Christianity, Hinduism, Judaism, Sikhism, and Zoroastrianism, privilege their foundational texts as sacred. Muslim rulers recognized this common principle by granting religious toleration to the ahl al-kitab (Peoples of the Book).

In its initial phase the rapid expansion of Islam beyond Arabia occurred on the basis of the Arab conquest of the Fertile Crescent and lands further afield in the century or so following the Prophet's death in 632. Faith in Islam and the Prophet's divine calling—as well as the desire for booty—united the Arabian tribes into a formidable fighting machine. They defeated both the Byzantine and Sasanian armies, opening part of the Byzantine Empire and the whole of Persia to Muslim conquest and settlement. At first Islam remained primarily the religion of the "Arab". Muslim commanders housed their tribal battalions in separate military cantonments outside the cities they conquered, leaving their new subjects (Christian, Jewish, or Zoroastrian) to regulate their own affairs so long as they paid the jizya (poll-tax) in lieu of military service. The process of Islamization occurred gradually, through marriage, as the leading families of the subject populations sought to join the Muslim elites. It also occurred as impoverished or uprooted sub-

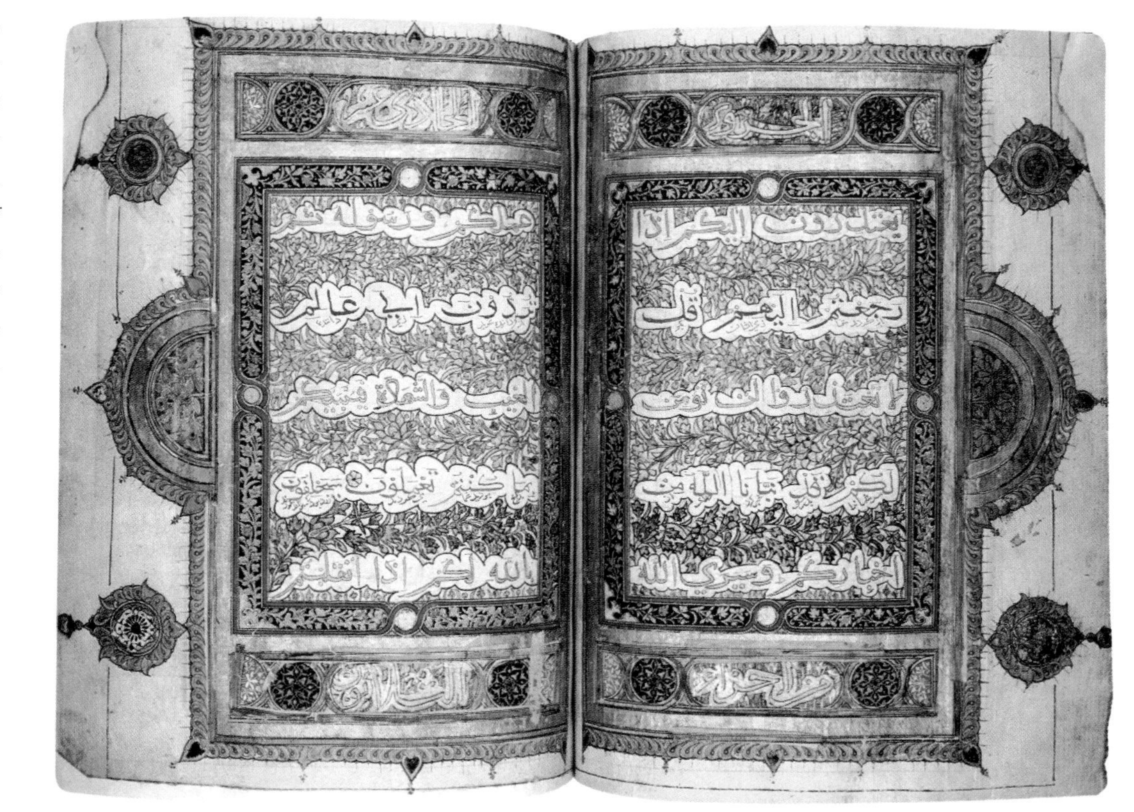

The illuminated double page from the Koran in the Bihari script. This copy was completed in 1399, the year after Timur's conquest of Delhi. The passage, from the Al-Tawba (Sura of Repentance), refers to the Prophet's bedouin allies who are not to be excused for failing to join one of his campaigns.

jects found support in the religion of their rulers, or as people disenchanted with their former rulers finding a congenial spiritual home in one that honored their traditions while representing their teachings in a new, creative synthesis. The role of early Muslim missionaries was also crucial in this process.

Muslim theology, however, did have one dynamic cultural dimension, which may help to explain its evolution of an "Arab" religion into a universal faith. As the quintessential "religion of the Book," which represented the divine Word as manifested in a written text, Islam carried with it the prestige of learning and literacy into illiterate cultures. The cult of the book, like Voltaire's definition of hypocrisy, was the compliment, not of vice to virtue, but of illiteracy to learning. The prophet himself is supposed to have been illiterate (although some scholars question this, since he was an active and successful merchant). His epiphany came in the form of language. Time and again the nomadic peoples on the fringes of the Muslim empires would take over the centers of power, and in so doing civilize themselves, becoming in turn the bearers of Muslim cultural prestige. After the disintegration of the great Abbasid Empire, the dream of a universal caliphate embracing the whole of the Islamic world (and, indeed, the rest of humanity) ceased to be a viable project. The lines of communication were too long for the center to be able to suppress the ambitions of local dynasts. But the prestige of literacy, symbolized by Koran and its glorious calligraphic elaborations on the walls of mosques and other public buildings, as well as in the meticulously copied versions of the book itself, was powerful. Even Mongol invaders, notorious for their cruelty, would succumb to the spiritual and aesthetic power of Islam in the western part of their dominions.

The maps in this book do not aim to provide a comprehensive account of the shifting patterns of state and religious authority that prevailed during the case sweep of Islamic history from the time of the Prophet to the present. But it is hoped that the will illuminate important aspects of this history, by opening windows into significant areas of the distant and recent pat, thereby helping to explain the legacy of conflicts—as well as opportunities—the past has bequeathed to the present. Geography is vital for the understanding of Islamic history and is problematic relationship with modernity.

As the maps in this Atlas illustrate, the central belt of Islamic territories stretching from the Atlantic Ocean to the Indus Valley were perennially at the mercy of nomadic or semi-nomadic invaders. In premodern times, before gunpowder weapons, air power, and modern systems of communication brought peripheral regions under the control of central governments (usually under colonial auspices), the cities were vulnerable to attack by nomadic predators. The genius of the Islamic system lay in providing the converted tribesmen with a system of law, practice and learning within a foundation of faith to which they became acculturated over time.

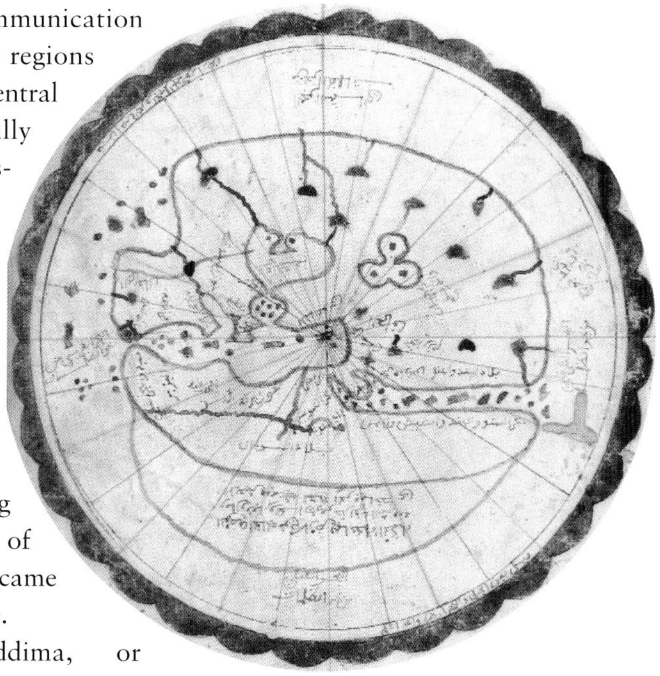

A world map drawn in 1571–72 by the al-Sharafi al-Sifaqsi family in the town of Sfax, Tunisia.

In his Muqaddima, or "Proglomena" to the History of the World, the Arab philosopher of history, Ibn Khaldun (1332–1406), developed a theory of cyclic renewal and state formation, which analyzed this process in the context of his native North Africa. According to his theory, in the arid zones where rainfall is sparse, pastoralism remains the principal mode of agricultural production. Unlike peasants, pastoralists are organised along the "tribal" lines (patrilineal kinship groups). They are relatively free from government control. Enjoying greater mobility than urban people, they cannot be regularly taxed. Nor can they be brought under the control of feudal lords who will appropriate a part of their produce in return for extending protection. Indeed, in the arid lands it is the tribesmen who are usually armed, and who, at times, can hold the city to ransom, or conquer it. Ibn Khaldun's insights tell us why it is usually inappropriate to speak of Muslim "feudalism," except in the strictly limited context of the great river valley systems of Egypt and Mesopotamia, where a settled peasantry farmed the land. In the arid regions, pastoralists move their flocks seasonally across the land according to complex arrangements with other users. Usufruct is not ownership. Property and territory are not coterminous, as they became in the high rainfall regions of Europe. Here feudalism and its offshoot, capitalism, took root and eventually created the bourgeois state that would dominate the countryside, commercializing agriculture and subjecting rural society to urban values and control. In most parts of Western Asia and North Africa, in contrast, the peoples at the margins continued to elude state control until the coming of air power. Even now the process is far from complete in places like Afghanistan, where tribal structures have resisted the authority of the central government.

Urbane Moroccans had a revealing term for the tribal regions of their country: bled al-siba—the land of insolence—as contrasted with bled al-makhzen, the civilized center, which periodically falls prey to it. The superiority of the tribes, in Ibn Khaldun's theory, depends on asabiya, a term which is usually translates as group feeling or social solidarity. This asabiyya derives ultimately from the harsher environment of the desert or arid lands, where there is little division of labor and humans depend for their survival on the bonds of kinship. City life, by contrast, lacks a common or corporative asabiyya. The absence of bourgeois solidarity, in which the corporate group interests of the burghers transcend the bonds of kinship, may partly be traced to the operations of Muslim law. Unlike the Roman legal tradition, the Sharia contains no provision for the recognition of corporate groups as fictive "persons."

In its classic formulation, Ibn Khaldun's theory applied to the North African milieu he knew and understood best. But it serves as an explanatory model for the wider history of Western Asia and North Africa, from the coming of Islam to the present. The key to the theory is the dialectical interraction between religion and asabiyya. Ibn Khaldun's concept of asabiyya, which is central to his theory of Muslim social and political history, can be made to mesh with modern theories of ethnicity, whether one adopts a "primordial" or "interractive" model. The key to Ibn Khaldun's theory may be found in two of his propositions singled out by the anthropologist and philosopher, Ernest Gellner: (1) "Leadership exists only through superiority, and superiority only through group feeling (asabiyya)" and (2) "Only tribes held together by group feeling can live in the desert."

The superior power of the tribes vis-a-vis the cities provided the conditions under which dynastic military government and its variants, royal government underpinned by mamlukism or institutionalized asabiya, became the norm in Islamic history prior to the European colonial intervention. The absence of the legal recognition of corporative bodies in Islamic law prevented the artificial solidarity of the corporation, a prerequisite for urban capitalist development, from transcending the "natural" solidarities of kinship. In precolonial times the high cultural traditions of Islam constantly interacted with these primordial solidarities or ethnicities: they did not replace them.

Formally the ethic of Islam is opposed to local solidarities, which privilege some believers above others. In theory there exists a single Muslim community—the umma—under the sovereignty of God. In practice this ideal was often modified by recognition of the need to enlist asabiya (tribal ethnicity) in the "path of God." Islamic orthopraxy ritualizes communitas through regular prayer, and pilgrimage, and other devotional practices, and given time, generates the urban scripturalist piety of the high cultural or "Great" tradition. But it does not of itself, forge a permanent congregational community strong enough to transcend the countervailing dynamic of local ethnicities. Be they secular, based on the tribal, village, or even craft-based ethnicities of urban migrants, or sectarian-religious, based on divisions between the different Sunni madhabs (schools of jurisprudence), the various Sufi orders (which tend to be structured, not "communally" but along kinship or parakinship lines) or Sunnis and Shiites.

Like Baptists in the United States, Islam (especially that of the Sunni mainstream, comprising about 90 percent of the world's Muslims) is a conservative, populist force, which resists tight doctrinal or ecclesiastical controls. While Muslim scripturalism and orthopraxy provide a common language which crosses ethnic, racial, and national boundaries—creating the largest "international society" known to the world in premodern times—it has never succeeded in supplying the ideological underpinning for a unified social order that can be translated into common national identity. In the West the institutions of medieval Christianity, allied to Roman legal structures, created the preconditions for the emergence of the modern national state. In Islamdom the moral basis of the state was constantly undermined by the realities of tribal asabiya. These could be admitted de facto, but never accorded de jure recognition. This may be one reason why a civilization that by the tenth and eleventh centuries, far ahead of its Christian competitor, eventually fell behind, to find itself under the political and cultural dominance of people it regarded—and which some of its members still do regard—as infidels.

The Islamic system of precolonial times, embedded in the memory of contemporary Muslims, was brilliantly adapted to the political ecology of its era. Even if the strategy of "waging jihad in the path of God" were adopted for pragmatic or military reasons, Islamic faith and culture were the beneficiaries. The nomad conquerors, Mamluks (soldier-slaves), imported from peripheral regions to keep them at bay, became Islam's foremost champions, defenders of the faith-community and patrons of its cultures and systems of learning.

The social memory of this system exercises a powerful appeal over the imaginations of many young Muslims at this time. This is especially true when the more recent memory of modernization through colonization can be represented as a story of humiliation, retreat, and betrayal of Islam's mission to bring universal truth and justice to a world torn by division and strife. The violence that struck America on September 11th, 2001, may have been rooted in the despair of people holding a romantic, idealized vision of the past and smarting under the humiliation of the present. While those who planned the operation were, almost certainly, educated, sophisticated men, fully cognizant with the workings of modern societies, it does not seem accidental that most of the fifteen hijackers were Saudi citizens, and came from the province of Asir. This impoverished mountainous region close to the modern borders of Yemen was conquered by the Al Saud family in the 1920s, and still retains many of its links with the Yemeni tribes. Like all decent people, Ibn Khaldun would have been horrified by the indiscriminate slaughter of 9/11: but it is doubtful that he would have been surprised.

Foundational Beliefs and Practices

In the majority of Islamic traditions, all Muslims adhere to certain fundamentals. The most important is the profession of faith, a creedal formula that states: "There is no God but God. Muhammad is the Messenger of God." Stated before witnesses, this formula—called the Shahada—is the sufficient requirement for conversion to Islam and belonging to the Umma.

Muslims affirm *tawid* (the Unity and Uniqueness of God). They believe that God has communicated to humanity throughout it's history by way of Messengers, who include figures like Abraham, Moses, and Jesus, and that Muhammad was the final Messenger to whom was revealed the Koran. In personal and social life, Muslims are required to adhere to a moral and ethical mode of behavior for which they are accountable before God.

The Koran also articulates a framework of practices which have become normative for Muslims over time.

One of them is worship, which takes several forms, such as salat (ritual prayer), personal dhikr (contemplative prayer), or dua (prayers of exhortation and praise). Muslims performing salat prostrate themselves in the direction of the Kaba, the square temple covered in an embroidered cloth of black silk that stands at the center of the sacred shrine in Mecca. Salat is performed daily: early morning, noon, mid-afternoon, sunset and evening or combined according to circumstance. Prayer may be performed individually, at home, in a public place such as a park or street, or in the mosque (an English word derived from the Arabic masjid, "place of prostration") and other congregational places. The call to prayer (adhan) is made from the minaret which stands above the mosque. It includes the takbir (allahu akbar "God is most great"), as well as shahada and the imperative: "Hurry to salat". In the past, the beautifully modulated sounds of the adhan delivered by a muezzin (Arabic muadhdhin) from the minarets five times a day. Nowadays, most minarets in Muslim cities are supplied with loudspeakers whose power often distorts the beauty of the muezzin's voice. The noon salat on Friday is the congregational service, and is accompanied by a khutba (sermon) spoken by the Imam, or prayer leader or other religious notable. In the early centuries of Islam, the name of the caliph or ruler was pronounced with the khutba. When territories changed hands between different rulers (as frequently happened), the official indication of a change of government came in the form of the proclamation of the new ruler's name in the country's leading mosques.

Another foundational practice is zakat, sharing of wealth (not to be confused with voluntary charity or sadaqa). In the past, zakat was intended to foster a sense of community by stressing the obligation of the better-off to help the poor, and was paid to religious leaders or to the government. At present, different Muslim groups observe practices specific to their tradition.

Sawm is the fast in daylight hours during the holy month of Ramadan, when believers abstain from eating, drinking, smoking, and sexual activity. Abu Hamid al-Ghazali, the medieval mystic and theologian, listed numerous benefits from the discipline of fasting. These included purity of the heart and the sharpening of perceptions that comes with hunger, mortification and self-abasement, self-mastery by overcoming desire, and solidarity with the hungry: the person who is sated "is liable to forget those people who are hungry and to forget hunger itself." Ramadan is traditionally an occasion both for family reunions and religious reflection. In many Muslim countries, the fast becomes a feast at sundown—an occasion for public conviviality that lasts well into the night. Ramadan is the ninth month in the hijri (lunar calendar) which falls short of the solar year by 11 days: thus Ramadan, like other Muslim festivals, occurs at different seasons over a 35-year cycle. In most places, the ordeal of fasting is harsher in summer, since the days are longer. Should Ramadan fall in the middle of June, Muslims who live in northern latitudes such as Norway or Canada, would endanger their health if they observed the daylight rule as punctiliously as their co-religionists in countries such as Egypt or Saudi Arabia. Muslim scholars have found various solutions to this difficulty. One involves distinguishing between direct and indirect (ambient) sunlight; another approach is based on the argument that Islamic rules are designed for Muslim majority countries, most of which fall in the temperate zone. A Muslim living in the far north should follow the pattern of observance prevailing in the nearest Muslim majority country.

Another significant ritual practice is the Hajj or pilgrimage to Mecca, that practicing Muslims are required to perform at least once in their lifetimes, if able to do so. Historically the Hajj has been one of the principal means by which different parts of the Muslim world remained in physical contact. In pre-modern times, before mass transportation by steamships and aircraft brought the Hajj within the reach of people of modest or average means, returning pilgrims enjoyed the honored title of Hajji and a higher social status within their communities than non-Hajjis. As well as providing spiritual fulfilment, the Hajj sometimes created business opportunities by enabling pilgrims from different regions of the world to meet each other. It also facilitated movements of religio-political reform. Many political movements were forged out of encounters that took place on the pilgrimage—from the Shiite rebellion that led to the foundation of the Fatimid caliphate in North Africa (909) to modern Islamist movements of revival and reform. The end of Ramadan is marked by the Id al-Fitr (the Feast of Fast Breaking), while the climax of the Hajj involves the Id al-Adha (Feast of Sacrifice) in which all Muslims participate by sacrificing animals. These two Feasts are the major canonical festivals observed by Muslims everywhere. There are, in addition, many other devotional and spiritual practices among Muslims that have developed over the centuries, based on specific interpretations of the practice of faith and its interaction with local traditions.

Geophysical Map of the Muslim World

Although lands of the Islamic world now occupy a broad belt of territories ranging from the African shores of the Atlantic to the Indonesian archipelago, the core regions of Western Asia where Islam originated exercised a decisive influence on its development. Compared to Western Europe and North America, the region is perennially short on rainfall. During the winter, rain and snow born by westerlies from the Atlantic fall in substantial quantities on the Atlas and Riffian Mountains, the Cyrenaican massif, and Mount Lebanon, with the residue falling intermittently on the Green Mountain of Oman, the Zagros, the Elburz, and the mountains of Afghanistan. But the only rains that occur with predictable regularity fall in the highlands of Yemen and Dhufar, which catch the Indian Ocean monsoons, and the Junguli region lying south of the Caspian Sea under the northern slopes of the Elburz, which catches moisture-laden air flowing southward from Russia.

Originally built in the fourteenth century, the mosque at Agades, in Niger, is made of mud. Its structure is constantly renewed by workers bearing new mud who climb up the wooden posts that protrude from the sides and serve as scaffolding.

Before recent times, when crops such as wheat, requiring large amounts of water, appeared in the shape of food imports, and underground fossil water (stored for millions of years in aquifers) became available through modern methods of drilling, agriculture was highly precarious. A field that had yielded wheat for millennia would fail when the annual rainfall was one inch instead of the usual twenty. Ancient peoples understood this well, and provided themselves with granaries. However, agriculture did flourish in the great river valleys of Egypt and Mesopotamia (now Iraq). Here the annual flooding caused by the tropical rains in Africa and melting snows in the Anatolian and Iranian highlands produced regular harvests and facilitated the development of the complex city-based cultures of ancient Sumer, Assyria, and Egypt. The need to manage finely calibrated systems of irrigation using the nutrient-rich waters of the Tigris, the Euphrates, and the Nile required complex systems of recording and control, making it necessary for literate priestly bureaucrats to govern alongside the holders of military power. Together with the Yellow River in China and the Indus Valley, the three great river systems of the Fertile Crescent are at the origins of human civilization. The first states, in the sense of orderly systems of government based on common legal principles, appeared in these regions more than five millennia ago.

The limited extent of the soil water necessary for agricultural production had a decisive impact on the evolution of human societies in the arid zone. Though conditions vary from one region to another, certain features distinguish the patterns of life from those of the temperate zones to the north or tropical zones to the south. Where rainfall is scarce and uncertain, animal husbandry—the raising of camels, sheep, goats, cattle, and, where suitable, horses—offers the securest livelihood for substantial numbers of humans. The "pure deserts" or sand seas of shifting dunes shaped by the wind, which cover nearly one-third of the land area of Arabia and North Africa, are wholly unsuitable for human and animal life, and have generally been avoided by herdsmen, traders, and armies. But in the broader semi-desert regions complex forms of nomadic and seminomadic pastoralism have evolved. In winter the flocks and herds will range far into the wadis or semidesert areas, to feed on the grasses and plants that can spring up after the lightest of showers. In the heat of summer they will move, where possible, to pastures in the highlands, or cluster near pools or wells.

Unlike peasant cultivators, a portion of whose product may be extracted by priests in the form of offerings or by the ruler in taxes, nomadic pastoralists will often avoid the confines of state power. People are organized into tribes or patrilineal kinship groups descended from a common male ancestor. Military prowess is encouraged because, where food resources are scarce, tribal or "segmentary" groups may have to compete with each other, or make raids on settled villages, in order to survive. Property is held communally, classically in the form of herds, rather than in the form of crop-yielding land. Property and territory are not coterminous (as they tended to become in regions of higher rainfall) because the land may be occupied by different users at different seasons of the year. Vital resources such as springs or wells in which everyone has an interest are often considered as belonging to God, and are entrusted to the custodianship of special families regarded as holy.

As Islam established itself along the Silk Road, mosques were built for travelers and local converts. This mosque in the Xinjiang province of China reflects the Central Asian influence in its design.

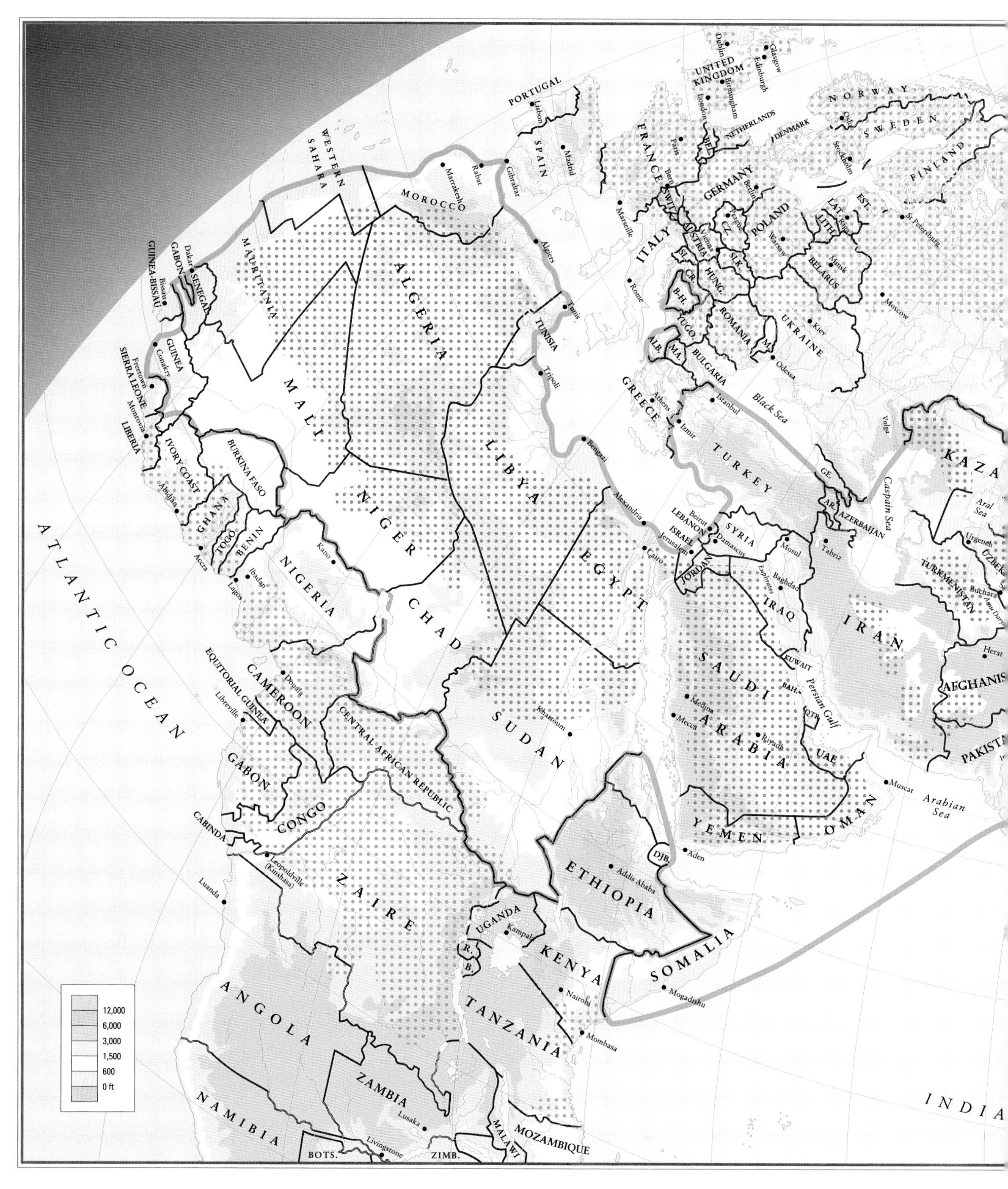
ATLANTIC OCEAN
INDIA
WESTERN SAHARA
MOROCCO
ALGERIA
TUNISIA
LIBYA
EGYPT
MAURITANIA
MALI
NIGER
CHAD
SUDAN
SENEGAL
GAMBIA
GUINEA-BISSAU
GUINEA
SIERRA LEONE
LIBERIA
IVORY COAST
BURKINA FASO
GHANA
TOGO
BENIN
NIGERIA
CAMEROON
EQUITORIAL GUINEA
GABON
CONGO
CABINDA
CENTRAL AFRICAN REPUBLIC
ZAIRE
ANGOLA
NAMIBIA
ZAMBIA
BOTS.
ZIMB.
MALAWI
MOZAMBIQUE
TANZANIA
KENYA
UGANDA
R.
B.
SOMALIA
ETHIOPIA
DJB.
YEMEN
OMAN
UAE
QTR.
BAH.
KUWAIT
SAUDI ARABIA
IRAQ
IRAN
SYRIA
LEBANON
ISRAEL
JORDAN
TURKEY
GE.
AR.
AZERBAIJAN
KAZA
UZBEK
TURKMENISTAN
AFGHANIS
PAKIST
PORTUGAL
SPAIN
FRANCE
UNITED KINGDOM
NETHERLANDS
DENMARK
NORWAY
SWEDEN
FINLAND
GERMANY
POLAND
CZ.
SLK.
AUSTRIA
HUNG.
ITALY
SL.
CR.
B-H.
YUGO.
ALB.
MA.
ROMANIA
M.
BULGARIA
GREECE
UKRAINE
BELARUS
LITH.
LAT.
EST.
Black Sea
Caspian Sea
Aral Sea
Persian Gulf
Arabian Sea
Volga
Euphrates
Amu Darya
Lisbon
Madrid
Gibraltar
Rabat
Marrakesh
Algiers
Tunis
Tripoli
Bengazi
Alexandria
Cairo
Khartoum
Dakar
Bissau
Conakry
Freetown
Monrovia
Abidjan
Accra
Lagos
Ibadan
Kano
Douala
Libreville
Leopoldville (Kinshasa)
Luanda
Lusaka
Livingstone
Kampala
Nairobi
Mombasa
Mogadishu
Addis Ababa
Aden
Muscat
Mecca
Medina
Riyadh
Baghdad
Mosul
Tabriz
Damascus
Beirut
Jerusalem
Istanbul
Izmir
Athens
Odessa
Kiev
Moscow
Minsk
Warsaw
Riga
St Petersburg
Stockholm
Oslo
Berlin
Prague
Vienna
Rome
Marseille
Paris
London
Birmingham
Dublin
Edinburgh
Glasgow
Urgench
Bukhara
Herat
12,000
6,000
3,000
1,500
600
0 ft

R U S S I A
TAN
MONGOLIA
Karakorum
RGHIZIA
Kashgar
Beijing
Kaifeng
Luoyang
C H I N A
Lhasa
NEPAL
BHU.
Delhi
Ganges
BANGLA DESH
BURMA (MYANMAR)
N D I A
Bay of Bengal
Hanoi
LAOS
VIETNAM
THAILAND
CAMBODIA
Canton
TAIWAN
Tropic of Cancer
N. KOREA
Kaesong
S. KOREA
Yellow Sea
East China Sea
Sea of Japan
JAPAN
Sea of Okkhotsk
Lena
Amur
Huang He
Chang Jiang
PACIFIC OCEAN
PHILIPPINES
SRI LANKA
CEAN
MALAYSIA
I N D O N E S I A
New Guinea
Papua New Guinea
Muslim lands
Arid zone
Northern and southern forest zones
Muslim population 50% or more

Muslim Languages and Ethnic Groups

There are approximately one billion Muslim people—about one-fifth of humanity—living in the world today. Of these the largest single-language ethnic group, about 15 percent, are Arabs. Not all Arabs are Muslims—there are substantial Arab Christian minorities in Egypt, Palestine, Syria, and Iraq, and small numbers of Arabic-speaking Jews in Morocco—although the numbers of both these communities have rapidly declined in recent decades, mainly through emigration. As the language of the Koran, of Islamic scholarship and law, Arabic long dominated the cultures of the Muslim world, closely followed by Persian—the language of Iran and the Mughal courts in India.

The spread of Islam among non-Arab peoples, however, has made Arabic a minority language—although many non-Arab Muslims read the Koran in Arabic. An ethnographic survey published in 1983 lists more than 400 ethnic/linguistic groups who are Muslim. The largest, after the Arabs, in diminishing order, are Bengalis, Punjabis, Javanese, Urdu speakers, Anatolian Turks, Sundanese (from Eastern Java), Persians, Hausas, Malays, Azeris, Fulanis, Uzbeks, Pushtuns, Berbers, Sindhis, Kurds, and Madurese (from the island of Madura, northeast of Java). Each of these groups numbers between nearly 100 million (Bengalis) down to 10 million (Sindhis, Kurds, and Madurese). Of the hundreds of smaller groups listed, the smallest—the Wayto hunter gatherers in Ethiopia—number fewer than 2,000. However, three of the languages spoken by more than 10 million—Javanese, Sundanese, and Madurese—are in the course of being overlaid by Bahasa Indonesia, the official language taught in Indonesian schools. With Indonesians constituting the world's largest Muslim-majority nation, Bahasa Indonesia could soon overtake Arabic as the most widely spoken Muslim language.

In addition to Muslims living in their countries of ethnic origin, there are now millions of Muslims residing in Europe and North America. Given that English is the international language of commerce, scholarship, and science, with second-generation European, American, and Canadian Muslims speaking English (as well as French, German, Dutch, and other European tongues) the growth of English among Muslims is a significant recent development.

The modern nation-state, based on internationally recognized boundaries, a common language (in most cases), a common legal system, and representative institutions (whether these are appointed or elected) is a recent phenomenon in most of the Muslim world. Often imposed by arrangements between the European powers, modern boundaries cut across lines of linguistic/ethnic affiliation, leaving peoples such as Kurds and Pushtuns divided into different states. Before the colonial interventions began to lock them into the international system of UN member states, Muslim states tended to be organized communally rather than territorially. States were not bounded by lines drawn on maps. The power of a government did not operate uniformly within a fixed and generally recognized area, as happened in Europe, but rather "radiated from a number of urban centers with a force which tended to grow weaker with distance and with the existence of natural or human obstacles." [Albert Hourani *A History of the Arab Peoples* London, Faber, revised ed. 2002, p. 138]. Patriotism was focused, not as in Renaissance Italy, England, or Holland, on the city, city-state, or nation in the modern territorial sense, but on the clan or tribe within the larger frame of the umma, the worldwide Islamic community. Local solidarities were reinforced by endogamous practices such as marriage between first cousins, a requirement in many communities. Clan loyalties were further buttressed by religion, with tribal leaders often justifying their rebellions or wars of conquest by appealing to the defense of true Islam against its infidel enemies.

Viewed from the perspective of modern Western history the systems of governance that evolved in the arid region were divisive and unstable. In Europe, a region of high rainfall, the state emerged out of constitutional struggles between rulers and their subjects animated by conflicts between social classes, within ethnically homogeneous populations sharing common national, political, and cultural identities (although these were sometimes contested, as in Ireland). In the arid zone dominant clans or tribally based dynasties exercised power over subordinate groups or tried to ensure their dominance by importing Mamluks (slave-soldiers), from distant peripheries, who had minimal social contacts with the indigenous populations. Peasant cultivators and townsfolk remained vulnerable to the predations of nomadic marauders—the proverbial "barbarians at the gates." The asabiyya (loyalties or group solidarity) that bound the clans was stronger than urban solidarity. Lacking the corporate ethos of their Western counterparts the Muslim urban classes failed to achieve the "bourgeois" or capitalist revolutions that gave rise to the modern state systems of Europe and North America.

There is, however, a different way of viewing the same historical landscape. Given the predominance of pastoral nomadism in the vast belt of territories where Islam took root, stretching from the Kazakh steppes to the Atlantic shores (and in similar regions in northern India and south of the Sahara) the inability of relatively weak agrarian states to tax nomadic predators or control them through military power was balanced by the moral force and cultural prestige of Islam. Time and again in precolonial times the predators were converted into Islam's most trusted defenders. To borrow a phrase of the academic Ernest Gellner, "the wolves become sheepdogs." Just as the prophet Muhammad had tamed the Arabian tribes by his personal example, the eloquence of the Koran, and the system of governance that proceeded from it, so the Sharia (divine) law and human systems of fiqh (jurisprudence) to which it gave rise mediated the perennial conflicts between pastoral predators, cultivators, and townsfolk. The system, embedded in the social memory of today's Muslim populations, was based on the duty of the ruler to uphold social justice by governing in accordance with Islamic law. The formidable task facing contemporary Muslim states is to harness political and social traditions forged in a very different context to modern-day conditions.

A Tuareg policeman in the Sahel region south of the Sahara. From their center at Timbuktu, the Tuareg controlled the trade routes between the Mediterranean and West Africa.

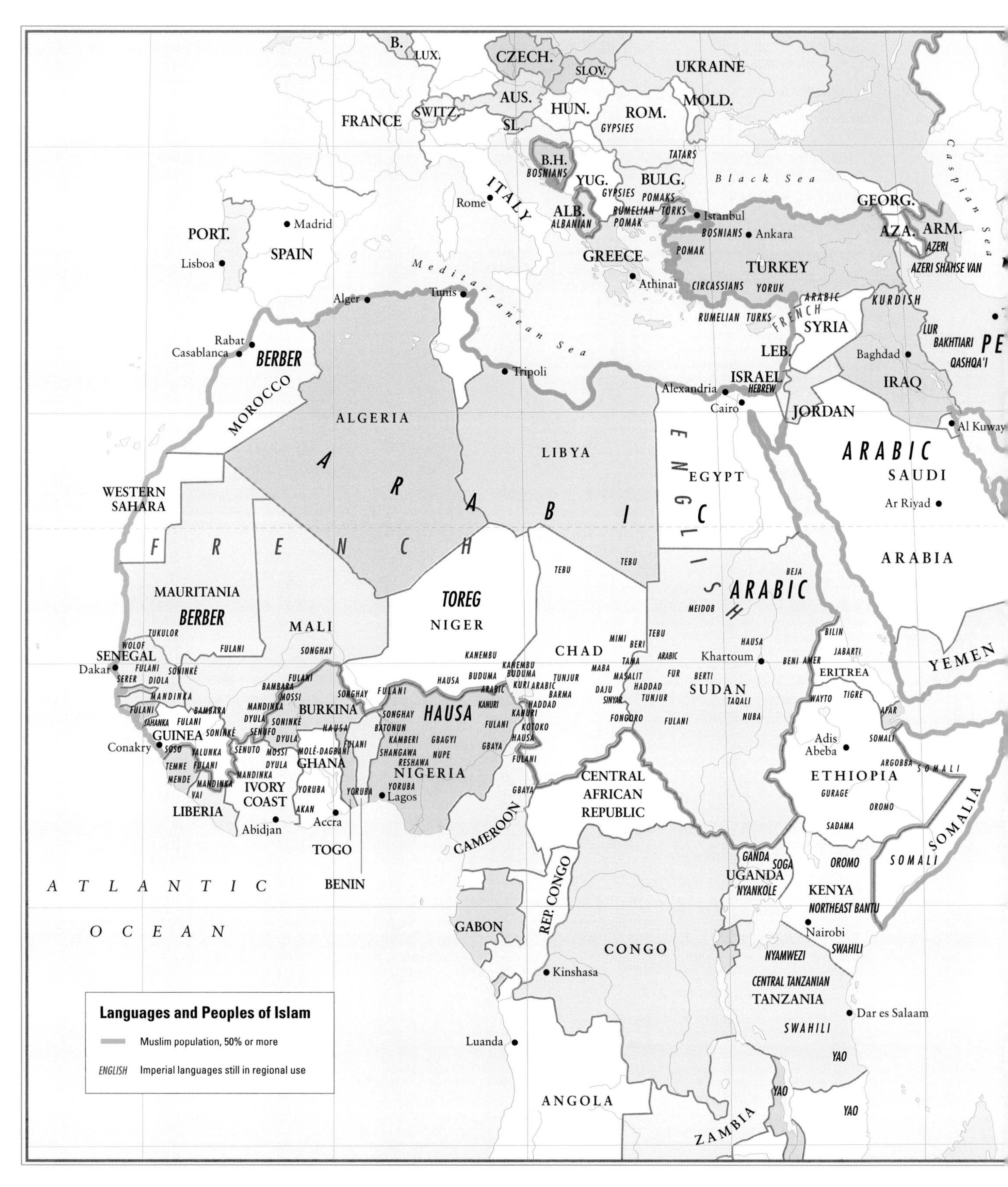

Languages and Peoples of Islam
Muslim population, 50% or more
ENGLISH Imperial languages still in regional use
ATLANTIC OCEAN
Mediterranean Sea
Black Sea
Caspian Sea
FRANCE
SPAIN
PORT.
ITALY
GREECE
TURKEY
SYRIA
IRAQ
JORDAN
ISRAEL
LEB.
EGYPT
LIBYA
ALGERIA
MOROCCO
WESTERN SAHARA
MAURITANIA
MALI
NIGER
CHAD
SUDAN
ETHIOPIA
SOMALIA
KENYA
UGANDA
TANZANIA
NIGERIA
GHANA
SENEGAL
GUINEA
LIBERIA
IVORY COAST
BURKINA
TOGO
BENIN
CAMEROON
CENTRAL AFRICAN REPUBLIC
GABON
REP. CONGO
CONGO
ANGOLA
ZAMBIA
ERITREA
YEMEN
SAUDI ARABIA
ARABIC
FRENCH
ENGLISH
BERBER
TOREG
HAUSA

KAZAKHS
UYGUR
KIRGHIZ.
KIRGHIZ
TURKMEN
KIRGHIZ
TAJIK.
TAJIK
TAJIK
QIZILBASH
PASHAI
Kabul
KHO
SHING
BALTIS
HAZARAS
KOHISTANIS
KASHMIRIS
PERSIANS
AFGHAN.
Lahore
PUSHTUN
BRAHUI
GUJARS
PAKISTAN
JAT
BALUCH
Delhi
SINDHIS
MEOS
URDU
Karachi
Ahmadabad
GUJARATIS
INDIA
MAHARASHTRIANS
DECCANI
ORISSANS
Bombay
Hyderabad
MAPPILLA
Bangalore
Madras
TAMIL
LABBAI
TAMIL
SRI LANKA
INDIAN OCEAN
MONGOLIA
CHINA
NEPAL
BH.
Dhaka
Calcutta
BANGLA-DESH
BURMA (MYANMAR)
Harbin
Shenyang
Beijing
Tianjin
N. KOREA
Seoul
S. KOREA
Pusan
Chengdu
Wuhan
Shanghai
Guangzhou
Taiwan
Hong Kong
PACIFIC OCEAN
Hainan
LAOS
VIETNAM
Yangon
THAILAND
Bangkok
CAMB.
Luzón
Manila
Ho Chi Minh
PHILIPPINES
Mindanao
BRUNEI
BAJAU
ACEHNESE
GAYO
BATAK
MALAYSIA
MINANGKABAU
GORONTALESE
TOMINI
Sumatra
Borneo
Sulawesi
WAND
OGAN-BESEMAH
BUGIS
INDONESIA
Jakarta
Java
Timor
N

Late Antiquity Before Islam

This rock relief from Magshi-i Rus Van depicts Ardeshir I, founder of the Sasanian dynasty, facing a hostile Parthian warrior.

The Muslim community emerged in seventh-century Arabia in a region dominated by ancient civilizations, empires, cultures, and ethnic groups. Traces of Mesopotamian culture still survived in the Tigris and Euphrates valleys, and the areas bordering the Mediterranean and the Gulf had long felt the impact of the adjoining powers that plied the maritime trade in these waters. Byzantium, the Eastern Roman and Orthodox state based in Constantinople, was the primary Christian kingdom in the region and at odds with the powerful Zoroastrian Sasanian Empire based in Persia (modern Iran). The ebb and flow of conflict between the various major states influenced trade as well as relations with the prosperous region of Arabia to the south. The history of some of the ancient Arab kingdoms is still preserved in archaeological remains, such as those of the Nabateans at Petra (1st century BC–1st century AD), Palmyra (2nd–3rd century AD), and of the Ghassanids in later centuries, whose patrons were the Byzantines and the Lakhmids, who gave allegiance to the Sasanian Empire.

A major influence on intellectual life that was to emerge in the Muslim world came from the academies and learning institutions that preserved influences from Persia, Greece, and India. In particular, the Hellenistic and Persian legacies in the fields of medicine, the sciences, and philosophy would bring about a strong tradition of intellectual inquiry in Muslim societies.

The cultures in the regions were influenced by the cosmopolitan nature of this Mediterranean world to different degrees, preserving the heritage of classical antiquity and the Hellenistic legacy in its various forms, architectural, philosophical, artistic, urban, and agricultural. Of the major religions in the region, Christianity in its orthodox form also held sway in southern Arabia while Zoroastrianism predominated in Iran and Mesopotamia. Judaism had a long history in the Near East and small Jewish communities had also settled in Yemen and the oases of Arabia, such as Medina. The inherited values, literature, and practices of all these traditions coexisted in this vast, multifaith and multiethnic milieu, which within a century of the death of the prophet Muhammad would be overtaken by Muslim conquest. Over time it would form part of a larger set of civilizations linked by the faith of Islam, while still preserving continuities with the various heritages of antiquity.

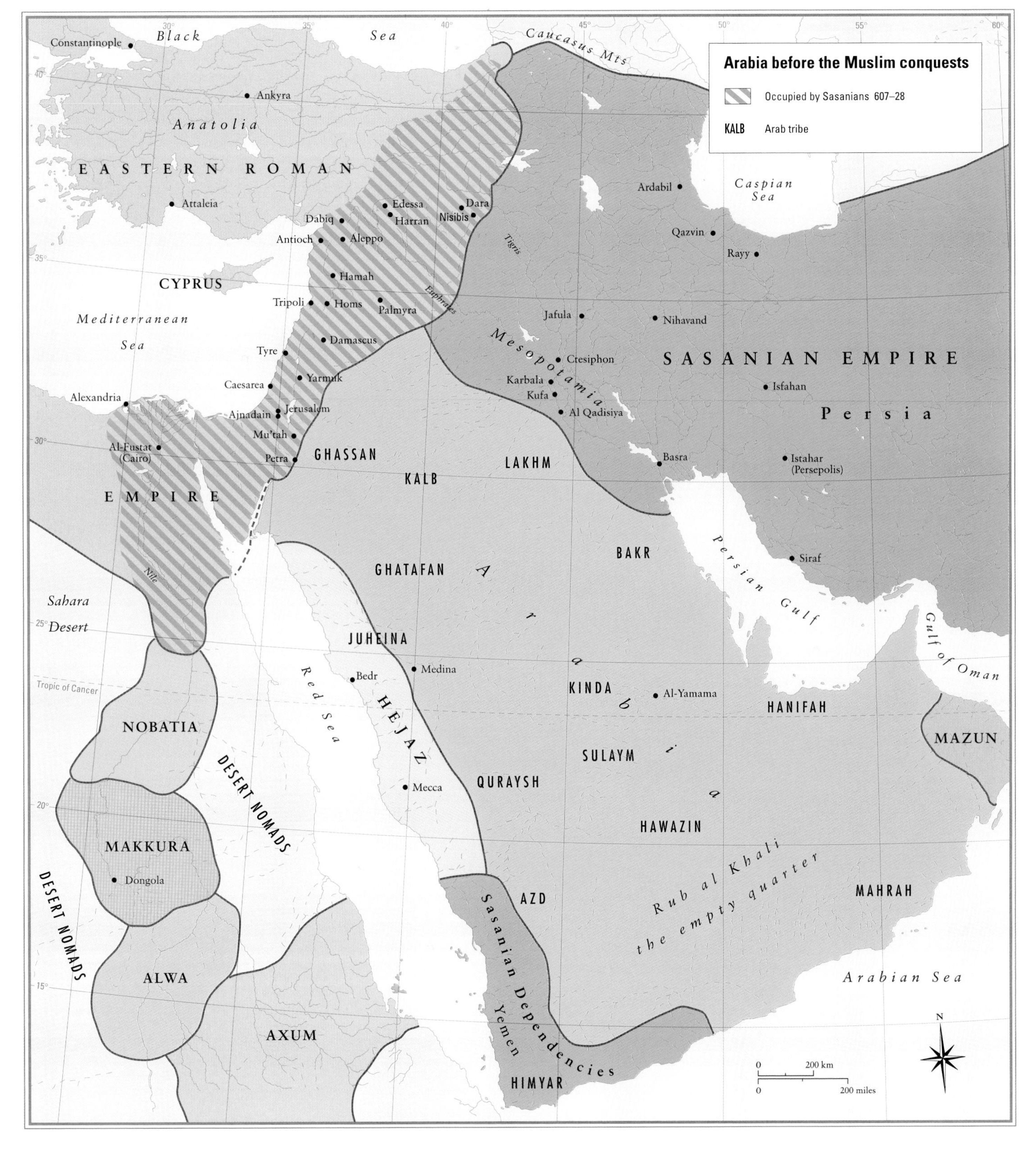

Arabia before the Muslim conquests
Occupied by Sasanians 607–28
KALB Arab tribe
Black Sea
Caucasus Mts
Caspian Sea
Constantinople
Ankyra
Anatolia
EASTERN ROMAN EMPIRE
Attaleia
CYPRUS
Mediterranean Sea
Edessa
Harran
Dara
Nisibis
Dabiq
Antioch
Aleppo
Hamah
Tripoli
Homs
Palmyra
Damascus
Tyre
Yarmuk
Caesarea
Alexandria
Ajnadain
Jerusalem
Mu'tah
Al-Fustat (Cairo)
Petra
Tigris
Euphrates
Ardabil
Qazvin
Rayy
Jafula
Nihavand
Mesopotamia
Ctesiphon
Karbala
Kufa
Al Qadisiya
SASANIAN EMPIRE
Isfahan
Persia
Basra
Istahar (Persepolis)
GHASSAN
LAKHM
KALB
BAKR
Persian Gulf
Siraf
Gulf of Oman
Nile
Sahara Desert
Tropic of Cancer
GHATAFAN
Arabia
JUHEINA
Medina
Bedr
Red Sea
HEJAZ
KINDA
Al-Yamama
HANIFAH
MAZUN
NOBATIA
SULAYM
DESERT NOMADS
Mecca
QURAYSH
MAKKURA
Dongola
HAWAZIN
Rub al Khali
the empty quarter
MAHRAH
AZD
Sasanian Dependencies
Yemen
ALWA
AXUM
HIMYAR
Arabian Sea
N
0 200 km
0 200 miles

Muhammad's Mission and Campaigns

Although Muhammad's image is considered taboo, pictures of the heroic deeds of his uncle, Hamzea, and others were circulated to show the first epic battles of the Muslims. This painting from India c. 1561–76 is from a series of large format illustrations shown to audiences while the epic stories were read aloud.

Islam is an Arabic noun from the verb aslama, to surrender oneself. In its primary sense the active participle muslim means someone who surrenders himself or herself to God as revealed through the teachings of the prophet Muhammad (c. 570–632). Muhammad is believed by Muslims to have communicated God's revelation in the Koran, a text Muslims regard as the final revelation of God to humankind. Collected under the third of Muhammad's successors, the Caliph Uthman (r. 644–656), the Koran is composed of 114 chapters, or suras. These are said to have been revealed in Muhammad's native city of Mecca, where he was a respected merchant, and suras also date from the period of his sojourn in Medina (622–632).

In Mecca, the Koran's condemnation of the sins of pride, avarice, and the neglect of social duties, its warnings of divine judgement, and its attacks on pagan deities brought Muhammad and his followers into conflict with the leaders of his own tribe, the Quraish. His fellow clansmen were boycotted, with Muslim converts subjected to persecution, and a number took refuge in Axum (Ethiopia). However, Muhammad's fame as a prophet and trusted man of God spread beyond Mecca. He was invited to act as judge and arbitrator between the feuding tribal factions of Yathrib, later renamed Madinat al-Nabi ("the city of the Prophet"), usually shortened to Medina, an oasis settlement about 250 miles northeast of Mecca. The hijra (migration) of the Muslims in 622 marks the beginning of the Muslim era. The passages in the Koran dating from the Medina period, when Muhammad was the effective ruler, contain some of the legislative material (such as rules regarding marriage and inheritance) that would form the basis of what became Islamic law. After a series of campaigns against the Meccans, the Muslims emerged victorious. In the last year of his life Muhammad returned in triumph to Mecca, receiving the submission of the tribes along the way. He reformed the ancient ceremonies of the hajj (pilgrimage), discarding their animist aspects and reorienting them to what he believed to be the original monotheism of Abraham. After further expeditions he returned to Medina. He died there after a short illness in 632.

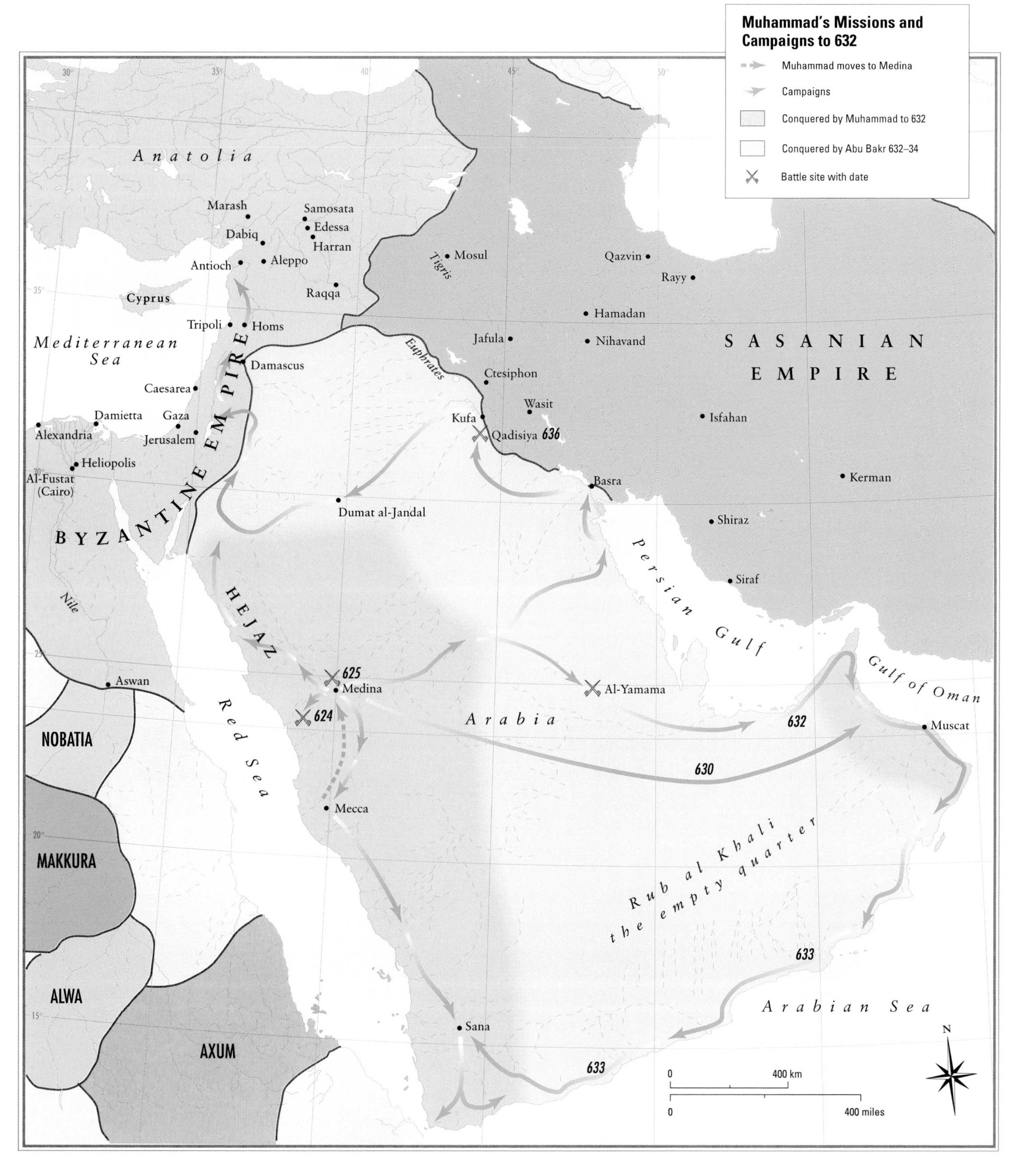
Muhammad's Missions and Campaigns to 632
Muhammad moves to Medina
Campaigns
Conquered by Muhammad to 632
Conquered by Abu Bakr 632–34
Battle site with date
Anatolia
Marash
Samosata
Edessa
Dabiq
Harran
Antioch
Aleppo
Raqqa
Cyprus
Tripoli
Homs
Mediterranean Sea
Damascus
Caesarea
Damietta
Gaza
Alexandria
Jerusalem
Heliopolis
Al-Fustat (Cairo)
BYZANTINE EMPIRE
Nile
HEJAZ
Aswan
NOBATIA
MAKKURA
ALWA
AXUM
Red Sea
Mosul
Tigris
Euphrates
Qazvin
Rayy
Hamadan
Jafula
Nihavand
SASANIAN EMPIRE
Ctesiphon
Wasit
Kufa
Qadisiya 636
Isfahan
Kerman
Basra
Dumat al-Jandal
Shiraz
Siraf
Persian Gulf
Gulf of Oman
625
Medina
624
Al-Yamama
Arabia
632
Muscat
630
Mecca
Rub al Khali
the empty quarter
633
Arabian Sea
Sana
633
0 400 km
0 400 miles
N

Expansion of Islam to 750

Muhammad's death left the Muslim community without an obvious leader. One of his oldest companions, Abu Bakr (r. 632–634), was acknowledged by several leaders as the first caliph, or successor. Under Abu Bakr and his successor, Umar (634–644), the tribes, who had begun to fall away on the death of Muhammad, were reunited under the banner of Islam and converted into a formidable military and ideological force. The Arabs broke out of the peninsula, conquering half the Byzantine provinces as well as defeating the armies of Sasanian Persia. Ctesiphon, the Persian capital, fell in 637, Jerusalem in 638. By 646, under Umar's successor Uthman (r. 644–656) the whole of Egypt had come under Arab Muslim control. Acquiring ships from Egypt and Syria, the Arabs conducted seaborne raids, conquering Cyprus in 649 and pillaging Rhodes in 654. Religious differences between the Byzantine rulers and their subjects in Egypt and Syria ensured that the Muslims were met with indifference, or even welcomed by fellow monotheists embittered by decades of alien Byzantine rule. But secular factors were also important. The Arabs were motivated by desire for plunder, as well as religious faith. In previous eras nomadic predators would have taken the plunder or held onto land, dispersing as landlords or peasants among the conquered peoples. In a farsighted decision Caliph Umar encouraged the tribes to settle with a system of stipends paid from the common treasury, which took control of the conquered lands. The Arabs were kept apart from the population in armed camps that evolved into garrison cities such as Basra and Kufa in Iraq. Although the tensions over the distribution of booty would erupt into open civil war the overall control exercised by the fledgling Islamic government remained under dynastic rule. Though individual dynasties would often be challenged as ruling contrary to Islamic principles of equality and justice, the dynastic system of governance fitted the prevailing form of social organization, the patriarchal kinship group, and remained the norm until modern times. Under the Umayyads the remarkable expansion of Islam continued, with the Arab raiders reaching as far as central France and the Indus valley.

The Dome of the Rock in Jerusalem, built by the Caliph Abd al-Malik in 691–92, is the first great building to have been constructed after the Arab conquest. Embellished with Koranic quotations proclaiming the unity of God, the building surrounds the rock from where Muhammad is believed to have embarked on his miraculous "night journey" to heaven.

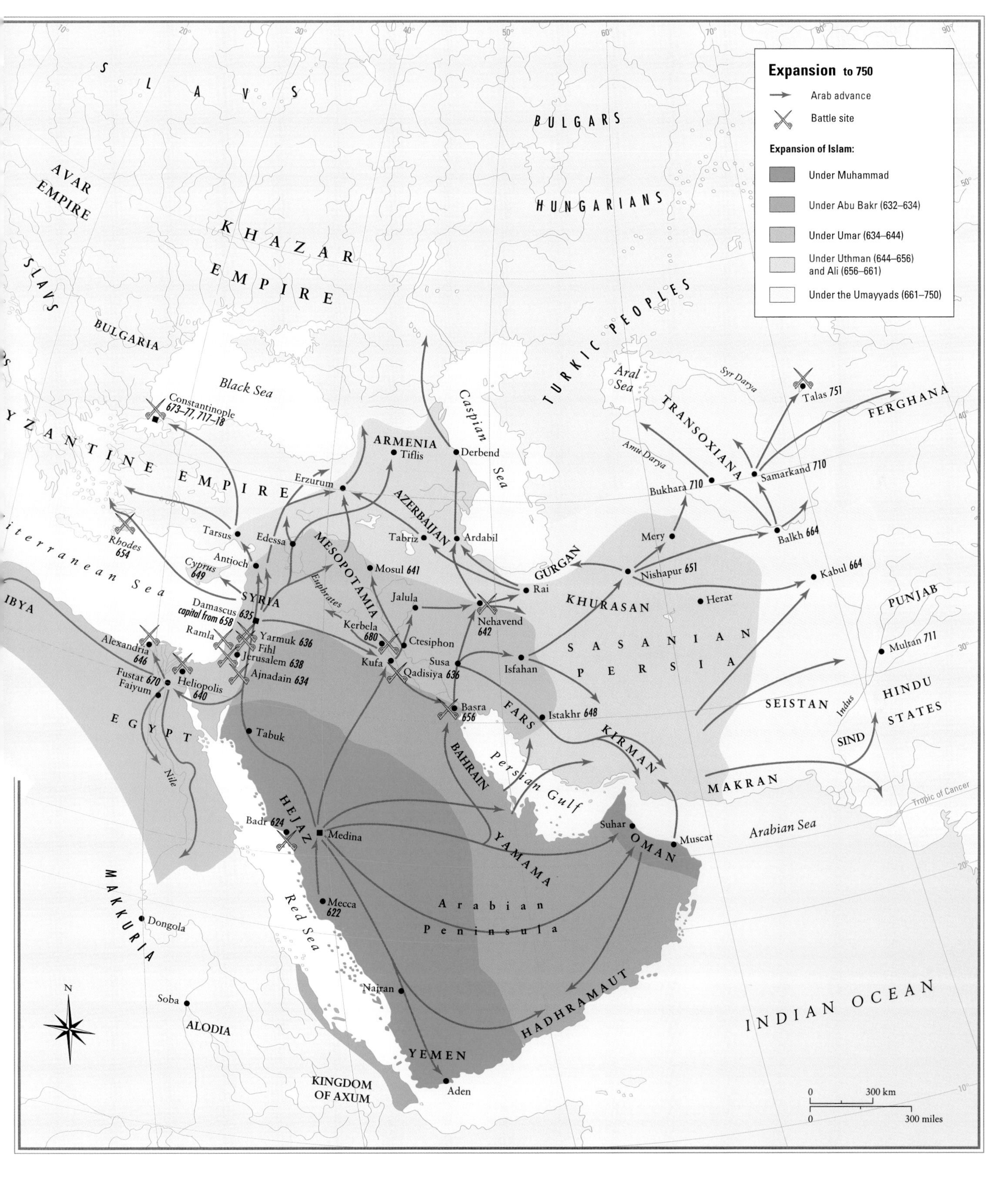
Expansion to 750
Arab advance
Battle site
Expansion of Islam:
Under Muhammad
Under Abu Bakr (632–634)
Under Umar (634–644)
Under Uthman (644–656) and Ali (656–661)
Under the Umayyads (661–750)
SLAVS
BULGARS
HUNGARIANS
AVAR EMPIRE
KHAZAR EMPIRE
SLAVS
BULGARIA
TURKIC PEOPLES
Black Sea
Constantinople 673–77, 717–18
BYZANTINE EMPIRE
Caspian Sea
Aral Sea
Syr Darya
Amu Darya
Talas 751
FERGHANA
TRANSOXIANA
Samarkand 710
Bukhara 710
ARMENIA
Tiflis
Derbend
Erzurum
AZERBAIJAN
Tabriz
Ardabil
Tarsus
Edessa
Rhodes 654
Cyprus 649
Antioch
MESOPOTAMIA
Mosul 641
Euphrates
Mediterranean Sea
GURGAN
Merv
Balkh 664
Nishapur 651
Kabul 664
Rai
KHURASAN
Herat
PUNJAB
LIBYA
Damascus 635 capital from 658
SYRIA
Jalula
Nehavend 642
Kerbela 680
Ctesiphon
SASANIAN PERSIA
Multan 711
Alexandria 646
Ramla
Yarmuk 636
Fihl
Jerusalem 638
Ajnadain 634
Kufa
Qadisiya 636
Susa
Isfahan
Fustat 670
Faiyum
Heliopolis 640
Basra 656
FARS
Istakhr 648
SEISTAN
Indus
HINDU STATES
EGYPT
Tabuk
BAHRAIN
KIRMAN
SIND
Nile
Persian Gulf
MAKRAN
Tropic of Cancer
HEJAZ
Badr 624
Medina
YAMAMA
Suhar
OMAN
Muscat
Arabian Sea
MAKKURIA
Dongola
Red Sea
Mecca 622
Arabian Peninsula
Najran
HADHRAMAUT
INDIAN OCEAN
Soba
ALODIA
YEMEN
KINGDOM OF AXUM
Aden
N
0 300 km
0 300 miles

Expansion 751–1700

The tower of the great mosque in Kairouan, now in Tunisia, dates from the ninth century. Built near the site of ancient Carthage, the design of three superimposed towers is based on the lighthouses and watchtowers of classical antiquity.

Islam expanded by conquest and conversion. Although it was sometimes said that the faith of Islam was spread by the sword, the two are not the same. The Koran states unequivocally, "There is no compulsion in religion" (2:256). Following the precedent established by the Prophet, who allowed the Jews and Christians to keep their religion if they paid tribute, the caliphs granted all the people of the Book (including Zoroastrians) the right to maintain their religious practices provided they paid the jizya tax (tribute), a payment in lieu of military service. Initially Islam remained the religion of the Arabs, a badge of unity and mark of superiority. When conversions did occur the converts were required to become mawali (clients) of the Arab tribes, the assumption being that the Arabs retained a hegemonic role.

Many factors, however, encouraged conversion after the initial conquests. For those Christians who were tired of centuries of erudite theological wranglings over the precise balance between Christ's divine and human natures, Islam provided the hospitality of a religion in which Christ had an honored place as a forerunner to Muhammad. Likewise for Jews Islam could appear as a reformed faith in the tradition of Abraham and Moses. For Zoroastrians who, like the Jews, believed in the eschatological idea of a Messiah sent to rescue humanity from the forces of darkness, it would have been relatively easy to identify the coming savior, in Islamic guise, as belonging to the House of Ali, in accordance with the beliefs of the Shia. Eschatological ideas have a universal appeal, and are found in nearly all religious traditions. After the Islamic conquests in India, the Awaited Imans of the Shiite eschatology would sometimes be identified with a forthcoming avatar of Vishnu. In the metropolitan areas converts from the older traditions helped to detribalize the Arabian religion, by asserting their rights as Muslims, by emphasizing the universality of its message, and by stressing its legitimizing function in the establishment of the new social order and forms of political power. Further afield the simplicity of the conversion process (the mere utterance before witnesses of the formula: "There is no god but

God. Muhammad is the Messenger of God") would contrast favorably with the often complex conversion procedures of the mystery religions. In Subsaharan Africa local spirits could be Islamized by incorporating them into the Koranic storehouse of angels, djinns, and devils. Ancestor cults could be accommodated by grafting local kinship groups onto Arab or Sufi spiritual lineages.

There were also more worldly considerations behind many conversions. Islamic marriage rules are weighted in favor of spreading the faith, for while a woman from one of the ahl al-dhimma (protected communities) who marries a Muslim is not required to change her religion, the converse does not apply, and the children are expected to be brought up as Muslims, ensuring the Islamization of subsequent generations. This demographic advantage would have carried considerable weight in societies where it was customary for the victors to marry the women of defeated tribes. More generally, there exists the natural tendency of bright and ambitious individuals to enter the ranks of the ruling elites. As Islamic society developed in metropolitan areas such as the cities of Iran and Iraq, knowledge of the Law and the Traditions of the Prophet, alongside secular learning in such fields as literature, astronomy, philosophy, medicine, and mathematics, became the mark of distinction among the patrician classes. Conversions inspired by social ambition should not be dismissed as mere opportunism: at its high point in the classical era, the Islamic world was the most developed and sophisticated society outside China. The models of urbane sobriety and order it offered would have exercised their own appeal quite apart from conscious missionary activity. Peoples on the fringes of the core regions would have encountered the faith in numerous guises: educated, literate merchants, wandering scholar-teachers, charismatic dervishes, native princes with impressive retinues, sophisticated intellectuals and dais (missionaries) from esoteric traditions who specialized in tailoring their message and rituals to suit audiences of widely different cultural backgrounds. Lacking a centrally directed missionary program, the religion has proved itself sufficiently adaptable to spread organically.

This Koran, written using muhaqqaq script, was produced in Baghdad in 1308. The large format indicates that this manuscript was a presentation copy, used for public recitation in the mosque.

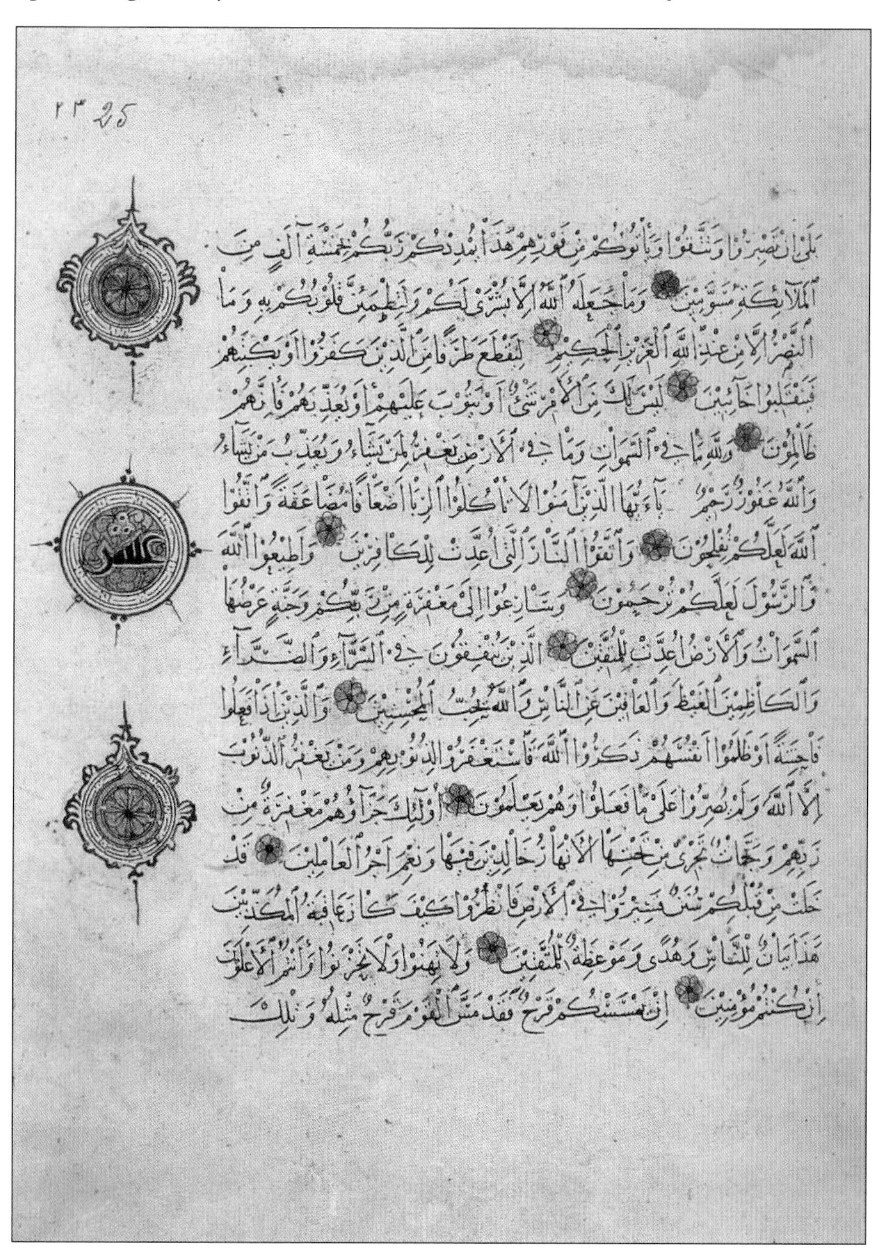

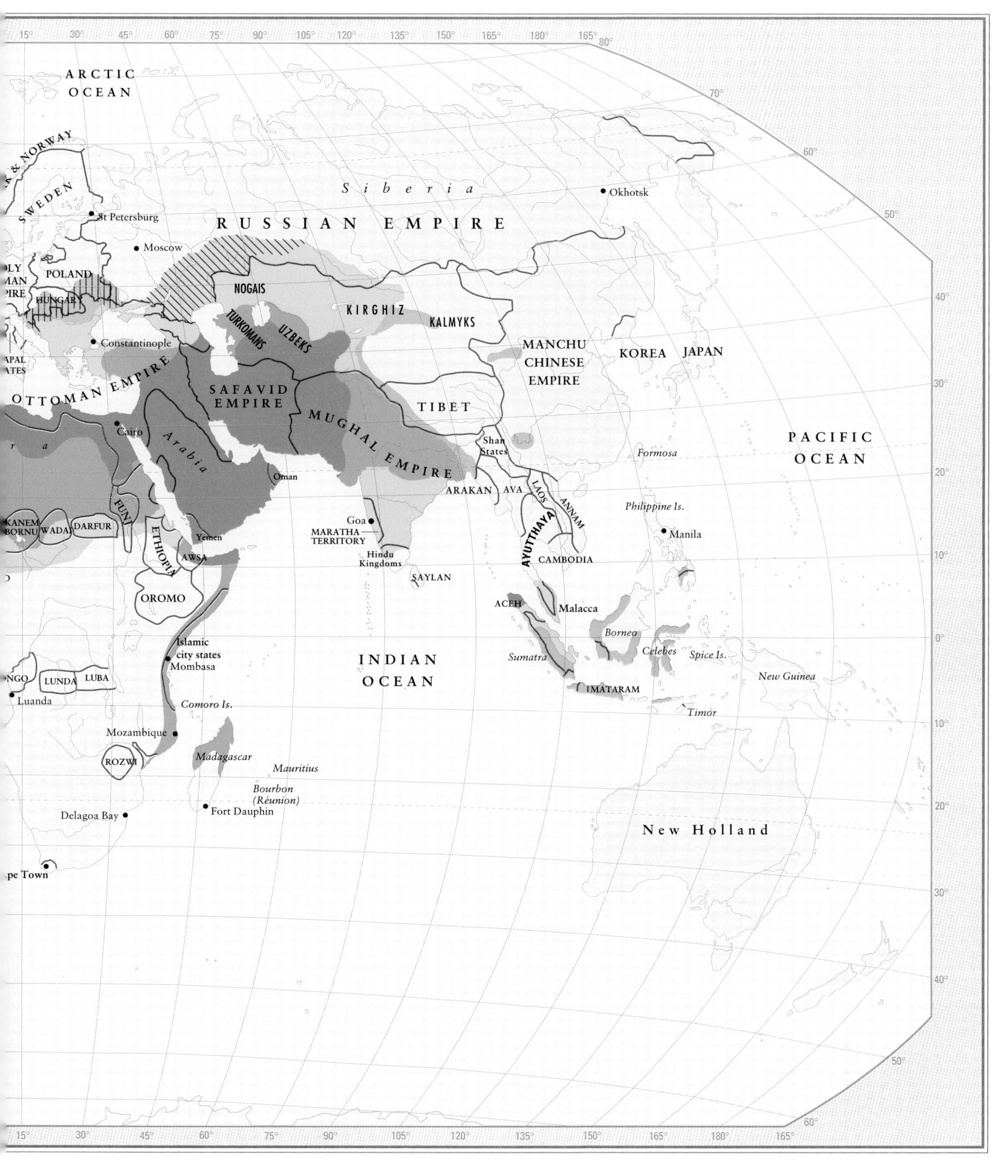
ARCTIC OCEAN
Siberia
RUSSIAN EMPIRE
Okhotsk
SWEDEN
St Petersburg
Moscow
POLAND
HUNGARY
NOGAIS
KIRGHIZ
KALMYKS
TURKOMANS
UZBEKS
Constantinople
OTTOMAN EMPIRE
SAFAVID EMPIRE
MUGHAL EMPIRE
TIBET
MANCHU CHINESE EMPIRE
KOREA
JAPAN
Cairo
Arabia
Oman
Shan States
Formosa
PACIFIC OCEAN
ARAKAN
AVA
LAOS
ANNAM
Philippine Is.
FUNJ
DARFUR
WADAI
Yemen
ETHIOPIA
AWSA
Goa
MARATHA TERRITORY
Hindu Kingdoms
SAYLAN
AYUTTHAYA
CAMBODIA
Manila
OROMO
ACEH
Malacca
Borneo
Celebes
Spice Is.
Islamic city states
Mombasa
INDIAN OCEAN
Sumatra
MATARAM
New Guinea
Timor
LUNDA
LUBA
Luanda
Comoro Is.
Mozambique
ROZWI
Madagascar
Mauritius
Bourbon (Réunion)
Fort Dauphin
Delagoa Bay
New Holland

Sunnis, Shia, and Khariji 660–c. 1000

The major divisions of Islam, revolving around the question of leadership, go back to the death of the Prophet but were intensifiedby the first civil war (656–661) and its aftermath in the following generation (680–81). The first caliph, Abu Bakr, had been one of the Prophet's oldest companions and the father of his youngest wife, Aisha. On the Prophet's death he had been chosen by acclamation with the powerful support of Umar, an early convert and natural leader. When Abu Bakr died Umar's caliphate was generally acknowledged, and it was during his ten-year reign that the Muslim state began to take shape. Under Umar the tensions resulting from the conquests, over the distribution of booty and the status of tribal leaders in the new Muslim order, began to surface. The tensions were kept in check under Umar's stern and puritanical rule but would surface disastrously during the reign of his successor, Uthman, who was murdered in Medina by disgruntled soldiers returning from Egypt and Iraq. Though renowned for his commitment to the new religion as an early convert, Uthman was linked to the Umayyad clan in Mecca that had originally opposed Muhammad's message. He was accused of favoring his fellow clansmen at the expense of more pious Muslims. The latter congregated around Ali, the Prophet's cousin and closest surviving male relative, who was already regarded by some of his followers as the originally designated successor to the Prophet, and who now assumed the role of caliph. Ali's failure to punish Uthman's assassins provoked a rebellion by two of Muhammad's closest companions, Talha and Zubayr, supported by Aisha. Though he defeated Talha and Zubayr, Ali failed to overcome Uthman's kinsman Muawiya, the governor of Syria, at the Battle of Siffin. His eventual decision to seek a compromise with Muawiya provoked a rebellion among his more militant supporters, who came to be known as Kharijis (seceders). Though Ali defeated the Kharijis in July 658, enough of them survived to continue the movement, which has lasted to this day in a moderate version known as Ibadism. One of the Khariji leaders, Ibn Muljam, avenged his comrades by murdering Ali in 661. Ali's elder son Hasan made an accommodation with the victorious Muawiya who became the first Umayyad caliph. On Muawiya's death in 680, when the succession passed to Muawiya's son, Yazid, Ali's younger son Hussein made an unsuccessful bid to restore the caliphate to the prophet Muhammad's closest descendants. The massacre of Hussein and a small group of followers at Karbala in 680 by Yazid's soldiers provoked a movement of repentance among Ali's supporters in Iraq. They became known as the Shia, the "partisans" of Ali.

The Mughal emperors and their descendants had an abiding interest in the history and wisdom of their faith. This was expressed both in their memoirs and in their paintings. By the mid-1600s, the Emperor Jahangir's artists had developed a format in which two or more sages, or holy men, were depicted seated in discussion. Mughal artists did not shrink from depicting fabled holy men from the past as if they were still alive. The figures in this painting represent the Muslim orthodoxy, with the only nonconformist being the bare-headed dervish seated at the lower left.

Abbasid Caliphate under Harun al-Rashid

A romanticized nineteenth-century portrait of Harun al-Rashid with Ottoman-style mosque in the background. The revival of the caliphate by the Ottoman sultans was intended to grant them rights over the Muslim subjects of European powers to balance the rights claimed by the latter over the sultan's Christian subjects.

The reign of caliph Harun al-Rashid (r. 764–809) marked the height of military conquests and territorial acquisition under the Abbasids, with the caliphate extending from the boundaries of India and Central Asia to Egypt and North Africa.

Harun rose through the ranks as a military commander before assuming the caliphate from his murdered brother al-Hadi (r. 785–86) and served variously as governor of Ifriqiya (modern-day Tunisia), Egypt, Syria, Armenia, and Azerbaijan. His military campaigns against the Byzantines kept them at bay. Upon becoming caliph in 764, Harun established diplomatic relations with Charlemagne (r. 742–814), the Byzantine emperor. Diplomatic and commercial ties were also established with China.

Harun's reign is often referred to as the Golden Age, a period of significant cultural and literary activity during which the arts, Arabic grammar, literature, and music flourished under his patronage. Al-Rashid figures prominently in the famous literary compilation *One Thousand and One Nights*. Among his courtiers were the poet Abu Nuwas (d. 815), who was renowned for his wine and his love poetry, and the musician Ibrahim al-Mawsili (d. 804). al-Kisai (d. 805), who was tutor to al-Rashid and his sons, was the leading Arabic grammarian and Koran reciter of his day. The classical texts were translated from Greek, Syriac, and other languages into Arabic. Harun was famous for his largesse: a well-turned poem could earn the gift of a horse, a bag of gold, or even a country estate. His wife Zubaida was famous for her charities, especially for causing numerous wells to be dug on the pilgrimage route from Iraq to Medina.

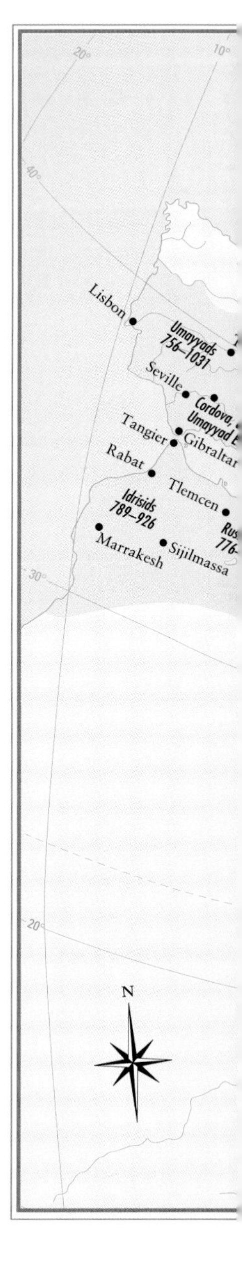

But piety was not neglected. Sufism (Islamic mysticism) flourished under the caliph. The famous ascetic and mystic Maruf al-Karkh (d. c.815) was among the leading expositors of Sufism in Baghdad. By contrast, Harun instituted a policy of repressing the Shiites.

The latter half of Harun's reign was marked by political instability. The granting of semiautonomy to the governor of Ifriqiya, Ibrahim b. al-Aghlab, in 800, followed by Harun's destruction of the all-powerful al-Barmaki family led to a period of political and territorial decline. Harun's decision to divide the empire between his two sons al-Amin and al-Mamun, appointing the elder al-Amin (r. 809–813) as his successor, contributed to a two-year civil war that was followed by periods of continued instability and insurrection. The reign of al-Mamun (r. 813–833), though intellectually brilliant, was marked by territorial decline and the waning of Abbasid influence.

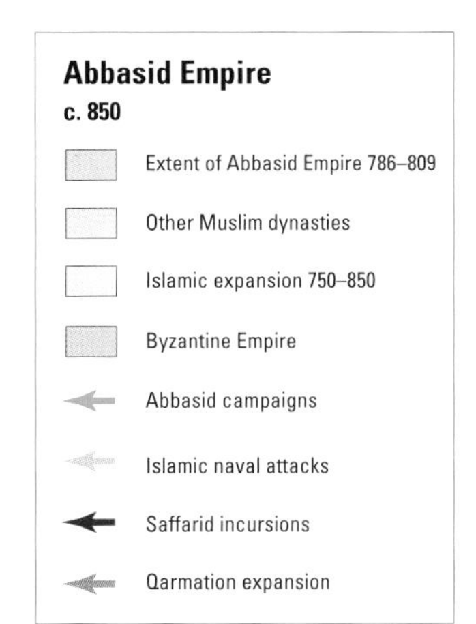

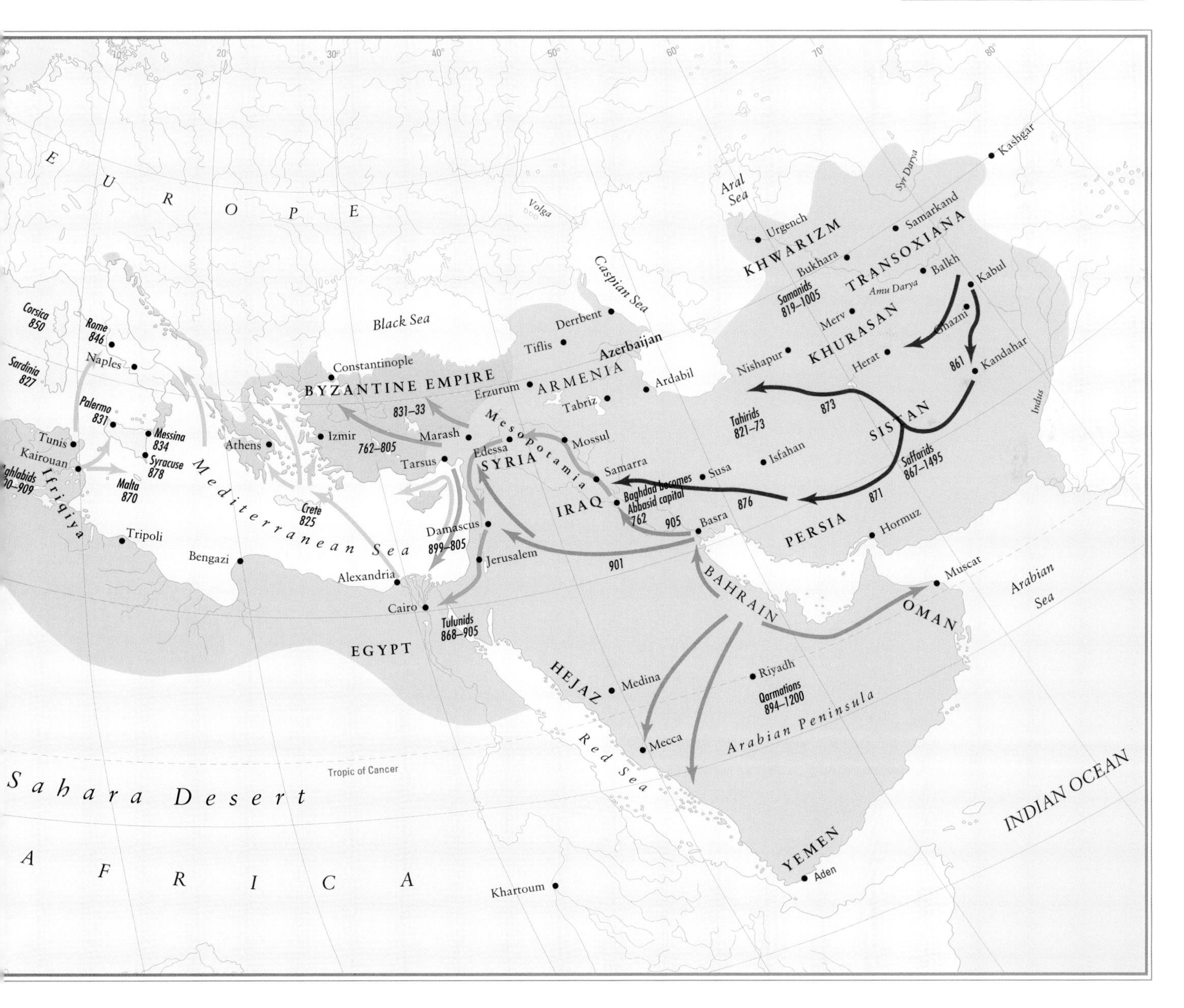

Spread of Islam, Islamic Law, and Arabic Language

The rapid spread of Islam acted as a formidable force of change in the Old World. By the end of the reign of Umar ibn al-Khattab (d. 644), the whole of the Arabian Peninsula was conquered, together with most of the Sasanian Empire, as well as the Syrian and Egyptian provinces of Byzantium. Following the tragic battle of Karbala, which led to the death of Imam al-Hussein (AD 680), a new phase was ushered in with the making of the Umayyad Empire (661–750), which eventually extended its dominion from the Ebro River in Spain to the Oxus Valley in Central Asia. Claiming universal authority over far-reaching frontiers, the Umayyad dynasty took Damascus as its capital city, and remained virtually unchallenged in its reign until the rise of the Abbasid caliphate with its capital in Baghdad (749–1258). While Spain continued to be under Umayyad rule (756–1031), new regional powers confronted the Abbasid hegemony, like the Fatimids in Egypt (909–1171), the Saljuqs in Iran and Iraq (1038–1194), along with waves of Crusader invaders in the Levant.

Numerous traditions in thought flourished, like the Sunni schools of legal reasoning (hanafi, maliki, shafii, hanbali) and the "Twelver Shiite" lineage descending from the Imam Ali ibn Abi Talib (d. 661). The upsurge in intellectual activities was also marked by the founding of the mutazila and ashari methods of kalam, in addition to the maturation of philosophy, the sciences, and mysticism. Many notable centers of learning were established, along with associated productions of manuscripts, like al-Azhar in Cairo, the Zaytuna in Tunis, the Qarawiyyin in Fez, the coteries of Córdoba in Andalusia, the schools of Najaf and Karbala in Iraq, and those of Qumm and Mashhad in Iran.

Being the language of the Koran, Arabic was carried to the new converts. Becoming the *lingua franca* of medieval Islam, the distinctiveness of Arabic was evident in all spheres of high culture, from religious to legal, official, intellectual, and literary dictions. While in the western provinces Arabic dominated the vernacular dialects, Persian remained in use eastward; witnessing a literary revival in the tenth century AD with the unfurling of an Arabo-Persian idiom, which became prevalent across Iran as well as Transoxiana and northern India.

A theme that recurs in this formative period of Islamic thought is the relationship, often tense, between revelation and reason. Under the Abbasid caliph al-Mamun (r. 813–833) there existed a group of theologians known as the Mutazila. They had absorbed the work of Greek philosophers and adopted a rationalist style of argumentation that equated God with pure reason. For the Mutazila the world created by God operated according to rational principles humans could understand by exercising reason. As free agents, humans were morally responsible for their actions, and since good and evil had intrinsic value, God's justice was constrained by universal laws. They held to the view that the Koran was created in time, inspired by God in Muhammad, but not part of his essence. Their opponents, the hadith scholars, insisted that the Koran was "uncreated" and coeternal with God. They believed it was not for man to question God's injunctions or explore them intellectually, and that all human action was ultimately predetermined. The Mutazili view, buttressed by the mihna (an "inquisition" or test applied to ulama and public officials), held sway for a period. However, it was reversed under his successor al-Mutawakil (r. 847–61) as a result of populist pressures focused on the heroic figure of Ahmad ibn Hanbal (d. 855) who resisted imprisonment and torture to defend the Uncreated Koran. A kind of compromise between reason and revelation was reached in the work of Abul Hasan al-Ashari (d. 935). He used rationalistic methods to defend the Uncreated Koran and allowed for a degree of human responsibility. However, the consequences of the Mutazili defeat were far reaching. The caliphs ceased to be the ultimate authorities in doctrinal matters. Mainstream Sunni theologians espoused the command theory of ethics: an act is right because God commands it, God does not command it because it is right. Mutazilism is a term of abuse for many conservative Islamists, especially in Saudi Arabia, which follows the Hanbali tradition in law.

The courtyard at al-Azhar in Cairo, founded by the Shiite Fatamids in 970, became the foremost center of Sunni scholarship and an important source of manuscripts.

Successor States to 1100

This clay model clearly shows the physical features that Arab and Persian commentators noted as typical of the Turkish soldiers recruited by the caliphs.

Even at its maximum extent the Abbasid Empire failed to contain the whole Islamic world. In Spain an independent dynasty had been founded by an Umayyad survivor, Abd al-Rahman I (r. 756–788). A grandson of the Caliph Hisham, he escaped the massacre of his kinsmen and after various adventures made his way to the peninsula. Here he persuaded feuding Arabs and Berbers to accept him as their leader, instead of the governor sent by the Abbasids. In what is now Morocco, a descendant of Ali and Fatima, Idris bin Abdullah, who escaped from Arabia after the failure of a Shiite revolt in 786, arrived at the old Roman capital of Volubilis. Here he formed a tribal coalition, which rapidly conquered southern Morocco. His son Idris II founded Fez in 808. In Tunisia (Ifriqiya) the descendants of Ibrahim ibn Aghlab, Harun al-Rashid's governor, who had been granted autonomy in return for an annual tribute, founded a dynasty that lasted until 909. The puritanical Kharijis, who held to the principle of an elected imam or caliph, established independent states based in Wargala oasis, Tahert, and Sijilmassa. Of Tahert, destroyed

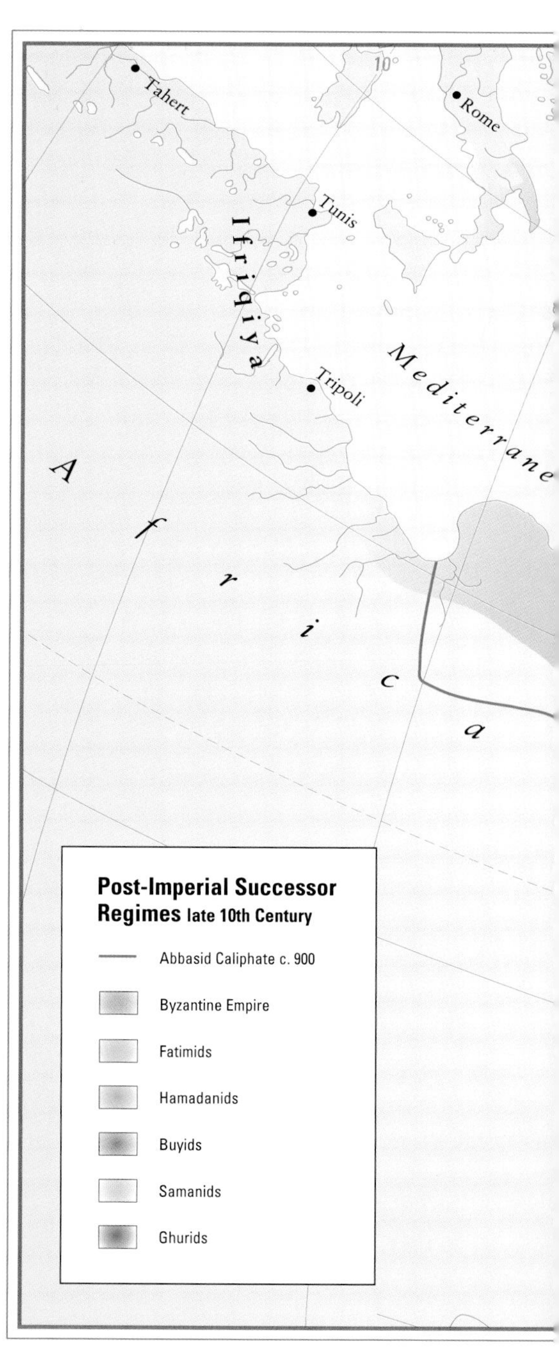

by the Fatimids in the tenth century, the chronicler Ibn Saghir wrote:

"There was not a foreigner who stopped in the city but settled among them and built in their midst, attracted by the plenty there, the equitable conduct of the Imam, his just behavior toward those under his charge, and the security enjoyed by all in person and property."

At the heart of the empire, however political and religious tensions were rife. The disputed succession between Harun's sons Amin and Mamun led to a civil war that lasted a decade, weakening the Abbasid armies and the institution of the caliphate. Though Mamun won the war, his attempt to impose a version of Islamic orthodoxy, sometimes

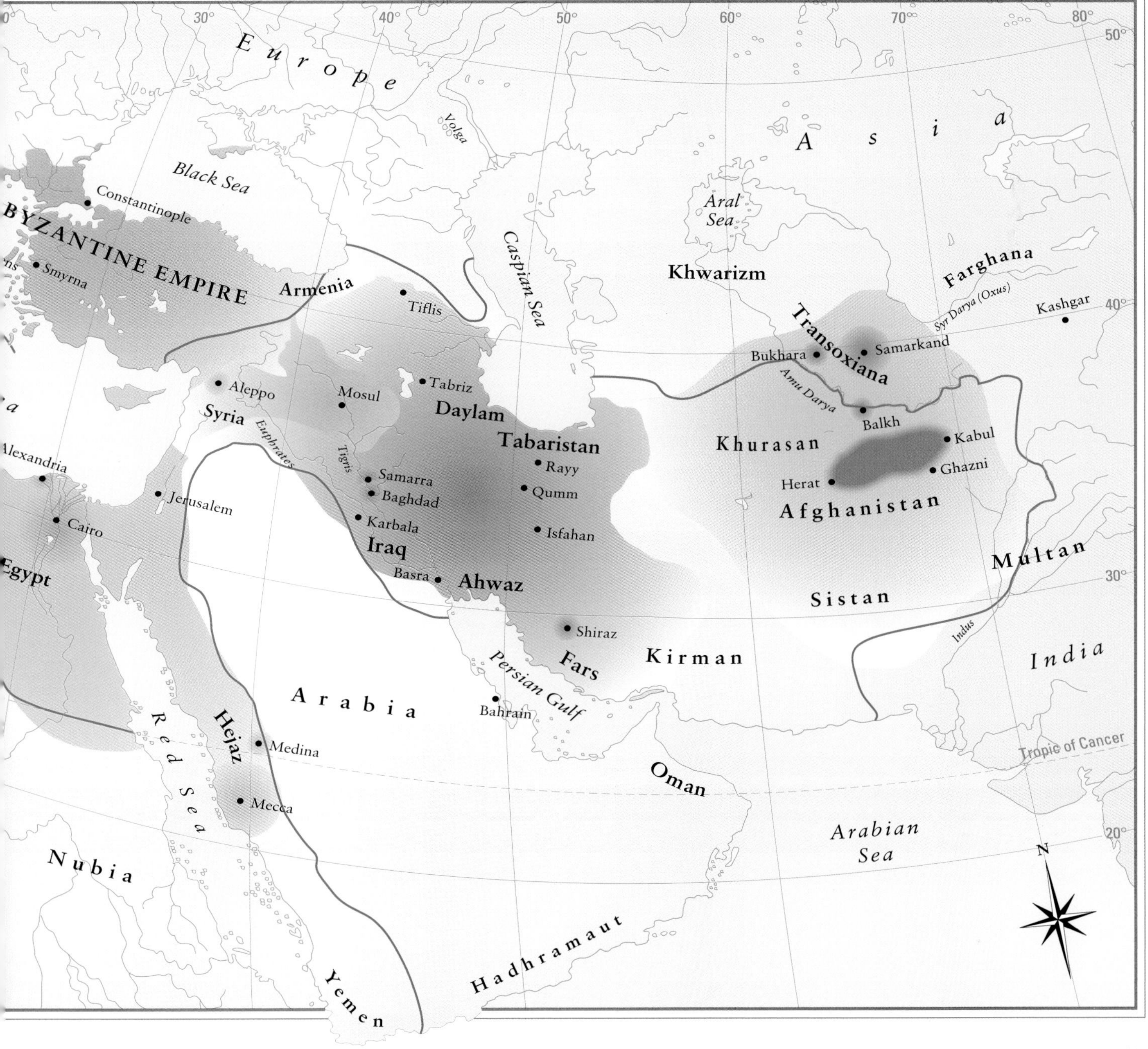

seen as rationalistic, based on the doctrine that the Koran had been "created" in time, met with strong resistance from populist ulama (religious scholars) grouped around Ahmad Ibn Hanbal. The latter saw the divine text as "uncreated" or eternal: the doctrine of the created Koran derogated from the idea of the Koran as God's speech. They looked to the Koran and the emerging corpus of hadiths (traditions or reports about the prophet Muhammad) as the sole sources of religious authority, with themselves as qualified interpreters. They regarded the caliph as the executive of the will of the community, not the source of its beliefs.

As the caliph's religious authority weakened, so did his political and economic control. In cultivated regions including Iraq the system of iqta (tax-farming) built up a class of landlords at the expense of central government. In Iran and the eastern provinces Mamun's most effective general, Tahir, established a hereditary governorate. To offset the power of the Tahirids Mamun's successor Mutasim relied increasingly on mercenaries recruited from Turkish-speaking tribes in Central Asia—a practice that hastened the breakup of the empire and the establishment of de facto tribal dynasties. The construction of a new capital at Samarra further isolated the caliph from his subjects. By the end of the tenth century the Abbasid caliphs were mainly titular monarchs, their legitimacy challenged by claimants in the line of Ali. The most radical of these movements, the Qaramatians, fomented peasant and nomad rebellions in Iraq, Syria, and Arabia in the name of a mes-

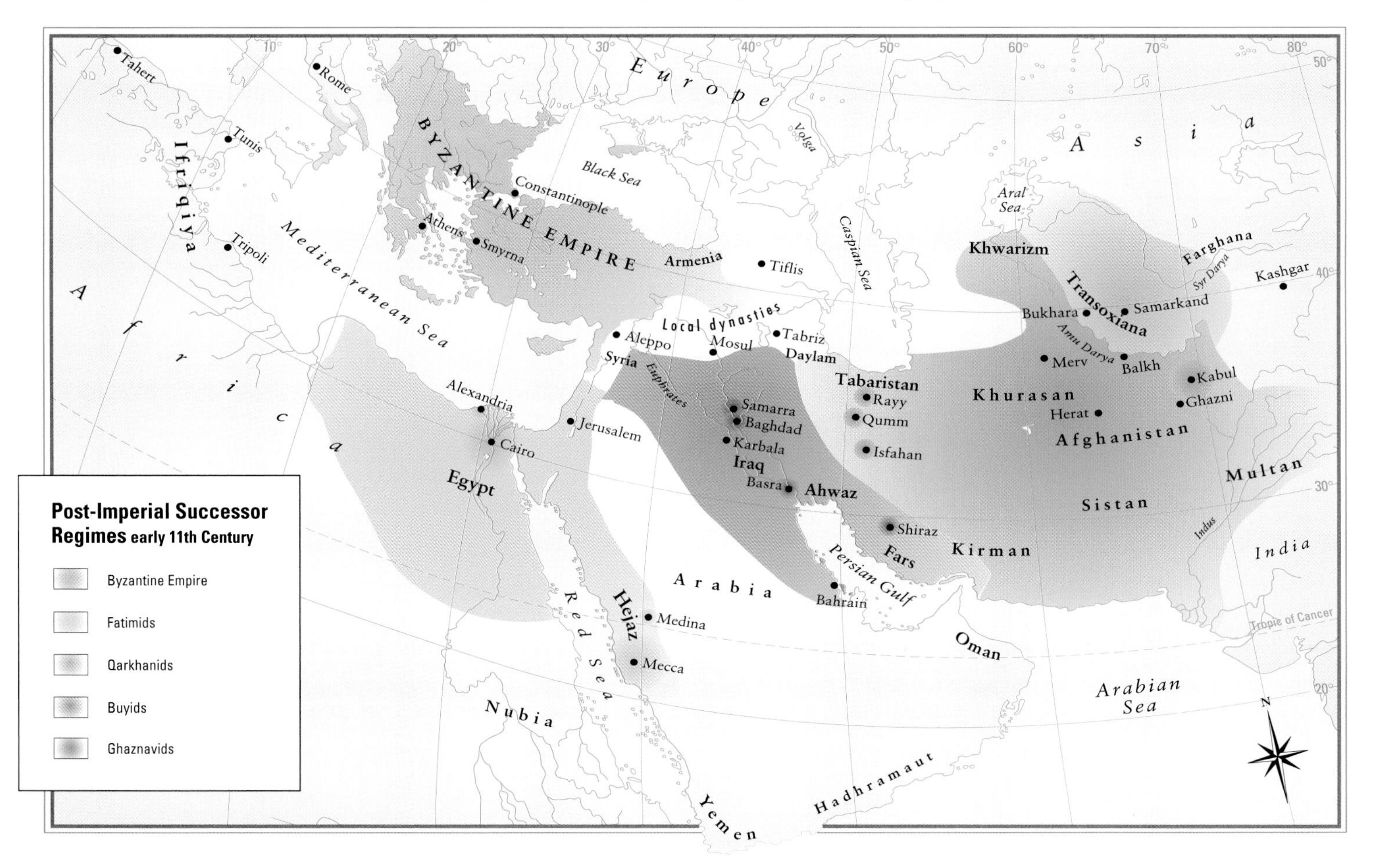

siah descended from Ali through his descendant Ismail bin Jaafar. In the 920s the Qaramatians, who created an independent state in Bahrain, shocked the whole Muslim world by pillaging Mecca and carrying off the Black Stone. In 969 Egypt—already semi-independent under Ibn Tulun and his successors, the Ikhshids—was taken over by the Ismaili Fatimids, who established a new caliphate under a living imam descended from Ali and Ismail. In northern Syria and the Upper Tigris the bedouin Arab Hamdan family—also Shiite—ruled a semi-autonomous, sometimes independent, state. In Khurasan and Transoxiana the Samanid family replaced the Tahirids as defenders of the mixed Arab-Persian high culture against incoming nomadic tribes. Even in the central heartlands of the empire—Iraq and western Iran—the caliphs were virtual prisoners of the Shiite Buyids, a warrior clan from Daylam, south of the Caspian.

In Inner Asia, where the Samanids had established a flourishing capital in Bukhara, the adoption of Islam by Turkish-speaking tribes subverted the role of the Samanids as ghazis. These were frontier warriors entrusted with the defense of Islam against nomadic incursions. The practice of recruiting warrior-slaves, known as Mamluks or ghulams, from mountainous or arid regions hastened the disintegration of the empire. When power declined at the center, the Mamluks went on to establish their own "slave-dynasties." Thus the Ghaznavids who supplanted their former Samanid overlords in Khurasan started as slave-soldiers in the frontier region of Ghazni, south of Kabul. When the Samanid regime collapsed in 999, Mahmud of Ghazni (r. 998–1030), son of a slave-governor, divided their territory with the Turkish tribe of Qarluqs, led by the Qaraqanid dynasty, which he did his best to confine to the Oxus basin in the north. Mahmud crossed the Indus Valley, establishing permanent rule in the Punjab, and conducted raids into northwestern India, plundering cities and destroying numerous works of art as idolatrous. This earned him a fearsome reputation as a ghazi against the infidel. On his western front, in the lands of "old Islam" he pushed the Buyids back almost to the frontiers of Iraq.

Mahmud of Ghazni crosses the Ganges. The Ghaznavids, Turkish military governors, enjoyed great renown in later times as the first to extend Muslim power into India. This image is from the Compendium of Chronicals, *composed for the vizier Rashid al-Din, in the early fourteenth century.*

The Saljuq Era

Despite challenges to their authority and the loss of military and effective political power, the Abbasid caliphs retained immense prestige in the eyes of most townspeople and many of the tribes as the lawful successors to the Prophet and heads of the Muslim community. The division of the world into Dar al-Islam and Dar al-Harb facilitated the spread of Islam centripetally as well as centrifugally: when tribes from the margins who encountered Muslim merchants, scholars, or wandering Sufis, accepted Islam the caliphs tended to legitimize their rule, appointing their leaders as governors. Conversion civilized the nomadic and pastoral peoples by subjecting them formally (if not always in practice) to the Sharia law, reducing the cultural differences between the peoples of the desert and steppes and those of the cities and settled regions. Tribes recently converted often became the greatest builders and patrons of Islamic high culture in art, architecture, and literature. At the same time conversion made it difficult for rulers to defend their heartlands from nomadic predators, since if the nomads were no longer infidels the jihad (struggle or "holy war") launched against them lost its *raison d'être*.

Following the rapid advance of the Saljuqs into Anatolia, Konya (formerly Iconium) became their capital. This elaborately decorated portal from the Ince Minare Madrasa shows the extraordinary richness of the Saljuq style. The "Slender Minaret" from which the school takes its name, was partially destroyed by lightning in 1900.

Two Turkish-speaking peoples, the Qarluqs and the Oghuz, established states that made significant contributions to this process. In Transoxiana the Qaraqanid dynasty accepted the nominal authority of the Abbasid caliphs, becoming the patrons of a new Turkish culture derived in part from Arab and Persian models. After defeating the Ghaznavids the Oghuz people, led by the Saljuq family, became the rulers of Khurasan, laying the foundations of the Saljuq Empire. Defeating the Buyids in 1055 they took control of Baghdad where the caliph crowned their leader Tughril Beg Sultan ("hold-

er of centuries"). In exchange for formal recognition, the sultans agreed to uphold Islamic law and defend Islam from its external enemies. The massive defeat inflicted by the Saljuqs on the Byzantine army at Manzikert in 1071 was one of the factors leading to the First Crusade in 1096. Although the Saljuqs conquered half of Anatolia, laying the foundations for later Ottoman-Turkish rule, their system of authority was too fragmented to maintain the unity of the empire, or to defend the frontiers of Islam against further nomadic incursions.

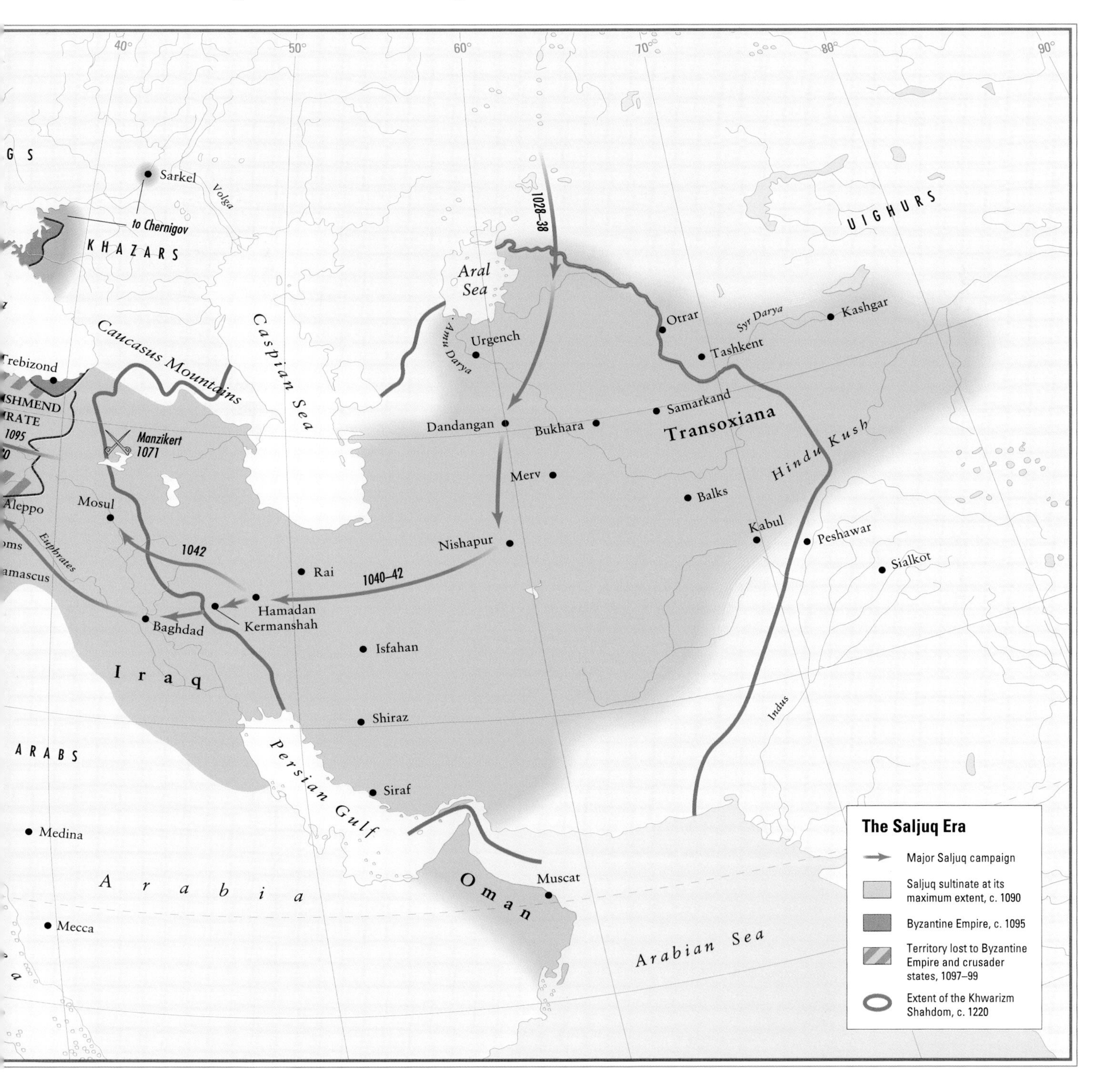

Military Recruitment 900–1800

The recruitment of armies from the peripheral regions, mainly from the steppelands of Inner Asia, the Caucasus, and the Balkans, became the most distinctive feature of the Islamic systems of governance until modern times. Known as Mamluks—"owned ones"—these warriors were purchased as slaves from the highlands and steppes or captured from defeated tribes. Brought in as the sultan's private armies and palace bodyguards, they were taught the rudiments of Islamic faith and culture and trained in the military arts. Attaching the word "slave" to Mamluks (as in "slave-warriors" or "slave-dynasties") is somewhat misleading. Though Mamluks and ghulams (household slaves) were bought and sold as personal property, their social position reflected that of their masters, rather than their own servile status. Eventually manumitted they became freedmen, clients of their former masters entitled to property rights, marriage, and personal security, with some of them rising to become rulers.

The practice of mamlukism started with the Abbasid caliphs who recruited tribes from Transoxiana, Armenia, and North Africa to offset the power of the Tahirids. They balanced these tribes with Turkish ghulams who were purchased individually before being trained and drafted into regiments under individual commanders. Since they were housed in separate cantonments, with their own mosques and markets, their allegiance was to their commanders, rather than to the caliphs. In the breakup of the empire after 945 the practice was adopted by the de-facto rulers who inherited the political power of the Abbasids. All the post-Abbasid states in the East—the Buyids, Ghaznavids, Qaraqanids, and Saljuqs—were created by ethnic minorities, including mercenaries from the Caspian region, Turkish, and other nomadic peoples from Inner Asia. Since new military rulers had no ethnic, cultural, linguistic, or historical connection with the peoples over whom they ruled, society tended to develop outside the purview of the state, with the ulama—the religious scholars and experts on law—merging with merchant and landowning families to form elites of notables whose prestige was dependent on religious knowledge. While allowing a form of civil society to develop separately from the military state, the practice of mamlukism militated against the type of communal loyalties or patriotisms that would emerge in Western Europe at a later period. The pattern

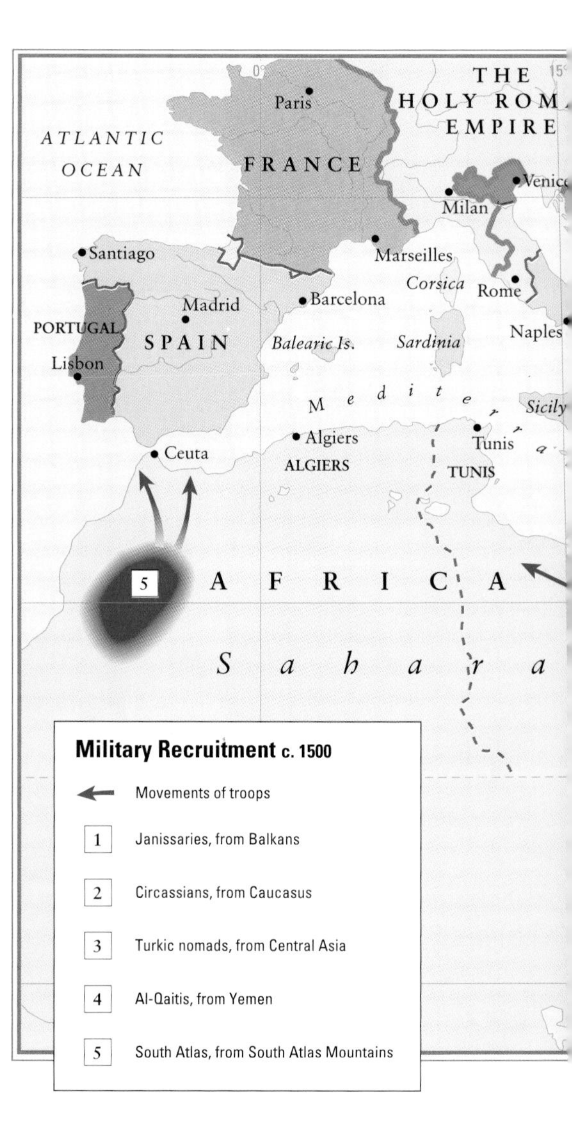

of recruiting erstwhile nomadic predators to defend society against other nomads—of making "wolves into sheepdogs"—is found throughout the Muslim heartlands, from the Maghreb to the Indus Valley.

The system of military slavery reached its fullest development in Egypt, a densely populated country of peasant cultivators without an indigenous military class. The system was institutionalized so successfully that Mamluk rule lasted for more than two and a half centuries (1250–1517), and resurfaced in a modifed form under the Ottomans (1517–1811). By constantly replenishing their ranks from abroad (firstly from among the Kipchak Turks from Central Asia, later from among the Circassians in the Caucasus) the Egyptian Mamluks resisted becoming absorbed into the ranks of the indigenous elites. For the most part they remained a one-generation aristocracy, without ties of blood with the rest of Egyptian society.

Under the Ottomans military slavery evolved in a somewhat different direction. From the late fourteenth century the sultans began to offset the power of their sipahi cavalry units levied from the estates of the nobility or recruited as mercenaries from Arabic, Kurdish, and Farsi-speaking nomads, an infantry corps of "new troops", Janissaries, levied mainly from its Christian provinces in the Balkans. The levy (known as the

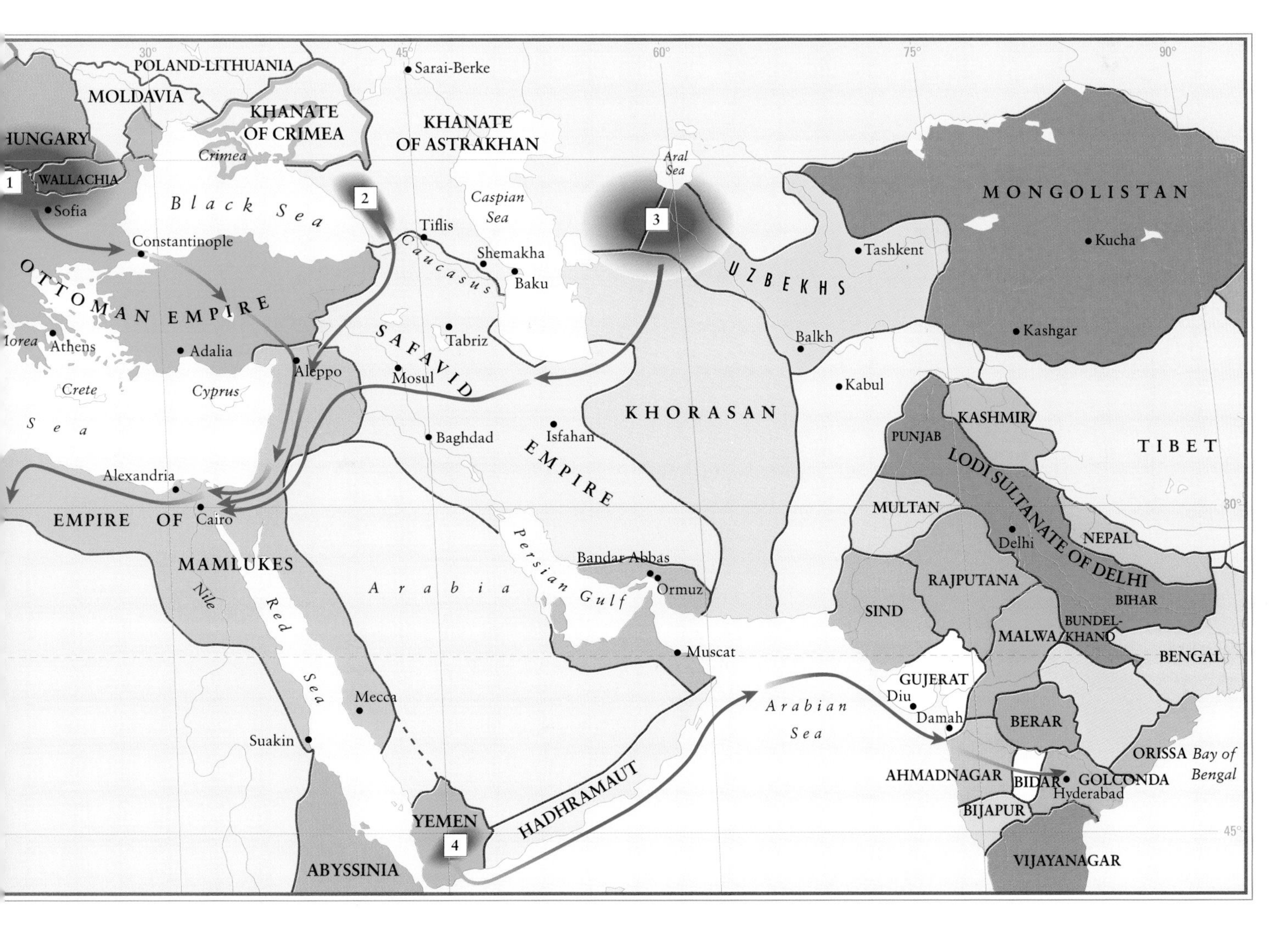

devshirme) was conducted in the villages about every four years: the towns were usually exempt, as the sons of townsfolk were considered too well educated or insufficiently hardy. Boys between 13 and 18 were selected (although there are reports of children as young as 8 being chosen). Since married men were exempt, the Orthodox peasants often married off their children very young to avoid the levy. The selected boys (estimates are put at around 20 percent) were given Muslim identities and trained in the arts of war, with the brightest selected for personal service to the sultan, where they often rose to be rulers of the empire. Although slave recruitment ceased in the 1640s the Janissaries continued to prosper, with increasing numbers of Muslim-born boys joining their ranks. Having substantial commercial interests, salaries, and state-funded pensions they became a privileged and tyrannical elite, resistant to change. In 1826 Sultan Mahmud II used his newly formed military force to slaughter most of them at a muster in Istanbul.

The Janissary corps, dressed in their gold finery, parade at a court reception. Originally recruited from the Christian Balkans, became a formidable power within the state. Sultan Mahmud II abolished the Janissaries in 1826, as part of his program of modernization.

Fatimid Empire 909–1171

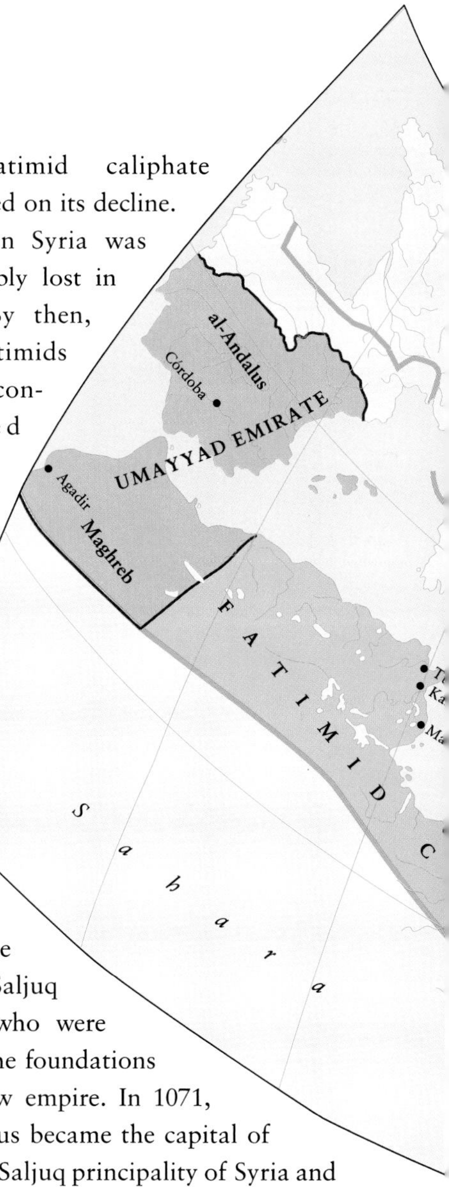

The Shiite Ismaili caliphate of the Fatimids was established in Ifriqiya in the Maghreb, when a group of Kutama Berbers accepted the claims of Abdallah al-Mahdi to be the rightful descendant of Ali and Fatima and rose against the Aghlabids in 909. By 921, al-Mahdi had settled in his new capital city of Mahdiyya on the coastline of Ifriqiya. As successors to the Aghlabids, the Fatimids also inherited their fleet and the island of Siqilliyya (Sicily). By the end of al-Mahdi's reign (909–934), the Fatimid state extended from present-day Algeria and Tunisia to the Libyan coast of Tripolitania. The third Fatimid caliph, al-Mansur (r. 946–953) built a new capital city named Mansuriyya, after himself. Situated near Sabra to the south of Qayrawan, Mansuriyya served as the Fatimid capital from 948 until 973.

Fatimid rule was firmly established in North Africa only during the reign of the fourth member of the dynasty, al-Muizz (r. 953–975), who transformed the Fatimid caliphate from a regional power into a great empire. He succeeded in subduing the entire Maghreb, with the exception of Sabra, before concerning himself with the conquest of Egypt, an objective attained in 969. A new Fatimid capital city was built outside Fustat, initially called Mansuriyya, but renamed al-Qahira al-Muizziyya (Cairo), "The Victorious City of al-Muizz," when the caliph took possession of his new capital in 973. The extension of Fatimid power in Syria became the primary foreign policy objective of al-Muizz's son and successor al-Aziz (r. 975–996). By the end of his reign, the Fatimid Empire had attained, at least nominally, its greatest extent, with Fatimid suzerainty being recognized from the Atlantic and the western Mediterranean to the Red Sea, the Hejaz, Syria, and Palestine. By 1038, the Fatimids had also extended their authority to the emirate of Aleppo.

In the long reign of al-Mustansir (1036–94), the Fatimid caliphate embarked on its decline. Northern Syria was irrevocably lost in 1060. By then, the Fatimids were confronted with the growing menace of the Saljuq Turks, who were laying the foundations of a new empire. In 1071, Damascus became the capital of the new Saljuq principality of Syria and Palestine. By the end of al-Mustansir's rule, of the former Fatimid possessions in Syria and Palestine, only Ascalon and a few coastal towns, like Acre and Tyre, still remained in Fatimid hands. By 1048, the Zirids, ruling over Ifriqiya on behalf of the Fatimids, placed themselves under Abbasid suzerainty. By 1070, when they lost Sicily to the Normans, Barqa had become the western limit of the Fatimid Empire, which soon became effectively limited to only Egypt. Ascalon, the last Fatimid foothold in Syria-Palestine, was lost to the Franks in 1153. Fatimid rule ended in 1171, when Salah al-Din (Saladin), who became the last Fatimid vizier after taking over Egypt, had the khutba (sermon) read in Cairo in the name of the reigning Abbasid caliph while the last Fatimid caliph, al-Adid (r. 1160–71), lay dying in his palace.

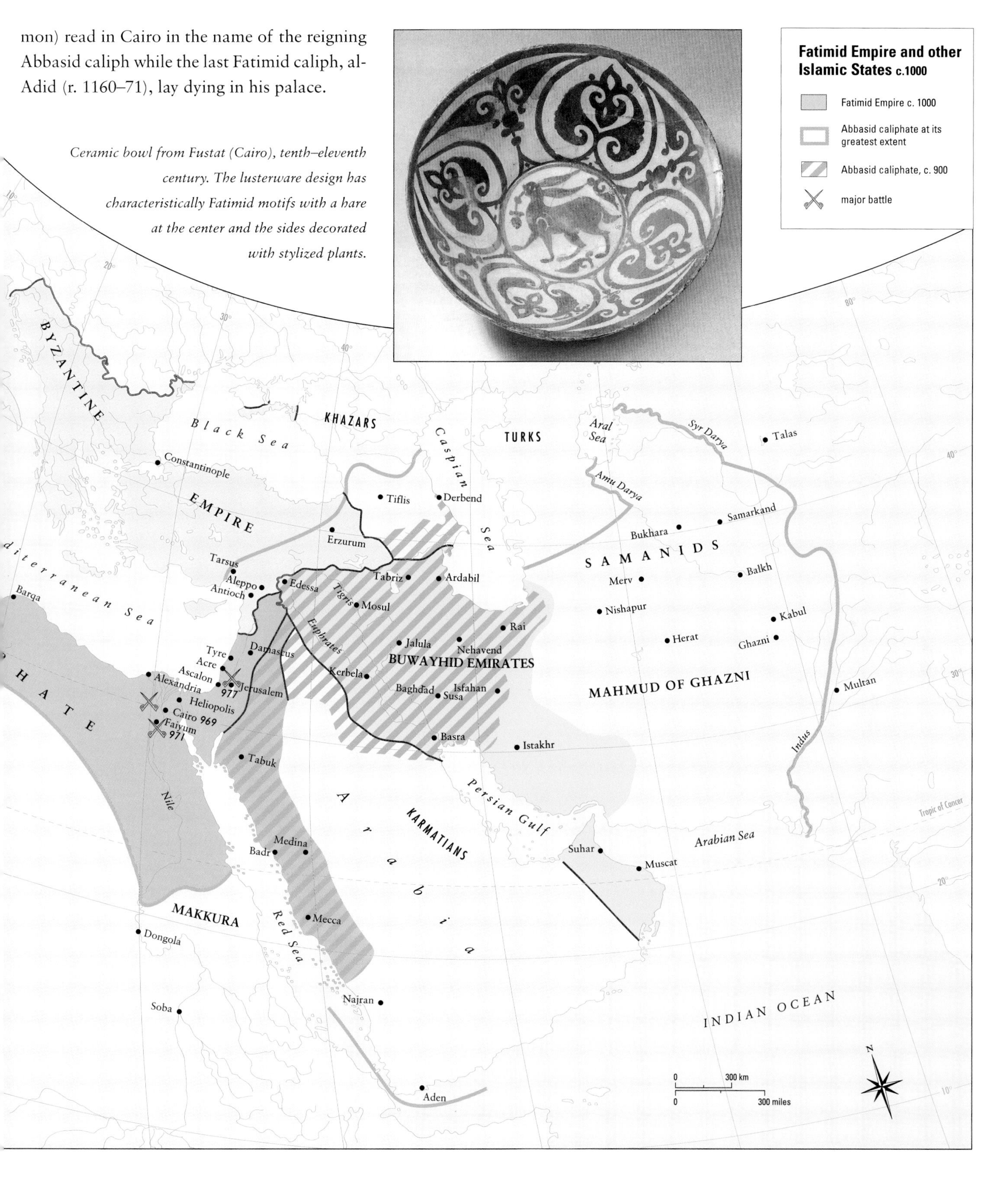

Ceramic bowl from Fustat (Cairo), tenth–eleventh century. The lusterware design has characteristically Fatimid motifs with a hare at the center and the sides decorated with stylized plants.

Trade Routes c. 700–1500

Muhammad is said to have traveled outside Arabia as a merchant. His tribe, the Quraish, who led the Arab conquests, were among the foremost traders in the peninsula. Merchants continued to be held in high esteem, often marrying into the families of ulama, who they supported by endowing their educational institutions. Islamic rituals favor commercial activity. Mosques are often adjacent to markets, and though Friday is the day for congregational prayer, it was not treated as a sabbath until recent times. Markets opened before and after the noonday prayer. Since the whole male population was gathered in town, Fridays were good days for doing business. Similarly, the pilgrimages to Mecca (umra and hajj), where Muslims from distant parts of the world meet each other, have always been a facilitator of trade. Pilgrims would finance the long and arduous journey (which in premodern times could take half a lifetime) by trading goods or working as artisans. Merchants would join the pilgrim caravans to sell their goods in the Hejaz.

By bringing vast areas of territory and coastlands under a single government, the Arab conquests created an enormous area of free trade, facilitating the expansion of trade far beyond the empire's borders. The extent of this trade has been revealed by archaeology, with significant numbers of coins from Abbasid times discovered in Scandinavia, and Chinese silks and ceramics found in burial sites in western Asia. Muslim merchants were not subject to tariffs within the empire. Foreign merchants who entered the lands of Islam were subject to the same rates imposed on Muslim merchants in their homelands. The new elite of the caliphal courts, with their demand for luxury goods, boosted trade. Though the breakup of the empire led to economic decline in some areas, with rival dynasties augmenting their budgets by imposing extra taxes and tariffs, the frequency with which such measures were denounced as illegal, oppressive, and unjust indicates that the general temper remained favorable to mercantile activity, even under adverse political conditions.

Initially the Arab conquest had the effect of bringing two oceanic trade routes—through the Persian Gulf and Red Sea—within a single market based on common law, language, and currency. Under the Abbasids the most attractive route for goods from East and South Asia to the Mediterranean went up the Tigris to Baghdad, or up the Euphrates to an easy portage to Aleppo and from there to a Syrian port such as Antioch. The towns along these routes depended on the exchange of commodities for their existence.

The Mesopotamian cities absorbed luxury goods from India and China. These were sold in the markets alongside necessities such as food grains, fuel, timber, and cooking oils. Mesopotamia was also the terminus of the chief land route to China and India as well as north to the Volga basin and the well-watered lands of Eastern Europe, sources of fur, amber, metal goods, and hides. In the earliest period Muslim ships from ports such as Basra or Hormuz went all the way to China, returning after two or three years with cargoes such as silk, porcelain, jade, and other valuables. However as the trade became more sophisticated merchants no longer traded directly with Guangzhou (Canton) and Hangzhou but acquired goods from China at ports in Java, Sumatra, or the Malibar coast.

Muslim merchants from the Maghreb were active in the gold trade, which took them across the Sahara Desert to the Sahel cities of Timbuktu and Gao, and beyond, to the goldfields of western Africa. The chain of commercial centers established by Muslim traders on the eastern African coast, including Lamu, Malindi, and the island of Zanzibar extended as far south as Sofala in modern Mozambique. Intrepid Muslim travelers penetrated the African interior in search of gold, slaves, ivory, rare woods, and precious stones centuries before Europeans followed in their paths.

When the decline of Abbasid power and the incursions of Turkish tribesmen made the trans-Syrian route less secure the alternative water route, via the Red Sea and the Nile, came into prominence. It was the more difficult as the land route from the Gulf of Suez to the Nile was more arduous than the route across Syria, except for a brief period when the Mamluk sultans revived an ancient canal originally dug by the pharaohs. Red Sea ports such as Aden, Jidda, Aydhab, and Qulzum, benefited from this trade, as did Cairo and Alexandria. Trade on the Indian Ocean was monopolized by Muslims until the arrival of the Portuguese, followed by the English and Dutch from the sixteenth century onward.

The land routes linking western Asia and the Mediterranean with eastern and southern Asia were just as important as the maritime routes. With many cities landlocked or distant from rivers and oceans, even bulky items had to be carried by animals. Careful planning was needed before the caravans set out on long journeys. Food had to be procured for animals and humans, and nomadic tribes had to be hired as guards. In remote areas networks of khans (overnight resting places) or khaniqas (Sufi lodges) provided food and hospitality. Some were built like fortresses for defense against bedouin marauders. The vast distances over rough terrain, combined with the breakdown in territorial authority, made road construction impracticable. Even by late Roman times, wheeled traffic had all but disappeared. The results can be seen in many of the cities of western Asia and North Africa. Before modern times few of them had boulevards broad enough for carts or carriages.

By the 1500s, the Ottoman Empire, with its capital at Constantinople, had become one of the Islamic world's most important trading centers. The sultan's court, together with his advisors, took careful account of annual trade.

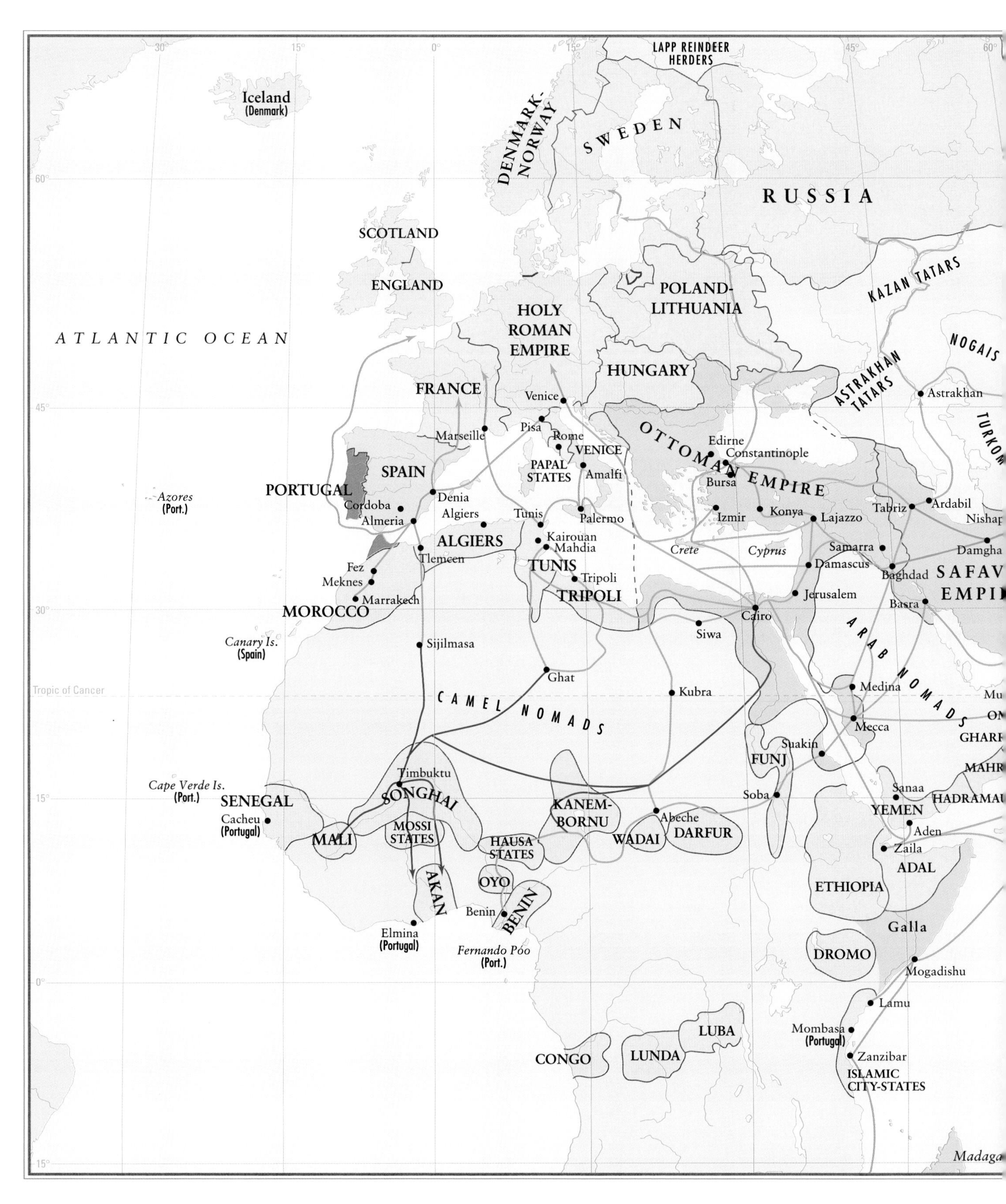
LAPP REINDEER HERDERS
Iceland (Denmark)
DENMARK-NORWAY
SWEDEN
RUSSIA
SCOTLAND
ENGLAND
POLAND-LITHUANIA
KAZAN TATARS
ATLANTIC OCEAN
HOLY ROMAN EMPIRE
NOGAIS
HUNGARY
ASTRAKHAN TATARS
Astrakhan
FRANCE
Venice
TURKOM
Marseille
Pisa
Rome
VENICE
PAPAL STATES
Amalfi
OTTOMAN EMPIRE
Edirne
Constantinople
Bursa
SPAIN
PORTUGAL
Azores (Port.)
Cordoba
Almeria
Denia
Algiers
Tunis
Palermo
Izmir
Konya
Lajazzo
Tabriz
Ardabil
Nishap
ALGIERS
Kairouan
Mahdia
Tlemcen
Crete
Cyprus
Samarra
Damascus
Damgha
Fez
Meknes
TUNIS
Tripoli
Baghdad
SAFAV
EMPI
Marrakech
MOROCCO
TRIPOLI
Jerusalem
Basra
Cairo
Siwa
Canary Is. (Spain)
Sijilmasa
ARAB NOMADS
Tropic of Cancer
Ghat
Medina
Kubra
CAMEL NOMADS
Mecca
Suakin
FUNJ
Timbuktu
Cape Verde Is. (Port.)
SENEGAL
SONGHAI
KANEM-BORNU
Soba
Sanaa
HADRAMAU
YEMEN
Cacheu (Portugal)
MALI
MOSSI STATES
HAUSA STATES
WADAI
Abeche
DARFUR
Aden
Zaila
ADAL
OYO
AKAN
ETHIOPIA
Benin
BENIN
Elmina (Portugal)
Fernando Póo (Port.)
Galla
DROMO
Mogadishu
Lamu
LUBA
Mombasa (Portugal)
CONGO
LUNDA
Zanzibar
ISLAMIC CITY-STATES
Madaga
30°
15°
0°
15°
45°
60°
60°
45°
30°
15°
0°
15°

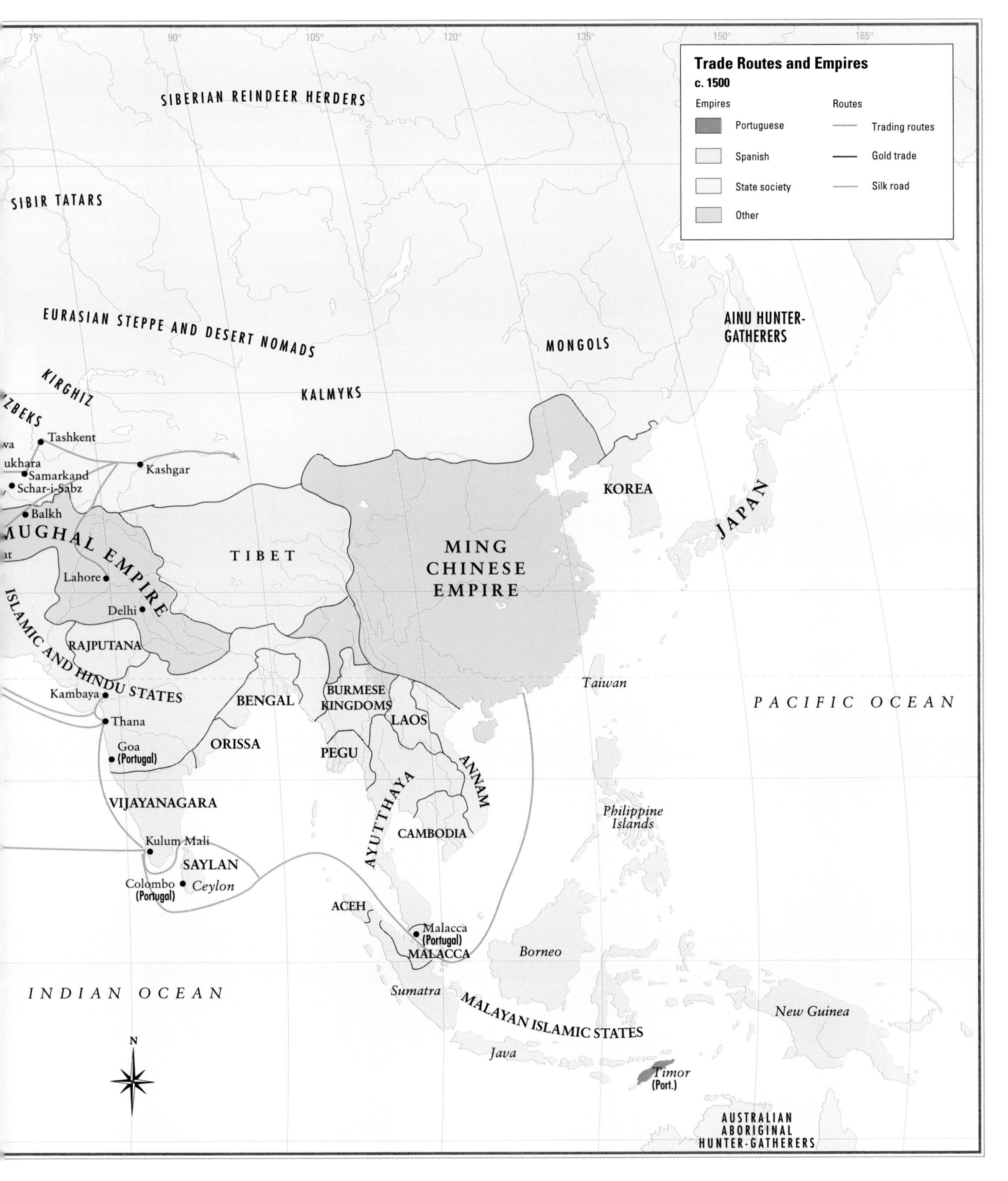

Trade Routes and Empires
c. 1500
Empires
Portuguese
Spanish
State society
Other
Routes
Trading routes
Gold trade
Silk road
SIBERIAN REINDEER HERDERS
SIBIR TATARS
EURASIAN STEPPE AND DESERT NOMADS
KIRGHIZ
KALMYKS
MONGOLS
AINU HUNTER-GATHERERS
Tashkent
Samarkand
Schar-i-Sabz
Kashgar
Balkh
MUGHAL EMPIRE
TIBET
MING CHINESE EMPIRE
KOREA
JAPAN
Lahore
Delhi
ISLAMIC AND HINDU STATES
RAJPUTANA
Kambaya
Thana
Goa (Portugal)
BENGAL
ORISSA
BURMESE KINGDOMS
LAOS
PEGU
ANNAM
AYUTTHAYA
CAMBODIA
Taiwan
PACIFIC OCEAN
VIJAYANAGARA
Philippine Islands
Kulum Mali
SAYLAN
Colombo (Portugal)
Ceylon
ACEH
Malacca (Portugal)
MALACCA
Borneo
INDIAN OCEAN
Sumatra
MALAYAN ISLAMIC STATES
New Guinea
Java
Timor (Port.)
AUSTRALIAN ABORIGINAL HUNTER-GATHERERS
N

Crusader Kingdoms

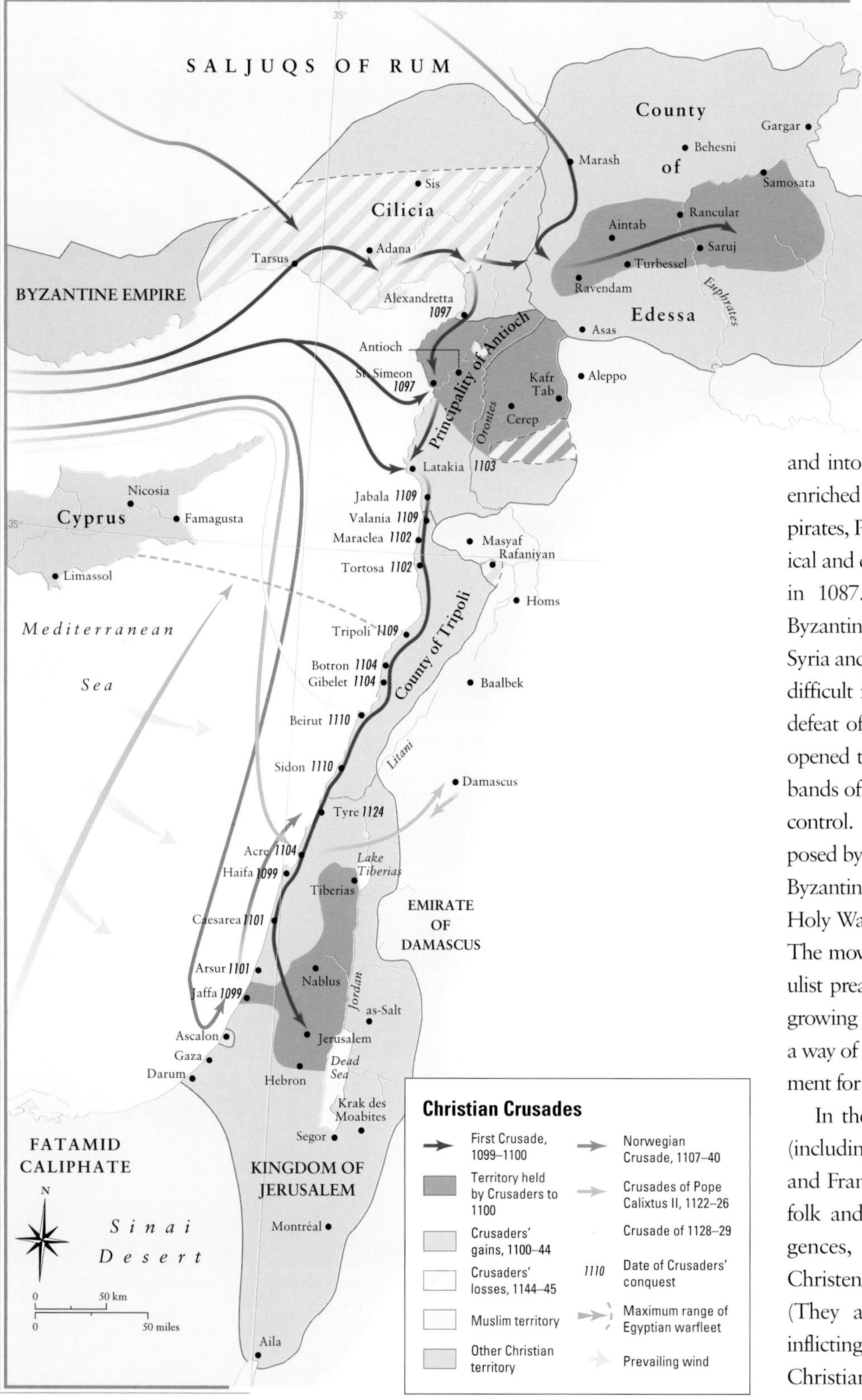

The Crusades occurred at a time of Islamic disunity and retreat. There were Christian advances in Spain—Toledo fell in 1085—and in Sicily, which the Normans conquered in 1091–92. Economically, the decline of the Abbasid caliphate and the Saljuq invasions had diverted the East Asian trade away from Baghdad and Constantinople. Sending it through Egypt and into the hands of Italian merchant shipping, it enriched the Italian cities. Harassed by Muslim pirates, Pisa and Genoa destroyed Mahdia, the political and commercial capital of Muslim North Africa in 1087. The fluctuating frontiers between the Byzantine and Fatimid Empires allowed the cities of Syria and Palestine considerable autonomy, making it difficult for them to unite against the invaders. The defeat of the Byzantine army at Manzikert in 1071 opened the rich Anatolian pastures to migration by bands of Oghuz Turks, not all of them under Saljuq control. Alarmed at the danger to Christendom posed by the Turks as well as by Norman attacks on Byzantine lands in Italy, Pope Urban II launched a Holy War for the defense and unity of Christendom. The movement was stimulated by charismatic, populist preachers such as Peter the Hermit and by the growing popularity of the pilgrimage to Jerusalem as a way of earning spiritual merit or as an act of atonement for sins such as murder.

In the event, the knights from the Latin West, (including England, Scandinavia, Germany, Italy, and France) supported by ragtag armies of townsfolk and peasants lured by the promise of indulgences, were not wholly interested in saving Christendom by helping their Orthodox brethren. (They actually sacked Constantinople in 1202, inflicting untold damage on the capital of Eastern Christianity.) They wanted to carve out feudal domains in the well-watered lands of the Mediterranean littoral. The remarkable success of the First Crusade, culminating in the capture of Jerusalem from the Fatimids in 1099, contained the seeds of the Byzantine Empire's eventual demise. The need to support the intrusive Latin states whose existence depended on Muslim disunity overrode the need to maintain Byzantium's eastern frontiers. For the most part the Franks, as the invaders were known, were hated as oppressors by Muslims and local Christians alike—not to mention the Jews, who lost the protection they had enjoyed under Muslim rule, and were massacred in Palestine as they had been in Europe. Far from checking the Turkish advance on Christian domains, the Crusaders' attacks on Byzantium helped to destroy the only polity that could have prevented it. Though the Latin kingdoms were eventually eliminated, their existence damaged the previously good relations that had existed between the eastern churches, their Muslim protectors, and local Islamic communities, leaving a legacy of mistrust of the West that has lasted to the present.

Entry of the crusaders into Damietta, Egypt, in June 1249. After losing Jerusalem, the Crusaders made several attacks on Egypt in the hope of regaining territory in the Holy Land. From an illuminated manuscript painted in Acre shortly after 1277. This school of illuminators was probably founded by Louis IX during his stay in Palestine, 1250–54.

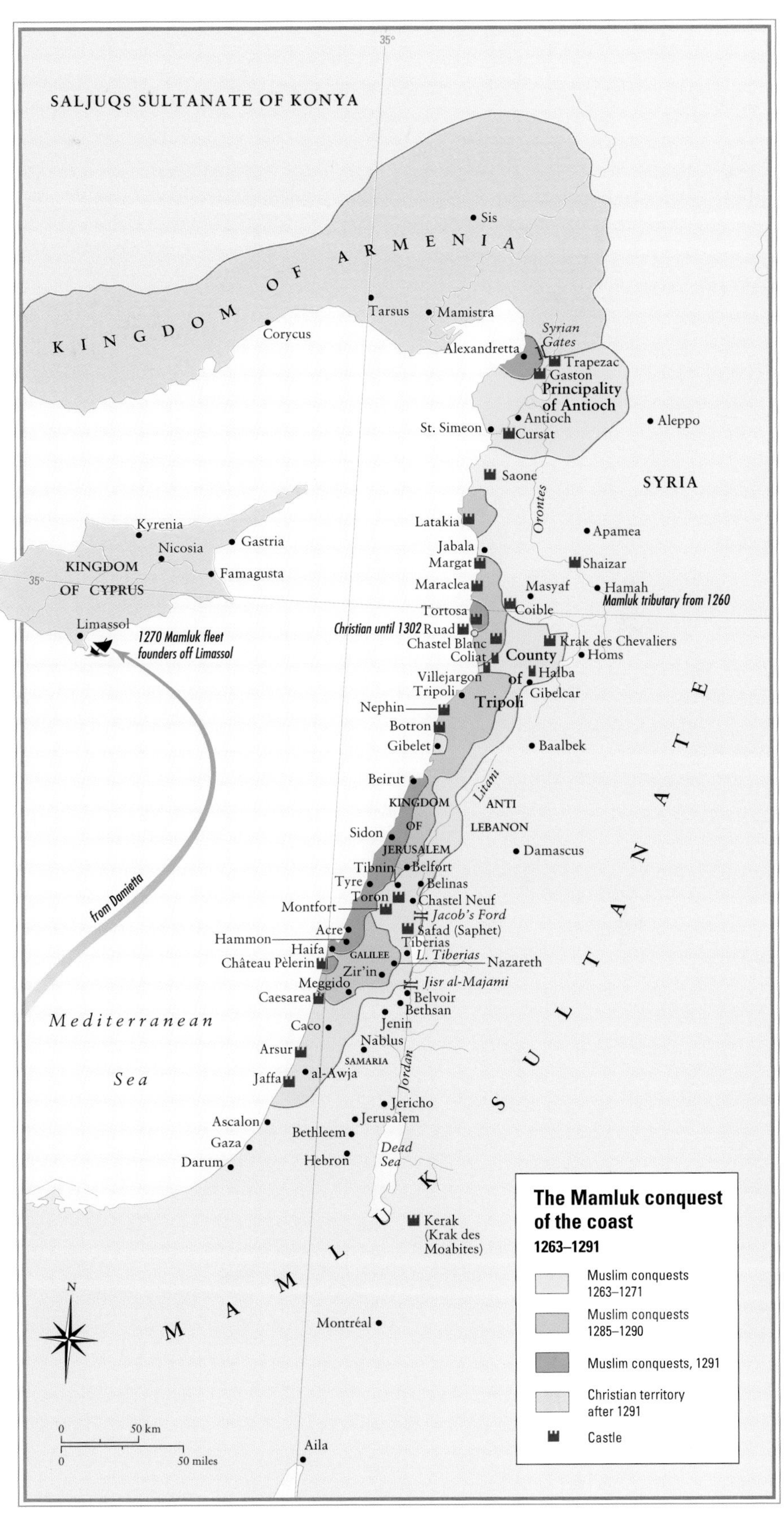

Sufi Orders 1100–1900

The Sufi orders were and remain the most important organized expression of Islamic spirituality. The word Sufism (from the Arabic *Sufi*, one who wears wool), is thought to derive from the coarse woolen garments worn by early Muslim ascetics who sought to develop an inner spirituality. This was sometimes expressed as the quest for union with God and it set them apart from believers who were content with the formal observance of Islamic law and ritual. Early adepts, sometimes known as "drunken" Sufis, cultivated mental states that would lead them to experience annihilation of the self in the divine presence. The desire for ecstatic union with the divine, and the pain of separation from it, is the theme of much Sufi poetry. Drunken Sufism sometimes displayed itself in extravagant displays aimed at demonstrating contempt for the flesh, such as piercing the body with iron rings or handling dangerous animals. Sober Sufism—exemplified in the teachings of Abu Hamid al-Ghazali (d. 1111)—insisted that the path to spiritual fulfillment lay firmly within the boundaries of normative legal and ritual practice.

Present from the beginnings of Islam, all Sufi movements would claim to have their origins in the religious experience of Muhammad and his closest Companions Abn Bakr and Ali. Organized Sufism, however, was consolidated in the twelfth and thirteenth centuries, gaining ground rapidly in Asia in the aftermath of the Mongol invasions when the institutional fabric of Muslim life was severely dislocated. Internally the Sufi orders cemented the sociopolitical order by providing rulers with popular sources of religious legitimacy, supplementing the formal authority conferred by the ulama. Many rulers were patrons of Sufi orders and placed themselves under the spiritual guidance of Sufi masters from whose baraka (blessedness or charismatic spiritual power) they derived benefit. Further afield the Sufi orders were instrumental in spreading Islam in peripheral regions, such as the Malay archipelago, Central Asia, and Subsaharan Africa. Access to the normative, textual Islam of the ulama, based on the Koran, hadith, fiqh (jurisprudence), and tafsir (hermeneutics), required knowledge of Arabic, restricting its appeal. The Sufi shaikhs and pirs, however, were adept at spiritual improvisation and were able to convey Islamic teachings verbally, using local languages. The esoteric Sufi rituals, known as dhikrs (ceremonies held in remembrance of God), allowed them to develop spiritual techniques that meshed with practices derived from non-Islamic traditions, such as ritual dances or controlled yoga-style breathing practiced in India. In Africa Sufis and Marabouts (from the Arabic murabit) were able to propagate Islam by assimilating local deities or spirits to the numinous forces, such as djinns and angels referred to in the Koran. Ancestor cults could be accommodated by adding local kinship structures onto Arab lineages or Sufi silsilas, chains of spiritual authority linking the shaikhs and Marabouts to the Prophet and his Companions. In peripheral regions such as the High Atlas these silsilas provided a quasi-constitutional framework through which segmentary tribal groups achieved a basic minimum of cooperation, with leaders of saintly families acting as arbiters in intertribal conflicts. In all parts of the Muslim world Sufi holy men (and occasionally women) became the objects of popular veneration. In due course such cults became the targets of reformers who regarded the excessive devotion given to saintly mediators as a violation of the Islamic prohibition on idolatry.

A group of Mevlevi Sufis or dervishes (mendicants) perform their traditional whirling ritual. The "dance," a dhikr, or "remembrance of God," brings the adept closer to the divine, balancing spiritual ecstasy with formal discipline. The Mevlevi order was founded by Jalal al-Din Rumi (1207–73), the famous Sufi poet and mystic.

In contrast to the ulama who tended to reflect the consensus of the learned, the Sufi tariqas developed elaborate hierarchical organizations with spiritual power concentrated into the hands of the leader—known variously as the shaikh, murshid, or pir. Murids (members or aspirants) were bound by the baya, oath of allegiance, to the leader or murshid who headed a hierarchy of ranks within the order based on ascending spiritual stages. Although the systems varied considerably with some tariqas more exclusive and tightly controlled than others, the combination of devotion to the leader and rankings within the organization made it possible for the tariqas to convert themselves into formidable fighting forces. In the Caucasus the Imam Shamil waged his campaign against the Russians from 1834–39 under the spiritual authority of his murshid and father-in-law, Sayyid Jamal al-Din al-Ghazi-Ghumuqi, shaikh of the Khalidiyya branch of the Naqshbandiyya. In North Africa Abd al-Qadir, a shaikh of the Qadiriyya, took the lead in the struggle against the French; in Cyrenaica the Sanusiyya were at the forefront of resistance against the Italian occupiers. In other regional contexts, however, the tariqas ran with the flow of colonial power. In Morocco during the late nineteenth and early twentieth centuries the influential Tijaniyya order accepted lavish subsidies from the French, who used the order to further their colonial interests. In Senegal the Muridiyya order founded by Amadu Bamba (c. 1850–1927) turned away from resistance to develop a work ethic based on peanut cultivation that brought economic stability to the country under the French-dominated regime.

The tariqas, in many cases, provided the leadership for the reform and revival movements that swept through the Islamic world in the nineteenth and twentieth centuries. The term "neo-Sufism" is sometimes applied to movements that place more emphasis on "outward" political activity than to "inner" spiritual experience, with the structure of the tariqa providing the vehicle for the transmission and implementation of ideas. A well known example is the Nurculuk movement in Turkey founded by Said Nursi (1876–1960). A Naqshbandi-trained preacher and writer, he sought to revitalize Islamic thought by integrating science, tradition, theology, and mysticism in a new version of the Naqshbandi slogan of "the hand turned to work and the heart turned to God." In contrast to the Muslim Brotherhood in Egypt, which was also influenced by Sufi ideas, the movement works with the grain of Turkey's secular state.

In recent decades Sufi ideas and devotional practices have come under attack from two quarters—modernists, who regard Sufism as retrograde, and Wahhanbi-inspired Islamists, who have taken over many Islamic insitutions with financial support from Saudi Arabia and other oil-rich countries. Though the two agendas are somewhat different, the consequences are the same. Modernists, adapting the ideas of the European Enlightenment, began with demands for a "rational" religion. They ended by turning against religion altogether. The Islamists, reacting against the modernists, are caught in the same "all-or-nothing" attitudes.

Sufism occupies the middle ground between modernism and fundamentalism, enabling religion to accommodate itself to changing social conditions. Without the mediating, adaptive power of Sufism, it is unlikely that the advocates of Political Islam (or "Islamism") will succeed in accommodating the variegated strands of Islam within the "restored" Islamic order that they seek.

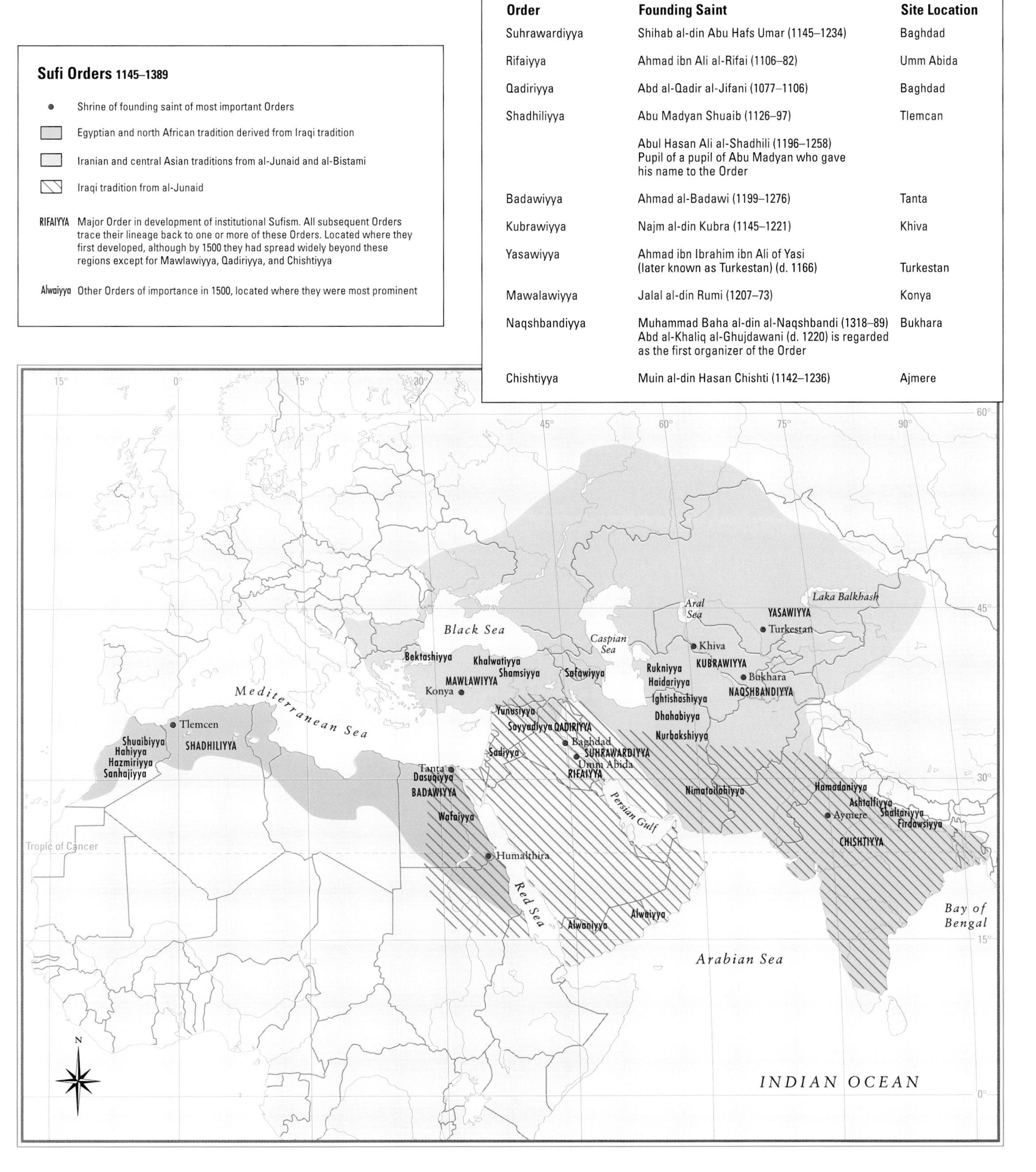

Order	Founding Saint	Site Location
Suhrawardiyya	Shihab al-din Abu Hafs Umar (1145–1234)	Baghdad
Rifaiyya	Ahmad ibn Ali al-Rifai (1106–82)	Umm Abida
Qadiriyya	Abd al-Qadir al-Jifani (1077–1106)	Baghdad
Shadhiliyya	Abu Madyan Shuaib (1126–97)	Tlemcan
	Abul Hasan Ali al-Shadhili (1196–1258) Pupil of a pupil of Abu Madyan who gave his name to the Order	
Badawiyya	Ahmad al-Badawi (1199–1276)	Tanta
Kubrawiyya	Najm al-din Kubra (1145–1221)	Khiva
Yasawiyya	Ahmad ibn Ibrahim ibn Ali of Yasi (later known as Turkestan) (d. 1166)	Turkestan
Mawalawiyya	Jalal al-din Rumi (1207–73)	Konya
Naqshbandiyya	Muhammad Baha al-din al-Naqshbandi (1318–89) Abd al-Khaliq al-Ghujdawani (d. 1220) is regarded as the first organizer of the Order	Bukhara
Chishtiyya	Muin al-din Hasan Chishti (1142–1236)	Ajmere

Ayyubids and Mamluks

Saladin, depicted here as the archetypically heroic Saracen by Gustave Doré (1884) was equally admired by the Muslims and his crusader foes for his sense of honor and humanity. His reputation in the West was enhanced by the popularity of Sir Walter Scott's novel The Talisman *(1825).*

Having established themselves in a fragmented part-Muslim world, the Crusader kingdoms eventually stimulated a united response. The revival can be traced to the seizure of Aleppo by the Saljuq governor of Mosul, Zangi, in 1128. His son, Nur al-Din, who ruled in Damascus from 1154–1174, consolidated his power in Syria and Mesopotamia, sending his Kurdish general Salah al-Din (Saladin) to take control of Egypt in 1169. Two years later Saladin assumed power symbolically by deposing the last of the Fatimid caliphs. He and his descendants, the Ayyubids, broadened the appeal of Sunnism in Egypt by allowing scholars from the different legal schools to work alongside each other, while popular devotion to the House of Ali was permitted at the mosque of Hussein, where the martyr's head is buried. From Egypt Saladin conquered Syria and upper Mesopotamia, restoring a unified state in the East for the first time since the early Abbasids. In 1187 he crowned his achievement by taking Jerusalem from the Franks.

Saladin's Ayyubid dynasty, however, was not to endure. In 1250 the last Ayyub sultan was killed by his Turkish Mamluk soldiers. They proclaimed their own general sultan, initiating more than two and a half centuries of Mamluk rule. Ten years later the brilliant Mamluk general, Baybars, defeated the Mongol invaders at Ayn Jalut in Syria. By 1291 his successors had reunited Syria, expelled the last Crusaders, and expanded the boundaries of their empire into the upper Euphrates valley and Armenia. The Mamluks kept their Turkish names and the exclusive right to ride horses and to own other Mamluks as slaves. For the most part they married the female slaves who had been imported with them. If they married local women or took on Muslim-Arab names, they lost caste among themselves. When the supply of Kipchak Turkish slaves began to run out the Kipchak Mamluks (known as Bahris) were replaced by Circassians (known as Burjis). Though most of the sultans tried to establish dynasties, their efforts were rarely successful, since minors or weaklings were invariably ousted by more powerful rivals. Nevertheless they demonstrated their devotion to Islam by patronizing scholarship and the Sufi orders, and by the magnificent buildings, including mosques, seminaries, and inns, which they lavished on Cairo in the distinct and ornate style that carries their name.

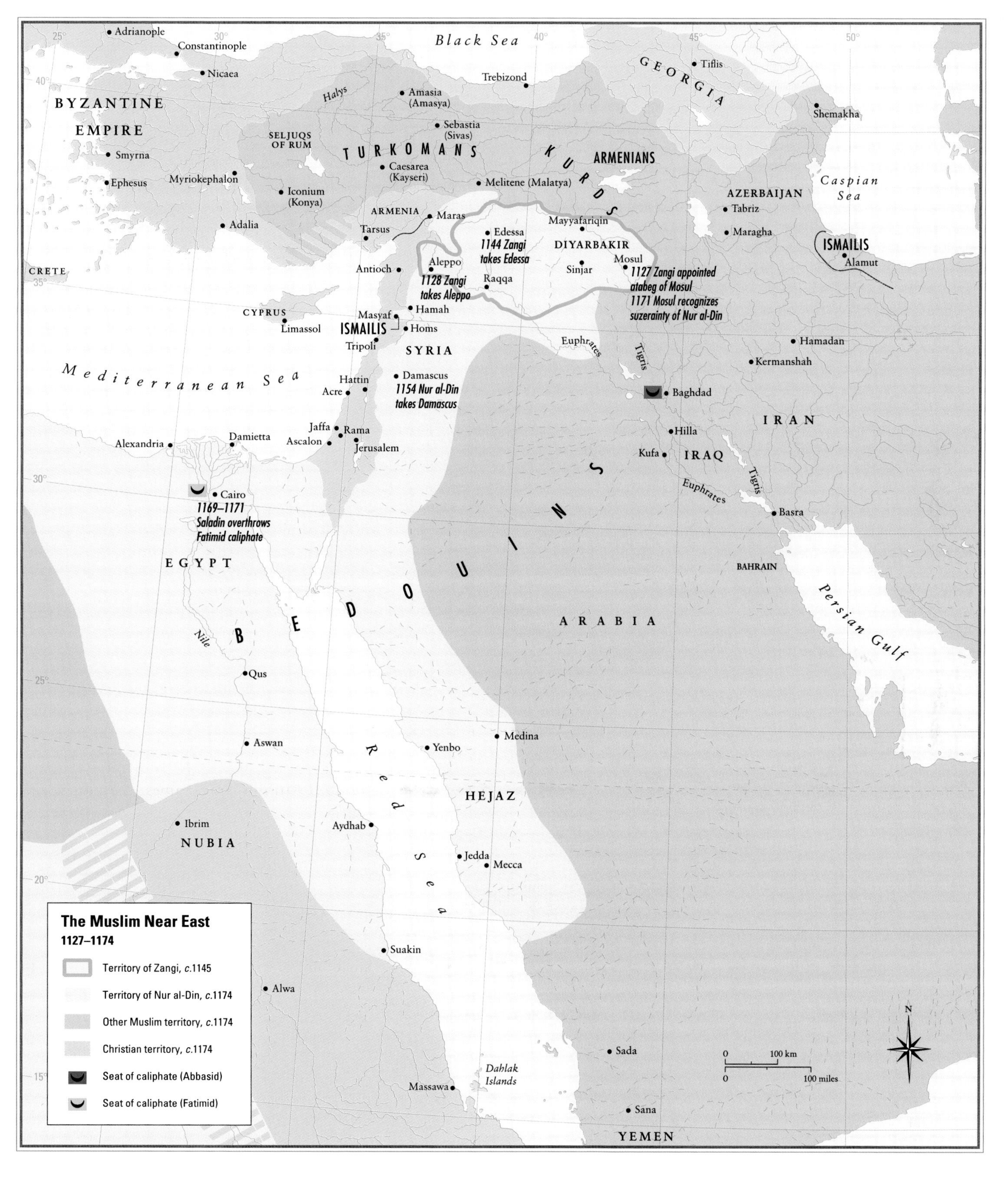
The Muslim Near East
1127–1174
Territory of Zangi, c.1145
Territory of Nur al-Din, c.1174
Other Muslim territory, c.1174
Christian territory, c.1174
Seat of caliphate (Abbasid)
Seat of caliphate (Fatimid)
Black Sea
Mediterranean Sea
Caspian Sea
Persian Gulf
Red Sea
BYZANTINE EMPIRE
SELJUQS OF RUM
TURKOMANS
KURDS
ARMENIANS
GEORGIA
AZERBAIJAN
ISMAILIS
ARMENIA
DIYARBAKIR
CRETE
CYPRUS
SYRIA
EGYPT
BEDOUINS
ARABIA
IRAQ
IRAN
BAHRAIN
HEJAZ
NUBIA
YEMEN
Adrianople
Constantinople
Nicaea
Smyrna
Ephesus
Myriokephalon
Iconium (Konya)
Adalia
Amasia (Amasya)
Sebastia (Sivas)
Caesarea (Kayseri)
Trebizond
Melitene (Malatya)
Tiflis
Shemakha
Tabriz
Maragha
Alamut
Maras
Tarsus
Edessa
1144 Zangi takes Edessa
Mayyafariqin
Mosul
1127 Zangi appointed atabeg of Mosul
1171 Mosul recognizes suzerainty of Nur al-Din
Sinjar
Raqqa
Aleppo
1128 Zangi takes Aleppo
Antioch
Masyaf
Hamah
Homs
Tripoli
Limassol
Hattin
Acre
Damascus
1154 Nur al-Din takes Damascus
Jaffa
Rama
Ascalon
Jerusalem
Damietta
Alexandria
Cairo
1169–1171 Saladin overthrows Fatimid caliphate
Halys
Euphrates
Tigris
Nile
Baghdad
Hilla
Kufa
Basra
Hamadan
Kermanshah
Qus
Aswan
Medina
Yenbo
Aydhab
Ibrim
Jedda
Mecca
Suakin
Alwa
Sada
Sana
Massawa
Dahlak Islands
0 100 km
0 100 miles
N

The Mongol Invasion

Ghenghis Khan in state surrounded by his attendants. However luxurious his court, as shown by this lavishly decorated yurt, the Great Khan remained a nomad to the end of his life.

Unlike the deserts of Arabia the steppelands of Inner Asia are comparatively well watered, with extensive grazing for horses. The horseback nomads who dwelt there were organized along similar lines to the Arabs in patrilineal tribal formations. Like the Arab and Turkish nomads they were able to construct large federations for successful raids on cities and areas of cultivation, creating substantial empires under formidable leaders: Attila, who ravaged central Europe in the fifth century with his Huns, is a well-known example. The Chinese emperors understood the dangers of these large formations of horse-borne invaders, and used their forces to break them up whenever strong enough to do so. The Great Wall had been built as a defensible barrier to keep them out.

Early in the thirteenth century a new formation developed among the Mongols in a remote region bordering the Siberian forests under Ghenghis Khan (c. 1162–1227). A clever and ruthless leader, he took command of a wide grouping of tribes from about 1206. By the time of his death he had dominated most of northern China and his armies had reached the shores of the Caspian. Divided between his sons, the empire continued to expand, overwhelming the rest of northern China and sweeping through eastern Europe as far as Germany. As with other nomadic formations, however, there were no clear rules of succession. The descendants of Ghenghis Khan competed for his legacy, creating several independent, sometimes mutually hostile, states. They included present-day Mongolia, northern China, the realm of the Golden Horde (centered in the Volga basin), the Chaghatay Khanate in the Oxus (Amu Darya) region, and the Ilkhan dynasty, which invaded Iran and destroyed Saljuq power in Anatolia.

The Mongols were not just ruthless and violent nomads. Their system of communications and knowledge of the latest warfare techniques were sophisticated enough to enable them to wreak unprecedented levels of destruction. In the initial conquests, entire populations of cities were massacred, without regard to age or gender. Buildings were leveled, rotting heads stacked in gruesome pyramids. Mongol cruelty was a form of psychological warfare designed to send the message that resistance was useless. As a strategy, terror was highly effective: the amirs who governed in the Iranian highlands hastened to demonstrate their homage. The local bureaucrats and families of notables actively collaborated, and even encouraged attacks on their Muslim enemies in order to gain favor with the conquerors. Members of the ulama rose to prominence and power. For instance, the historian al-Juvaini accompanied the Mongol army under the warlord Hulegu to Alamut, where the last Ismaili stronghold to survive the fall of the Fatimids, was destroyed in 1256. After the conquest of Baghdad two years later, the Sunni historian al-Juvaini became its governor. Within a generation the western Mongols had converted to Islam, opening a brilliant new era in the story of its development.

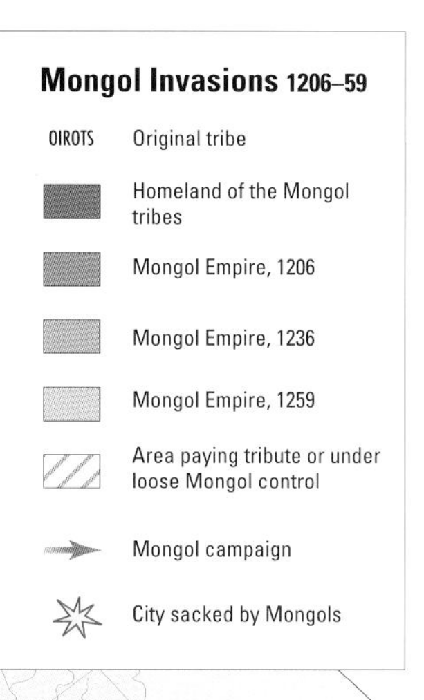

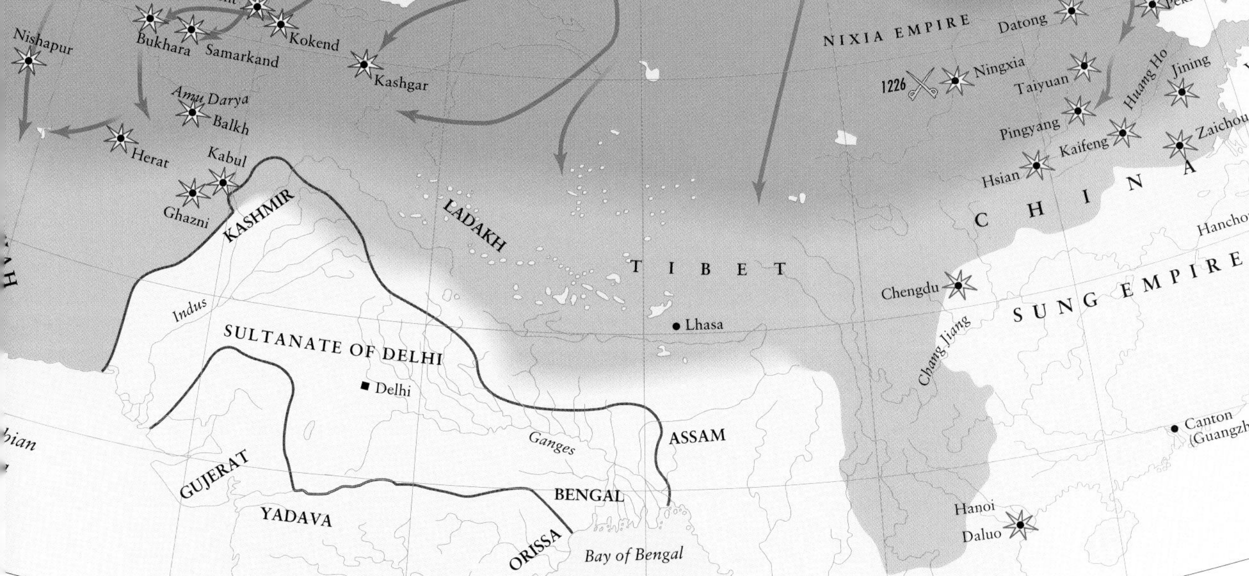

Maghreb and Spain 650–1485

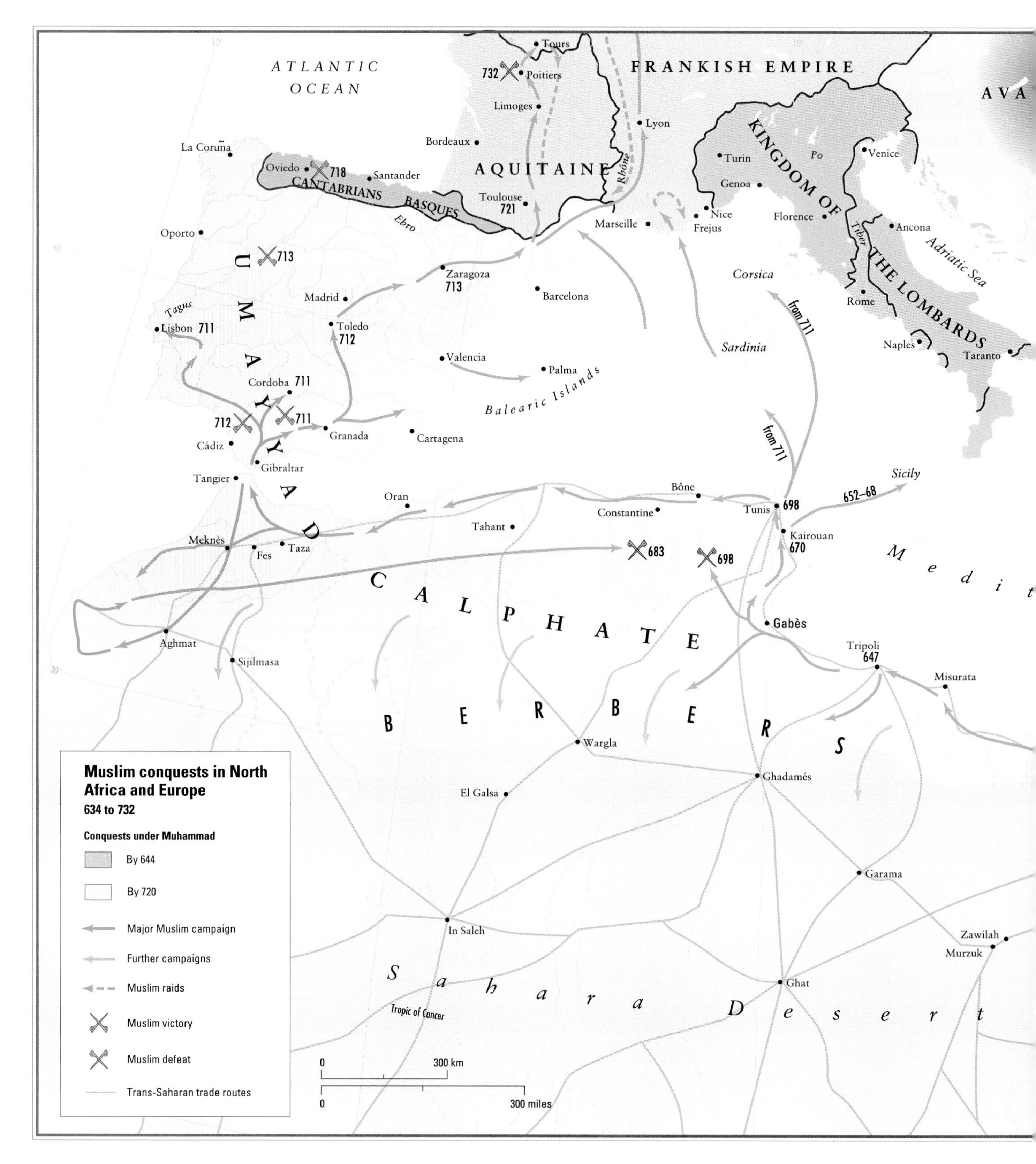

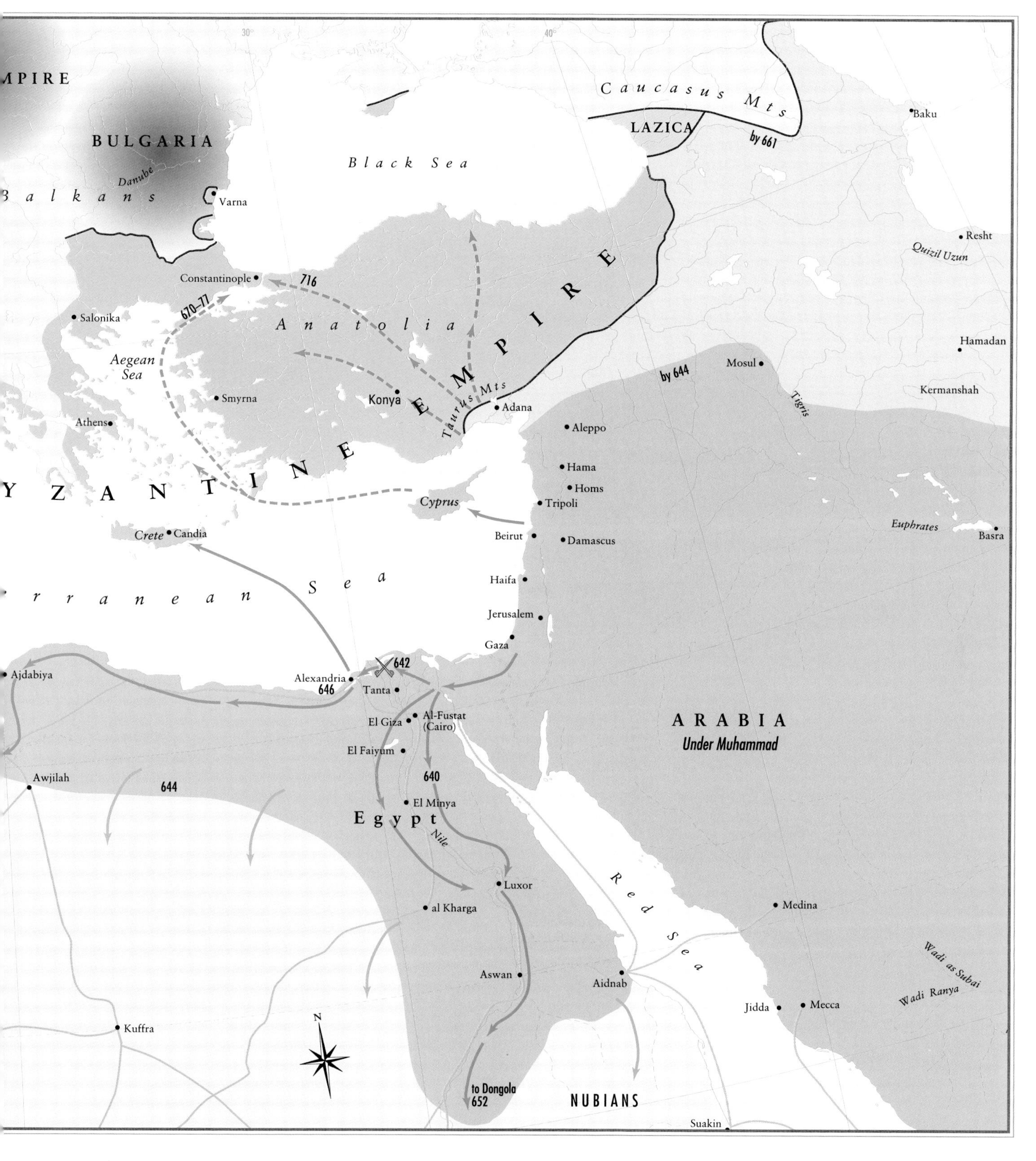

MPIRE
BULGARIA
Danube
Balkans
Varna
Black Sea
Caucasus Mts
LAZICA
by 661
Baku
Resht
Quizil Uzun
Constantinople
716
670–77
Salonika
Anatolia
BYZANTINE EMPIRE
Aegean Sea
Smyrna
Konya
Taurus Mts
Adana
by 644
Mosul
Tigris
Hamadan
Kermanshah
Athens
Aleppo
Hama
Homs
Tripoli
Cyprus
Crete
Candia
Beirut
Damascus
Euphrates
Basra
Mediterranean Sea
Haifa
Jerusalem
Gaza
642
Ajdabiya
Alexandria
646
Tanta
Al-Fustat (Cairo)
El Giza
El Faiyum
ARABIA
Under Muhammad
Awjilah
644
640
El Minya
Egypt
Nile
Luxor
al Kharga
Red Sea
Medina
Aswan
Aidnab
Wadi as Subai
Wadi Ranya
Jidda
Mecca
Kuffra
N
to Dongola 652
NUBIANS
Suakin

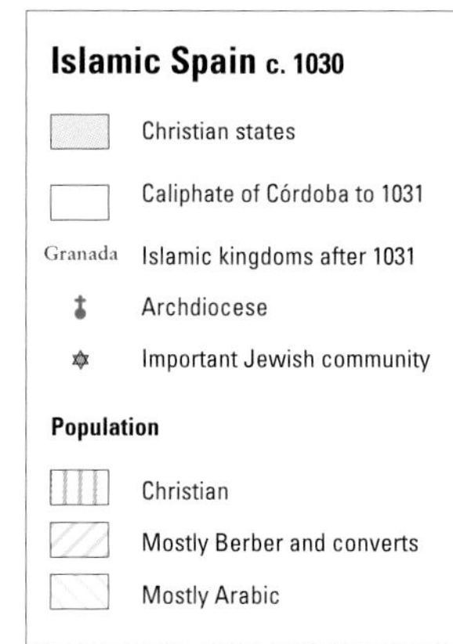

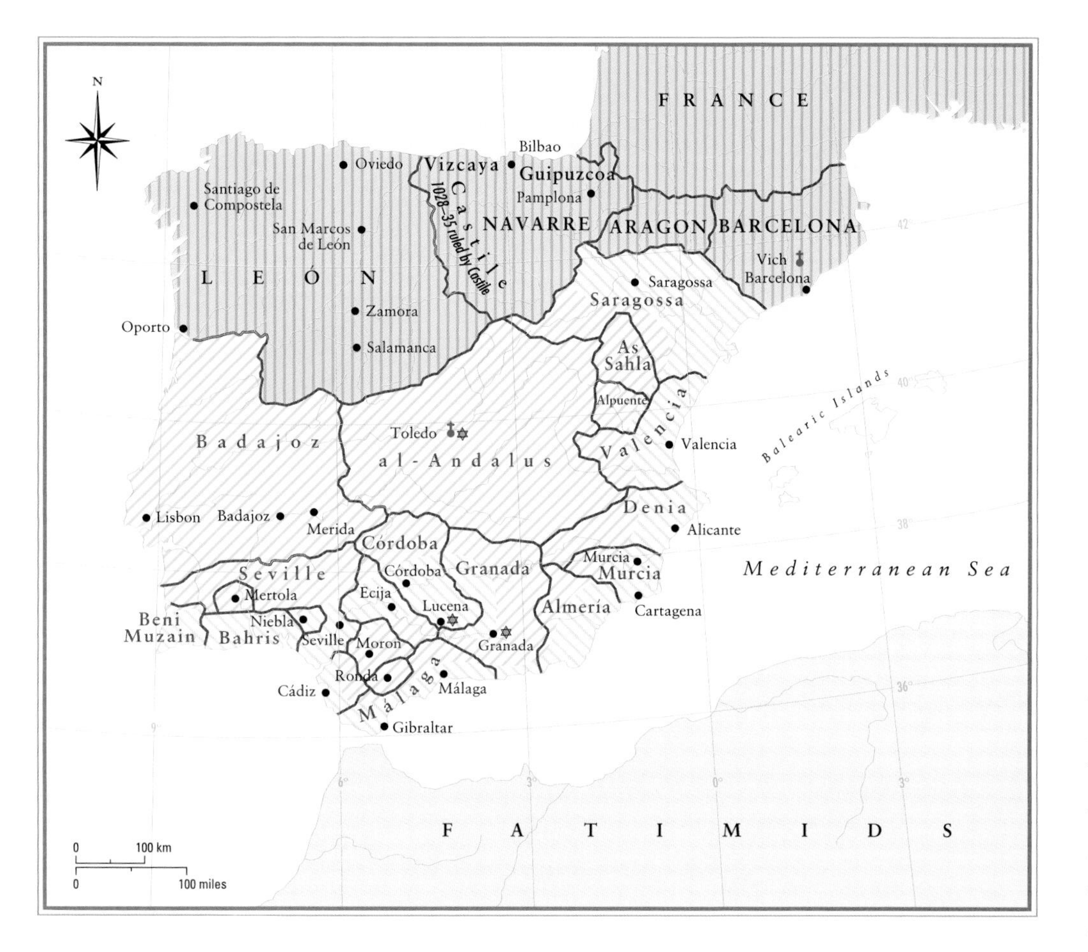

Al-Andalus is the Arabic name for territories in the Iberian Peninsula that came under Muslim rule and influence for nearly 800 years. The first Muslim contact with the region came in 711. A Muslim army crossed the Straits of Gibraltar from North Africa and by 716 a number of cities and kingdoms were defeated. The nature and extent of Muslim rule in the area was dramatically affected by the collapse of the Damascus-based Umayyad dynasty in 750. A member of the dynasty fled to Spain, became a governor, and initiated a ruling dynast, which eventually declared Iberia and North Africa as a separate Umayyad caliphate.

Inspired by a more orthodox vision of Muslim rule, the two movements arriving in North Africa established control over the region in the eleventh and twelfth centuries. They were the Almoravids (1056–1147) and the Almohads (1130–1269). By the end of Almohad rule, various Christian rulers had united to begin the period of *reconquista* and, except for the rule of the Nasridas in Granada until 1492, most of the Iberian Peninsula was lost to Muslim authority.

After the 1492 defeat of Granada, most Muslims and Jews fled to North Africa to avoid the Inquisition. Some submitted and converted to Christianity, while a small number were allowed to retain their faith, but under much more constrained circumstances. By the sixteenth century, however, the process of conversion and expulsion of Muslims was almost complete and the presence of Islam in the region remained only through cultural traces.

The civilization engendered in Muslim Andalusia was linked to the broader developments in the Middle East and North Africa, but was distinctive in several respects. The art and architecture associated with the cities of Córdoba, Granada, Seville, and Toledo remain as landmarks. The literary heritage that flowered in the later period was also distinctive in its contribution to Romance literature. But perhaps the most enduring legacies were reflected in the philosophical, theological, and legal writings of Muslims and Jews, which would exercise a great influence on subsequent Latin scholasticism in Europe. Among this tradition's most outstanding reference points were Ibn Rushd (also known as Averroës), who died in 1198. Ibn Arabi (d. 1240), wrote many mystical works that influenced succeeding generations. The great Jewish thinker, Moses Maimonides (d. 1204), also worked in this most intellectually invigorating and culturally resplendant milieu.

The court of the lions in the Alhambra palace in Granada. The kingdom of Granada, the last Islamic outpost in Western Europe, held out for 250 years in the face of the Christian Reconquista. Despite the external pressures, under the Nasrid dynasty it remained a sophisticated and tolerant center where Islamic and Western cultures were blended in a brilliant, creative synthesis.

Subsaharan Africa—East

The southernmost outpost of Dar al-Islam until modern times, Kilwa had a population of about 10,000 in 1505, when the Portuguese took the island by storm. The first Muslim occupants were mariners and merchants from the Persian Gulf who settled around AD *800.*

From the time of the ancient pharaohs the Upper Nile regions of East Africa had belonged to the same cultural universe as Egypt. Ethiopia was Christianized by Coptic missionaries from the fourth century, and according to the earliest Islamic sources, the Christian Negus gave refuge to a group of persecuted Muslims from Mecca even before the Hijra. The Arab conquerors of Egypt reached Aswan in 641 and for centuries continued to move southward, giving the Upper Nile region its predominantly Arabic character. The Funj sultanate, which maintained a monopoly on the gold trade that lasted until about 1700, was created by herders moving downstream along the Blue Nile. It consolidated the Arabic influence by attracting legal scholars and holy men (known locally as *faqis*) from Egypt, the Maghreb, and Arabia.

PLAN OF THE GREAT MOSQUE AT KILWA

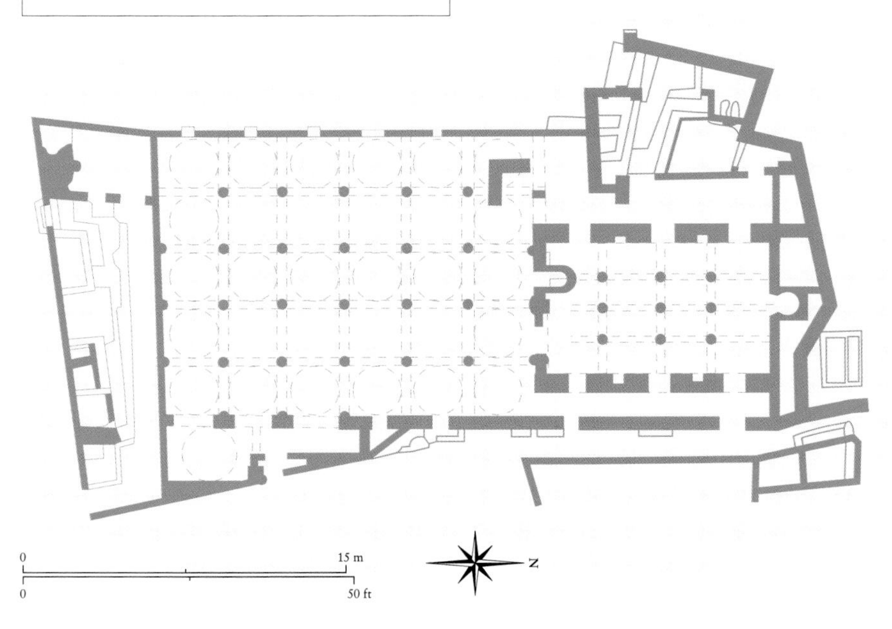

The Arab character of East African Islam was reinforced by the proximity of the coastal regions to the Hejaz and Yemen. From an early period Somali cattle-breeders acquired the most prestigious of all Islamic lineages in the form of Quraishi pedigrees, a trend that would emerge among other religious and tribal leaders. While Arabic and—in some cases—Persian brought by mariners retained their prestige as the language of "True Islam," vernacular languages developed rich oral literatures that would eventually acquire written form. The first Swahili text dates from 1652. The Swahili culture that dominates the thousand-mile coastal strip from Mogadishu to Kilwa is the fruit of many centuries of interaction between the ideas brought by Arab-Persian merchants, traders, and settlers, and the indigenous peoples of the eastern seaboard with whom they intermarried.

After Vasco da Gama rounded the Cape of Good Hope in 1498 the Portuguese systematically destroyed the prosperous Swahili cities that had sprung up along the coast. In 1505 Kilwa was captured and Mombasa was sacked. By 1530 the Portuguese controlled the entire coast from their fortresses on Pemba, Zanzibar, and other islands. In the 1650s, however, the Omani who were Ibadi Muslims expelled them from Muscat, restoring the eastern part of the Indian Ocean to Muslim rule. The Omanis built up the trade in cloth, ivory, and slaves between East Africa and India. In the nineteenth century, under the Sultan, Sayid bin Sultan (1804–56) Muscat and Zanzibar were briefly united under a single ruler, opening the way to settlement by new waves of Muslim immigrants from South Arabia. Much of Zanzibar was turned over to the commercial production of cloves and other spices, using slave-plantation methods similar to those employed in the United States. After the division of the empire between the sons of Imam

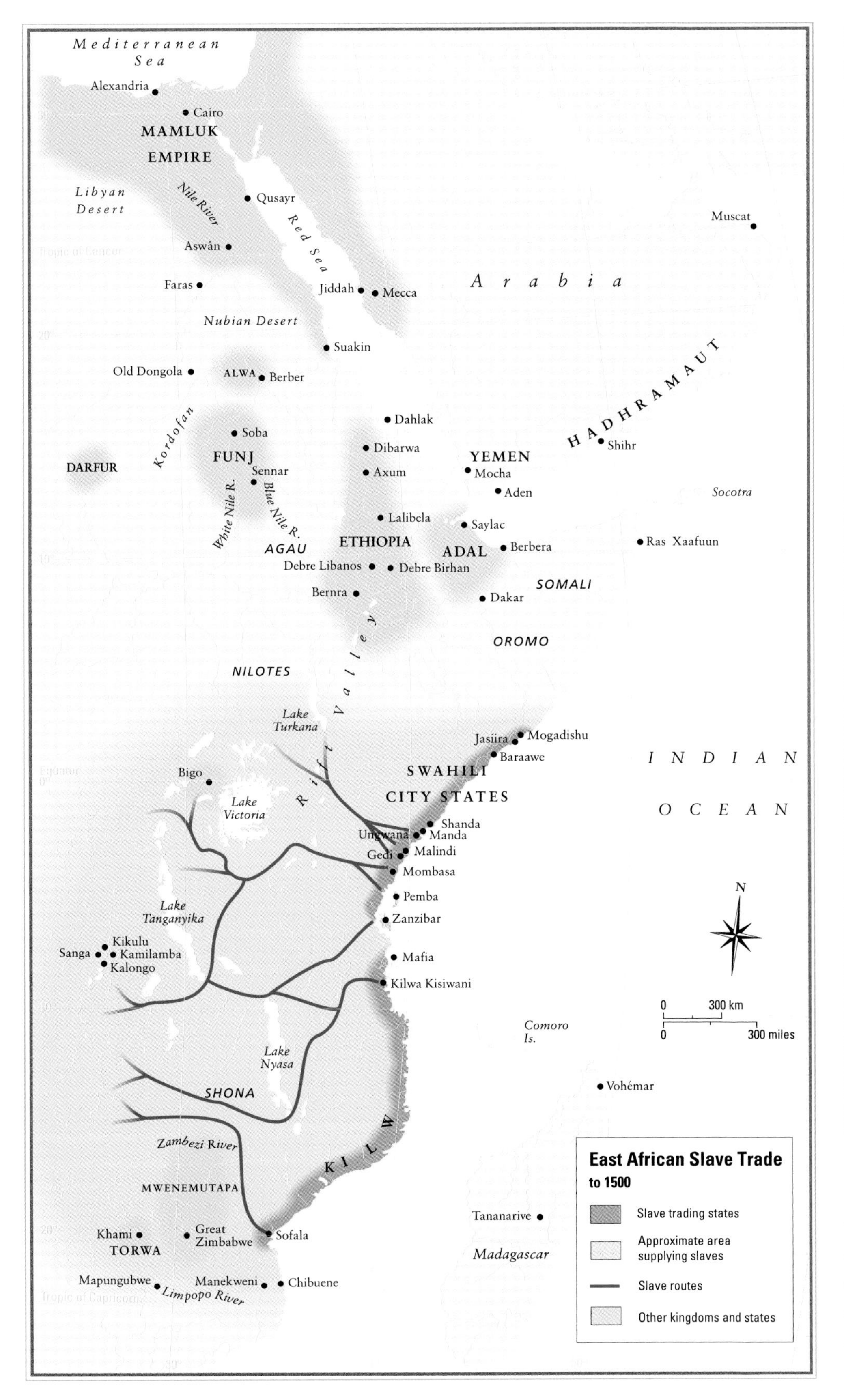

Sayid, Zanzibar came under increasing pressure to abolish slave trade by the British, who used their navy to enforce the antislave trade laws and to pursue their own commercial interests. After becoming a British protectorate, Zanzibar played host to a new wave of immigrants from British India. Many of these migrants were Muslims from minority communities including Momens,

The entrance to a private house in Stone Town, Zanzibar. The decorated portals carved from local hardwoods, or trees imported from the mainland, symbolized the social status of the house's owner. The walls are made from coral rag and need constant maintenance to prevent destruction by torrential monsoon rains.

Subsaharan Africa—West

Detail from a fourteenth-century Catalan map showing a king enthroned, with his royal regalia. The portrait may be of Mansa Musa of Mali, whose wealth made a great impression on his contemporaries when he traveled to Mecca in 1324–25.

The expansion of Islam in West Africa was largely peaceful. The introduction of camels for transportation into the Sahara sometime before AD 600 had established a growing network of caravan routes between the Maghreb and the Sahil (shore), the vast belt of grassy steppelands that lies between the Sahara and the tropical forests of Guinea. The principal export from the south was gold from Bambuko on the Senegal River, which was for centuries the principal source of gold for the Maghreb, West Asia, and Europe. Gold—along with slaves, hides, and ivory—was exchanged for copper, silver, handcrafted articles, dried fruits, and cloth. More significant than the trade, however, was the diffusion of ideas. Islam was brought south by merchants, teachers, and Sufi mystics the French had named Marabouts. The latter were often members of saintly families who acted as hereditary arbiters among rural tribesfolk.

In the eleventh century Murabits from the Lamtuna Berber group established a center in Mauretania for the propagation of Islam, from where they launched a jihad against kings of Ghana, rulers of the largest and wealthiest of the West African states. The reforming zeal of the Murabits (known as Almoravids in Spanish) carried them northward to Iberia, where they reunited the petty principalities of al-Andalus to ward off the threat of the Christian reconquest. There were some forcible conversions of Africans south of the Sahara, but these were mostly rare. The earliest converts were usually the royal families that had always relied on religious prestige to extract taxes or military service from subordinate clans and communities. As Muslim merchants settled in Sahil cities (most of which had their own Muslim quarters by the late tenth century) the royals would seek to benefit from the cultural prestige they carried by adopting Islam as the court religion.

For the most part local kingdoms continued to form and re-form under different tribal dynasties, with Islamic rituals and practice intermingling with tribal customs. With each new state the capital would become a center of wealth and Islamic learning, as rulers sought prestige by patronizing religious scholarship. The most spectacular cultural center was the Tuareg city of Timbuktu on the Niger. The Tuaregs were a camel-borne elite who grew rich from the trans-Saharan trade, using slaves to exploit the salt mines and settling serfs from African tribes to cultivate the oases along their routes.

The most celebrated Muslim ruler from Subsaharan Africa was Mansa Musa (1307–32), king of Mali. He made the pilgrimage to Mecca in 1324–25 in the grandest possible style, leaving an impression that would last for generations. Unlike the Nilotic Sudan where the Arabic language took root, Islam was diffused in local vernaculars from a relatively early stage. From around 1700 (and possibly earlier) scholars and teachers developed a modified version of Arabic script to convey Islamic teachings in Fulfulde and Hausa, the leading languages of the western Sahil.

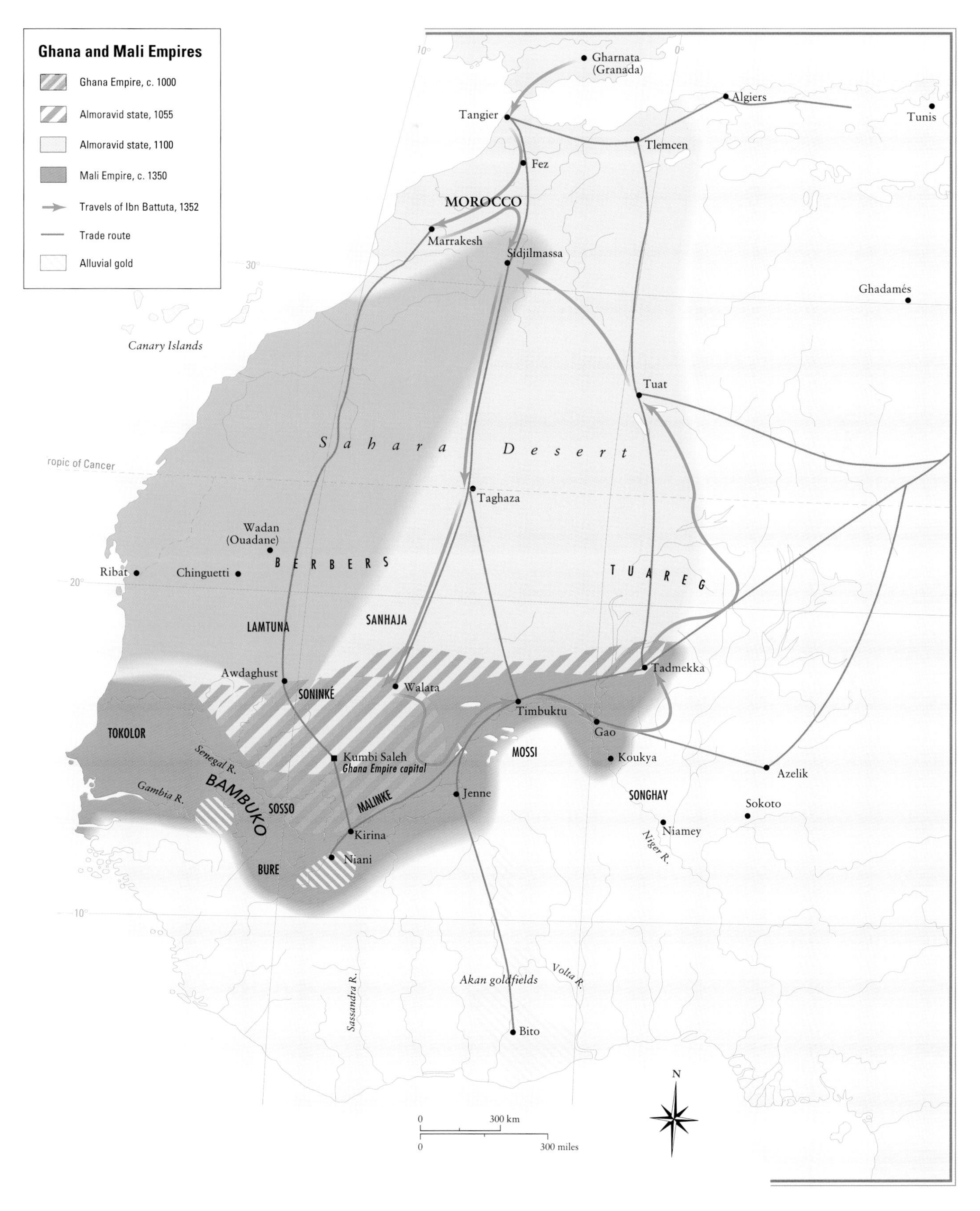
Ghana and Mali Empires
Ghana Empire, c. 1000
Almoravid state, 1055
Almoravid state, 1100
Mali Empire, c. 1350
Travels of Ibn Battuta, 1352
Trade route
Alluvial gold
Gharnata (Granada)
Algiers
Tunis
Tangier
Tlemcen
Fez
MOROCCO
Marrakesh
Sidjilmassa
Ghadamés
Canary Islands
Tuat
Sahara Desert
Tropic of Cancer
Taghaza
Wadan (Ouadane)
BERBERS
TUAREG
Ribat
Chinguetti
LAMTUNA
SANHAJA
Awdaghust
Tadmekka
SONINKÉ
Walata
Timbuktu
Gao
TOKOLOR
Senegal R.
Kumbi Saleh
Ghana Empire capital
MOSSI
Koukya
Azelik
Gambia R.
BAMBUKO
SOSSO
MALINKE
Jenne
SONGHAY
Sokoto
Niamey
Kirina
Niger R.
Niani
BURE
Volta R.
Akan goldfields
Sassandra R.
Bito
N
0 300 km
0 300 miles

Jihad States

From the seventeenth to the nineteenth century a series of jihad movements occurred in West Africa that led to the creation of a number of Islamic states and transformed the presence of Islam in the region. Most of these jihads involved rebellions by nomadic tribesmen against nominally Islamic rulers who held to traditional African concepts of divine kingship, mixing rituals of pagan origin with symbols

Mudbaked mosque at Djenne, Niger. Designed in the local vernacular style, the building fabric is constantly renewed from the material of which it is made.

derived from Islam. The leadership of these movements usually came from the literate class of ulama—scholars, teachers, and students—who had studied with Sufi masters locally or had acquired their reformist ideas in Mecca and Medina. Their followers were Fulani cattle-herders moving south in search of pasture who resented taxes imposed on them by the Hausa kings, joined by disgruntled peasants, runaway slaves, and other outcasts. Ibrahim Musa (Karamoko Alfa d. 1751), a Fulani torodbe (scholar), waged a struggle against the local rulers. This resulted in the creation of the state of Futa Jallon in the uplands of Senegambia. The jihad movement (which Ibrahim Musa's descendants exploited to capture slaves for export and work in plantations) spread to Futa Toro in the Senegal River valley. Here torodbes formed an independent Islamic state before merging with the local elites prior to the French conquest. The most famous of the West African jihad leaders was Uthman Dan Fodio (1754–1817) a mallam (religious scholar) from a well-established family of scholars in the independent Hausa kingdom of Gobir. After attacking the king for mixing Islamic and pagan practices, Dan Fodio followed the classical Muhammadan scenario of making the hijra beyond the borders of the kingdom, before waging jihad against the king and other Hausa rulers in the name of a purified

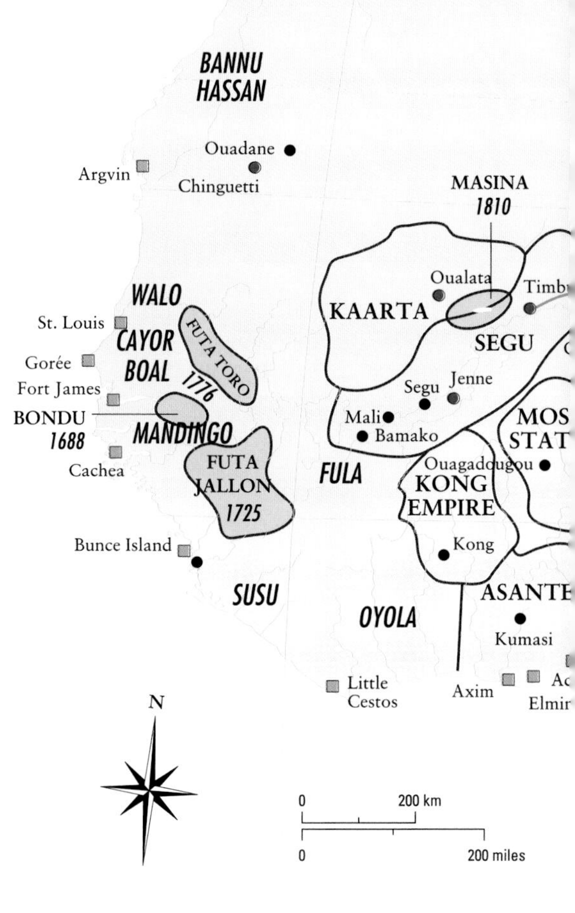

Islam. His preaching conveyed a powerful message of social justice in the classic manner of Muhammad, mixing theological attacks on idolatry with denunciations of illegal taxes, sequestration of property, compulsory military service, and the enslavement of Muslims. By 1808 the movement had overthrown most of the Hausa kingdoms; in the next two decades it expanded to include most of what is now northern Nigeria and the northern Cameroons. In 1817 Dan Fodio retired to a life of reading, writing, and contemplation leaving the empire to his son, Muhammad Belo. He became the Sultan of Sokoto—the most powerful Muslim emirate in what eventually became the British colony of Nigeria.

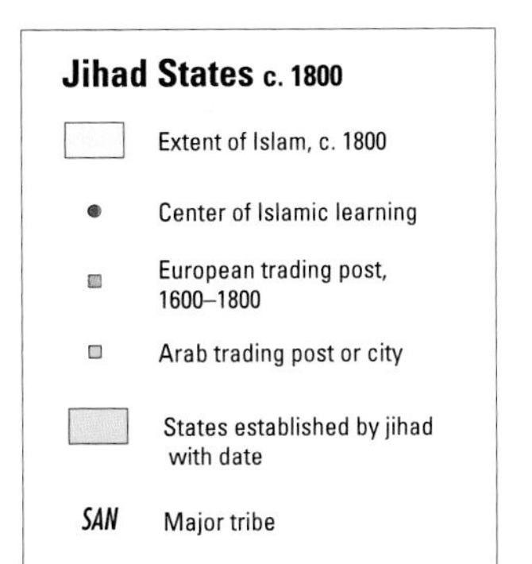

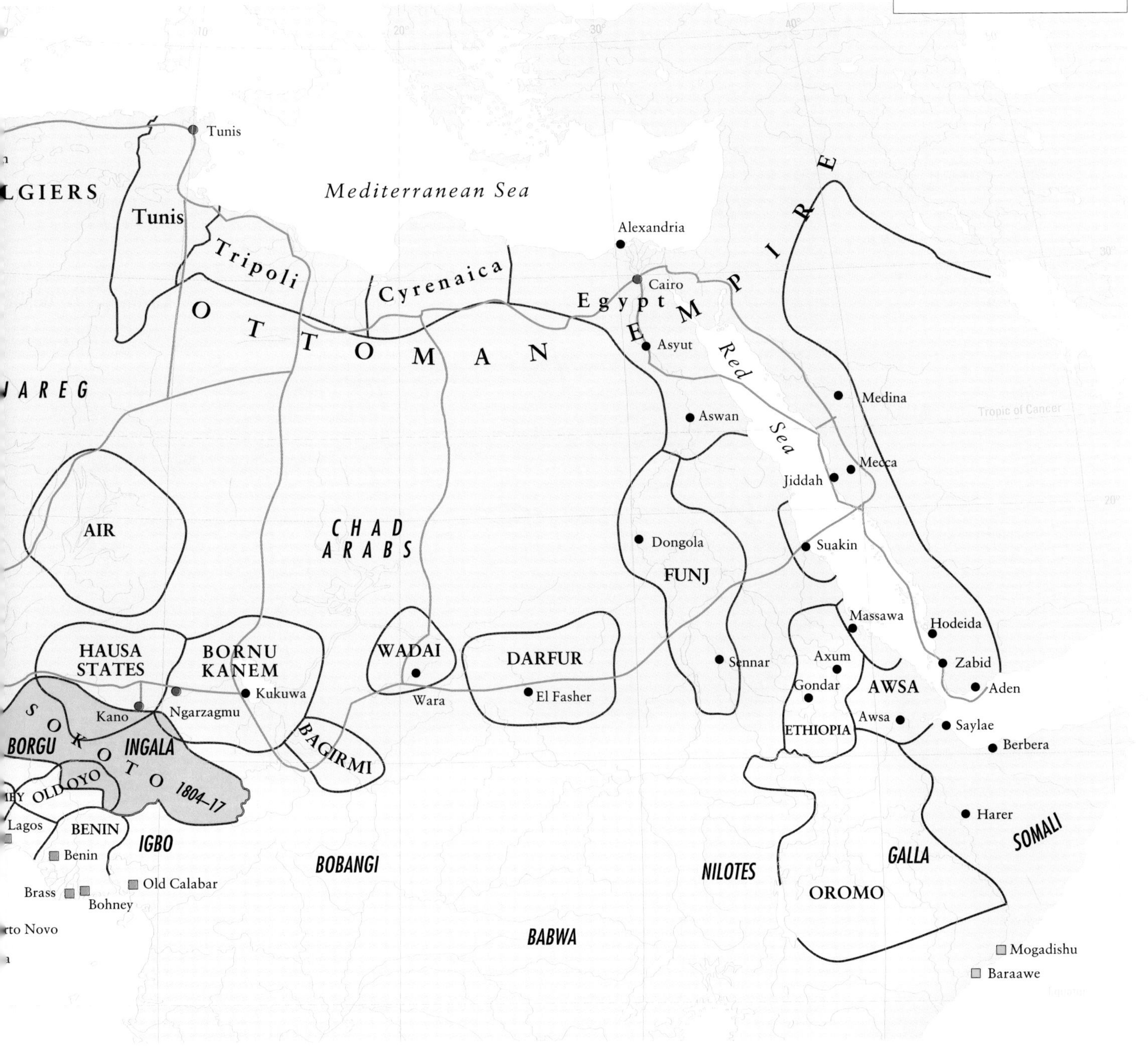

The Indian Ocean to 1499

Before the advent of Islam the Indian Ocean was part of an overlapping and interconnected, local, regional, and transcontinental network of trade routes stretching between China, Southeast Asia, East Africa, and the Mediterranean.

The *Periplus* (Circuit) *of the Erythrean Sea*, a Greek-language merchant-mariner's guide of the first century, describes two maritime trade routes commencing from ports on the Red Sea (i.e., Myus Hormus, Leuke Kome, and Berenike). These connected merchants of the classical Greco-Roman world engaged in the trade of items such as textiles, copper, spices, and slaves, to their partners on the western Indian Ocean littoral. One route went down through the Red Sea to southern Arabia by Muza (Mocha) and Dioscurides (Socotra), to northeast Africa (Adulis and Opone in Axum/Ethiopia), and down the coast of East Africa by way of Menouthias near Pemba as far as Rhapta (whose site is yet to be discovered, but may be Bagamoyo on the coast of modern Tanzania).

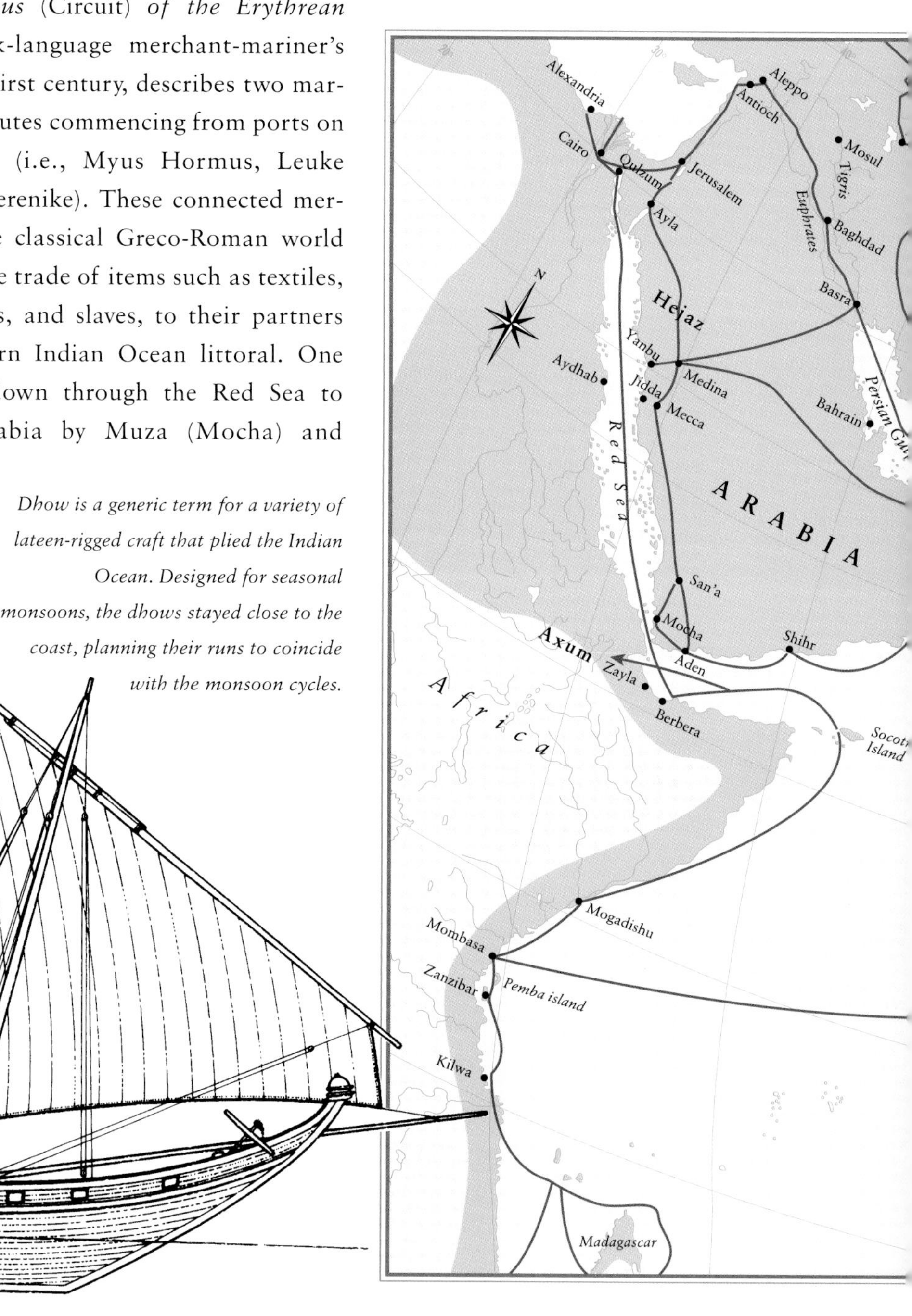

Dhow is a generic term for a variety of lateen-rigged craft that plied the Indian Ocean. Designed for seasonal monsoons, the dhows stayed close to the coast, planning their runs to coincide with the monsoon cycles.

The other route veered toward India's northwestern shores by Barygaza (Broach) and then south to Muziris Cranganore and Komar (Cape Comorin).

The movements of people and goods were regulated by the Indian Ocean's predictable monsoon cycle. The benign northeast or winter monsoon lasts approximately half the year (from November to March). Before the days of powered navigation, the northeast monsoon allowed the large lateen-rigged sails of the Arabian, Persian, and Indian dhows to sail such routes as Aden to Cochin with the sails trimmed to keep the ship pointing as closely as possible into the direction of the wind and then to trade up the Malabar coast of India on

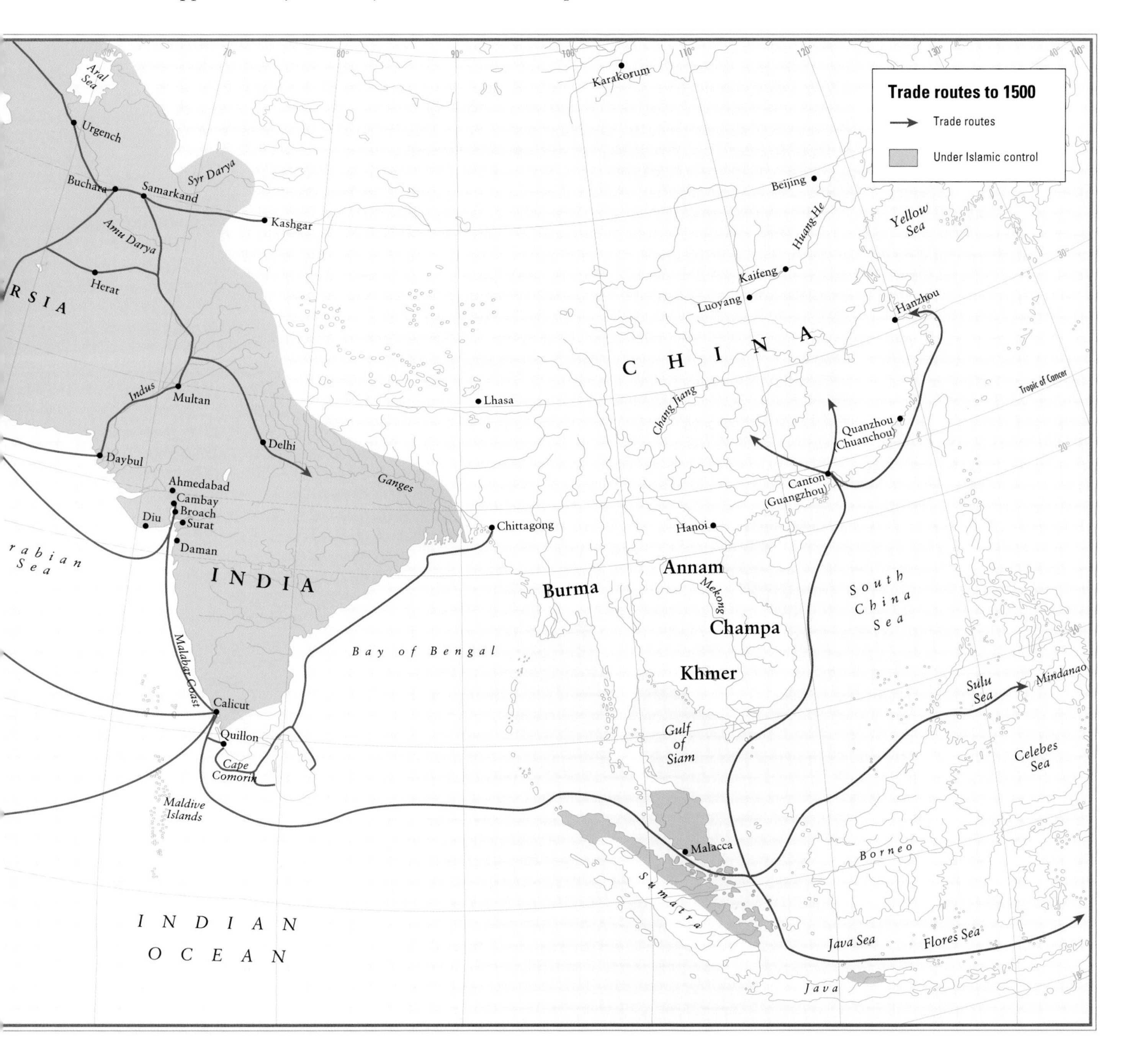

the opposite tack before returning with their sails full and their yard arms swinging free before the wind. The southwest monsoon, which brings rain to western India and generates more turbulent weather, was best avoided.

By the seventh century, the trading worlds described in *The Periplus* had long disappeared. Western Indian Ocean ports and trade routes were caught up in increasing rivalry between the Byzantine and Sasanian (Persian) Empires. The Byzantines supported Ethiopian raids on South Arabia from ports on the Red Sea, while the Persians secured their control over the Persian Gulf (Bahrain)

Saljuq ruler on his throne. Their position at the western end of the Silk Road enabled the Saljuq sultans to indulge their taste for luxuries, such as the finest Chinese silks and jewels, from Central Asia. Manuscript, 13th century

and southern Arabia at Aden, Suhar, and Daba. In between the two empires were the Quraish, who would become the first Muslims engaged in land-based trade at their sanctuary at Mecca.

The early trajectory of Muslim conquest and expansion was away from the Indian Ocean and toward the Mediterranean. But successive Muslim dynasties made efforts to gain political and economic control over the Indian Ocean. The Umayyad conquest and occupation of Daybul at Sind in 712 was a first step in this direction. Subsequently, the Abbasids' founding of their capital Baghdad in 762 near the Tigris, with its access via Basra to the Persian Gulf, provided further impetus to Muslim maritime trade and settlement from the shores of East Africa to southern China. Mariners' reports collected in the *Akhbar al-Sin Wal-Hind* (c. 850) provide a glimpse into what a typical round-trip mercantile sea voyage from Siraf (south of Shiraz) to Canton would have been like in Abbasid times. Contemporary maritime activity in the southwestern Indian Ocean, from Arabia to East Africa (Bilad al-Zanj), is attested to in the *Muruj al-Dhahab* of al-Masudi (d. 928).

In 969, the Fatimids conquered Egpyt and founded Cairo, posing a serious political and commercial challenge to the Abbasids. The Fatimids succeeded in diverting trade in the western Indian Ocean from Baghdad and the Persian Gulf to Fustat and the Red Sea. The commercial importance of Egypt and the Red Sea trade route to the western Indian Ocean was maintained by the Fatimids' successors, the Ayyubids and Mamluks. Documents from the Cairo Geniza collection offer evidence of the complex network of Fustat-based traders, stretching between North Africa and India via the western Indian Ocean, operating between the eleventh and thirteenth centuries.

Political and economic control over Indian Ocean trade routes by Muslim dynasties based in the Middle East was complemented by the growth of Muslim communities, mercantile centers, and independent states around the littoral, many of which have complex and multistranded histories that have yet to be studied. The eastern African coast, and its Swahili-speaking peoples, had multiple connections to the Arabian Peninsula, the Persian Gulf, and India. Muslim settlements (mosques and burial sites) at Shanga date to the latter half of the eighth century and there is evidence to support the presence of local Muslim dynasties controlling island settlements on Pemba, Zanzibar, Mafia, and Kilwa between c. 1000–1150. Many of these communities were thriving when Ibn Battuta visited the region by way of Mogadishu in 1331.

Ibn Battuta is also a source of information for the presence of Muslims along China's southern coastline up to Quanzhou (Zaitun), which he reached in 1347. At Quanzhou, burials and a mosque (c. 1009) mark the presence of a Muslim community at the trading port. The histories of Muslim communities in Southeast Asia are also informed by transoceanic trade. By the fifteenth century, it was the entrepot of Malacca on the Malay coast that emerged as a major maritime center in the larger Muslim Indian Ocean trading network, eclipsing centers on Java and Sumatra. Malacca had a sizeable Muslim population who had strong connections to western Indian merchants and ports such as Cambay (Gujarat). Ironically, Ibn Majid, the mariner credited with piloting Vasco da Gama through the Indian Ocean in 1498, provides an unfavorable description of Malacca. The port fell to the Portuguese in 1511, marking the firm establishment of the first European maritime power in the Indian Ocean.

The Indian Ocean 1500–1900

The forts guarding the entrance to the harbor of Muscat were originally built by the Portuguese in the sixteenth century on the site of earlier strongholds. After surviving Ottoman attacks, the Portuguese garrisons surrendered to the Omani Imam Sultan bin Saif in 1650.

Vasco da Gama's voyage around the Cape of Good Hope in 1498 was an epoch-making event, putting an end to the Muslim monopoly of trade in the Indian Ocean and opening the way for the British and Dutch Empires in South Asia and the East Indies. The era of European imperialism began with merchant adventurers who established trading posts in the southern seas, which became the bases for further expansion. The Portuguese were the pioneers, taking Kilwa and sacking Mombasa in 1505 before establishing bases in Zanzibar and Pemba. In 1509 they defeated a combined Egyptian-Indian fleet to take Goa on the Malabar coast. In 1515 they conquered Malacca and in the same year Hormuz on the Persian Gulf. Portuguese hegemony was soon replaced by that of the Dutch, whom the Portuguese had tried to exclude from the lucrative pepper and spice trade. The Dutch

Indian Ocean c. 1580

Portuguese possession with date of acquisition
Portuguese factory
Portuguese town
Portuguese trade routes

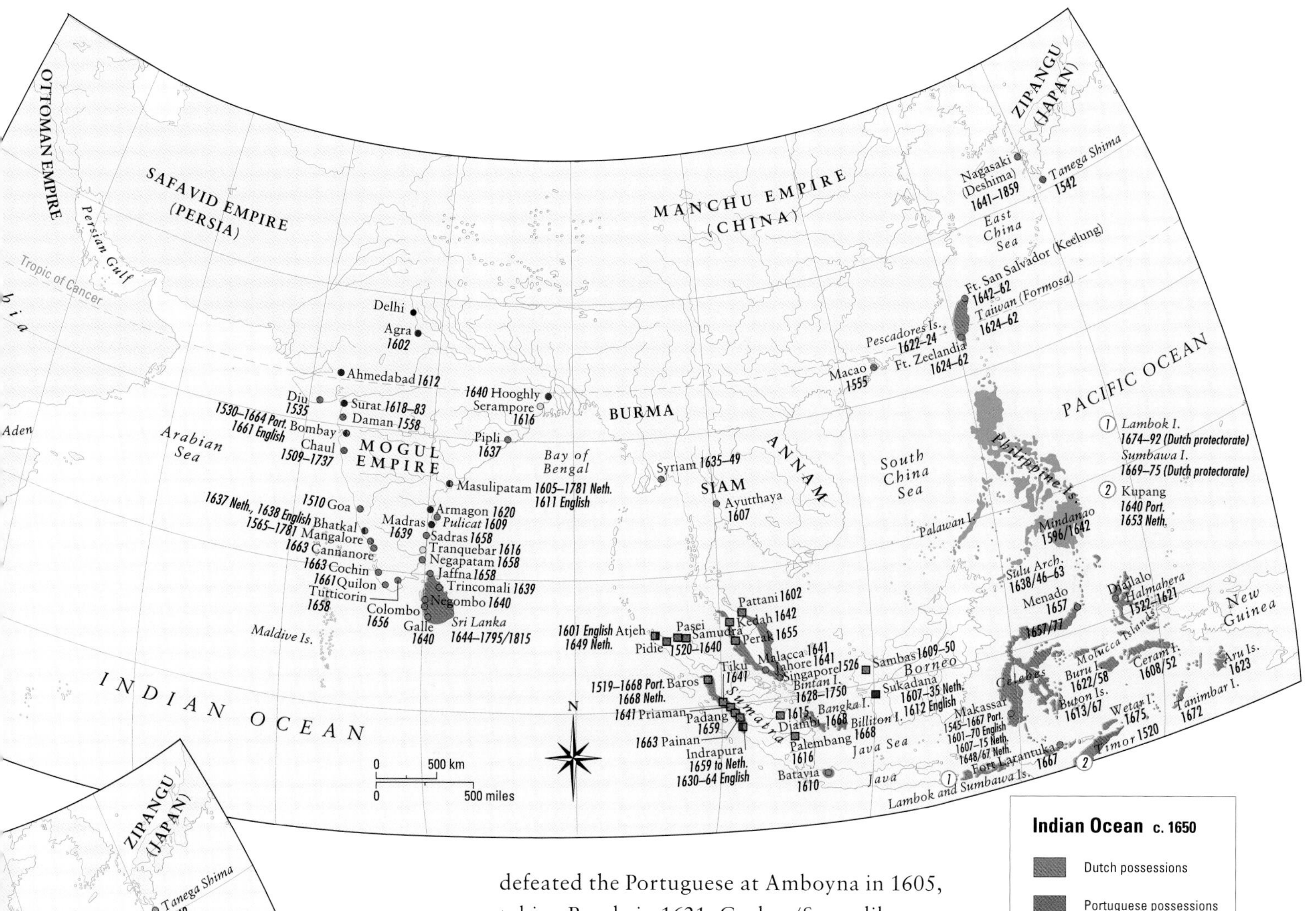

Indian Ocean c. 1650

- Dutch possessions
- Portuguese possessions
- Spanish possessions
- British possessions
- Danish possessions
- Factory

defeated the Portuguese at Amboyna in 1605, taking Banda in 1621, Ceylon (Sarandib, now Sri Lanka) in 1640, and Malacca in 1641. Batavia (now Jakarta), which would become the capital of the Dutch East Indies, was founded in 1619.

Although the process was a gradual one, the Portuguese intervention introduced changes in the patterns of trade and in the political economies of the Muslim states in the region. By the end of the seventeenth century England and Holland, two small countries perched on the Western periphery of Eurasia, had become (with France) the dominant forces in world trade. Cargos of raw commodities—timber, grain, fish, and salt—replaced the traditional trade in luxury goods. The shift in cargoes heralded even more far-reaching changes, whereby the world would be divided between colonies producing raw materials and industrial and

As the British began to establish themselves in India, they imported their own architectural styles, as shown in a watercolor of a house built at Chapra in 1796.

commercial centers producing high-value goods and services. Viewed from the perspective of the twenty-first century, Vasco da Gama's voyage represents the beginnings of a process that culminates in "globalization."

Two technological factors drove these changes: better sails and gunpowder. Their position on the eastern shore of the Atlantic had encouraged the Portuguese to develop powerful naval vessels capable of riding the Atlantic storms and sailing closer to the wind than the lateen-rigged Arab dhows. The Portuguese ships were larger and sturdier than their Arab and Persian counterparts, and thus able to hold more cargo and engage in longer runs. The new route around southern Africa to the Indies bypassed the West Asian trade routes, bringing goods from South Asia and the Indies—spices, cloths, and other valuable commodities—directly to Lisbon, enriching the merchants there but cutting out the intermediate beneficiaries of the trade between Europe and Asia (who had included the Venetians and Genoese who plied the waters of the eastern Mediterranean as well as the Muslim traders who carried goods by land). The gunpowder revolution—like the revolution in sailing techniques—was gradual, but reached equally far in its consequences. With the development of cannons, stone fortresses ceased to be impregnable, lending the military advantage to well-organized central powers that could afford to make the costly investment in artillery and firearms. As military technology advanced, a shift took place in the balance of power between the traditional warrior classes for whom military prowess was vested in notions of tribal solidarity, honor, prestige, and courage (classic virtues of the nomadic conquerors) and economic powers with sophisticated administrative centers capable of keeping up with the latest military technology. Under European pressure the fragmented Muslim states that followed in the wake of Arab caliphate and the Mongol invasions were consolidated into larger units dominated by the three great "gunpowder empires": Ottoman Eurasia, Safavid Iran, and Mughal India.

Indian Ocean 1800 – 1900

European, U.S., and Japanese territories in Asia
- British
- Allied to British administration
- French
- Dutch
- Portuguese
- German
- United States

Spheres of influence, c. 1907
- British
- French
- Russian
- German
- Japanese

- Russian Empire, 1855
- To Russia by 1900
- Occupied by Russia, 1900
- Treaty Port in China, with date of opening
- Major railway

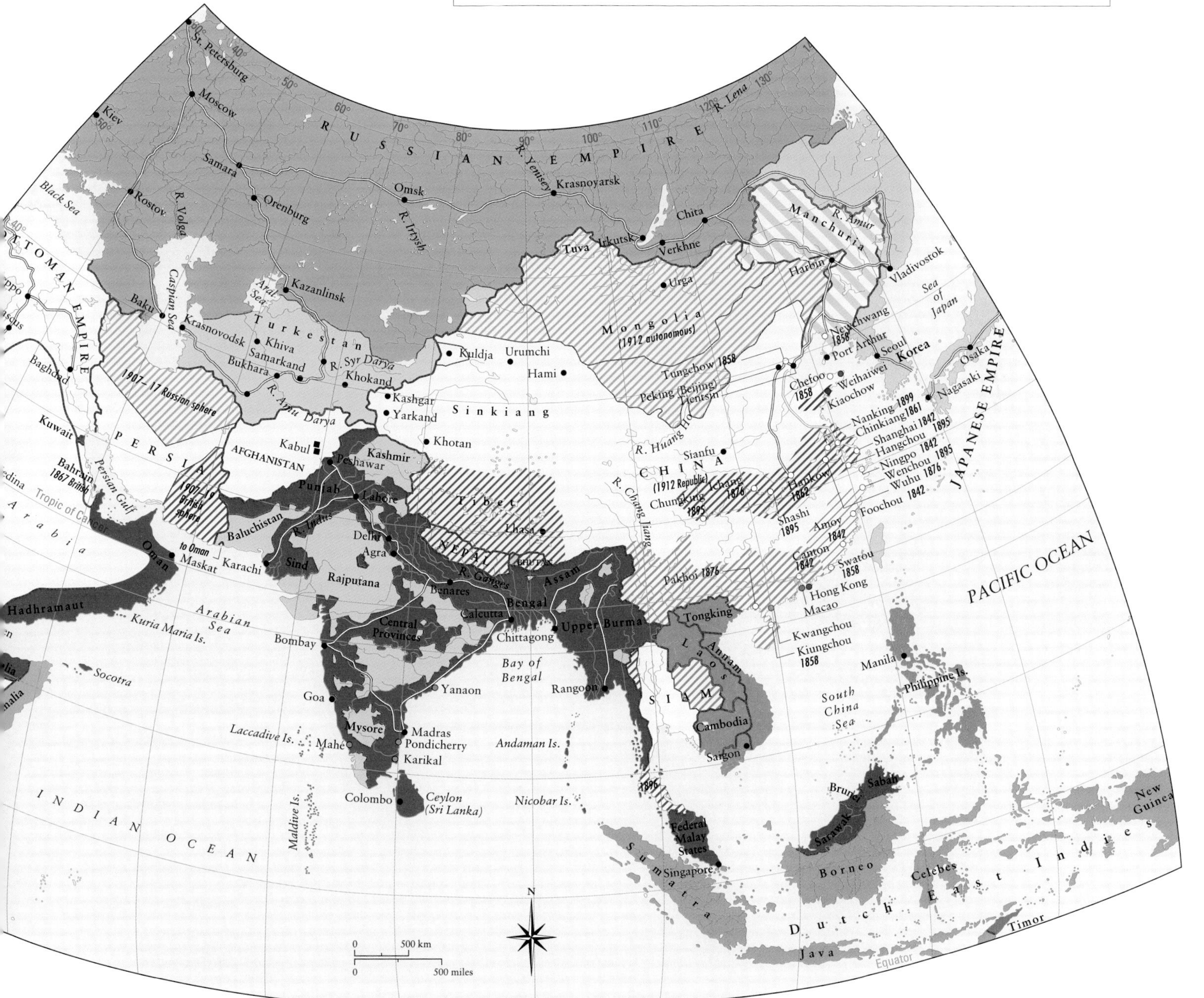

Rise of the Ottomans to 1650

The Ottoman Empire became the most far-reaching of all the Islamic states, it began its remarkable expansion as a frontier state conducting raids on Byzantine territories from Bithynia near the Sea of Marmara early in the thirteenth century. In 1242–43 the Mongols defeated the Saljuqs, making them vassals, pushing increasing numbers of Turkish nomads into the peninsula in search of pasturage and booty. The breakup of Saljuq power led to the creation of several petty states under loose Mongol overlordship. After taking Bursa, which they made their capital in

The great period of Ottoman expansion occurred during the reign of Suleiman I "the Magnificent." The painting below depicts an Ottoman fleet attacking the French town of Toulon in 1545.

1326, the Ottomans became players in the factional strife that beset the Byzantine Empire in its latter days. It was as auxiliaries to one of the contending parties that they first crossed the straits and occupied Byzantine territory in Europe. They occupied Greece, Macedonia, and Bulgaria, and finally established their control over the western Balkans by defeating the Serbs at the Battle of Kosovo in 1389. Successive campaigns involving coalitions of Latin and Orthodox powers

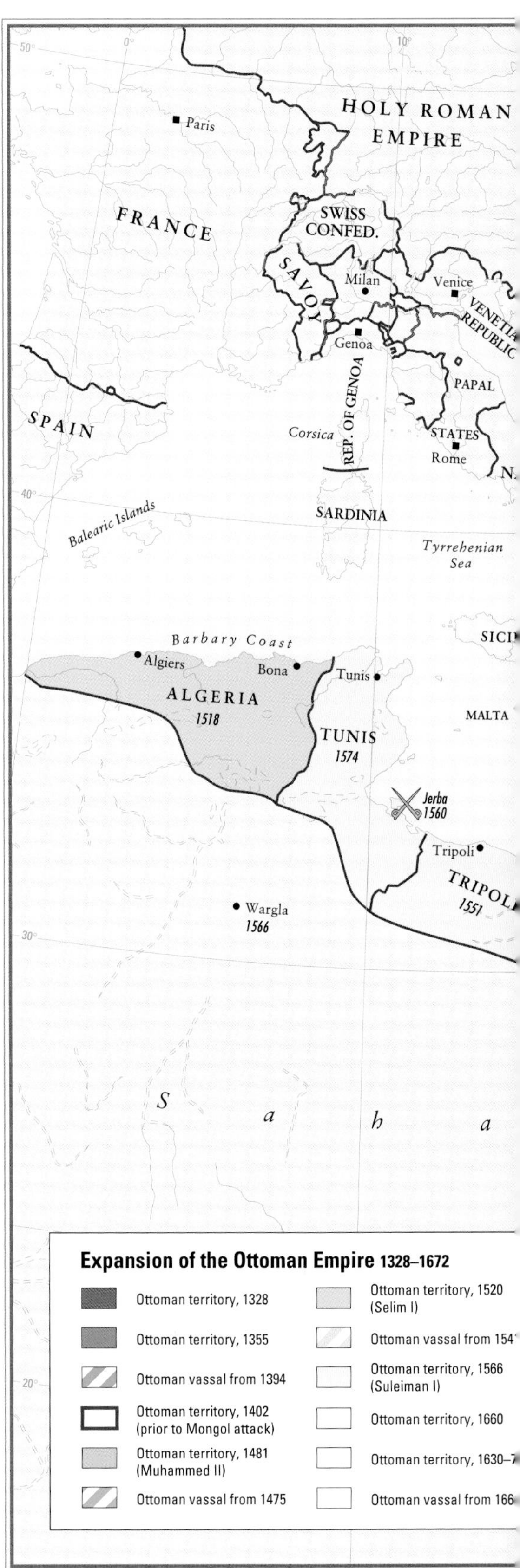

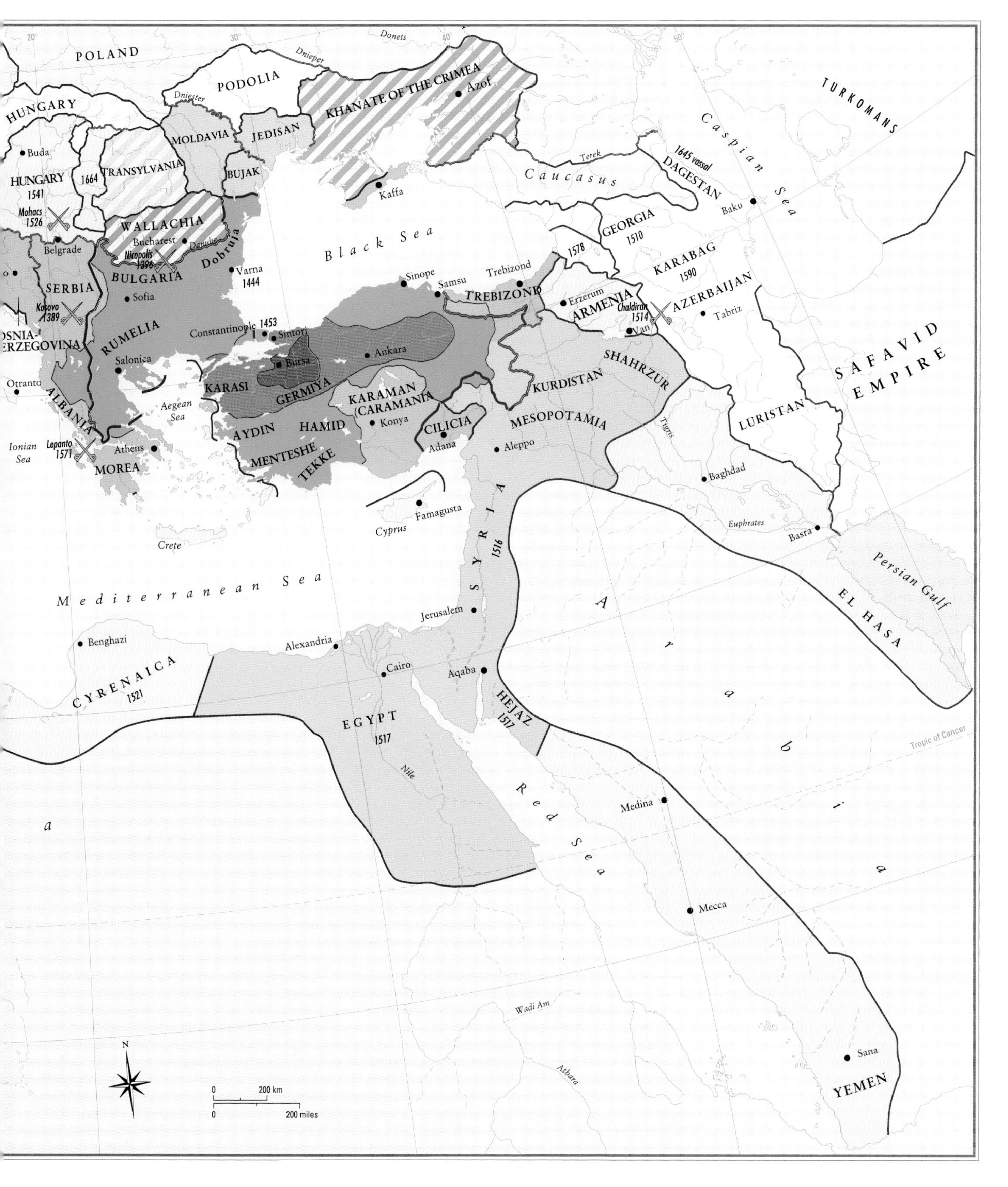
POLAND
HUNGARY
PODOLIA
KHANATE OF THE CRIMEA
Azof
TURKOMANS
Caspian Sea
MOLDAVIA
JEDISAN
TRANSYLVANIA
BUJAK
Kaffa
Caucasus
1645 vassal
DAGESTAN
Baku
Buda
HUNGARY 1541
1664
Mohacs 1526
WALLACHIA
Bucharest
Danube
Nicopolis 1396
Dobruja
Belgrade
Black Sea
GEORGIA 1510
1578
KARABAG 1590
SERBIA
BULGARIA
Varna 1444
Sofia
Kosovo 1389
Sinope
Samsu
Trebizond
TREBIZOND
Erzerum
ARMENIA
Chaldiran 1514
AZERBAIJAN
Tabriz
Van
RUMELIA
Constantinople 1453
Sintori
Bursa
Ankara
Salonica
KARASI
GERMIYA
KARAMAN (CARAMANIA)
Konya
KURDISTAN
SHAHRZUR
SAFAVID EMPIRE
Otranto
ALBANIA
Aegean Sea
AYDIN
HAMID
CILICIA
Adana
MESOPOTAMIA
Aleppo
LURISTAN
Tigris
Ionian Sea
Lepanto 1571
Athens
MOREA
MENTESHE
TEKKE
Baghdad
Famagusta
Cyprus
Crete
Euphrates
Basra
Persian Gulf
SYRIA 1516
Mediterranean Sea
Jerusalem
EL HASA
Arabia
Benghazi
Alexandria
CYRENAICA 1521
Cairo
Aqaba
EGYPT 1517
HEJAZ 1517
Nile
Tropic of Cancer
Red Sea
Medina
Mecca
Wadi Am
Atbara
Sana
YEMEN
0 200 km
0 200 miles
N

(including Naples, Venice, Hungary, Transylvania, Serbia, and Genoa) failed to stem the Ottoman advances into Europe. In 1453 Constantinople fell to the forces of Mehmet the Conqueror, fueling Ottoman imperial ambitions and providing the basis for further expansion. In 1521 the Ottomans captured Belgrade from the Hungarians. By 1529 they had reached the gates of Vienna, the Habsburg capital. By the time of the death of Suleiman the Magnificent in 1566 they controlled a swath of European territory from the Crimea to southern Greece.

Ottoman victories were even more spectacular in the lands of Islam. After defeating the Safavids at Chaldiran in 1514, they annexed eastern Anatolia and northern Mesopotamia, enabling them to control the central Asian trade routes linking Tabriz and Bursa. In 1516 and 1517 they took over the Mamluk Empire in Syria and Egypt, giving them control of the holy places of the Hejaz. Building on the Greek seamanship acquired from their Byzantine predecessors, they contested the power of Venice in the eastern Mediterranean and challenged the dominance of Habsburg Spain in the western Mediterranean, taking Algiers (1529), Tunis (1534–35), Jerba (1560), and the strategic island of Malta, the last Crusader stronghold, in 1565, as well as Cyprus in 1570. This string of naval victories finally provoked a successful counterattack. In 1571, the defeat of the Ottoman navy at the Battle of Lepanto by a Venetian–Habsburg coalition was celebrated all over Europe as a triumph for Christendom. Although the Ottomans refurbished their fleets and retook Tunis in 1574, a balance of power was achieved in the Mediterranean, confirming the frontiers that remained between the Muslim lands to the south and Christian lands to the north.

Paradoxically the early Ottoman state was both militantly Islamic and strongly influenced by Greek culture, heir to the Saljuqs but also to practices and structures derived from the Roman–Byzantine Empire it replaced. Straddling the Christian Balkans and the western reaches of Dar al-Islam, it was a bridge between rival civilizations. Being close to Constantinople, which had long been the goal of Muslim conquest, the state ruled by the Osmanli family (from which the English spelling Ottoman derives) attracted many of the ghazis (holy warriors) seeking glory in the jihad against Christendom. In Anatolia these Turkish incomers and pastoralists tended to be prejudiced against the Christian villagers, some of whom may have converted to avoid persecution. Among the incomers, however, there were also dervishes and members of Sufi brotherhoods from Inner Asia, such as Hajji Bektash (d. 1297). He preached versions of Islam that tended to merge Islamic beliefs, both Sunni and Shiite, with Christian beliefs and religious practices, facilitating the conversion of Greek and Armenian-speaking peoples. The Ottoman rulers assisted this process by excluding bishops and metropolitans from their sees, leaving the Christians without leaders, and by replacing the Orthodox infrastructure of hospitals, schools, orphanages, and monasteries with Islamic institutions staffed by Persian and Arab scholars. By the fifteenth century more than 90 percent of the Anatolian population had become Muslim, though substantial minorities of Christians and Jews remained in the cities. While the peasants were mostly converted, the nobility and civil servants of the old imperial system were integrated into the Ottoman armies and administration, giving the state a distinctly Byzantine character. Though a measure of religious autonomy was permitted through the millet system of self-governing minorities the Ottoman state was highly centralized. In other Muslim lands (including some of the Arab provinces that came under the looser forms of Ottoman dominion) the practice of

Islam in law and society was virtually self-regulating. The rulers appointed the qadis (judges) but in most other respects allowed the religious institutions such as the mosques and madrasas where the ulama were trained, the networks of Sufi lodges, and the guilds of artisans that were often connected to them, to flourish independently. By contrast with other Islamic regimes, the Ottomans dominated, controlled, and shaped the societies they governed. Though theoretically subject to the Sharia, the sultans supplemented the divine law with firmans (decrees) regulating the status and duties (including dress codes) of all their subjects. They brought the ulama, the Sufi lodges, and the guilds of artisans under state control by dictating appointments, grading, and licenses. Society was divided into two classes: the rulers and the ruled, the principal distinction being the right of the askeri (rulers) to exploit the wealth of the subjects through imposts and taxes. In theory all the land was the personal property of the sultan. The ruling elites were not confined to the ranks of pashas, beys, and ayan (Muslim notables) who dominated the empire in the provinces: they included patrician Greek families, ecclesiastical authorities, and prominent Jewish and Armenian bankers, as well as princely families from the Balkans.

This portrait was intended to show Suleiman to his royal peers in Europe. The Ottoman sultans did not display their images to their own subjects until late in the nineteenth century.

The Ottoman Empire 1650–1920

At its peak in the sixteenth century the Ottoman system was highly efficient. But it also contained crucial weaknesses, notably the system of succession. In nomadic societies the absence of a fixed mode of succession has a sound Darwinian rationale: after a struggle with his peers, a chief will emerge who is fittest to lead his tribe. Transferred to the center of an imperial system, the result will be civil war.

Abdul Hamid II was the last Ottoman sultan to wield effective power over the Empire. An absolute monarch and opponent of political liberalization, he nonetheless encouraged educational, legal, and economic reforms.

After a series of fratricidal struggles, the Ottomans dealt with the problem of the succession by confining the sultan's male relatives to the palace's Inner Courtyard or harem, thereby preventing future sultans from acquiring vital knowledge of military and secular affairs. From the seventeenth century the Ottoman sultans, who came to power as a result of "Byzantine" maneuvers and harem intrigues, lacked experience in the field and familiarity with the realities of politics. The power of the state and the army held up briefly under ruthless viziers such as Mehmed

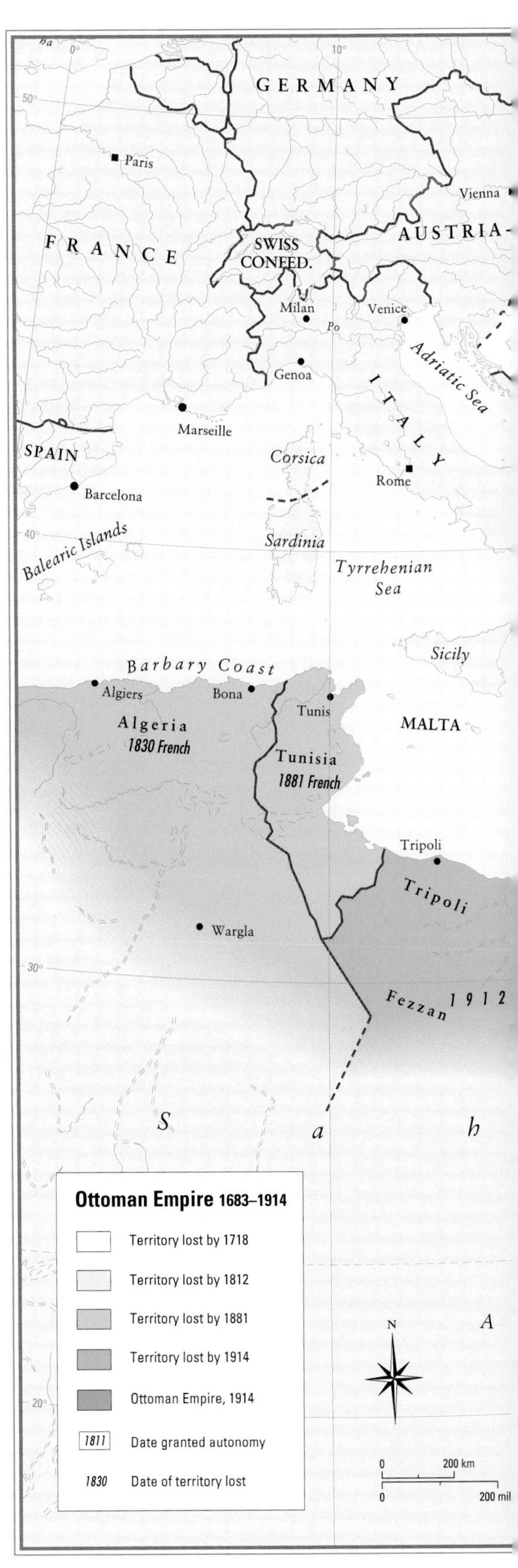

PODOLIA 1699
KHANATE OF THE CRIMEA 1774
JEDISAN 1792
BESSARABIA 1812
MOLDAVIA 1829
TRANSYLVANIA 1699
BANAT 1718
WALLACHIA 1829
DOBRUJA 1878
SERBIA 1878
Bulgaria
1878
1908
E. Rumelia
1913
Albania
Macedonia 1913
1881
GREECE 1830
Crete 1898
1912 to Italy
1878 to Britain
Cyprus
Black Sea
Caucasus
Caspian Sea
DAGESTAN 1723
GEORGIA 1730
KARABAG 1730
AZERBAIJAN 1730
ARMENIA
TREBIZOND
Anatolia
Mesopotamia
LURISTAN 1730
PERSIA
KUWAIT 1899 British protectorate
Persian Gulf
Bahrain 1687 to Britain
El Hasa
from 1853 to Britain
Arabia
Syria
Hejaz
Egypt
1811
1882 British Protectorate
Cyrenaica
Mediterranean Sea
Red Sea
YEMEN
Aegean Sea
Tropic of Cancer
Constantinople
Salonica
Athens
Bursa
Ankara
Konya
Adana
Aleppo
Baghdad
Basra
Erzerum
Van
Tabriz
Baku
Trebizond
Samsu
Sinope
Sevastopol
Kaffa
Azov
Varna
Sofia
Bucharest
Belgrade
Famagusta
Jerusalem
Alexandria
Cairo
Aqaba
Benghazi
Medina
Mecca
Sana
Sintori
Dniester
Danube
Tigris
Euphrates
Nile
Wadi Am
Atbara

Koprulu (r. 1656–61), son of an Albanian Christian, and his son Ahmed (r. 1661–76), allowing further expansion north of the Crimea and (after Ahmed's death) even a second siege of Vienna (1683). The process of decline, however, proved irreversible. The influx of Spanish silver from the Americas created a massive inflation problem, undermining the commercial classes and the ability of government to pay for troops whose modern weaponry (muskets and gunpowder) required cash rather than booty. Provincial governors and local magnates gained power at the expense of the center, hiring private armies or raising taxes for themselves. The Janissaries, who had evolved into a privileged body within the state, became enmeshed in large-scale nepotism and misrule. Land concessions that should have nurtured agriculture degenerated into tax-farms, driving cultivators off the land, creating gangs of rural bandits or urban migrants who drifted into cities already overcrowded and subject to famine, plague, and disorder. The millet system, which allowed the Christian and Jewish communities (and in Iraq the Shia) a high degree of administrative autonomy, undermined the legitimacy of the state by privileging Western traders and encouraging Greek and Balkan Christians to look toward the empire's enemies in Russia and Western Europe for inspiration and support.

Internally decentralized, the empire proved no match for the rising powers of Europe, whose military and economic systems were beginning to benefit from the revolution in scientific thought. During the last two decades of the seventeenth century, the European powers made significant advances at the empire's expense. Between 1684 and 1687 the Habsburgs took most of Hungary north of the Danube and took Serbia in 1689. The Venetians seized Dalmatia and southern Greece (Morea). Poland invaded Podolia, and the Russians, under the newly modernized army of Peter the Great, took Azov in the Crimea. Although the Ottomans regained some of these territorial losses during the first half of the eighteenth century, in the longer term they were unable to stem the tide of Russian advance. In 1768 the Russians began a new campaign, occupying Moldavia and Wallachia (modern Romania) and the Crimea. Under the humiliating terms of the treaty of Kuchuk Kaynarca (1774) the Ottomans were obliged to allow Russia a foothold on the Black Sea, as well as freedom of navigation and commerce, with access to the Mediterranean and to overland trade in the empire's Asian and European provinces. Although Moldavia and Wallachia remained technically under Ottoman suzerainty, the increased autonomy they were granted laid them open to Russian manipulation. Under Russian pressure a clause permitting the erection of a Russian church in Istanbul would be converted into a general right of Russian intervention on behalf of all the sultan's Orthodox Christian subjects.

The flow of ideas that followed in the wake of European victories would prove even more devastating than military defeats. Napoleon Bonaparte's brief occupation of Egypt in 1798 planted the seeds of modern scientific thought and revolutionary change in the empire's wealthiest (but most neglected) province. By defeating the neo-Mamluk amirs who governed Egypt under Ottoman authority, Napoleon opened the way for penetration of Western ideas under the modernizing dynasty of Mehmed Ali (r. 1805–48), an Albanian officer who seized power in 1805, making himself an independent ruler in all but name. The colonial ambitions of a restored French monarchy led to the loss of Algeria from 1830 and the establishment of a protectorate in Tunisia (1881). The winds of nationalism that tore through Europe in the wake of the French Revolution reached the Christian communities in the Balkans, starting with the Serbian revolt of 1804–13 and the Greek war of independence (1821–29). They culminated in the treaty of

San Stefano in 1878, by which the Ottomans were forced to concede the independence of Bulgaria, Serbia, Romania, and Montenegro. The final dismemberment of the empire was only postponed because of rivalries between the European powers, with Britain and France propping up the "sick man of Europe" against Russia in the Crimea (1854–56) while Austria competed with Russia for ascendancy in the Balkans. In 1911, Italy invaded Tripoli and Cyrenaica, forcing the Ottomans to concede their suzerainty. In 1912, the combined Balkan powers (Serbia, Bulgaria, Greece, and Montenegro) took all the remaining Ottoman territories in Europe, except for a strip of land around Istanbul, before arguing among themselves. In August 1914 the rivalries between the European powers in the Balkans erupted into a worldwide war, with the Ottoman Empire ranged alongside Austria and Germany against Britain, France, Italy, and Russia. The defeat of the Central Powers in 1918, the abdication of the sultan in 1922, the abolition of the caliphate in 1924, as well as the exchange of populations between Turkey and Greece in 1921 brought the Ottoman Empire to its end.

The Dolmabahçe Palace, Istanbul. The classical Venetian-style facade of this palace, like others built for the Ottoman sultans in the nineteenth century, reveals change in cultural orientation, as they abandoned their former seclusion and displayed their power like European monarchs.

Iran 1500–2000

The history of modern Iran began with the ruling Safavid dynasty (1501–1722), which established Twelver Shiism as the state religion. The dynasty's founder, Shaikh Safi al-Din (1252–1334), was a Sufi teacher and mujaddid (renovator) of Sunni allegiance who started a movement of reform among the tribes of eastern Anatolia and northwestern Iran. His descendant Shah Ismail (1487–1524) activated popular eschatological expectations in the period of disorder following the collapse of the Timurid Empire by proclaiming himself the Hidden Imam, a reincarnation of Ali and a manifestation of God. Led by a fearsome band of warriors known as Qizilbashis (red heads) from their distinctive red turbans, the movement enabled Shah Ismail, who proclaimed himself king in Tabriz in 1501, to conquer most of Iran in the course of the next decade.

Shah Suleiman and his courtiers with Western visitors, shown against a lyrical European-style landscape. The Safavid rulers exported carpets and silk to Europe as well as ceramics designed by Chinese craftsmen for the Western markets. They broke with the traditional religious hostility toward figurative painting by claiming that the Imam Ali, revered by the Shiites, had been a painter as well as a calligrapher.

The power of the Safavid state, based on the brilliant new capital built by Shah Abbas (1588–1629) in Isfahan, was limited. It relied for its authority on a network of uymaqs or smaller chieftains and the traditional iqta system of tax-farming, yet the Safavid strategy of religious consolidation gave Iran the distinctive Shiite character it retains to this day. Once the Qizilbashis had done their work Ismail's messianic claims were deemphasized, and Shiite scholars were imported from Syria, Iraq, Bahrain, and al-Hasa to promote the "official" version of Twelver Shiism, according to which the return of the Imam/Messiah is indefinitely deferred, while the ulama govern on his behalf. Popular versions of Sunnism were suppressed, with the tombs of Sufi saints desecrated and khaniqas (hostelries) given over to Shiite youth. Jews and Zoroastrians were subject to forcible conversion. The pilgrimage to Mecca was discouraged in favor of ziyaras (visits) to the lavishly endowed shrines of the Shiite imams.

Under the Qajar dynasty (1779–1925) the ulama acquired increased autonomy as an organized body of mujtahids (interpreters). Their powers were enhanced by zakat and khums (religious taxes), which were paid to them directly, while their custodianship over shrines and waqfs (charitable trusts) gave them access to rents from land and housing. The location of two of the most important shrines, at Karbala and Najaf in Iraq, in Ottoman controlled territory, further enhanced their independence by giving them a power base outside the domain of the state. The mourning ceremonies commemorating the martyrdom of the Imam Hussein at Karbala and the associated taziya passion plays became characteristic features of popular religiosity, making Shiism a component element in Iranian national identity.

As pressures from Russia and Britain began to impinge on Iran in the nineteenth century, the ulama came to the forefront of nationalist resistance. In 1873 they forced the shah to cancel far-reaching economic and financial concessions made to a British citizen, Baron de Reuter, and in the 1890s they led a national boycott against a tobacco monopoly granted to another Briton, Major Talbot. The political momentum engendered by the tobacco agitation culminated in the Constitutional Revolution of 1906 when a coalition of liberal ulama, merchants, and members of the westernized intelligentsia forced the shah to convene a national assembly and to submit to a form of parliamentary government. A brief period of constitutional rule, during which tensions between conservative ulama and the liberals came to the surface, was brought to an end by the Russians in 1911, who intervened to restore the shah's autocracy.

In 1925 Reza Khan Pahlavi, an officer in the Cossack Brigade, came to power after a period of instability following the Russian Revolution. Reza Shah instituted a radical modernizing regime that sought to break the power of tribal leaders and curb the autonomy of the ulama by introducing secular education and government supervision of religious schools. Secular courts were established depriving the ulama of their legal monopoly, which included the lucrative business of registering land transactions. During the Second World War Britain and Russia, who needed a compliant Iranian government to facilitate the passage of war materiel to the eastern front, forced Reza Shah to resign, replacing him with his son, the young Muhammad Reza. After the Second World War oil, first discovered in 1908 and leased to the British under generous concessions, became a bone of contention when the nationalist prime minister, Muhammad Mosaddeq, attempted to nationalize the Anglo-Iranian Oil Company. In the crisis engendered by a boycott of Iranian oil by western oil companies, the CIA intervened to help the army restore the autocratic Pahlavi regime.

The collapse of the regime in 1979 and the ensuing Islamic revolution was the result of a complex combination of economic, cultural, and political factors. Far from benefiting small tenants and landless peasants, the shah's ambitious land reforms in the 1960s favored large-scale enterprises and agribusiness (in which the ruling family had interests), while alienating the ulama, many of whom were themselves wealthy landowners or controlled extensive waqfs in land. The sudden increase in oil prices after 1973 increased wealth into the small modernized sector of the economy, while adversely affecting small businesses in the bazaari community, which had close links to the ulama. The corruption of the Pahlavi family and ruthless repression by SAVAK, the secret police, alienated the educated middle classes. The younger generation of students who had come under the influence of Marxism and the leftist versions of Islamic ideology promoted by Dr. Ali Shariati and Jalal Al-e-Ahmed, author of a highly influential tract entitled *Westoxification*, were especially disaffected. Poor rural migrants to the cities provided the tinder for revolution.

Under a deal reached between the shah and Saddam Hussein, Iraq expelled the dissident cleric Ayatollah Ruhallah Khomeini from the Shiite center of Najaf where his lectures, calling for a restored Islamic government under ulama supervision, found a receptive audience among ulama and students. From his place of exile in a Paris suburb, Khomeini had access to the international media, while taped copies of his fatwas and sermons denouncing the shah were smuggled into Iran. Early in 1979 a series of massive demonstrations, timed to coincide with the ritual of Ashura (the Day of Mourning for the Imam Hussein), forced the shah into exile, bringing Khomeini home to a tumultuous reception. For ten years Khomeini ruled the Islamic Republic as the supreme religious leader, until his death in 1989. His successor as guardian or supreme religious authority, the Ayatollah Khamenei, lacked Khomeini's charisma and religious authority, and power is now divided between a relatively liberal parliament and elected president, and the conservative Guardianship Council (controlled by Khamenei), which is proving increasingly resistant to change.

Central Asia to 1700

The Shah mosque (now Imam mosque) in Isfahan, with the names of God and Muhammad written in bold geometric characters on the minaret. Built between 1612 and 1630 its spectacular blue tiled decoration epitomizes the style and splendour of Shah Abbas.

The history of Inner Asia, like that of the Fertile Crescent where Islam originated, was dominated by the relationship between nomadic pastoralists and settled peoples. In the vast semiarid steppelands to the north and east of the Black and Caspian Seas lived peoples whose livelihoods depended mainly on cattle, horses, goats, sheep, camels, and yaks. They were organized into patriarchal kinship groups based on families, clans, and confederations or hordes, the greatest of which was that organized under the leadership of Ghenghis Khan and his successors. Under the leadership of Ghenghis Khan's son Batu (r. 1227–55) the Golden Horde of Mongol-Turkish people (who became known as Tatars in Russia) established its base from two sarays (palace headquarters) on the Volga River. From here they conquered the Ukraine, southern Poland, Hungary, Bulgaria, and Russia, creating a vast empire of which the ruler in Moscow was the principal tributary. Leading Tatar families became Muslims from the mid-thirteenth century after contact with the sedentary peoples of Iran, Khwarzm, and Transoxiana. Brought by the merchants and Sufi dervishes who traveled along the Silk Road, Islam in Inner Asia acquired a mystical, pluralistic character resulting from its encounters with Zoroastrianism, Buddhism, Nestorian Christianity, and older traditions of shamanism.

The conversion to Islam by Tarmarshirin (r. 1326–34), the ruler of the lands in Transoxiana bequeathed by Ghenghis Khan to his second son Chagatay, caused a split in his clan. This was cleverly exploited by Timur Lenk, a member respected by the impoverished clan of Turkomans. Though lame from birth Timur (r. 1370–1405), known as Tamerlane in the West, was a brilliant political strategist and military commander. By uniting Transoxiana and Iran (previously ruled by the Ilkhans, descendents of Hulegu) he regenerated Turkish-Mongolian power in central Asia, creating an empire that would stretch, at its height, from western India (including Delhi) to the shores of the Black Sea. After defeating the Ottomans at Ankara in 1402, where he captured the sultan, Bayazid I (r. 1389–1402), he became well known in Europe. The disruption of Ottoman power in Anatolia relieved the pressure on Constantinople (which survived for another half century) and reopened the trade routes to China, while his defeat of the Golden Horde assisted the rise of Christian Russia.

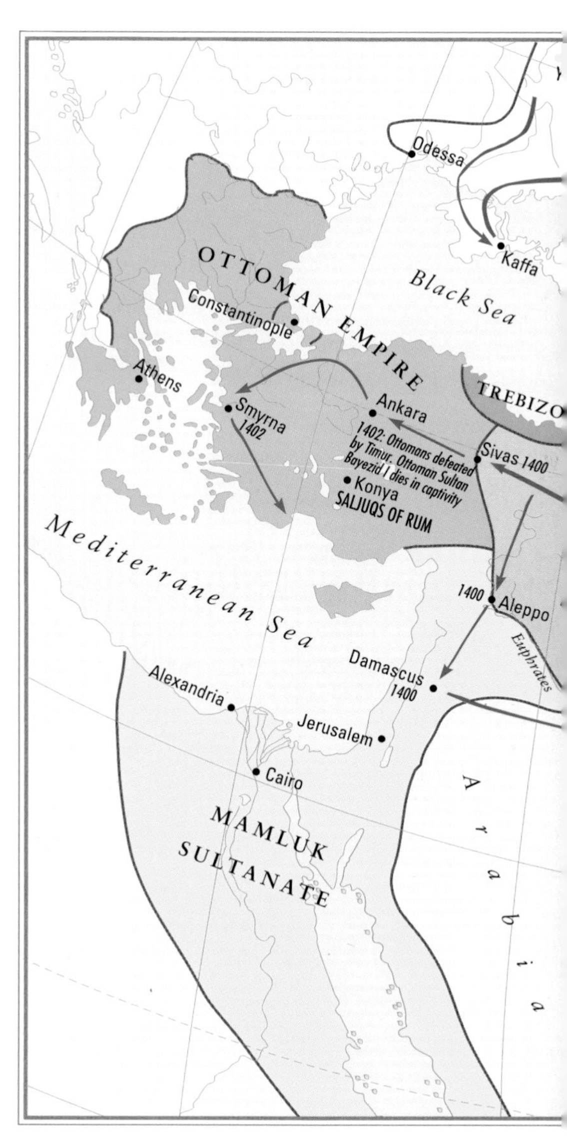

Under Timur, his successor Ulugh Beg (r. 1404–49), and the Uzbek Shaybanids (1500–c. 1700) who inherited Timurid power in Inner Asia, Herat, Samarkand, and Bukhara were transformed into world-class cities. They were embellished by the plunder and legions of skilled craftsmen and artisans Timur and his successors had imported from Persia, India, Iraq, and Syria. Though utterly ruthless and cruel (before taking Delhi, he had thousands of male prisoners executed so they would not be able to change sides) Timur was far from being an ignorant barbarian. He mastered Persian, and surrounded himself with some of the most distinguished scholars, artists, historians, and poets of his time, setting the stamp of "royal" Islamic high culture that would be imitated with rather more refinement by his successors. He was broad-minded on religious matters. Though a Sunni Muslim who launched his conquests in the name of the Sharia under the pretext that his enemies were apostates and traitors to Islam, he gave his protection to the Shiites. Shaiks (Sufi pirs) were his chief spiritual advisors. The Naqshbandi Sufi order, named after Baha al-Din Naqshband (d. 1389) who is buried near Bukhara, put down deep roots in inner Asia during this period.

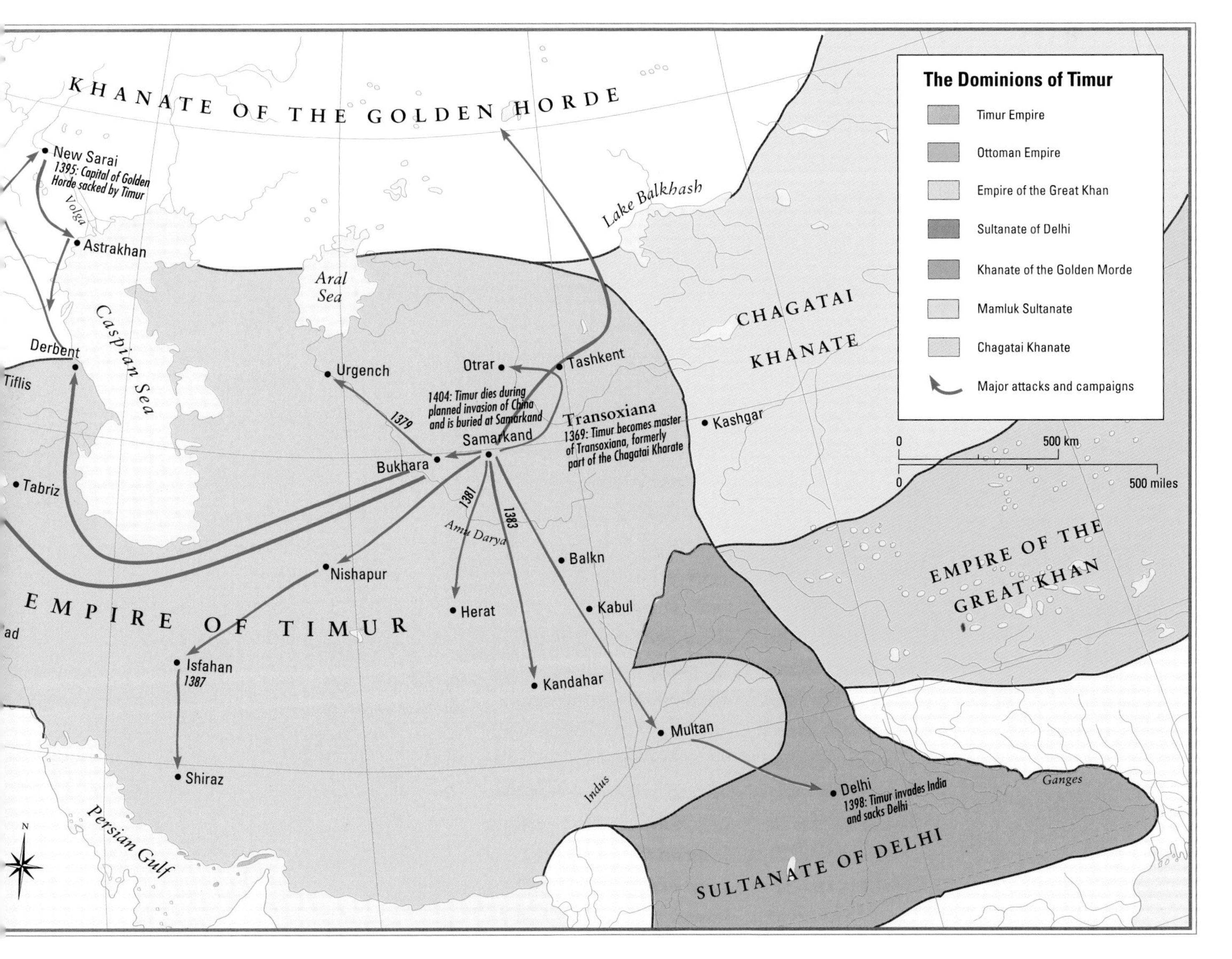

India 711–1971

Islam first appeared in the South Asia subcontinent with the Arab invasion of Sind (711–713). In the tenth century Fatimid dais (missionaries) from Cairo converted local rulers in Multan to Ismailism. However, these were replaced by Sunni governors appointed by the Ghurids in the aftermath of the conquest of the Punjab by Mahmud of Ghazna, who sacked Lahore and devastated northern India in 1030. The systematic conquest of the subcontinent began with the Ghurids who occupied Multan, Lahore, and Delhi (1175–92) before one of their generals, Qutb al-Din Aybeg, established the first of several independent sultanates in Delhi. These endured from 1206–1526 under a succession of different dynasties. The Delhi sultanates help to establish the distinctive character of Indian Islam, a legacy carried by the Timurid Mughal Empire founded by Timur's grandson Babur in 1526. This lasted more than three centuries until its dissolution by the British after the "Mutiny" or Great Rebellion in 1858. The Mughal Empire absorbed a number of independent Muslim dynasties that had been established in Bengal (1356–1576), Kashmir (1346–1589), Gujerat (1407–1572), and the Deccan (1347–1601). At the empire's greatest extent under Aurungzeb (r. 1658–1707) the emperor's name was read from the pulpits of mosques as far apart as Kabul and Mysore.

Some of the early Muslim rulers were fired with iconoclastic zeal against "idolators" and destroyed Hindu temples replacing them with large mosques intended to symbolize Islamic domination. The Tughluq dynasty (1320–1413), however, initiated a pattern of tolerance that would help to establish a pluralistic version of Islam in India that contrasted with the more rigid and austere varieties of earlier times. To counter the political influence of well-established Muslim families, the dynasty's founder Muhammad Tughluq (r. 1325–51) appointed non-Muslims to military and government offices, took part in local festivals, and allowed the construction of temples. While there was an initial period of Muslim immigration into India from Afghanistan and Central Asia after the conquests, the process of conversion and Islamization was slow and relatively limited. It is doubtful if more than 20 or 25 percent of the Indian population became Muslim, with the Muslim populations concentrated in the Indus Valley, the northwestern frontier region, and Bengal. While the ruling classes were the descendants of warriors from Afghanistan, Iran, and Inner Asia, most of the converts were from the lower Hindu castes or tribal and rural peoples whose lives were improved by joining the religious community of the rulers. The fullest diversity of Islamic faith, practice, and tradition came to be reflected among Indian Muslims, Sunni, Shiite, and Sufi, with a vast number of variations. The pluralistic character of Indian Islam is reflected in its magnificent architectural heritage where motifs drawn from Islamic and Hindu vernaculars were blended into a new, creative synthesis. Muslim devotional literature, including poetry, exists in a large number of Indian languages in addition to Arabic and Persian, the languages taught in the institutions of higher learning along with law, theology, and mysticism.

While the ruling dynasties reflected an urban pattern of Muslim life, which had much in common with the cosmopolitan culture of other Muslim regions such as Iran and Central Asia, rural Muslim populations retained a strong vernacular heritage, with local Hindu rituals and customs often mixed with Islamic beliefs and practices. Sufi teachers and religious orders played a particularly important role in the spread of Islam in South Asia. Among the most important tariqas were the Suhrawardiyya and the Chistiyya. Though organized hierarchically in a way that fitted the character of Indian society, the social roles of the tariqas differed greatly. Whereas the Suhrawardis maintained close relations with the Delhi sultans, benefiting from endowments and gifts of land that gave their leaders the status of

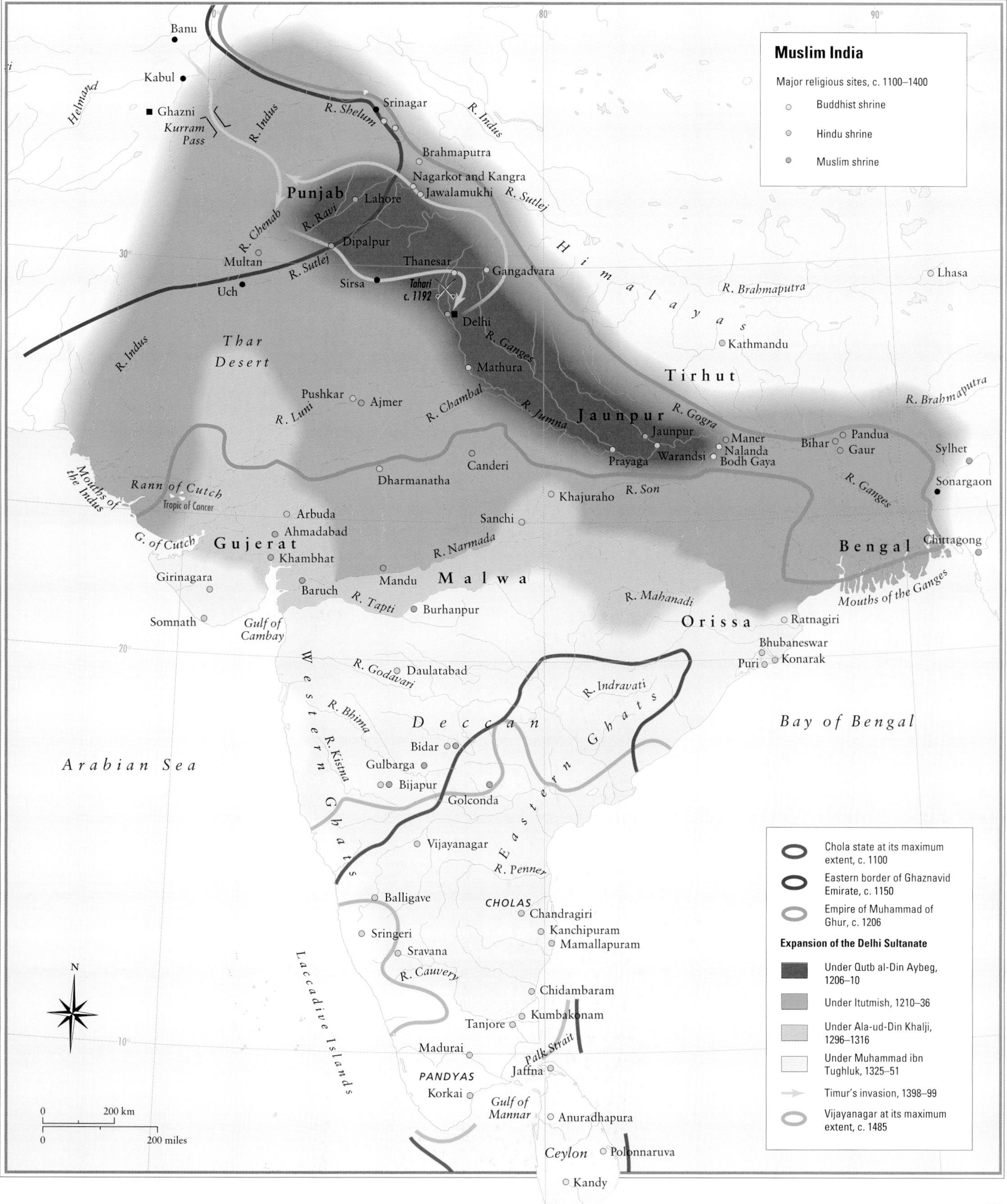

Muslim India
Major religious sites, c. 1100–1400
Buddhist shrine
Hindu shrine
Muslim shrine
Chola state at its maximum extent, c. 1100
Eastern border of Ghaznavid Emirate, c. 1150
Empire of Muhammad of Ghur, c. 1206
Expansion of the Delhi Sultanate
Under Qutb al-Din Aybeg, 1206–10
Under Itutmish, 1210–36
Under Ala-ud-Din Khalji, 1296–1316
Under Muhammad ibn Tughluk, 1325–51
Timur's invasion, 1398–99
Vijayanagar at its maximum extent, c. 1485
Banu
Kabul
Ghazni
Kurram Pass
Helmand
R. Indus
R. Shelum
Srinagar
Brahmaputra
Nagarkot and Kangra
Jawalamukhi
R. Sutlej
Punjab
Lahore
R. Ravi
R. Chenab
Dipalpur
Multan
R. Sutlej
Uch
Sirsa
Thanesar
Tahari c. 1192
Gangadvara
Delhi
Himalayas
R. Brahmaputra
Lhasa
Kathmandu
Thar Desert
R. Ganges
Mathura
Tirhut
Pushkar
Ajmer
R. Luni
R. Chambal
R. Jumna
Jaunpur
R. Gogra
Maner
Nalanda
Bodh Gaya
Warandsi
Prayaga
Bihar
Pandua
Gaur
Sylhet
Sonargaon
Canderi
Dharmanatha
Mouths of the Indus
Rann of Cutch
Tropic of Cancer
Khajuraho
R. Son
Arbuda
Ahmadabad
Sanchi
G. of Cutch
Gujerat
Khambhat
R. Narmada
Bengal
Chittagong
Girinagara
Mandu
Malwa
Baruch
R. Tapti
Burhanpur
R. Mahanadi
Mouths of the Ganges
Somnath
Gulf of Cambay
Orissa
Ratnagiri
Bhubaneswar
Puri
Konarak
R. Godavari
Daulatabad
R. Indravati
Western Ghats
R. Bhima
Deccan
Eastern Ghats
Bay of Bengal
R. Kistna
Bidar
Arabian Sea
Gulbarga
Bijapur
Golconda
Vijayanagar
R. Penner
Balligave
CHOLAS
Chandragiri
Kanchipuram
Mamallapuram
Sringeri
Sravana
Laccadive Islands
R. Cauvery
Chidambaram
Kumbakonam
Tanjore
Madurai
Palk Strait
Jaffna
PANDYAS
Korkai
Gulf of Mannar
Anuradhapura
Ceylon
Polonnaruva
Kandy
N
0 200 km
0 200 miles
80°
90°
30°
20°
10°

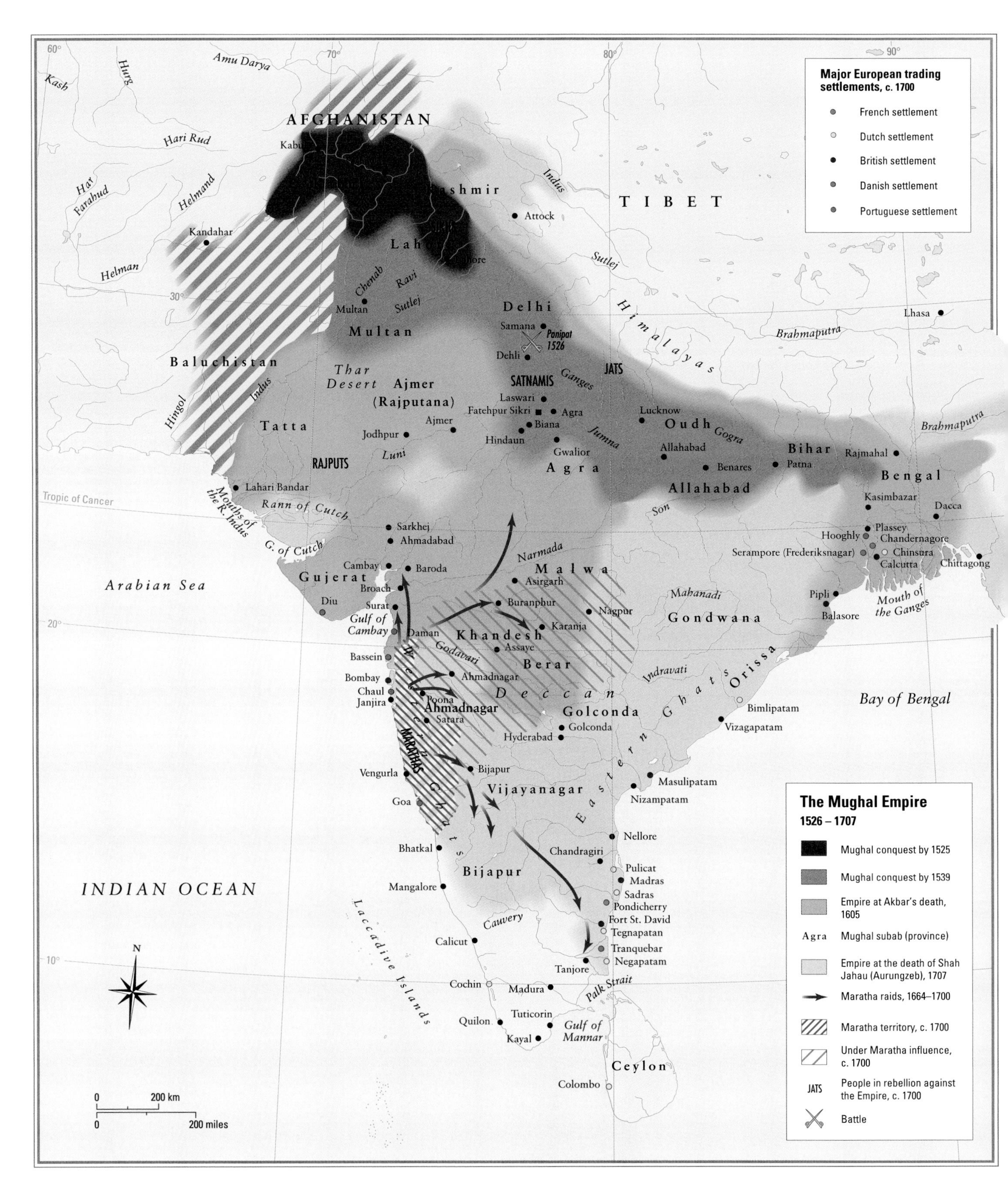

Major European trading settlements, c. 1700
French settlement
Dutch settlement
British settlement
Danish settlement
Portuguese settlement
The Mughal Empire 1526 – 1707
Mughal conquest by 1525
Mughal conquest by 1539
Empire at Akbar's death, 1605
Agra Mughal subab (province)
Empire at the death of Shah Jahau (Aurungzeb), 1707
Maratha raids, 1664–1700
Maratha territory, c. 1700
Under Maratha influence, c. 1700
JATS People in rebellion against the Empire, c. 1700
Battle
AFGHANISTAN
TIBET
Baluchistan
Multan
Delhi
Ajmer (Rajputana)
Tatta
Agra
Oudh
Allahabad
Bihar
Bengal
Gujerat
Malwa
Khandesh
Berar
Gondwana
Ahmadnagar
Golconda
Vijayanagar
Bijapur
Orissa
Deccan
Ceylon
Arabian Sea
Bay of Bengal
INDIAN OCEAN
Himalayas
Thar Desert
Eastern Ghats
Western Ghats
Laccadive Islands
Tropic of Cancer
Panipat 1526
SATNAMIS
JATS
RAJPUTS
MARATHAS
Kandahar
Attock
Multan
Samana
Dehli
Laswari
Fatehpur Sikri
Agra
Ajmer
Jodhpur
Biana
Hindaun
Gwalior
Lucknow
Allahabad
Benares
Patna
Rajmahal
Lhasa
Lahari Bandar
Sarkhej
Ahmadabad
Cambay
Baroda
Broach
Diu
Surat
Daman
Bassein
Bombay
Chaul
Janjira
Poona
Satara
Ahmadnagar
Asirgarh
Buranphur
Karanja
Assaye
Nagpur
Hyderabad
Golconda
Bijapur
Vengurla
Goa
Bhatkal
Mangalore
Calicut
Cochin
Quilon
Madura
Tuticorin
Kayal
Tanjore
Colombo
Nellore
Chandragiri
Pulicat
Madras
Sadras
Pondicherry
Fort St. David
Tegnapatan
Tranquebar
Negapatam
Masulipatam
Nizampatam
Vizagapatam
Bimlipatam
Pipli
Balasore
Kasimbazar
Dacca
Plassey
Hooghly
Chandernagore
Serampore (Frederiksnagar)
Chinsura
Calcutta
Chittagong
Amu Darya
Hari Rud
Helmand
Helman
Har Farahud
Hurg
Kash
Indus
Sutlej
Chenab
Ravi
Ganges
Jumna
Gogra
Brahmaputra
Son
Luni
Narmada
Godavari
Mahanadi
Indravati
Cauvery
Hingol
Rann of Cutch
Mouths of the R. Indus
G. of Cutch
Gulf of Cambay
Mouth of the Ganges
Palk Strait
Gulf of Mannar
200 km
200 miles

provincial notables, the Chistis made a point of refusing endowments and rejecting government service, living by cultivating wastelands and from donations by their devotees.

The pirs (Sufi shaikhs) who won converts among tribal or marginal peoples or from the lower Hindu castes used local languages (including ritual languages) to convey the Islamic message in social and religious milieus that were very different from those prevailing in the regions where Islam originated. At a popular level it mattered little if a holy man presented himself as a Muslim or a devotee of Shiva: what inspired bakhti (devotion) was his individual aura of holiness. At an intellectual level the philosophical justification for religious collaboration between Islam and what would come to be known as Hinduism (a term invented by Europeans in the nineteenth century) could be found in the writings of the great Andalusian mystic Ibn al-Arabi, whose doctrine of "unity of being" could be harmonized with the spiritual teachings of the Vedas and the Upanishads. The high point of Hindu-Muslim religious harmony was reached during the reign of Akbar I (1556–1605), a supporter of the Chistis who instituted the Din-i-Ilahi (divine religion). This was an imperial cult with Akbar at its center combining the roles of Sufi master and philosopher-king.

In due course, however, practices seen by the ulama as syncretic or idolatrous would become the targets of reformist movements inspired by more orthodox teachings emanating from the centers of Islam to the west. The leaders of this tendency were Shaikh Ahmad Sirhindi (1564–1624) and his follower Shah Wali Allah (1702–63). The public form of this reaction began under Akbar's grandson Aurungzeb, who reversed the policy of accommodation with Hindus. He imposed the jizya (poll tax) on non-Muslims, ordered the destruction of Hindu temples, and founded Muslim colleges for the study of the Sharia, as well as banning music at court. The reformist currents helped to preserve a distinctive Muslim identity during a century of Mughal decline, when the British became the dominant power in India. Reformers in the tradition of Shah Wali Allah encouraged Muslims to avoid collaboration with power or social mixing with non-Muslims. While Sufi devotional practices (including worship at the shrine of saints and colorful popular festivals) continued to attract the poor, the reformist currents gained ground among the emerging class of literate professionals. The reform college of Deoband, founded in 1867, used the new technology of print in Urdu and the burgeoning rail network to reach a mass Muslim audience throughout the subcontinent,

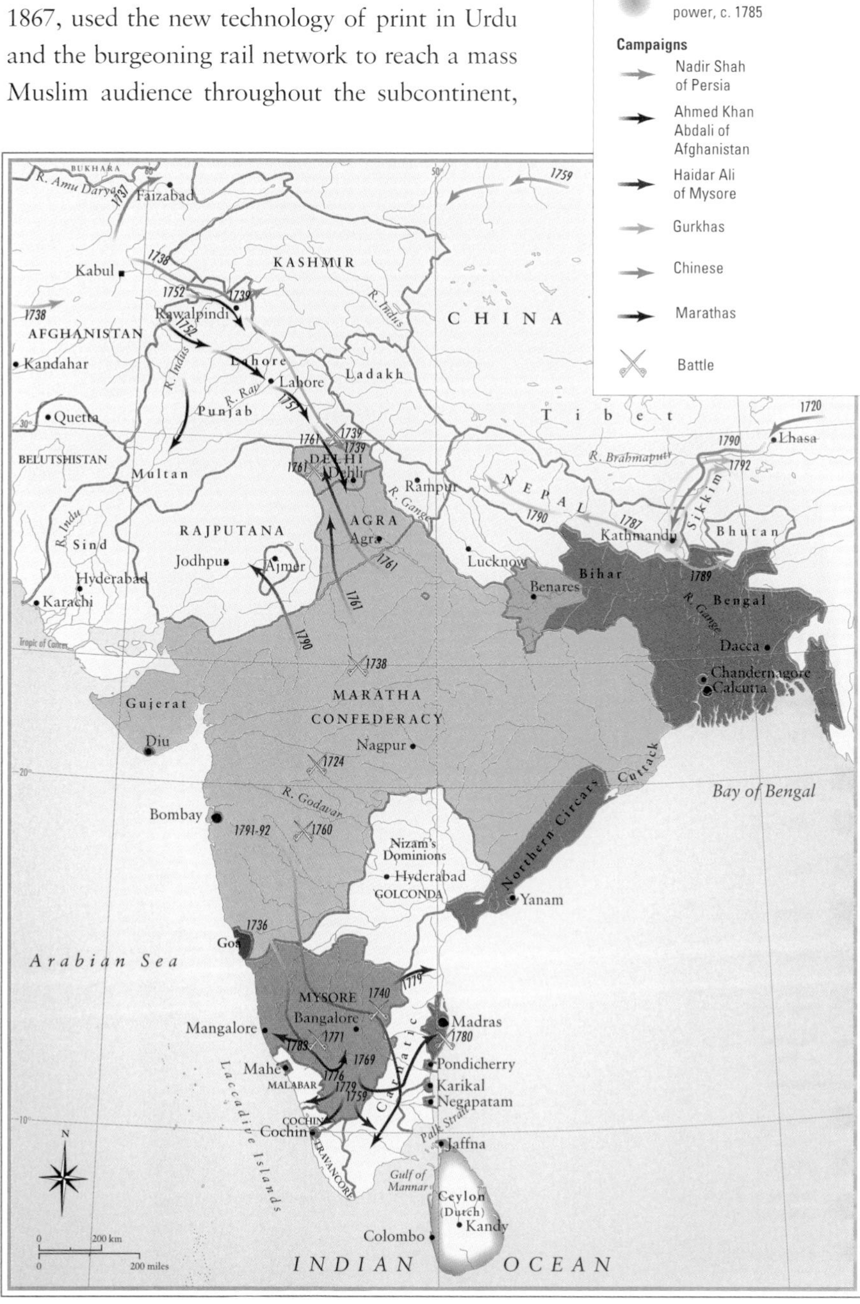

reinforcing Muslim communal distinctiveness. "To like and appreciate the customs of the infidels," wrote a leading Deobandi scholar Maulana Ashraf Ali Thanawi, "is a grave sin."

The sense of Muslim separateness was encouraged by the British, who tended to stress the importance of religious ties over family, lineage, language, caste, regional, or class affiliations among India's variegated communities. The Indian Councils Act of 1909 institutionalized separate Hindu and Muslim electorates at local level, thereby consolidating a separate identity of Muslims legally and politically. From there the "two-nations" theory, which held that Muslims and Hindus constituted distinct and separate nations, was a small but inevitable step. The same logic decreed that the Muslims of India were entitled to their own territorial homeland. The state of Pakistan created on Indian independence in 1947 was constructed out of a disparate vari-

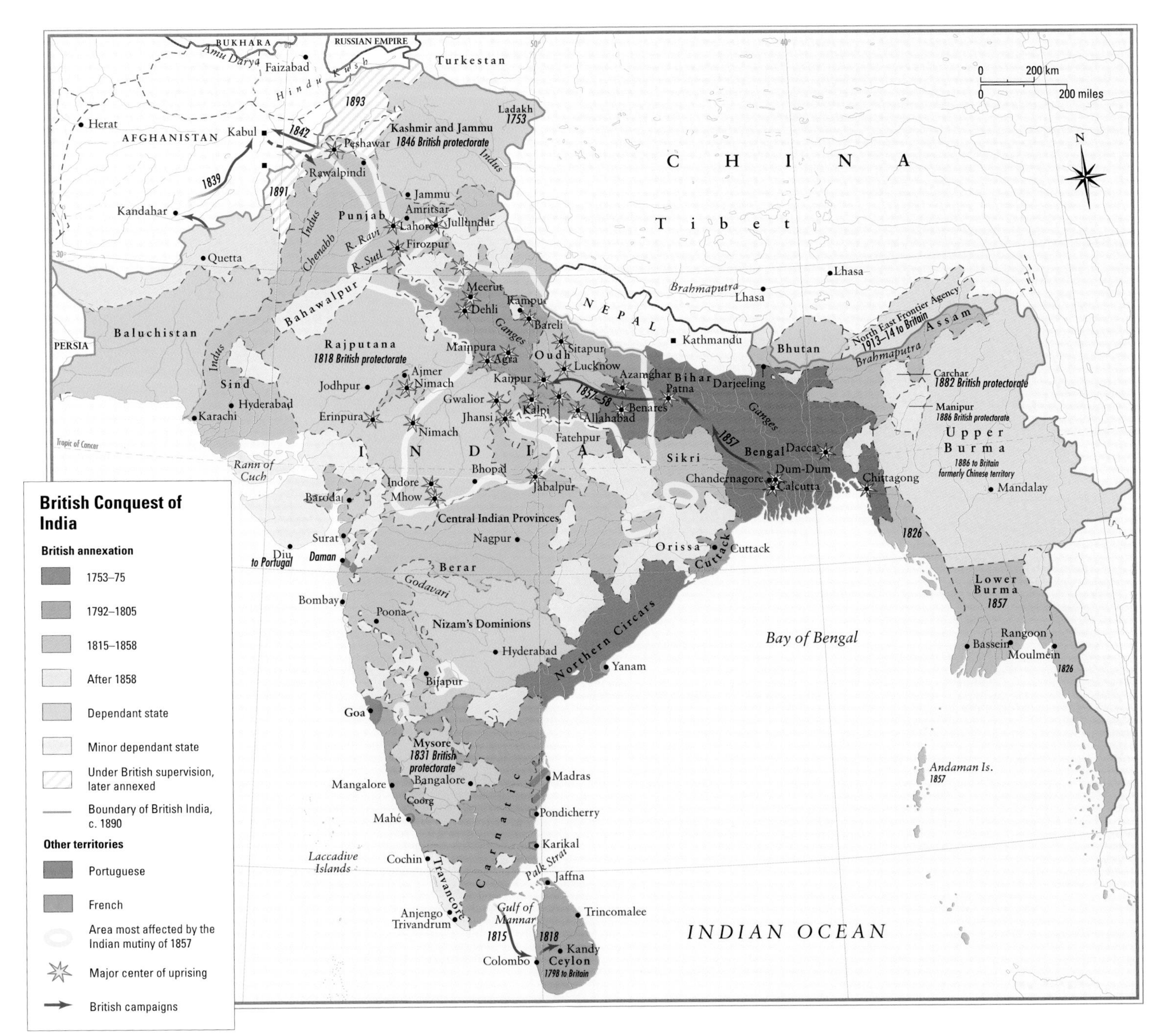

ety of Muslim communities located in the territories of Sind, Baluchistan, the Northwest Frontier province, the western half of the Punjab, and a part of Bengal, a mainly Muslim territory located more than a thousand miles to the east, separated by Indian territory. In western Pakistan, more than half the people were Punjabis, some 20 percent were Sindhis, 13 percent were Pashtuns, 3–4 percent were Baluchis, with the remainder, apart from small Hindu and Christian minorities, Muhajirs, or refugees from India. The exchange of populations following partition led to a massive bloodbath, in which hundreds of thousands of people were killed in communal rioting. The unresolved dispute over Kashmir, where the Hindu ruler chose to accede to the Indian Union against the wishes of his Muslim subjects, has contributed to three wars between India and Pakistan in 1949, 1965, and 1971, as well as a continuing cycle of insurgency and repression. Pakistan's political fragility was reflected by the succession of military governments that alternated with periods of precarious democratic rule by parties accused of corruption and lacking Islamic legitimacy. In the final analysis the army, controlled by the British-trained Punjabi officer class, proved the only institution capable of holding the country together. In 1971 with military help from India, East Pakistan broke away from western Pakistan to form the independent Muslim state of Bangladesh. The fractious relationship between India and Pakistan (both of them now nuclear powers that have fought three major wars since 1947) has yet to be resolved. The erosion of India's secular culture consequent on Hindu political revival and official Islamophobia occasionally tolerated in some states has made the position of the Muslim minority remaining in India—which numbers some 120 million, about 10 percent of the population—more vulnerable than at any time since partition. The legacy of the Muslim conquests has yet to be fully absorbed in Indian popular consciousness. A mosque in Ayodhya, said to have been built by Babur on the site of a temple devoted to the hero-deity Rama, and destroyed by Hindu militants in 1991 is still a powerful source of contention between India's Hindu and Muslim communities. In the ensuing communal riots, thousands of Muslims were killed—a story tragically repeated in 2003 when Hindu pilgrims returning from Ayodhya were attacked by Muslims in Gujerat causing widespread communal conflict in the region.

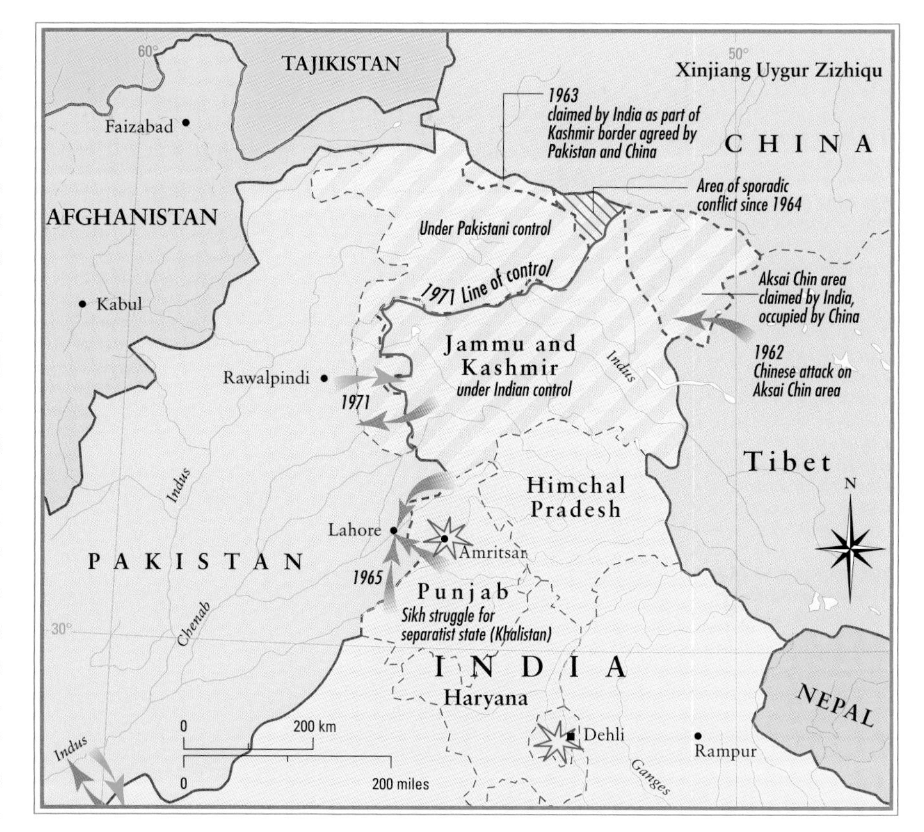

Conflict over Kashmir
1949 – 1971

- Pakistani attacks
- Indian attacks
- Religious unrest and rivalry

The Taj Mahal, Agra, India (completed 1653). One of the world's best known monuments, it is the most enduring emblem of Mughal rule in India. It was built by the Emperor Shah Jahan in memory of his wife Mumtaz Mahal. Shah Jahan ,who was deposed by his son Aurungzeb, is also buried there.

Russian Expansion in Transcaucasia and Central Asia

The Russian expansion into Transoxiana and the Caucasus region, which would culminate in the incorporation of more than fifty million Muslim peoples into the Soviet Union, began in the fifteenth century when the rulers of Moscow threw off the Tatar yoke. By the 1550s Moscow had absorbed the autonomous Muslim states of Kazan and Astrakhan, giving it control of the Volga and the northern shores of the Caspian Sea and opening the way for the conquest of the Kazakh steppes. The Kazakhs had pulled out of the confederation of Turkish-Mongol tribes that had created the Timurid and subsequent empires, remaining qazaq (freely roaming) lords of the steppes. The Russians built a string of forts between the Ural and the Irtysh rivers. This enabled them to bring the whole region under Russian control, a process marked by the abolition of the Kazakh khanates in the 1820s. However, Kazakh resistance, inspired by Islam, would last until the 1860s.

Imam Shamil of Daghestan (c. 1797–1871), on horseback, from a Russian engraving of c. 1850. Shamil waged a heroic campaign (1834–59) against the Russians under the spiritual authority of his father-in-law, a shaikh of the Naqshbandiyya Sufi order. Though eventually defeated and sent into exile, his memory remained alive in Daghestan and Chechnya, where it has inspired successive anti-Russian and anti-Soviet revolts up to the present day.

In its earlier phases Russian rule over its Muslim populations was extremely harsh. The Tatar nobility was subjected to forced conversion and expelled from important cities. Their lands were given over to the Russian nobility and monasteries, who planted them with Orthodox serfs and monks. The policy was relaxed under Catherine the Great, who regarded Islam as a more civilizing influence than Christianity. Muslims were guaranteed religious freedom, mosques were built with state sponsorship, and institutions created with broad authority over the Muslim population. The situation, however, was not to last. In the Crimea, which Russia had acquired from the Ottomans in 1783, the Russians took over Tatar lands and confiscated waqfs (religious endowments) for the benefit of European colonists. Further east the mainly pastoral peoples of Inner Asia fell prey to the colonizing ambitions of Russian generals and the desire of the tsars to secure trading advantages with Iran, India, and

China, forestalling potential British rivalry. Tashkent was occupied in 1865, Samarkand in 1868, and Bukhara was forced to open its frontiers to Russian traders. In the north Caucasus the Russians overcame resistance inspired by the Naqshbandi and Qadiri orders, overthrowing the Islamic state established by Imam Shamil in 1859. By 1900 the tsarist conquest of Transcaucasia and Central Asia was virtually complete.

Far from leading to the dissolution of the tsarist empire in Asia the Bolshevik revolution of 1917–18 led to its consolidation. In their struggle against their own conservative religious establishments, intellectual advocates of Islamic reform, known as jadidists, joined the Communist Party. They hoped to modify Russian policies to meet the needs of the Muslim populations and to promote versions of Muslim nationalism in alliance with Soviet Russia. The Muslim nationalists were outmaneuvered by Stalin and the party centralizers. Their leading advocate, Mir Said Sultan Galiev (b. 1880), was arrested in 1928 and disappeared soon afterward. However, a sense of shared values between Islam and communism (social justice, the priority of public over private interest, of community over the individual) encouraged them to work for their interests within the party by adopting a strategy of taqiya (dissimulation). But official Islam suffered serious assault during the 1930s when Stalin launched his "second revolution" from above. Mosques were placed in the hands of the Union of Atheists, to be turned into museums or places of entertainment, while two of the five "pillars" of the Islamic faith, the pilgrimage to Mecca and the collection of zakat (the religious dues used to maintain mosques and provide funds for the needy), were effectively forbidden. The ban on Arabic script and its replacement by Latin and later Cyrillic scripts ensured that future Soviet generations would have much less access than in the past to the canonical texts of Islam.

The potential for political solidarity among Soviet Muslims was attacked by a deliberate policy of divide and rule. Central Asian states of today owe their territorial existence to Stalin. He responded to the threat of pan-Turkish and pan-Islamic nationalism by parceling out the territories of Russian Turkestan into the five republics of Uzbekistan, Turkmenistan, Kazakhstan, Kyrgyzstan, and Tajikistan. The prosperous Fergana Valley, which lies at the core of the region and had always been a single economic unit, was divided between Uzbeks, Tajiks, and Kyrgyz. Stalin's policies demanded that subtle differences in language, history, and culture between these mainly Turkic peoples be emphasized in order to satisfy the Leninist criteria on nationality, which required a common language, a unified territory, a shared economic life, and a common culture. To the new territorial configurations were added the straitjackets of collectivization and monoculture. Under Khruschev's Virgin Lands scheme vast tracts of Kazakhstan were given over to cereal production, and when the mainly pastoral Kazakhs resisted, Slavs and other nationalities were imported to do the work. In Uzbekistan more than 60 percent of gross domestic production was turned over to cotton. This served the interests of the ruling party elites, some of whose members became involved in gargantuan frauds based on the systematic falsification of production figures. However, it also left a devastating environmental legacy by starving noncotton crops of irrigation and drying up the rivers and lakes, including the Aral Sea.

Distrusting the loyalty of Muslims during

the Second World War, some of whom did collaborate with the Germans, Stalin deported the whole population of Chechnya-Ingushia and the entire Tatar population of the Crimea to Central Asia.

Although there were undoubted benefits resulting from industrialization and the introduction of almost universal literacy, the retreat of Soviet power following the jihad in Afghanistan inevitably saw an upsurge of non-communist ideologies, including local nationalisms, pan-Turkism, and militant forms of Islam. The resurgence of Islamic activity after 1989 after more than half a century of repression may partly be accounted for by the mystical Sufi traditions. Originating in Central Asia, they had retained their roots. Naqshbandi Sufism, in particular, was able to survive official persecution as the tradition of "silent" rituals enabled meetings to take place under other guises. Additionally old family networks based on the asabiya of extended kinship groups persisted or even flourished by taking control of communist institutions. In Chechnya where Russia has fought two brutal wars 1994–96 and 1999–2002 to suppress local independence movements, the persistence of Sufi networks and allegiances after seven decades of Soviet rule provides a better explanation for anti-Russian activity than the foreign-funded Islamist or "Wahhabi" militants targeted by spokesmen in the Kremlin.

In Central Asia, despite the retreat of Russia, general disillusionment with Soviet rule, and the collapse of the local economies, the old communist nomenklaturas have managed to cling to power under new, so-called democratic labels that barely conceal the reality of bureaucractic authoritarian rule.

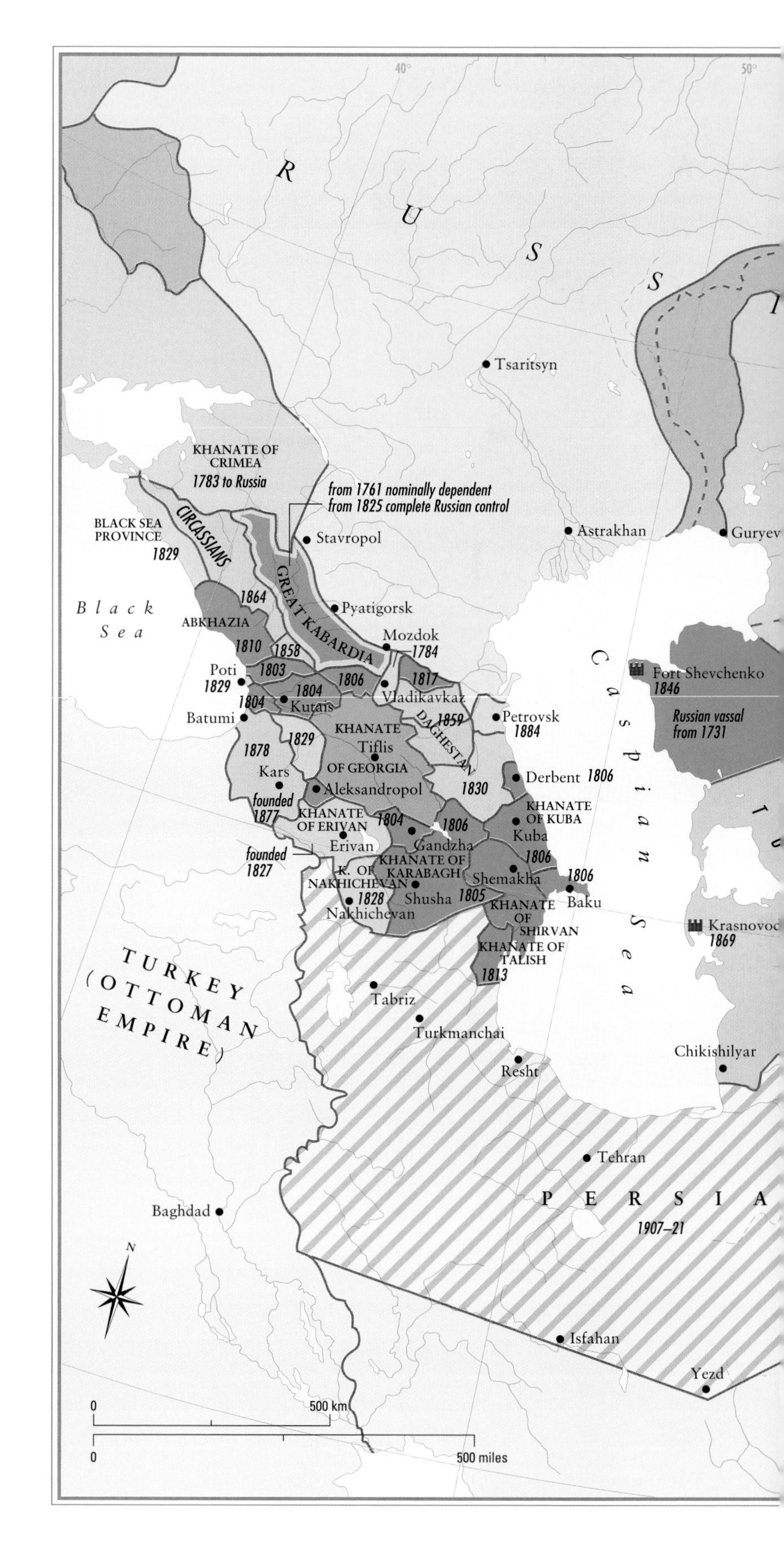

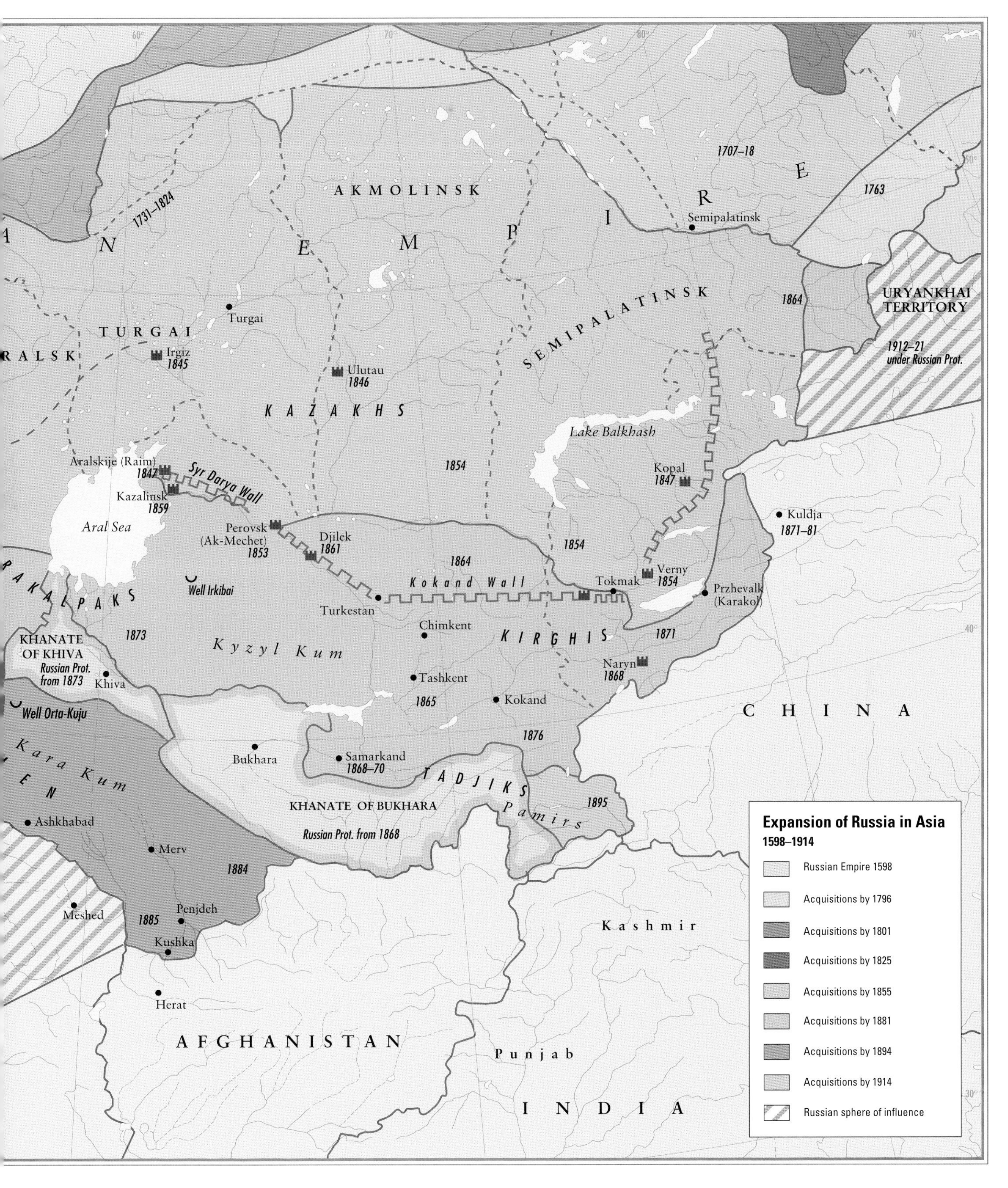
Expansion of Russia in Asia
1598–1914
Russian Empire 1598
Acquisitions by 1796
Acquisitions by 1801
Acquisitions by 1825
Acquisitions by 1855
Acquisitions by 1881
Acquisitions by 1894
Acquisitions by 1914
Russian sphere of influence
AKMOLINSK
SEMIPALATINSK
TURGAI
KAZAKHS
KIRGHIS
TADJIKS
E M P I R E
Semipalatinsk
Turgai
Irgiz 1845
Ulutau 1846
Aralskije (Raim) 1847
Syr Darya Wall
Kazalinsk 1859
Aral Sea
Perovsk (Ak-Mechet) 1853
Djilek 1861
Kokand Wall
Well Irkibai
Turkestan
Chimkent
Tashkent
Kokand
Kyzyl Kum
Lake Balkhash
Kopal 1847
Verny 1854
Tokmak
Przhevalk (Karakol)
Naryn 1868
Kuldja 1871–81
URYANKHAI TERRITORY
1912–21 under Russian Prot.
KHANATE OF KHIVA
Russian Prot. from 1873
Khiva
Well Orta-Kuju
Kara Kum
Ashkhabad
Merv
Meshed
Penjdeh
Kushka
Herat
Bukhara
Samarkand 1868–70
KHANATE OF BUKHARA
Russian Prot. from 1868
Pamirs
AFGHANISTAN
Kashmir
Punjab
INDIA
CHINA
1731–1824
1707–18
1763
1864
1854
1871
1873
1865
1876
1895
1884
1885

Expansion of Islam in Southeast Asia 1000–1800

As in other regions peripheral to the Islamic heartlands, Islam came to Southeast Asia by trade rather than conquest. In some cases Muslim merchants, who carried the prestige of Islamic high culture, married into local ruling families, providing them with wealth, diplomatic skills, and knowledge of the wider world. Adoption of Islam made it easier for chiefs in the coastal regions to resist the authority of the Hindu rulers who held sway in central Java. Sufi teachers, some of them also merchants, who arrived from Arabia and India, were able to present Islamic teachings in forms that people raised in Hindu traditions could understand. As trade expanded the adoption of Islam made it easier for smaller communities to become part of larger societies, favoring the further expansion of trade.

The development of Islam in this largely peaceful, organic fashion was disrupted, but not reversed, by the appearance of the Portuguese, who established themselves as a

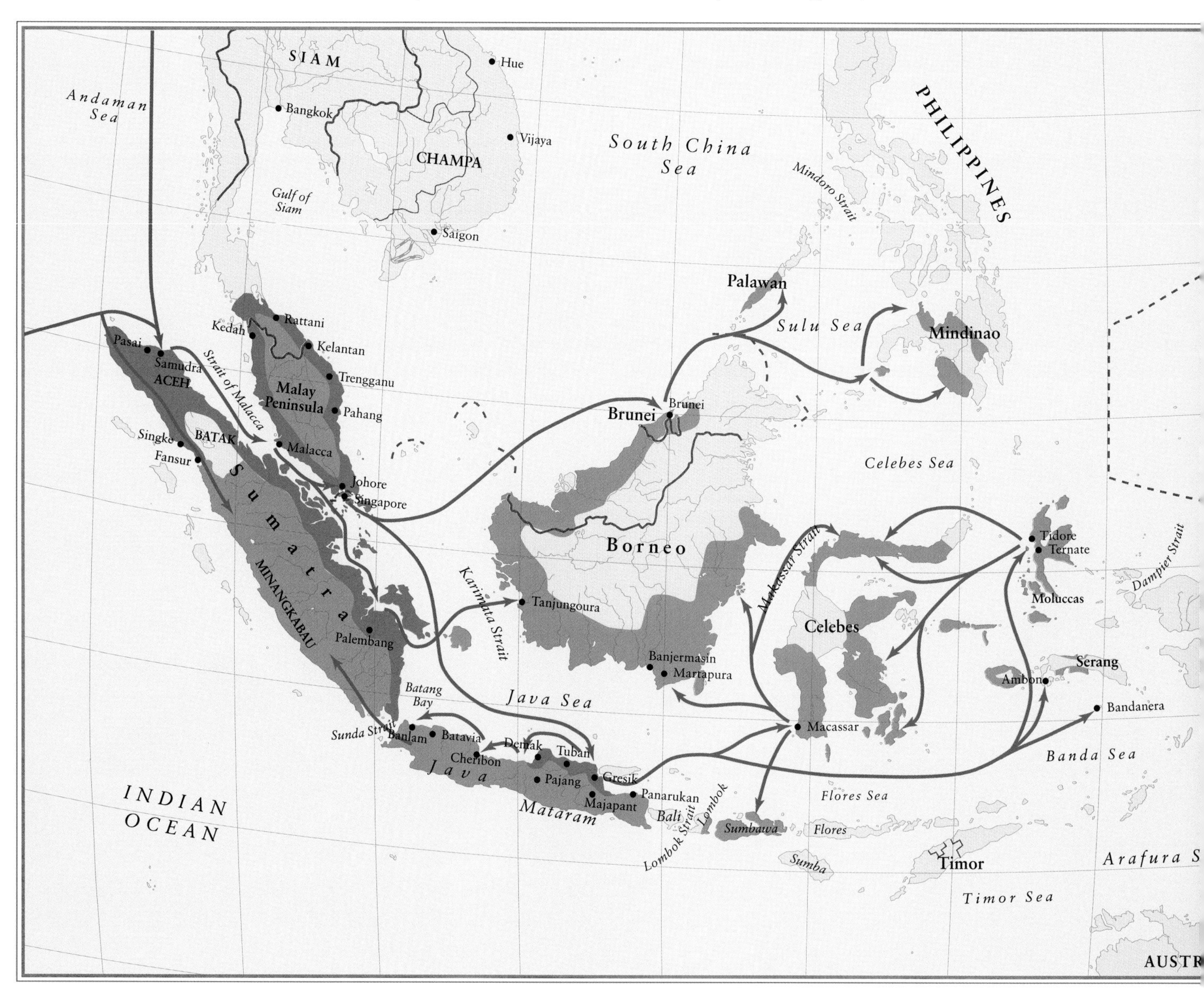

leading maritime power from the sixteenth century. Having taken Goa in 1509, the Portuguese conquered Malacca on the Malay Peninsula in 1511. Paradoxically, this aided the spread of Islam by sending Muslim teachers and missionaries to the courts of rulers in Acheh and Java, which became centers of resistance to the Portuguese. The appearance of the Dutch (who founded Batavia, later Jakarta, in 1619) in search of pepper, cloves, nutmeg, and tin complicated the picture, but did not reverse the spread, or appeal, of Islam in the region. Indeed conflict with the Dutch and Portuguese along with the expansion of trade had the reverse effect, bringing contact with the Ottoman Empire and an influx of scholars and Sufis from Mughal India especially in Acheh.

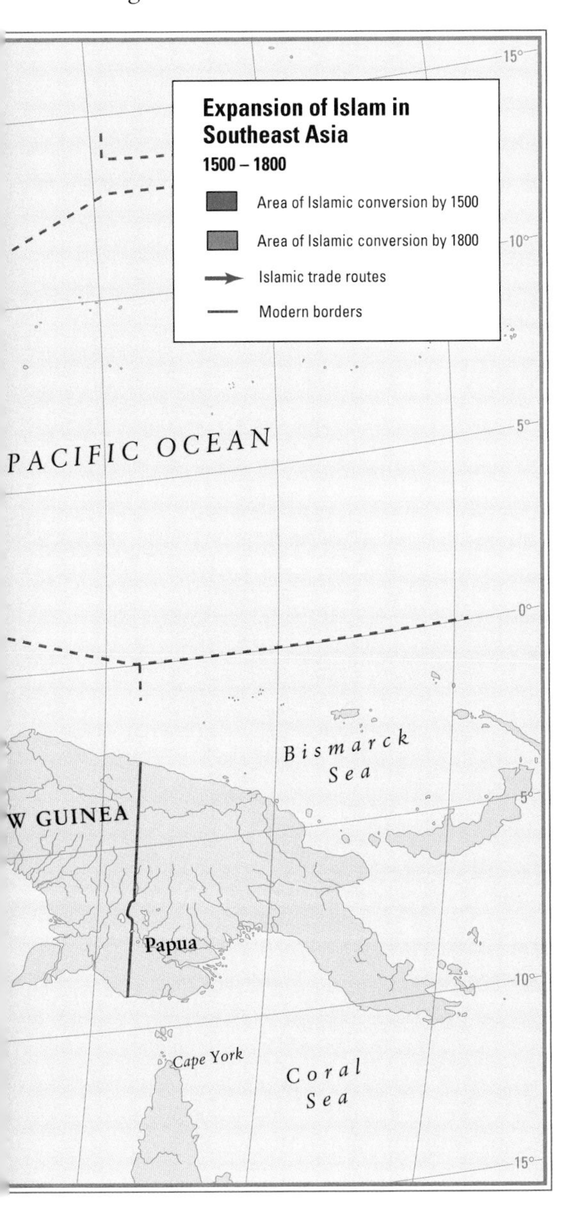

Differences between the coastal regions and the interiors, the legacies of Hindu and Buddhist kingships, the varying impacts of Portuguese, Dutch, and British rule, and the different degrees of resistance they engendered produced contrasting Islamic styles throughout the Malay Peninsula and Indonesian archipelago. A common element is the rainfall and rich tropical soil that makes much of the land highly productive—feeding colonial appetites for cash crops such as coffee and, later, rubber. In Southeast Asia Islam encountered societies of settled cultivators and relatively ancient polities whose deep territorial roots contrast strikingly with the flows of pastoral peoples that dominate Islamic history in Central or Western Asia. In some instances the tides of the faith coming from India and Arabia left a residue of ritual and practice that combined with the older traditions. In Java, for instance, villagers will describe themselves as Muslim, but their actual culture combines Islamic with Hindu and animist elements. Elsewhere, as in Minangkabau, after a period of economic upheaval in the eighteenth century, reformist currents preaching closer adherence to the Sharia became dominant, generating social conflicts that resulted in Dutch intercession and conquest (1839–45). Generally, the Islamic legacy in Indonesia has crystallized into two broad tendencies—the rural abangan style, which allows a tolerance for non-Sharia customs including matrilineal forms of inheritance, and the stricter santri tradition of the cities. Though modern Islamists in both Malaysia and Indonesia generally oppose pluralism and cultural mixing, the fact remains that both nations have undergone successful industrial revolutions that have placed them well ahead of Iran, Pakistan, and the Arab-Muslim countries in terms of economic development.

British, French, Dutch, and Russian Empires

The enormous increase in the power of the European countries that began to take over the Muslim world from about 1800 can be traced back to the scientific revolution of the seventeenth century and the industrial revolution to which it gave birth. Before the mid-1600s Western and Muslim civilizations were on relatively equal terms, militarily and economically. By 1800, however, the balance had shifted decisively and permanently toward what would come to be thought of as "the West." Napoleon's ill-fated expedition to Egypt was not halted by the neo-Mamluks, whom he defeated at the Battle of the Pyramids, but by the British admiral, Nelson, who destroyed the French fleet at Aboukir Bay. Henceforth it would be competition—military and economic—between European nations rather than conflicts between the Islamic world and the West that would determine the historical agenda for the Muslim peoples.

Numerous explanations have been advanced to account for the cumulative rise in European power. These range from the spirit of capitalism engendered by the Protestant reformers and the sudden access to wealth brought back from the Americas, to the radical methodology of questioning everything advocated by the French philosopher René Descartes, one of the progenitors of the scientific revolution. Whatever the causes, the effects were far reaching and irreversible. European capital was systematically reinvested to finance technical innovation in industrial methods of production, such as cotton spinning, which could destroy traditional methods by competition. European military power, benefiting from constant technical improvements, was deployed to protect and extend markets for manufactured products, leading to the collapse of local economies and the capacity of non-European powers to offer resistance. From the perspective of previous eras (for example, that of the Crusader Kingdoms and the gradual loss of al-Andalus to the Christians) the process was extraordinarily rapid. By 1920 European power encompassed virtually the whole of the planet, except for regions considered too unpopulated, poor, or remote to be worthy of imperial designs.

Muslim leaders, both spiritual and secular, were at the forefront of resistance to European world conquest. In Java Prince Dipanegara, a member of one of the ruling families that succumbed to Dutch influence and pressures from European cultivators, launched a revolt embracing displaced peasants and religious leaders that lasted from 1825 to 1830. In Bengal, where the British East India Company had been trading since the early 1600s, the defeat of a local ruler, Nawab Siraj al-Dawla, who tried to curb the power of the company at the Battle of Plassey (1757), opened the way to the British conquest of Bengal. After further defeat at Buksar in 1764 Muslim resistance shifted to the large, formerly Hindu kingdom of Mysore, where Haidar Ali, a Punjabi soldier, created with French assistance a disciplined force along European lines. His son and successor Tipu Sultan (1750–99) secured a notable victory over a British army at the battle of Conjeveram, near Madras, before eventually being killed at Seringapatam in 1799, a battle that effectively ended resistance to British rule in southern India. Afterward resistance shifted to the Northwest Frontier or to within the ranks of the British-led Indian army. In the late 1820s Sayyid Ahmed Barelwi (1786–1831), a missionary preacher in the reformist Naqshbandi tradition who had spent three years in Mecca, tried to rally the Yusufzai Pashtuns in the Northwest Frontier province as part of a broader campaign of reform in Indian Islam. His aim of creating an Islamic state on liberated territory outside British control was frustrated by the Sikhs, who defeated him at Balakot in 1831. The Northwest Frontier, however, continued to be the focus of resistance to British rule long after Barelwi's death. Between 1847 and 1908 there were no less than sixty rebellions against the British. Many of them had millennarian overtones and nearly all were legitimized as jihads against infidel rule.

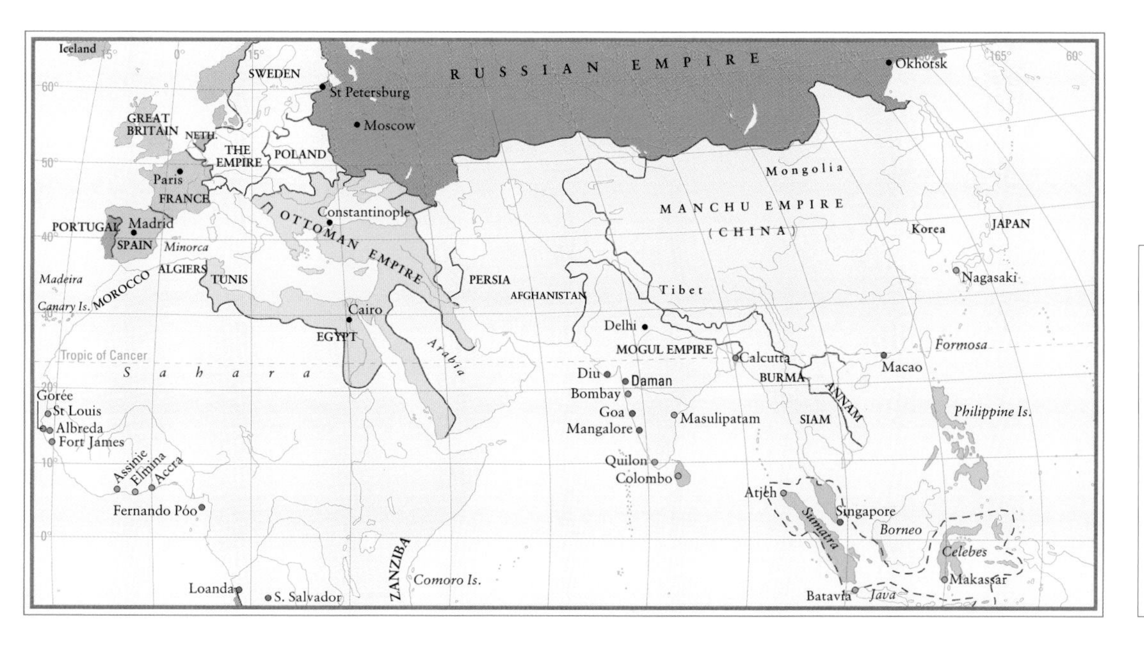

Many of these movements against European imperialism were led by men trained in the disciplines and hierarchies of the Sufi tariqas. In the Caucasus the Imam Shamil, a leader in the Naqshbandi tradition, waged a campaign against Russian penetration lasting from 1834 to 1839. Although the Islamic state he founded was eventually incorporated into the tsarist empire, Shamil's memory remained vibrant among the peoples of Daghestan and Chechnya who mounted successive revolts against Russians in 1863, 1877, 1917–19, during the Second World War, and against the post-communist administrations of Boris Yeltsin and Vladimir Putin. In Cyrenaica the Sanusiya order, who had accepted Ottoman suzerainty, became the source of organized resistance after the Italian invasion in 1911.

The British and French encountered similar movements of resistance throughout Muslim Africa. Abd al-Qadir, a shaikh of the Qadiriyya order, led the resistance to French rule after the conquest of Algiers in 1830. He established an Islamic state in the western Sahara. This lasted until 1847, when the French finally overwhelmed it and sent him into exile. In 1881 Muhammad Ahmad, a shaikh of the Sammaniya branch of the Khalwatiya, proclaimed himself Mahdi in the Upper Nile region, and launched a jihad against the Egyptian government and its foreign backers who were penetrating the region under European commanders. The defeat of the Mahdi's successor at Omdurman in 1898 was hailed by Winston Churchill, who witnessed the battle as "the most signal triumph ever gained by the arms of science over barbarians." The "arms of science" on this occasion were the British machine guns. Familiar weapons in small-scale punitive expeditions in much of Africa in the 1890s, here they were used for the first time against an army of more than fifty thousand men.

Nineteenth-Century Reform Movements

The tajdid (reform) movements, which have dominated Islamic thought and practice since the eighteenth century, have internal and external dimensions. Internally the example of Muhammad's attacks on the pagan idolaters of Mecca in the name of the "original" monotheistic religion taught by God to Adam, Ibrahim, and Ismail, followed by the hijra to Medina, the building of a new society, and his purging of Mecca's infidelities after his triumphant reconquest, is in itself a paradigm of religious reform. Throughout Islamic history the Prophetic scenario has been adopted by men of renowned learning and piety who have attacked or replaced corrupt rulers in the name of restoring the true Islam of Muhammad and his generation. Many such movements occurred in the eighteenth and nineteenth centuries. Some of these movements were religious responses to local practices, such as the custom of praying at the tombs of Sufi saints, condemned by the Arabian Wahhabis. Others, such as the reform movements in the Senegambian region of West Africa, involved local resistance to non-Muslim political elites; many others, such as the jihad movements on India's Northwest Frontier or the Mahdiya in the Nilotic Sudan were responses to European penetration.

Most of the militant movements of resistance and reform, however, occurred among tribal peoples in peripheral regions. Even when led by men of learning, such as the Mahdi Muhammad Ahmad or Uthman Dan Fodio, they could only succeed if backed by military-tribal power. Once it became clear that military solutions were not going to work because of the overwhelming power of the West, Muslim thinkers began to interpret the reformist scenario intellectually. Where the tribally-based movements distinguished between correct religious practice and unacceptable innovations, intellectual reformers sought to regenerate Islam by distinguishing between usul (fundamentals) of Islam, which were timeless and adaptable, and the details of furu (revelation), which applied to particular circumstances. All of the reformers recognized that if Islam was to survive and prosper under modern circumstances, Muslims must embrace modern learning and modern education. In India Sir Sayyed Ahmed Khan (1817–98) founded a college at Aligarh aimed at creating a modern generation of Muslim officials, lawyers, and journalists—men who in the course of time would become leaders of the Pakistan movement. A more conservative group of Indian ulama founded the academy at Deoband in 1867, which combined the study of revealed knowledge (Koran, hadith, and law) with rational subjects like logic, philosophy, and science. By taking advantage of the railroad system to distribute printed materials in Urdu, the Deobandis were able to reach all parts of Muslim India. This made Deoband the center of a new kind of Muslim consciousness that spread to other countries, with many students coming from Afghanistan, Central Asia, Yemen, and Arabia. A graduate of Deoband, Maulana Muhammad Ilyas, founded the reformist Tablighi Jamaat (preaching association) in 1927. Originally aimed at converting the Mewatis, a peasant community near Delhi, to stricter Islamic observance it combined strict adherence to the Sharia with Sufi meditations on the spirit of Muhammad as practiced by the Chisti order, to which Ilyas himself belonged. The Tablighi Jamaat, which formally eschews involvement with politics, is one of the fastest growing Islamic movements worldwide, with branches in more than ninety countries.

In Egypt the most influential reformer was Muhammad Abduh (1849–1905). Originally a disciple of the anti-British pan-Islamic activist, Jamal al-Din al-Afghani (1839–1970), Abduh accompanied Afghani to exile in Paris after the British occupation where they coedited a short-lived but influential Arabic pan-Islamist journal *Al-urwa al-wuthqa* "The Strongest Link." In 1885 Abduh

A locomotive drags its crowded carriages up the narrow-gauge Darjeeling Railway, c 1900. The Deobandi reformist movement took advantage of the railroad network to disseminate Islamic literature throughout the country, adding to the sense of Muslims as a distinct community in India.

broke with his mentor's hostility to imperialism and returning to Egypt via Syria, decided like Ahmad Khan to work with the grain of British power, seeing in it a necessary force for modernization. After rising in the legal service to become chief mufti or law officer of Egypt Abduh sought to modernize the Sharia and to introduce subjects such as modern history and geography into the curriculum of al-Azhar in Cairo, the foremost academy of Sunni Islam. He paid particular attention to the principle of maslaha (public interest) to enable the law to be changed in accordance with modern requirements, stating, "If a ruling has become the cause of harm which it did not cause before, then we must change it according to the prevailing conditions." Abduh believed that, properly understood, revelation must be in harmony with reason, because Islam was "natural religion" designed by God to fit the human condition. Like Ahmed Khan he sought to distinguish between the essentials and nonessentials of revelation, preserving the fundamentals while discarding those aspects that were historically contingent or time-specific. He tirelessly opposed what he saw as the hidebound conservatism of the traditional ulama and like Ahmad Khan emphasized the need for new applications of the principle of ijtihad (individual judgement) to meet modern conditions. Abduh's views were disseminated through his legal rulings, writings, and lectures and after his death through the periodical *al-Manar* ("the Lighthouse"), published by his Syrian disciple Rashid Rida, a member of the reformist Naqshbandi order, which ran from 1897–1935. As a mujaddid (reformer or renovator) of modern Islam his influence can hardly be underestimated. In Southeast Asia the Java-based missionary Muhammadiyah movement founded in 1912 by Ahmad Dahlan, which now has several million male and female adherents, owes much to Abduh's ideas. In the Arab world Dahlan is regarded, with Afghani, as the founder of the Salafiyya movement, inspired by the example of the "pious forebears," classically thought of as the first three generations of Muslims who received the message of Islam in its original context. Modern Salafists who can claim a part of Abduh's intellectual legacy range from militant activists who seek to establish modern Islamic states, if necessary by violent means, to secular nationalists who interpret Abduh's ideas as requiring a complete separation between political and religious realms.

Modernization of Turkey

The modernization of Turkey extends back at least two centuries when the Ottoman Sultan Selim III (1789–1807) attempted to introduce a series of educational and military reforms. His efforts threatened the interests of the ulama and Janissaries and he was deposed. But after a string of defeats in the Caucasus and Greece his successor, Mahmud II (r. 1807–39), made new efforts at reform by introducing new western-oriented schools, destroying the Janissary corps and dissolving the Bektashi Sufi order linked to it. The autonomy of the ulama was weakened by the state takeover of waqf (religious endowments), Sharia courts, and schools. A symbolic separation of religion and state was effected by a decree abolishing the wearing of turbans. For everyone except the official ulama turbans, often the mark of allegiance to one of the Sufi tariqas were replaced by the fez, the red-felt cylindrical hat, imported from the Maghrib. Mahmud's ambition to create a centralized, absolutist state (along the lines of prerevolution France or Prussia) was carried on by his successors in a series of programs known as the Tanzimat-i Hairiye (Auspicious Reorderings) that lasted from 1839–76. Modern postal systems, telegraph, steamship navigation, and railroads were introduced alongside radical legal reforms with western-style courts and law codes. A new civil code, the Mejelle, followed the Sharia law in content, but differed from tradition by being administered by state courts.

In 1855 the jizya (poll tax)—a formal mark of religious inferiority—was replaced by a tax on exemption from military service. The new centralized government that was coming into being was founded on a social base of new professionally-trained bureaucrats. The small urban middle class enjoyed a rising economic status that enabled it to challenge the religion-based power-structure of the religious communities. The Tanzimat reforms altered the previous basis of Ottoman society by abolishing the autonomy of Islamic educational and judicial institutions, bringing them under state control.

British troops at Gallipoli, together with other Western Allies, were deployed on the peninsula from 25 April 1915 until 9 January 1916. Their objective was to threaten Constantinople and to open a supply route to Russia across the Black Sea. The Turkish forces were commanded by Lieutenent Colonel Mustafa Kemal, whose drive and energy thwarted the Allied plan. His success would lead him to the office of National President.

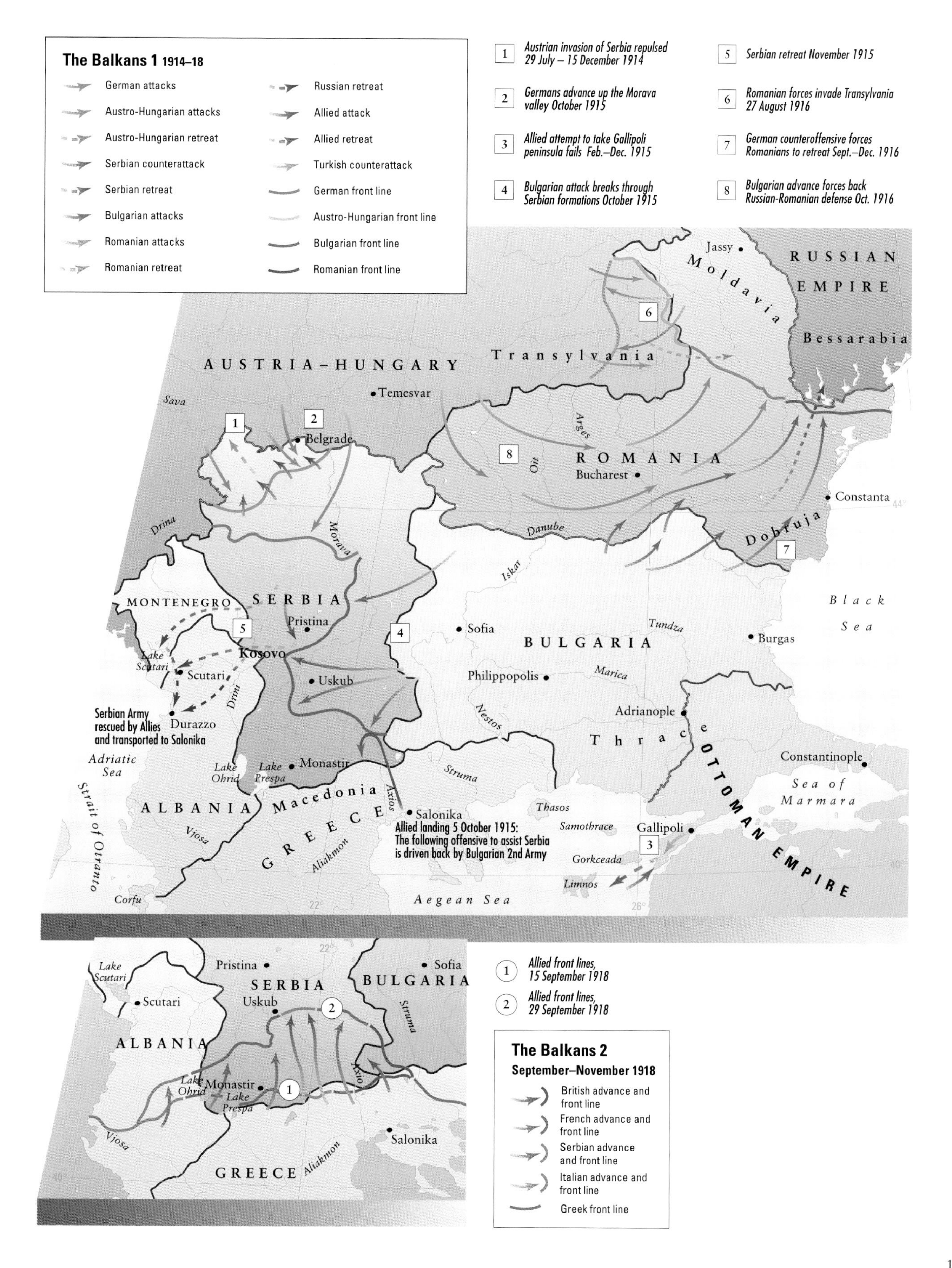

The Balkans 1 1914–18
German attacks
Austro-Hungarian attacks
Austro-Hungarian retreat
Serbian counterattack
Serbian retreat
Bulgarian attacks
Romanian attacks
Romanian retreat
Russian retreat
Allied attack
Allied retreat
Turkish counterattack
German front line
Austro-Hungarian front line
Bulgarian front line
Romanian front line
1 Austrian invasion of Serbia repulsed 29 July – 15 December 1914
2 Germans advance up the Morava valley October 1915
3 Allied attempt to take Gallipoli peninsula fails Feb.–Dec. 1915
4 Bulgarian attack breaks through Serbian formations October 1915
5 Serbian retreat November 1915
6 Romanian forces invade Transylvania 27 August 1916
7 German counteroffensive forces Romanians to retreat Sept.–Dec. 1916
8 Bulgarian advance forces back Russian-Romanian defense Oct. 1916
RUSSIAN EMPIRE
Jassy
Moldavia
Bessarabia
Transylvania
AUSTRIA-HUNGARY
Temesvar
Sava
Belgrade
Arges
Olt
ROMANIA
Bucharest
Constanta
Drina
Danube
Morava
Dobruja
Iskar
Black Sea
MONTENEGRO
SERBIA
Pristina
Sofia
Tundza
BULGARIA
Burgas
Lake Scutari
Kosovo
Scutari
Uskub
Philippopolis
Marica
Drini
Serbian Army rescued by Allies and transported to Salonika
Durazzo
Nestos
Adrianople
Thrace
Adriatic Sea
Lake Ohrid
Lake Prespa
Monastir
Struma
Constantinople
Sea of Marmara
Strait of Otranto
ALBANIA
Macedonia
Axios
OTTOMAN EMPIRE
Thasos
Salonika
Vjosa
GREECE
Allied landing 5 October 1915: The following offensive to assist Serbia is driven back by Bulgarian 2nd Army
Samothrace
Gallipoli
Aliakmon
Gorkceada
Limnos
Corfu
Aegean Sea
Lake Scutari
Pristina
Sofia
SERBIA
BULGARIA
Scutari
Uskub
Struma
ALBANIA
Axios
Lake Ohrid
Monastir
Lake Prespa
Vjosa
Salonika
GREECE
Aliakmon
1 Allied front lines, 15 September 1918
2 Allied front lines, 29 September 1918
The Balkans 2
September–November 1918
British advance and front line
French advance and front line
Serbian advance and front line
Italian advance and front line
Greek front line

The reforms stimulated the emergence of the "Young Turks," a movement among the intelligentsia who wished to move in a European direction. In 1908 the vanguard of this movement the Committee for Union and Progress (CUP), which had infiltrated the army, came to power in a military coup. The sultan was forced to restore the constitution he had suspended in 1876 and there was a front of parliamentary government. The real power remained with the army and the CUP, which embarked on a radical program of secularization, reducing the powers of the shaikh al-Islam (the chief religious functionary), imposing government control over Sharia courts and Muslim colleges. Though nationalist in outlook the Young Turks aimed to keep control of the eastern part of the Empire. With help from Germany whose military advisers were driving reforms in the army, the Berlin–Baghdad railroad was constructed. The first decade of the twentieth century also saw the construction of the famous Hijaz railroads from Damascus to Medina (the link to Mecca was never completed). While facilitating the passage of pilgrims to the holy places of Islam, the railroad was also designed to speed the passage of troops into the Peninsula to control tribal revolts in Syria and Arabia. The Ottomans continued to lose territory during the second decade of the twentieth century with the loss of Libya, Albania, and most of its European possessions in the Balkan wars. The *coup de grace* came with the First World War (1914–18). Having joined the Central Powers (Austria and Germany) against Britain, France, and Russia, the Empire lost its remaining Arab provinces to the three-pronged attack launched by Britain in Iraq and Palestine, and by the Arab tribes led by the Sharif of Mecca's son Faisal with the help of the British adventurer T. E. Lawrence.

Mustafa Kemal Atatürk, 1881–1938, founder of the Turkish secular state.

Despite the loss of its Arab provinces Turkey itself retained its independence as a Muslim country after the First World War, thanks to the efforts of Mustafa Kemal (later to be called Atatürk, "Father of the Turks"). A Young Turk general , he had saved Istanbul by defending the Gallipoli Peninsula from invasion by the British imperial forces in 1915. After forming a provisional nationalist government Atatürk mobilized the Turkish people against the partition of the Anatolian heartland, and losses to French-controlled Syria and to Greece, as well as to Kurds and Armenians (whose proposed state in the northeast was effectively partitioned between Turkey and the newly emergent Soviet Republic). Having defeated the Greeks (who had been awarded the mainly Greek area around Smyrna (Izmir) under the humiliating terms of the 1920 Treaty of Sèvres) Kemal won international recognition for complete and undivided Turkish sovereignty in Anatolia,

Adrianople (Edirne), and eastern Thrace (European Turkey) at the Treaty of Lausanne in 1923. Atatürk resolved his problems with Greece by the brutal but effective means of an exchange of populations.

Having established his authority as the victor or ghazi-warrior over Turkey's enemies, Atatürk embarked on a radical program of modernization. In 1923 the sultanate was separated from the caliphate, and the former abolished. The following year the caliphate was abolished, along with the Sharia courts. Islamic law was replaced by adapting the Swiss civil code to Turkish needs. The Latin alphabet was introduced for the Turkish language (which had previously been written in Arabic script), with a view to separating Turkey from the Islamic past and making literacy more accessible. The Sufi orders were banned and driven underground. The fez, which had ironically acquired the status of an "Islamic" item of headgear, was abolished, to be replaced by the peaked cloth cap worn by European workers at that time.

The Muslim World under Colonial Domination c. 1920

The defeat of the Ottoman Empire in the First World War brought the vast majority of Muslim societies under direct or indirect colonial rule. By 1920 the only independent Muslim states were Turkey (revitalized under Kemal Atatürk), Persia, where the Qajar dynasty would shortly be replaced by the Pahlavis (1923), Afghanistan under the modernizing regime of King Amanullah (1919–29), northern Yemen, where the Zaidi Imam Yahya won control after the Ottoman defeat, Central Arabia (Najd), and the Hijaz, the Muslim holy land containing the cities of Mecca and Medina, still under control of the Hashemite family. The remainder of Dar al-Islam was either under direct colonial rule or under some form of internationally recognized European "protection." Two new principles were being established that would bring these former colonies or semi-colonies into the international system: the fixing of boundaries (usually for the convenience of European states) and in the case of shaikhdoms bound by treaty to Britain, the "freezing" of dynasties to ensure continuity of government (though not necessarily through the European system of primogeniture). Legitimacy of succession would prevent the disruptive disputes that often followed the death of a traditional ruler and bind his heirs into the existing treaty arrangements.

By 1920 France controlled the whole of northwestern Africa except for the coastal strips of Spanish Sahara and Spanish Morocco. Italy was extending its rule far beyond the coastal provinces of Tripoli and Cyrenaica (though this task would not be completed until 1934). Britain, which since 1882, had occupied Egypt, the cultural center of the Muslim world, permitted the former Ottoman province a nominal independence under a constitutional monarchy, but retained overall strategic control. This led to the paradox of a formally neutral country becoming host to thousands of British and Empire troops during the Second World War. Following Kitchener's destruction of the Islamic state, created by the Mahdi Muhammad Ahmad in 1898, Britain took control of the Anglo-Egyptian Sudan, whose realm now extended deep into Equatorial Africa. Having taken Tanganyika from Germany, Britain controlled most of the Swahili coast except for the portion that formed part of Italian Somaliland. From Aden Britain contested the Bab al-Mandeb—the strategic entrance to the Red Sea—with Italy, which ruled in Eritrea, while retaining its grip on the Arabian littoral from Aden to Basra, having locked the shaikhdoms south of Arabia and the Gulf into exclusive treaties that guaranteed British control of defense and foreign policy.

In the Indian subcontinent, the British had locked some 560 princely rulers—some of them

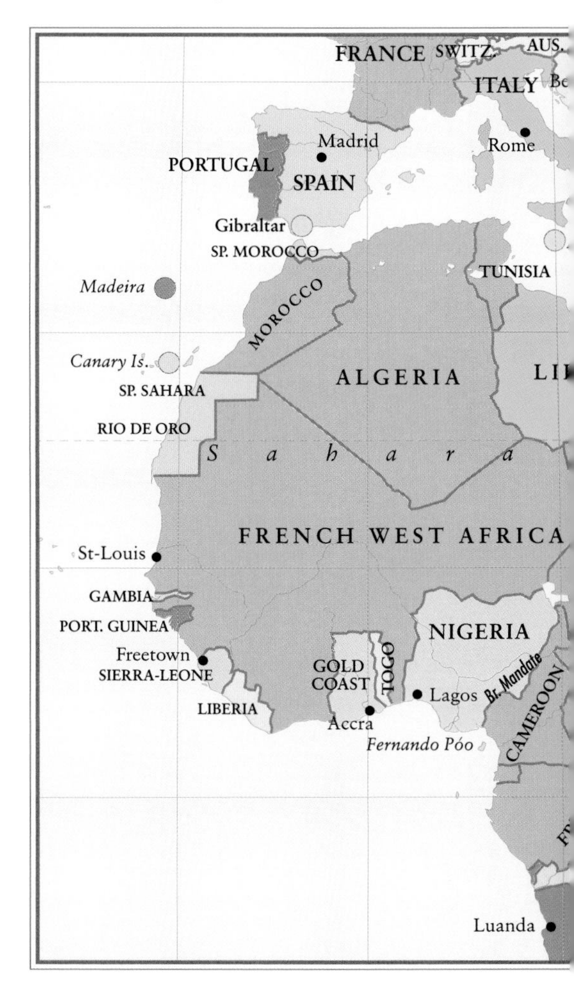

Muslims—into a mosaic of different treaties and agreements placing them and their Muslim subjects under the umbrella of British rule. In Southeast Asia Britain controlled the Malay states while the Netherlands had extended its sway beyond its original colonies in Java and Sumatra. In Muslim Central Asia and the Caucasus region, the Communist revolution and subsequent civil war had consolidated the power of Moscow within a new regional order.

In the core region of the Mashriq, Palestine had been opened to Jewish settlement under the terms of the Mandate granted to Britain by the League of Nations. Under the terms of the secret Sykes-Picot agreement reached with France in 1916 Britain also acquired Mandates —a euphemism for colonies—in Transjordan and Iraq, while France took control of Lebanon and Syria. Faisal ibn Hussein, son of the sharif of Mecca who had liberated Damascus from Ottoman Turkey with British help, had intended to make Syria an independent Arab state in accordance with a somewhat ambiguous undertaking his father had received from Sir Henry McMahon, the British High Commissioner in Egypt in 1915. In the aftermath of the war, however, it became clear that for the Muslim world imperial interests would supersede the national right of self-determination famously proclaimed by President Woodrow Wilson as the basis for the postwar settlement in Europe. Protest at the double standard that allowed the recognition of national rights for the subjects of Christian empires in Europe (including Czechs, Slovaks, Hungarians, Jews, and Irish, as well as former Ottoman subjects in the Balkans) while denying them to Muslims animated the anticolonial resentment that would surface throughout former Ottoman territories.

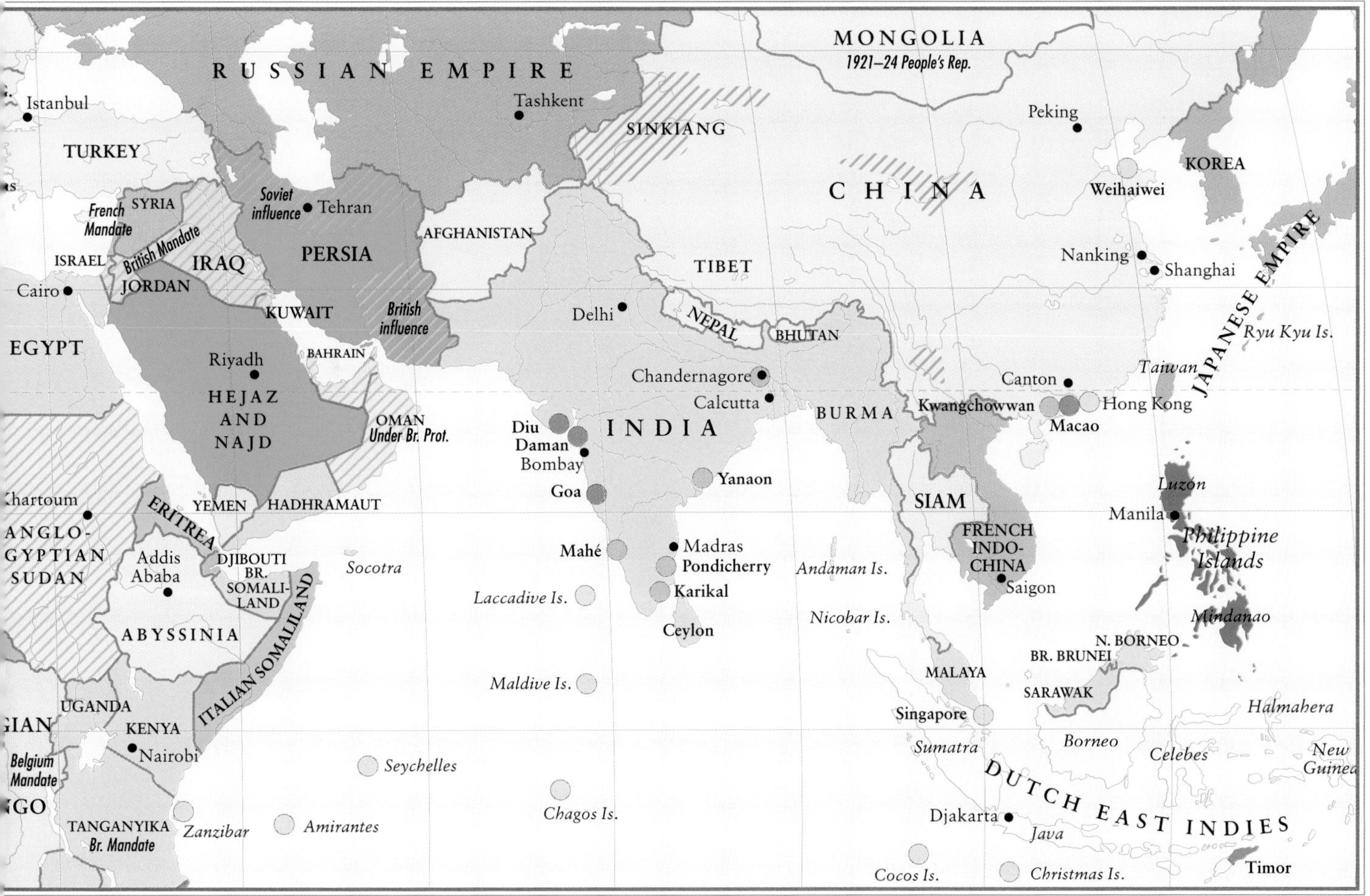

Balkans, Cyprus, and Crete 1500–2000

The Saljuq and subsequent Ottoman conquests in the Balkans left a residue of Muslims in Europe who arrived as settlers or adopted Islam by conversion. Unlike the conquest of Anatolia where the Byzantine ecclesiastical institutions were suppressed as imperial rivals, the Orthodox Church in the Balkans was given effective jurisdiction of the Christian communities. This factor may have limited conversions in the Christian Balkans as compared with Anatolia.

Stari Most bridge, Mostar, Bosnia-Herzegovina. Before its destruction by Bosnian-Croatian artillery fire in 1993, the bridge was one of the finest surviving examples of Ottoman engineering and design. Completed in 1566 by Khairuddin, a pupil of the great Ottoman architect Sinan, it spanned 30 meters with an arch rising to 27 meters above the Neretva River. The rebuilding of the bridge has become a symbol for the restoration of Bosnia's fractured community relationships.

The permanent Islamic presence in Europe was first established by Turkish migrants to northern Greece, Bulgaria, and Albania in the fourteenth and fifteenth centuries with the leading role played the tekkes (hospices) founded by Sufi holy men, which often became the nuclei of village communities. In rural areas conversions were facilitated by Sufi orders such the Mevlevis and Bektashis. They found ways of conveying Islamic ideas to peasants with Christian or "heretical" beliefs, such as those of the Bogomils, an initiatory gnostic sect whose influence spread throughout Catholic southern Europe in the eleventh and twelfth centuries. Conversion was greatest in Albania, Bosnia-Herzegovina, and Bulgaria, especially among the Pomaks of the Rhodopes, whose mountainous lands extend into the modern states of Greece and Macedonia, as well as Crete. Thanks to official Ottoman support for Orthodoxy, however, the fact that Christians remained the overwhelming majority in the Balkans would make them, initially, more susceptible than the empire's Muslim subjects to the forces of nationalism and revolution that swept through western Europe in the nineteenth century. A census conducted between 1520 and 1530 showed that 19 percent of the Balkan population was Muslim, 81 percent was Christian, and there was a small Jewish minority. The largest concentration of Muslims was in Bosnia (about 45 percent). Most of the Muslims lived in cities. For example, Sofia (now capital of Bulgaria) had a Muslim majority of 66.4 percent.

With the turning of the tide of conquest in Catholic Hungary, the rise of Orthodox nationalisms in Greece, Serbia, Romania, and Bulgaria, and the dismemberment of the Ottoman Empire in Europe, Muslims lost their political protection. Many of those who failed to retreat with the Ottoman armies were massacred or forcibly converted to Christianity. Large numbers migrated after the Russo–Turkish war of 1878, the Balkan wars of 1912–14, and after the First World War when there was a formal exchange of populations between Muslim Turks living in Greece (including Crete and the Dodecanese islands) and Greeks on mainland Anatolia. Cyprus, which like Crete had been taken by the Ottomans from the Venetians (1571), became part of the British Empire after the Congress of Berlin in 1878, preventing its Orthodox majority from opting for union with Greece (as Crete did in 1913) and thus excluding it from the exchange of populations in 1920. The island has been divided since 1972 when Turkey intervened militarily to prevent a nationalist military government from uniting the island with Greece.

Albania is still largely Muslim (70 percent) by

culture. After a prolonged antireligious campaign by the communist government, which declared the country to be the world's first officially atheist state, Islamic beliefs and practices are being revived. Substantial Muslim minorities remain in Bulgaria (13 percent), although the Bulgarian Turks (who number around 600,000) have migrated to Turkey in considerable numbers following a sustained campaign of Bulgarianization by communist and post-communist governments (including the elimination of Muslim first and family names).

In Bosnia Muslims constitute about 45 percent of the population. The civil war (1991–95) between the Serbs and the Muslim-Croat coalition led to a series of atrocities including massacres and attempts at "ethnic cleansing," which prompted intervention by NATO air forces and the signing of the 1995 Dayton Accords dividing Bosnia into separate Muslim-Croatian and Serbian states.

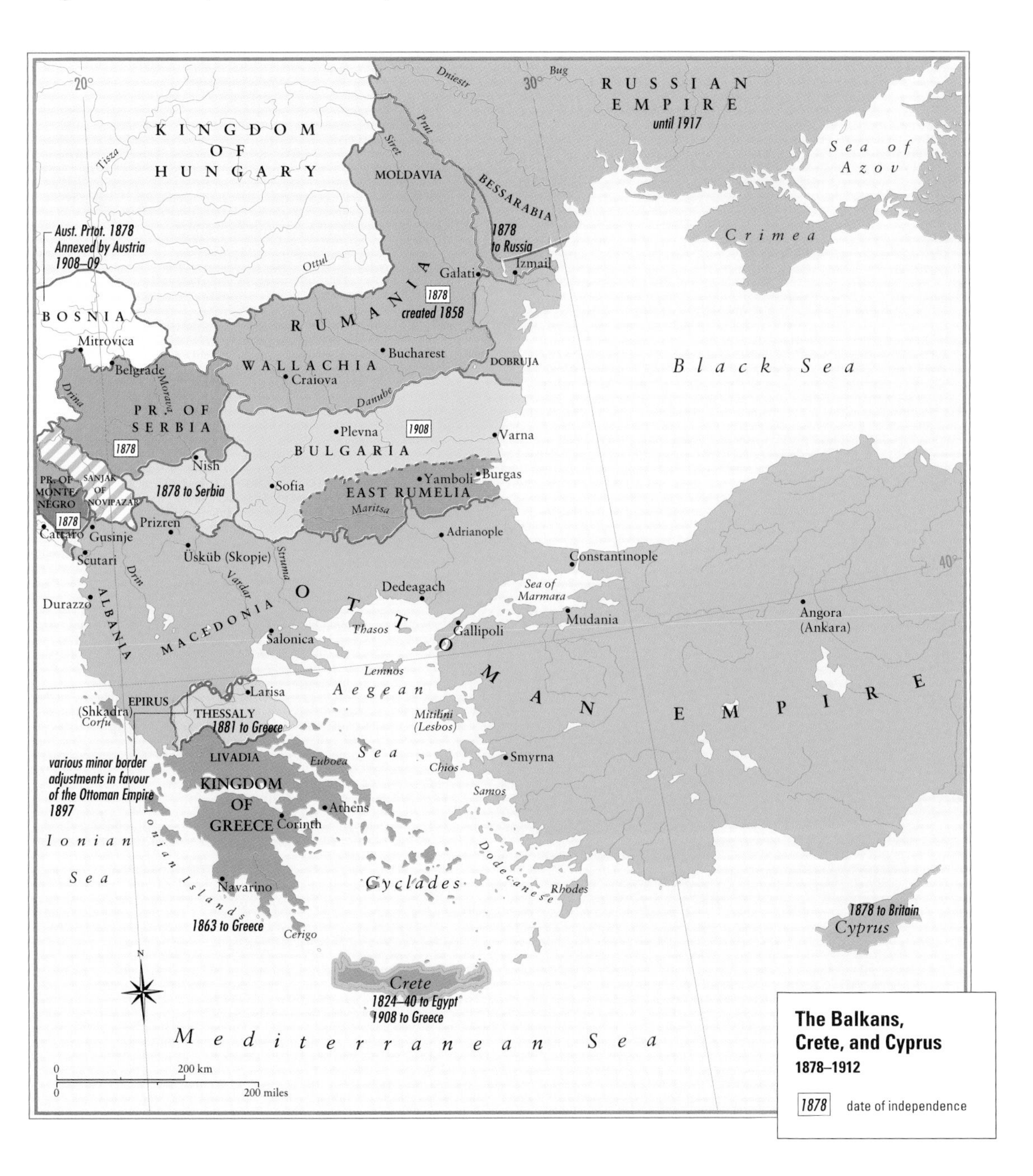

The Balkans, Crete, and Cyprus
1878–1912

1878 date of independence

The Balkans, Crete, and Cyprus
1912–13
Ottoman territory in 1913
1913 date of independence
RUSSIAN EMPIRE
until 1917
KINGDOM OF HUNGARY
MOLDAVIA
BESSARABIA
KINGDOM OF ROMANIA
BOSNIA
KINGDOM OF SERBIA
KINGDOM OF BULGARIA
K. OF MONTENEGRO
1913 to Montenegro
1913 to Romania
1913 to Bulgaria
1913 to Serbia
1913 to Greece
THRACE
1913 to Bulgaria
1915 to Bulgaria
PR. OF ALBANIA
1913
MACEDONIA
EPIRUS
THESSALY
KINGDOM OF GREECE
LIVADIA
PELOPONNESE
OTTOMAN EMPIRE
DOBRUJA
Black Sea
Aegean Sea
Ionian Sea
Mediterranean Sea
Sea of Marmara
Ionian Islands
Cyclades
Dodecanese
1912 Italian occupied
Annexed in 1914
Cyprus
Crete
Dniestr
Bug
Prut
Siret
Tisza
Ottul
Danube
Drina
Morava
Maritsa
Drin
Vardar
Struma
Galati
Izmail
Mitrovica
Belgrade
Bucharest
Craiova
Plevna
Varna
Nish
Sofia
Yamboli
Burgas
Adrianople
Cattaro
Gusinje
Djakova
Kumanovo
Üsküb (Skopje)
Scutari (Shkadra)
Durazzo
Constantinople
Dedeagach
Gallipoli
Mudania
Thasos
Salonica
Lemnos
Janina
Larisa
Corfu
Mitilini (Lesbos)
Smyrna
Chios
Samos
Euboea
Corinth
Athens
Tripolis
Navarino
Rhodes
Cerigo (Kythira)
20°
30°
40°
N
200 km
200 miles

The Balkans, Crete, and Cyprus
1920–23
demilitarized zone 1920–22
HUNGARY
U. S. S. R
ROMANIA
TRANSYLVANIA
MOLDAVIA
BESSARABIA
1918–20 to Romania
DOBRUJA
VOJVODINA
SLAVONIA
YUGOSLAVIA
SERBIA
BOSNIA
MONTENEGRO
ALBANIA
BULGARIA
THRACE
MACEDONIA
EPIRUS
THESSALY
GREECE
PELOPONNESE
TURKEY
Adrianople (1923 Edirne)
1920–22 to Greece
Constantinople (1923 Istanbul)
1920–22 to Greece
Dodecanese Italian
Black Sea
Sea of Marmara
Aegean Sea
Ionian Sea
Ionian Islands
Mediterranean Sea
Cyclades
Crete
Cyprus
Rhodes
Kythira
Thasos
Lemnos
Mitilini
Chios
Samos
Euboea
Corfu
Dniestr
Bug
Prut
Siret
Tisza
Ottul
Danube
Morava
Drina
Drin
Vardar
Struma
Maritsa
Izmail
Galati
Ploesti
Bucharest
Craiova
Mitrovica
Belgrade
Nish
Plevna
Varna
Sofia
Yamboli
Burgas
Cattaro
Gusinje
Djakova
Kumanovo
Üsküb (Skopje)
Scutari (Shkadra)
Durazzo
Dedeagach
Gallipoli
Mudania
Ankara
Salonica
Janina
Larisa
Smyrna
Corinth
Athens
Tripolis
Navarino
20°
30°
40°
N
0 200 km
0 200 miles

Muslim Minorities in China

This Chinese minaret symbolizes the adaptability of Muslim architecture to local vernacular forms. Unlike the traditional cathedral or church, there is no religiously-prescribed architectural form for the mosque other than the mihrab (a decorated niche) indicating the direction of prayer.

The Muslim communities of China are descended from Arab, Persian Central Asian, and Mongol traders who married Chinese women and mostly lived in small communities clustered around a central mosque. Their descendents, along with those of other incomers who arrived from Mongolia and Central Asia over the course of centuries, are known as the Hui. The Hui number roughly half of China's twenty million Muslims. Unlike other groups who tend to be concentrated in areas bordering on the Central Asian republics, they are spread throughout the country, though there is a particular concentration in the Ningxia Hui Autonomous region. The Hui are recognized by the state as a national minority—the third largest in China—and the only minority to be defined by religious affiliation. The other recognized Muslim minorities include the Uighurs of the Xinjiang region, and the Kazakhs, Kyrgyz, Uzbeks, Tatars, and Tajiks whose homelands are located in the territories of the former Soviet Union.

Though they developed a distinctive way of living as a Muslim minority outside the borders of Dar al-Islam the Hui were far from being isolated from the spiritual currents flowing from the Islamic heartlands. Sufism made substantial inroads from the seventeenth century with shaikhs from the Naqshbandiyya, Qadariyya, and Kubrawiyya orders establishing networks of tariqas and brotherhoods throughout mainland China. During periods of turbulence from the seventeenth to nineteenth centuries the orders helped organize a series of Muslim-led rebellions in Yunnan, Shaanxi, Gansu, and Xinjiang. Much of this unrest was the result of intra-Muslim violence caused by the impact on local Hui communities of reformist ideas imported from Arabia. For example, in 1781 a Naqshbandi shaikh, Ma Mingxin (b. 1719), who had studied in Arabia and Yemen for sixteen years, was executed after leading a movement, known as the New

Teaching or New Sect, which attacked the cult of saint-worship. In the 1860s and 70s another Naqshbandi shaikh, Ma Hualong, launched a major rebellion, which cut off the Qing (Manchu) Empire from the northwest, opening the way for rebellion of the Uighurs in Xinjiang. In more recent times a Wahhabi-inspired reformist movement at the turn of the twentieth century known as the Yihewani (from Arabic *ikhwan,* meaning brotherhood) was active in opposing practices deemed idolatrous. Such practices included the veneration of Sufi saints or the wearing of Chinese mourning dress. Under communist rule the Yihewani received more state patronage than the more traditionalist Hanafis known as Gedimu (from the Arabic *qadim,* meaning old). Though all Muslim groups were persecuted during Mao Zedong's Cultural Revolution (1966–76) with at least one major massacre of Hui in the wake of an uprising in Yunnan, state patronage of the Yihewanis has persisted under the more relaxed climate that followed the accession of Deng Xiaoping.

After the incorporation of Hong Kong into the People's Republic of China, the small Muslim community on the island has also built relations with other groups on the mainland.

The Levant 1500–2002

Unlike Egypt, which the Ottomans and their clients ruled as a single substate or province, the Levant, comprising Syria, Mount Lebanon, and Palestine, remained a patchwork of communities bound by a variety of tribal, ethnic, and religious affiliations under local leaders. The latter were formally subjects of the Ottoman sultans until the twentieth century when France and Britain divided the region into client states with precarious national identities. The Levant remained subject to occidental cultural influences long after the Crusades, with the Maronite Church based in the

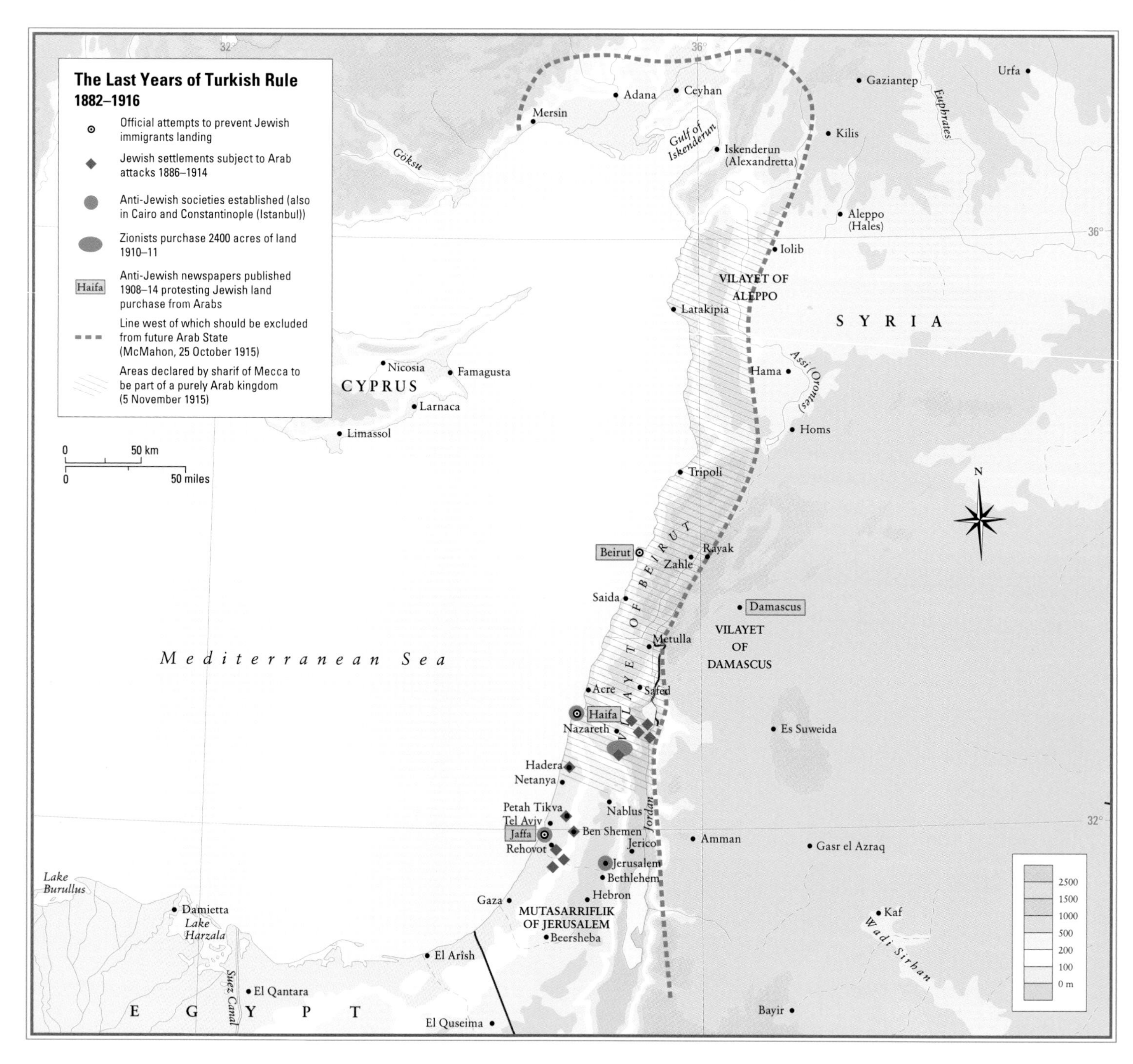

northern Lebanese highlands adopting Latin rites and acknowledging Papal supremacy. The southern highlands overlooking the plains of Galilee was homeland to the Druze people, a schismatic Shiite sect regarded as heretical by other Muslims. Under the Maan family (1544–1697) and the Shihabs (1697–1840), who replaced them, the division of power between Maronites and Druzes was relatively even, with Ottoman governors balancing the interests of both groups. However, the decline in Ottoman power from the eighteenth century saw increasing tension and sectarian rivalry between Maronites and Druzes, abetted by competition between France and Britain. This led to a succession of massacres and bitter sectarian wars between 1838 and 1860.

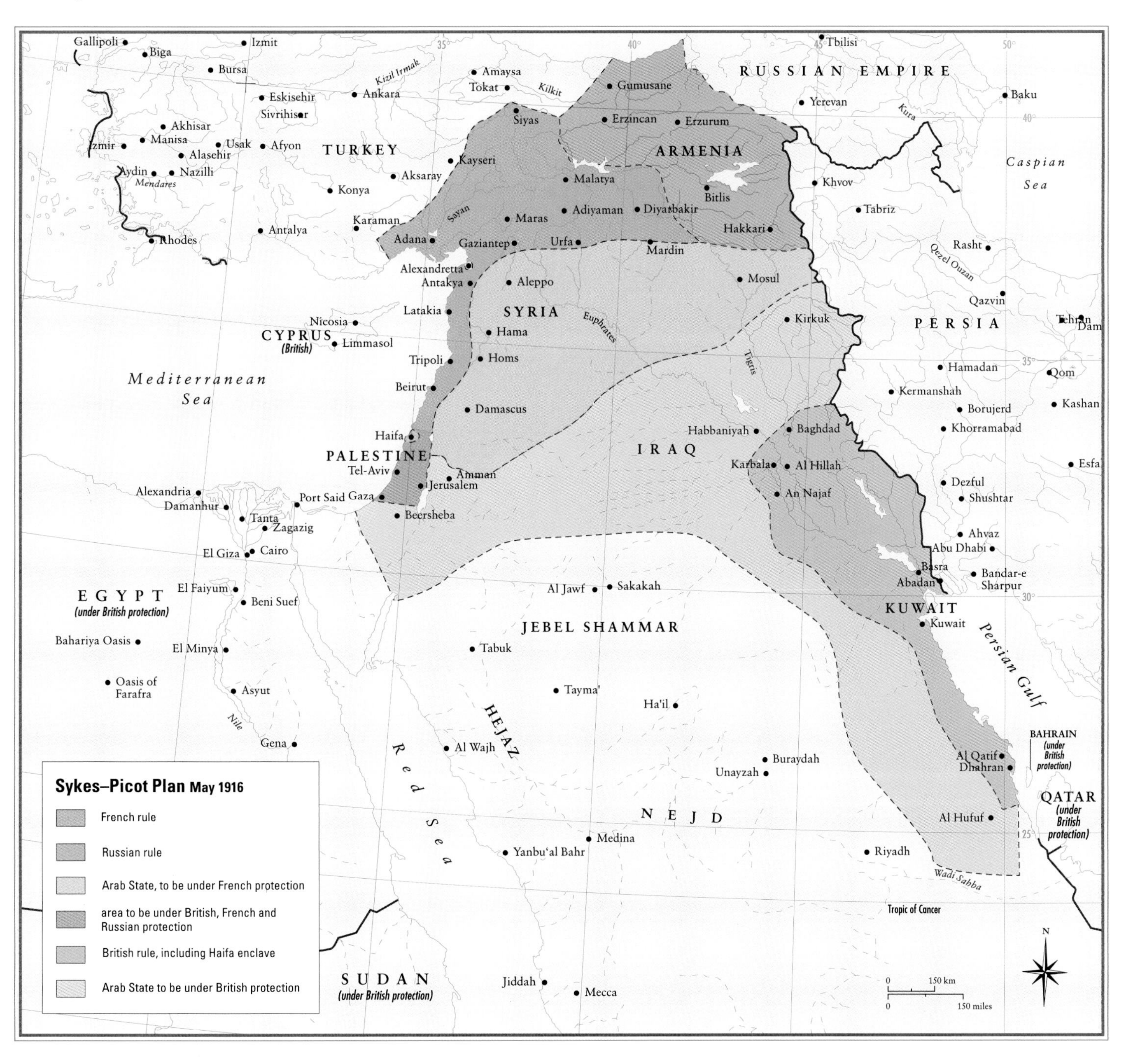

The Ottoman defeat in 1918 saw the division of the Levant between French and British spheres of influence, with the victorious allies creating four colonial dependencies—Iraq, Syria, Lebanon, and Palestine—out of the former Ottoman provinces. After ousting Faisal, son of the ruler of Mecca and leader of the Arab revolt against the Turks who had set up a provisional government in Damascus, the French imposed direct rule on Syria and Lebanon while Britain opened up Palestine for European Jewish settlement and established client monarchies in Transjordan and Iraq. While creating a modern bureaucracy in Syria along with an infrastructure of roads and communications networks, the French undermined national integration by creating administrative districts that reinforced ethnic and religious divisions. In particular they favored

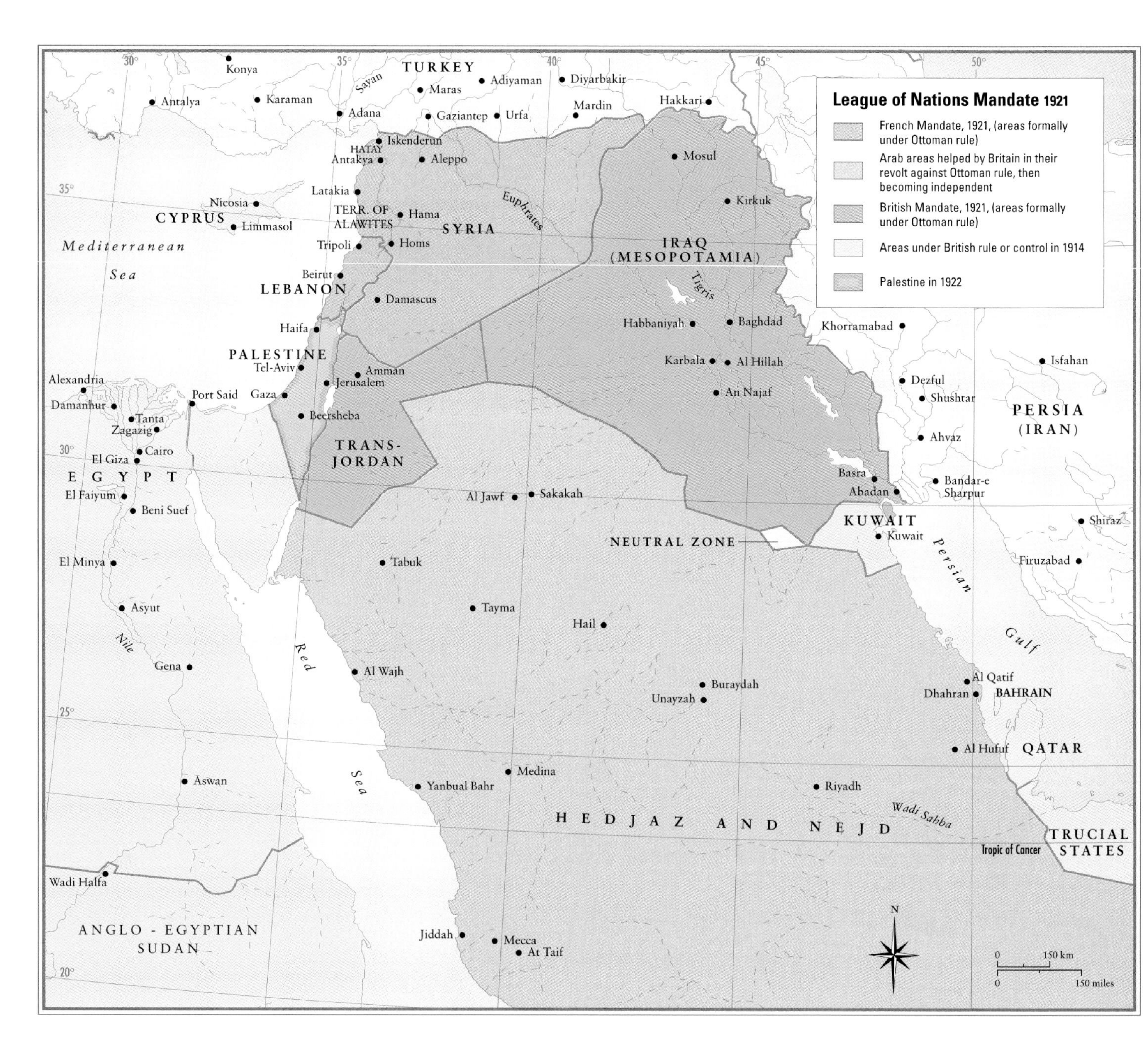

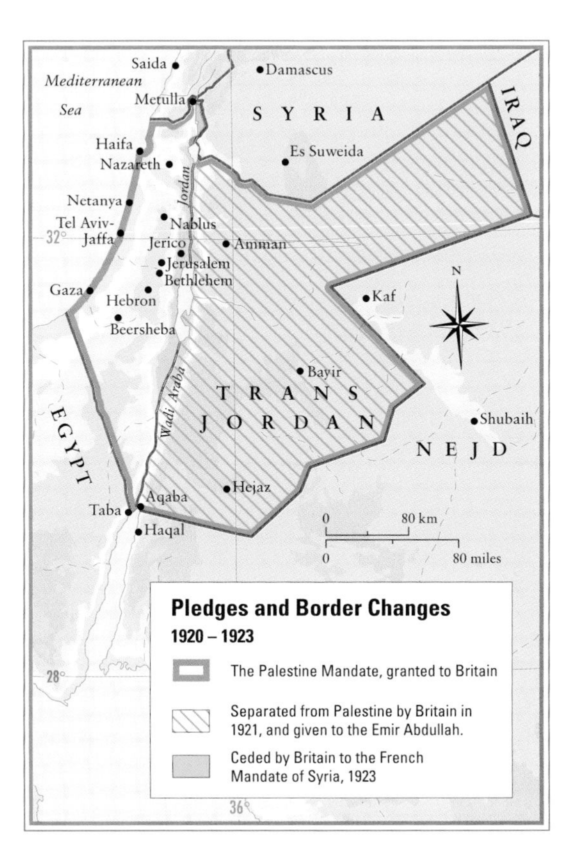

the military recruitment of the Alawi (Shiite) sectarians from the highlands above Latakia. After independence the Alawis were able to take control of the nationalist Baath (Renaissance) Party, establishing a sectarian dictatorship that combined socialist ideologies imported from Eastern Europe with the time-honored Arab system of asabiyya (group solidarity).

The French enlarged Lebanon by adding the districts of Tripoli, Sidon, the Biqaa valley, and South Lebanon to the smaller Ottoman province, substantially increasing the proportion of Muslims from the Sunni and Shiite communities. Building on Ottoman precedents they instituted a constitution by which power was divided between the main religious groups with Maronites retaining supreme power through the offices of president and commander-in-chief of the army, regardless of demographic changes. The division of power along sectarian lines was reaffirmed in the 1943 National Pact, which established the basis for rule after independence. The system ensured a modicum of social peace but militated against national integration. When Palestinians used Lebanese territory to launch attacks against Israel in the 1970s the Israeli reprisals reopened sectarian divisions leading to widespread civil war (1975–82) and the fragmentation of Lebanon into zones controlled by rival Christian, Shiite, Sunni, and Druze militias. The chaos was compounded by the 1982 Israeli invasion aimed at expelling the Palestinians and installing a Maronite regime allied to Israel. While the former objective was achieved with the expulsion of the Palestine Liberation Organization (PLO) from its Lebanese bases, the principal outcome of the invasion was the establishment of a de-facto Syrian hegemony and the emergence of the Shiite Hezbollah, backed by Syria and Iran—a more effective enemy to Israel than the Palestinians. The Israeli occupation of South Lebanon proved costly and ineffectual, provoking the government into making a unilateral withdrawal in 2002.

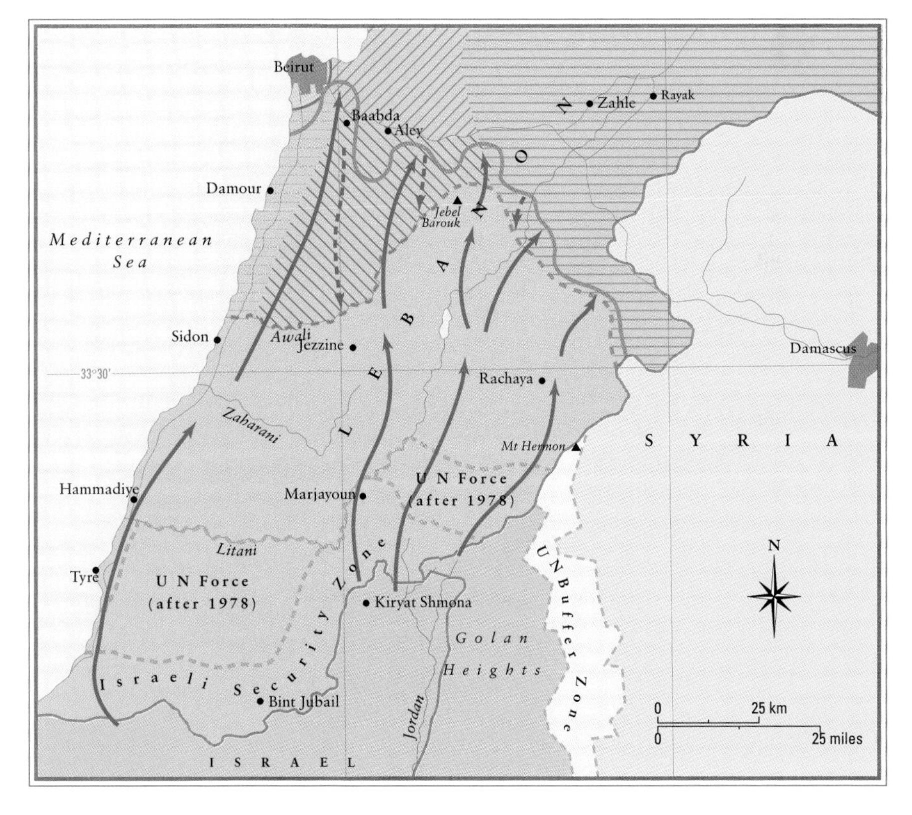

Prominent Travelers

Ibn Battuta spent more than a year in the Maldive Islands, where, with some reluctance, he accepted the post of qadi (judge). He regarded the people as "upright and pious" but disapproved of the way women were bare from the waist upwards.

The pilgrimage to Mecca gave rise to a rich genre of travel writing. Pilgrims kept journals of their travels or dictated their accounts to scribes, providing fascinating details about everything from food to architecture.

One of the most interesting accounts is the Safarnama (travelogue) of the Persian philosopher-poet Nasir Khusraw (1004–c. 1072) who journeyed to Cairo by way of Nishapur, Rayy, Lake Van, Aleppo, and Jerusalem. From Cairo he made two pilgrimages to Mecca before returning to Central Asia as the chief Ismaili dai (missionary) for the Fatimid Imam-caliph al-Mustansir (r. 1036–94). Attacked for his preaching by a Sunni crowd in the city of Balkh, (probably at the instigation of Saljuq officials) he took refuge in Badakhshan in the western Pamirs, where he spent the rest of his life under the protection of an Ismaili prince. The Ismailis of the Pamirs (located in eastern Afghanistan and the autonomous region of Gorno-Badakhshan in the former Soviet republic of Tajikistan) revere him as their founding saint. In local legend, he not only converted the people to the Ismaili faith, but named all their villages, canonizing the topography of places far removed from each other (in the same way that Ireland's patron saint is associated with regions as far apart as Mayo, Tipperary, Antrim, and Armagh). While his poems reflect the loneliness of exile, the rationalist temper of his philosophical writings made him acceptable to the communists who took over the region in 1920 and he retains his status as a national hero in Tajikistan.

The Cairo Nasir described in his book is a model for wise and just administration. The artisans are decently paid, leading to an improved quality of their products. The soldiers are paid regularly, making them less likely to molest the peasants. The judges get good salaries, ensuring fairness and sparing citizens from corruption and injustice. If a merchant is caught cheating a customer, according to Nasir, "he is mounted on a camel with a bell in his hand and paraded about the city, ringing the bell and crying out: 'I have committed a misdemeanor and am suffering reproach. Whoever tells a lie is rewarded with public disgrace.'"

The Arabic version of the pilgrimage-travelogue is known as a rihla. The genre was devised by the Andalusian Ibn Jubair (1145– 1217), who wrote a famous account of the two-year journey he made from Granada, starting in February 1183, to Mecca. Here he spent nine months before returning from the Muslim Holy Land by way of Iraq and Acre, where he boarded a Genoese ship bound for Sicily. After surviving a dramatic shipwreck in the Straits of Messina, he reembarked at Trapani, arriving safely at Granada in April 1185. Ibn Jubair's narrative provides an abundance of information about the countries and cities through which he passes, and is an invaluable source of information about the Crusades, the state of navigation in the Mediterranean, and the political and social conditions of the times. It served as a model for many other narratives, most importantly the rihla of the greatest of all Muslim travelers, the Moroccan Ibn Battuta (1304–c. 1370) whose journeys took him from his native Tangier to China and subsaharan Africa. Ibn Battuta made at least six pilgrimages to Mecca in the course of his travels and the earlier parts of his narrative conforms to the rihla genre. However as his journeys became more extended his book grew more comprehensive. They evolved into an unrivaled description of the known world. As with

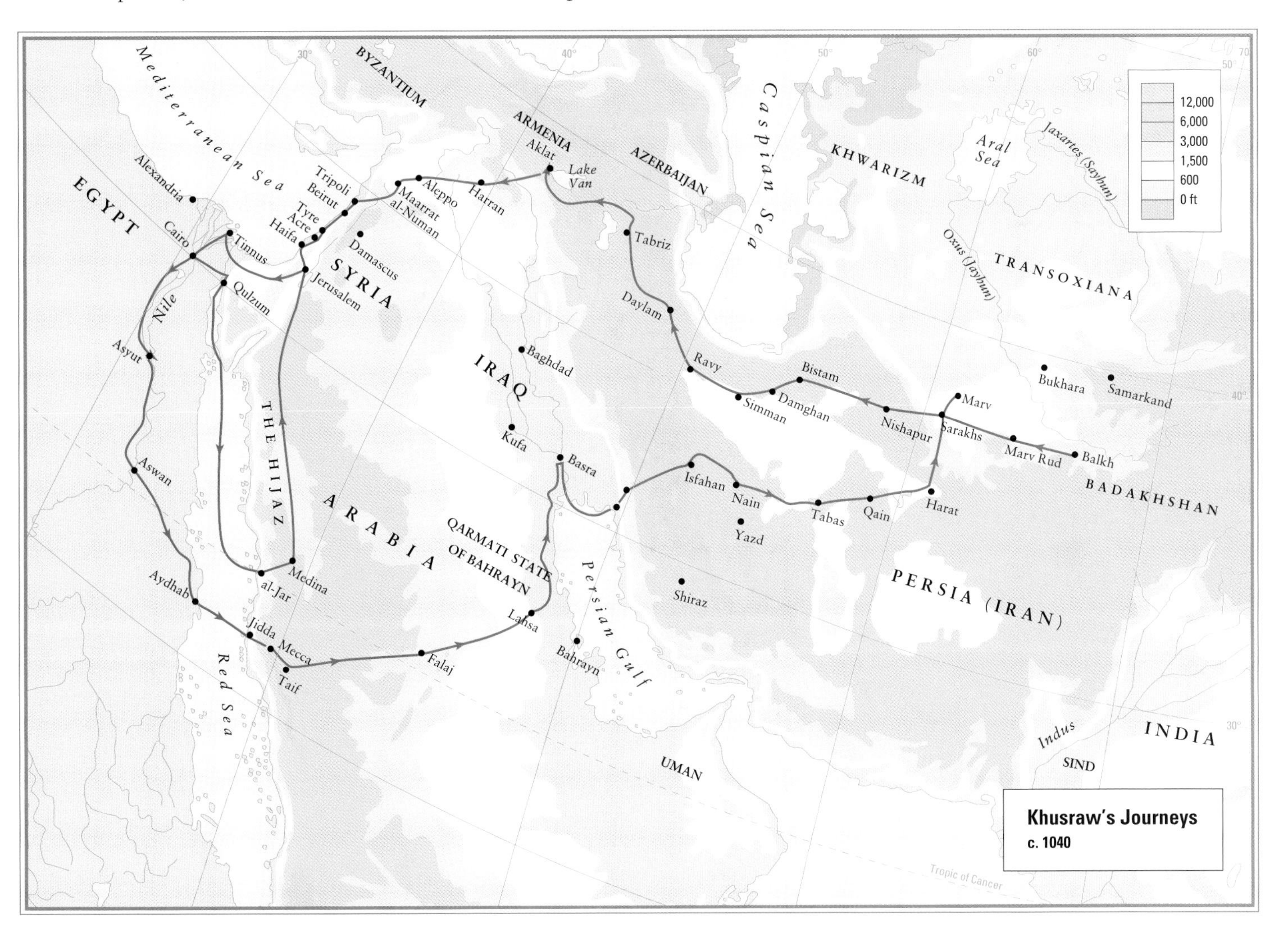

Marco Polo's equally famous travelogue, Ibn Battuta did not write his book himself but dictated it to a collaborator—in his case the Granadan scholar Ibn Juzay (1321–c. 1356). He wrote down Ibn Battuta's narrative at the behest of the ruler of Fez, Abu Inan (r. 1349–58). By the time the book was written the rihla genre had already become well established among educated people and questions arise (as with most other travelogues) as to the reliability of some of Ibn Battuta's descriptions. A modern scholar suggests that Ibn Juzay may have "systematically exaggerated in the direction of fantasy tendencies which in the original work were certainly more moderate" and rearranged some of Ibn Battuta's itineraries for stylistic reasons. Scholarly quibbles, however, cannot detract from Ibn Battuta's reputation as one of the greatest travelers of all time. The wealth of information he passed down to posterity about the world of his era is unparalleled. Like all great travelers, his observations tell us as much about his own social world as the countries in which he traveled. He had a sharp eye for detail. His curiosity takes his readers behind life's obvious appearances, with every sentence underpinned by a wealth of questioning: "The Chinese infidels eat the flesh of swine and dogs, and sell it in their markets. They are wealthy folk and well-to-do, but they make no display either in their food or in their clothes. You will see one of their principal merchants, a man so rich that his wealth cannot be counted, wearing a coarse

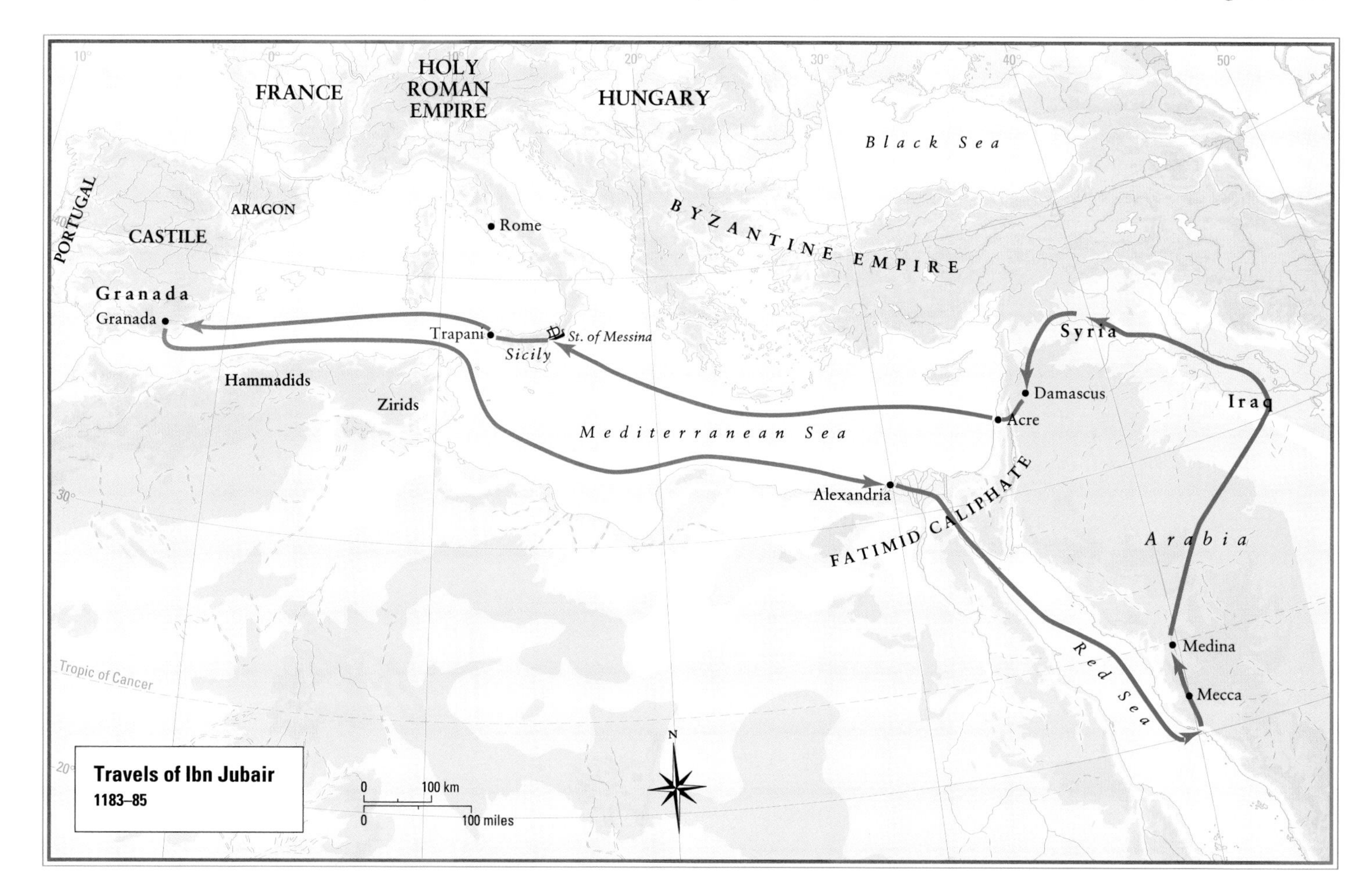

cotton tunic." The contrast with Muslim societies, where textiles were highly valued and the fabrics worn in public an important indicator of wealth and social status, is implicit. In the empire of Mali Ibn Battuta admires the Africans for their devoutness, and especially their zeal for learning the Koran by heart, "They put their children in chains if they show any backwardness in memorizing it, and they are not set free until they have it by heart." He disapproves, however, of their diet and their women's lack of attire: "Women go into the sultan's presence not properly covered, and his daughters also go about naked.... Another reprehensible practice among many of them is the eating of carrion, dogs, and asses."

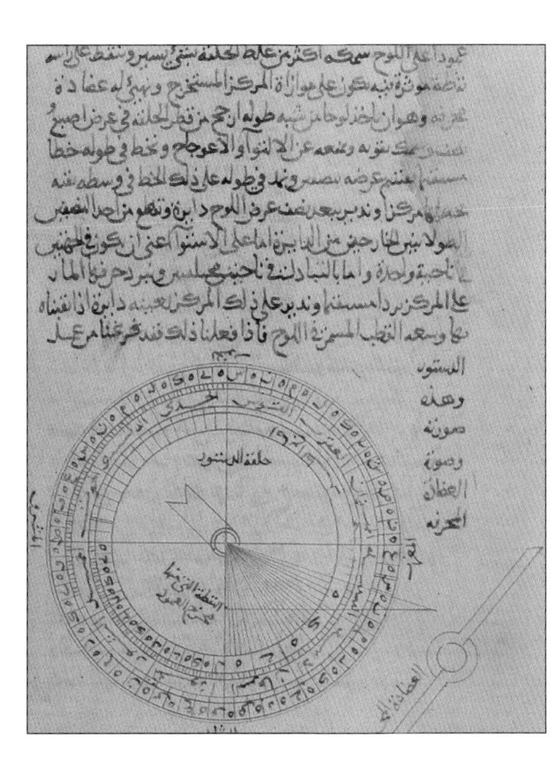

Construction of the astrolabe. This eleventh-century map was designed to establish the direction of Mecca—of great importance to Muslims at prayer.

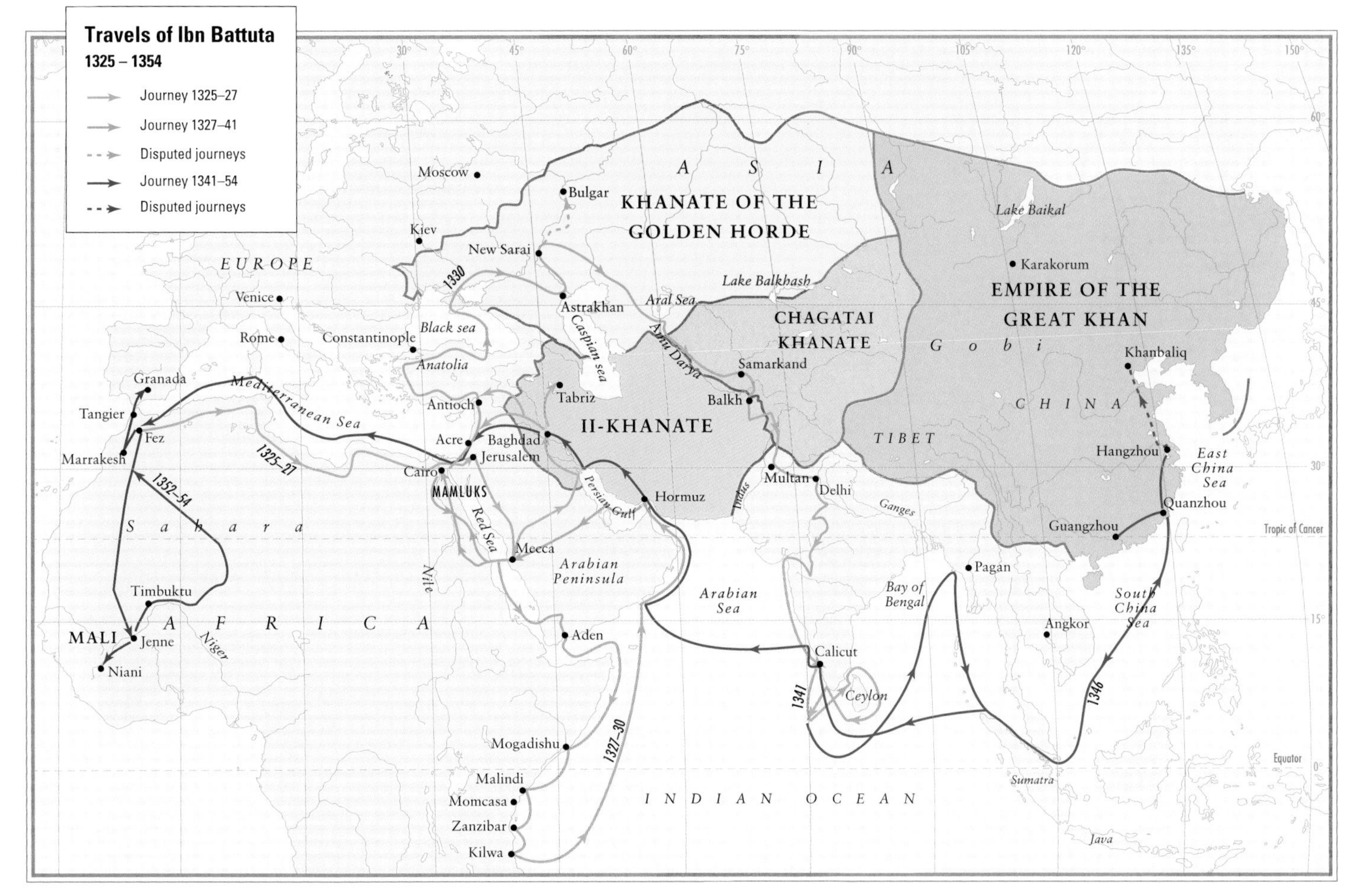

Britain in Egypt and Sudan in the 19th Century

General Charles George "Chinese" Gordon (1833–85) was killed by the forces of the Mahdi on the steps of the governor's house in Khartoum after a siege lasting 5 months. Seen by the British public as a Christian martyr, his death was avenged by Kitchener's re-conquest of Sudan in 1898. This drawing by the Victorian illustrator, Lowes Dickenson, is entitled "Gordon's Last Watch."

British control of Egypt began with the modernizing regime of Muhammad Ali—who was formally the Ottoman governor of Egypt but really an independent ruler—and his descendant Ismail Pasha (r. 1863–79), a passionate Europhile. His ambitious plans for economic development—including railroads and telegraph and the construction of the Suez Canal (opened 1869)—led to national bankruptcy and the imposition of a foreign-managed financial administration. A group of native Egyptian army officers, supported by ulama, landowners, journalists, and the pan-Islamist activist Jamal al-Din al-Afghani (1839–97) were opposed to the debt-management regime and took control of the war ministry, forming a parliamentary government under the "rebel" minister Urabi Pasha. William Gladstone, the British prime minister, bombarded Alexandria and landed troops who defeated Urabi at the Battle of Tel al-Kebir. Under the British resident Sir Evelyn Baring (later Lord Cromer), who held the financial reins of government, the Egyptian economy was managed efficiently—but in the imperial interest. Agricultural productivity improved, barrages were built to control the floodwaters of the Nile, and the railroad system was extended. Increasing quantities of raw cotton was grown for export but the British limited industrialization for fear of encouraging competition.

Egyptian penetration into Sudan began in the 1820s when Muhammad Ali overthrew the Funj sultanate as part of his bid to create an Egyptian empire in Africa. In 1830 Khartoum on the White Nile was founded as a new fortified capital. Using European officers to command local levies and Egyptian troops, Muhammad Ali's successors expanded their territory to the Upper Nile and equatorial provinces. Acting on the principles of administrative reform that were being applied in Egypt and the Ottoman Empire, the Egyptians imposed state trading monopolies—with slave raids becoming state business—while standardizing legal practice under the official Ottoman Hanafi code. This undercut the authority of local ulama (who were Malikis) as well as weakening local Sufi cults. Paradoxically this helped the spread of reformist tariqas including the Sammaniya and Khatmiya inspired by pilgrims returning from the Hijaz, where the reformist spirit had been strong since the eighteenth century.

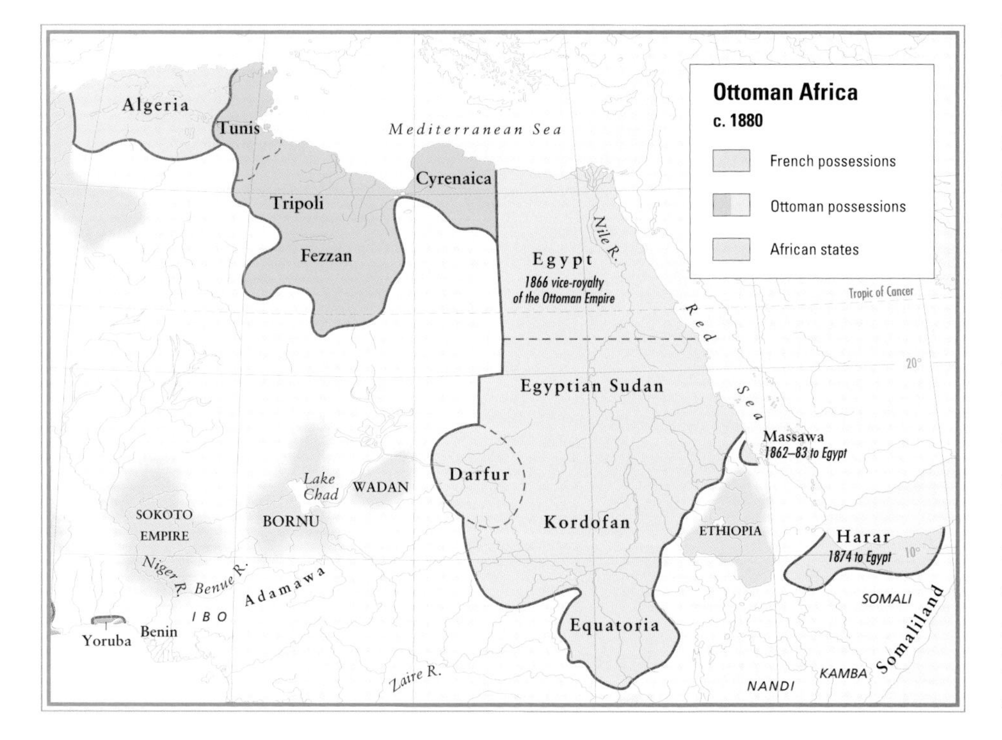

When the Egyptian state monopolies were abolished in the 1850s Europeans began entering Sudan to take over the trade in gum arabic, ostrich feathers, and ivory, damaging local business. Under pressure from Britain the government signed a convention abolishing the slave trade (1877). The ensuing resentments flared up in the great rebellion launched by Muhammad Ahmad. A shaikh of the Sammaniya, he enjoyed a

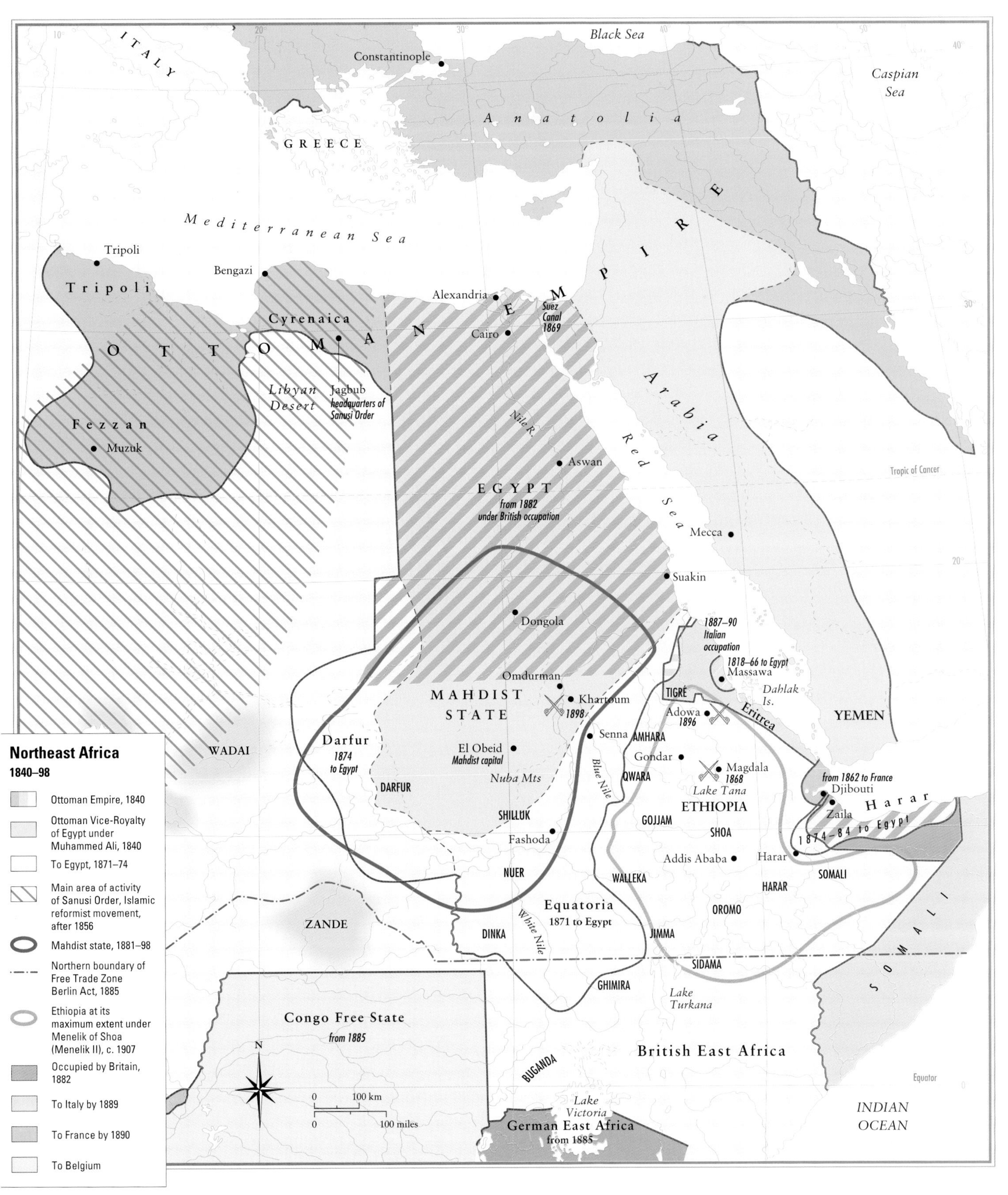

Northeast Africa
1840–98
Ottoman Empire, 1840
Ottoman Vice-Royalty of Egypt under Muhammed Ali, 1840
To Egypt, 1871–74
Main area of activity of Sanusi Order, Islamic reformist movement, after 1856
Mahdist state, 1881–98
Northern boundary of Free Trade Zone Berlin Act, 1885
Ethiopia at its maximum extent under Menelik of Shoa (Menelik II), c. 1907
Occupied by Britain, 1882
To Italy by 1889
To France by 1890
To Belgium
ITALY
Black Sea
Constantinople
Caspian Sea
Anatolia
GREECE
Mediterranean Sea
OTTOMAN EMPIRE
Tripoli
Bengazi
Tripoli
Cyrenaica
Alexandria
Suez Canal 1869
Cairo
Libyan Desert
Jagbub headquarters of Sanusi Order
Fezzan
Muzuk
Arabia
Nile R.
Red Sea
Aswan
EGYPT from 1882 under British occupation
Tropic of Cancer
Mecca
Suakin
Dongola
1887–90 Italian occupation
1818–66 to Egypt
Massawa
Omdurman
MAHDIST STATE
Khartoum
1898
TIGRÉ
Adowa 1896
Dahlak Is.
Eritrea
YEMEN
WADAI
Darfur 1874 to Egypt
Senna
AMHARA
El Obeid Mahdist capital
Gondar
Magdala 1868
Blue Nile
DARFUR
Nuba Mts
QWARA
Lake Tana
ETHIOPIA
from 1862 to France
Djibouti
Harar
Zaila
1874–84 to Egypt
SHILLUK
GOJJAM
SHOA
Fashoda
Addis Ababa
Harar
SOMALI
NUER
WALLEKA
HARAR
Equatoria 1871 to Egypt
OROMO
ZANDE
DINKA
White Nile
JIMMA
SOMALI
SIDAMA
GHIMIRA
Lake Turkana
Congo Free State from 1885
British East Africa
BUGANDA
N
0 100 km
0 100 miles
Lake Victoria
German East Africa from 1885
Equator
INDIAN OCEAN

great reputation for piety. Declaring himself to be the Mahdi (the Muslim messiah, widely expected to appear at the end of the thirteenth hijri century in November 1882), he roused the Baqqara cattle-herding tribes against the "infidel" Turko-Egyptian government. Having annihilated a force of 8,000 levies under Hicks Pasha at Sheikhan, the Mahdi went on to take Omdurman and Khartoum. General Gordon (who had disobeyed his instructions to evacuate the garrison) was killed here on the steps of the Governor's mansion. This left the Victorian public in Britain with a thirst for revenge. The Mahdi died (probably of typhus) six months after his triumphal entry into Khartoum. Under his successor, the Khalifa Abdullahi al-Taishi, the movement continued to expand southward into the Nuba Mountains and Bahr al-Ghazal regions. This brought many non-Muslim animists including the Nuer, Dinka, and others into their orbit, planting the seeds of future conflict.

Having challenged and humiliated British power in a strategically sensitive region where France also had imperial designs, the Mahdist state was doomed. In 1898 the Khalifa's army of 50,000 was massacred by an Anglo-Egyptian force commanded by General Herbert Horatio Kitchener. The Khalifa's spears and elderly rifles were no match for the new Gatling guns Kitchener had brought up the Nile in his flotilla of armored steamers.

The defeat of the Mahdi led to more than a half-century of British rule under the Anglo-Egyptian Condominium. The Mahdi's former followers—known as the Ansar, after Muhammad's original "helpers" in Medina—adopted the "peaceful" jihad, extending their influence in urban areas. In 1944 their leader Sayyid Abd al-Rahman, a son of the Mahdi, formed the Umma Party, which remained well-disposed to the British while working for independence. The Khatmiya formed the National Union Party, which favored a union with Egypt to counter the influence of the Ansar. Though the union was overwhelmingly rejected after the 1952 Egyptian revolution the bitter rivalry between the two religiously based parties persisted, opening the way for military rule under General Ibrahim Abbud (r. 1954–64) and later, under Jafar Numairi (r. 1969–85). Initially Numairi tried to heal the divisions between the Muslim north and predominantly non-Muslim (Christian and animist) south by granting limited autonomy to the Bahr al-Ghazal, Equatorial, and Upper Nile provinces. In 1983, however, Numairi radically switched directions, launching a campaign of total Islamization. He was supported by Hasan al-Turabi, leader of the National Islamic Front (the Sudanese version of the Muslim Brotherhood). Though overthrown in 1985 after becoming increasingly erratic and unstable, the program of Islamization continued under General Umar al-Bashir, who seized power with Turabi's support in 1989. Turabi's insistence on Arabizing and Islamizing the non-Muslim population, who were subjected to Islamic punishments, provoked increasing resistance among Southerners. Many joined or supported the Sudan People's Liberation Movement led by Colonel Garang. The struggle between north and south, Africa's longest-running civil war, has been described by a leading historian as a "civil war of genocidal proportions... with tactics that include starving the civilian populations and forcing them to migrate." [Ira Lapidus, *A History of Islamic Societies*, (2nd edition Cambridge, 2002): p. 768] Peoples adhering to African religions, such as the Nuer and Dinka, have been subjected to forcible conversion. Bashir used the NIFs program, which included purges and executions of non-Islamists in the top ranks of the army and civil service, to smash the power of the traditional political parties, dominated by the Sufi (mystical) brotherhoods. Ten years into the dictatorship, Turabi had served his purpose. In December 1999 the General ousted him in a "palace coup."

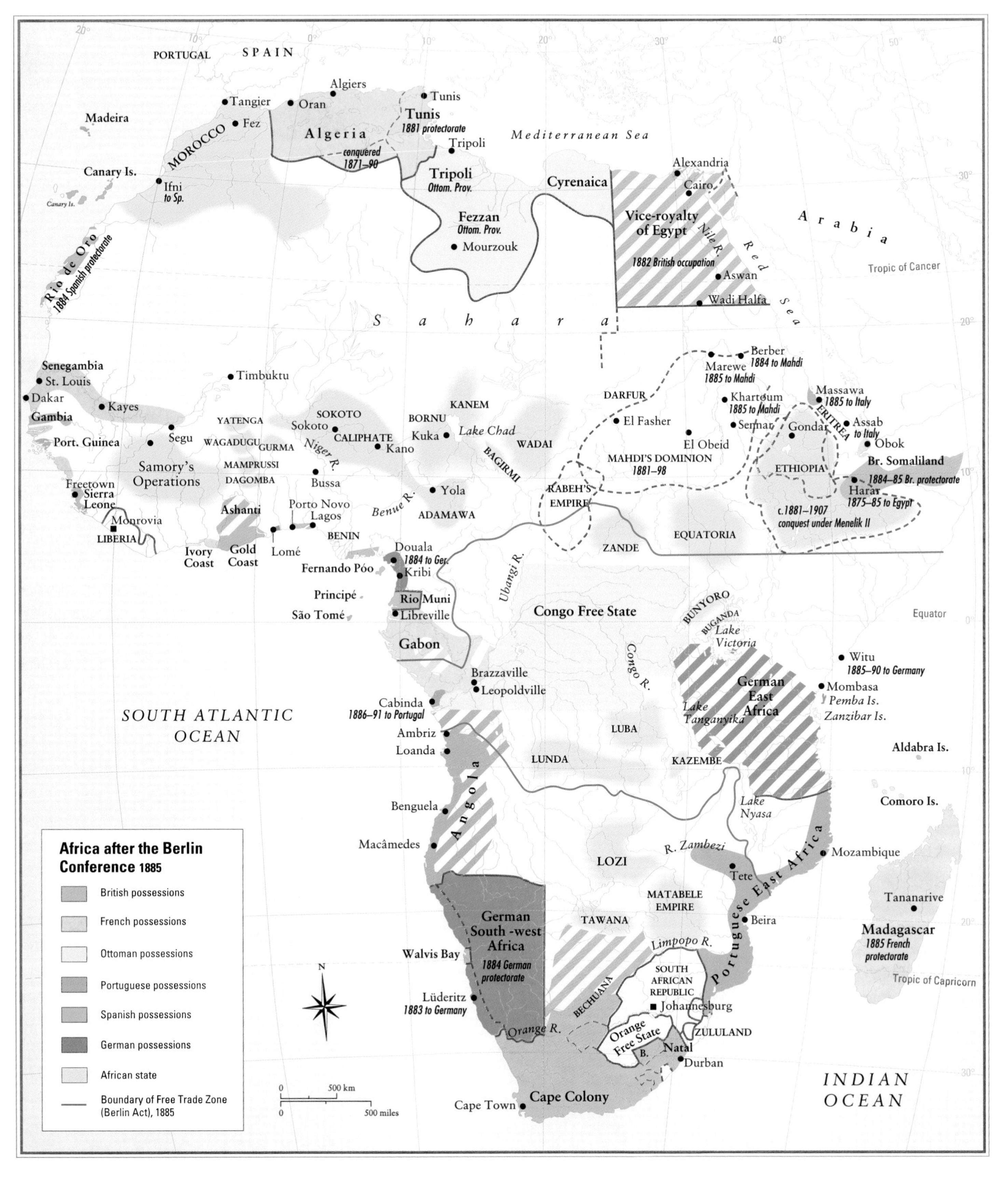
Africa after the Berlin Conference 1885
British possessions
French possessions
Ottoman possessions
Portuguese possessions
Spanish possessions
German possessions
African state
Boundary of Free Trade Zone (Berlin Act), 1885
PORTUGAL
SPAIN
Madeira
Tangier
Oran
Algiers
Tunis
Fez
MOROCCO
Algeria
conquered 1871–90
Tunis
1881 protectorate
Tripoli
Mediterranean Sea
Canary Is.
Ifni
to Sp.
Tripoli
Ottom. Prov.
Cyrenaica
Alexandria
Cairo
Fezzan
Ottom. Prov.
Mourzouk
Vice-royalty of Egypt
1882 British occupation
Nile R.
Aswan
Wadi Halfa
Red Sea
Arabia
Tropic of Cancer
Rio de Oro
1884 Spanish protectorate
Sahara
Senegambia
St. Louis
Dakar
Gambia
Timbuktu
Kayes
Segu
Port. Guinea
YATENGA
WAGADUGU
GURMA
MAMPRUSSI
DAGOMBA
Samory's Operations
SOKOTO
Sokoto
CALIPHATE
Kano
BORNU
Kuka
KANEM
Lake Chad
WADAI
BAGIRMI
Niger R.
Bussa
Freetown
Sierra Leone
Monrovia
LIBERIA
Ashanti
Porto Novo
Lagos
BENIN
Yola
Benue R.
ADAMAWA
Ivory Coast
Gold Coast
Lomé
Douala
1884 to Ger.
Kribi
Fernando Póo
Principé
São Tomé
Rio Muni
Libreville
Gabon
DARFUR
El Fasher
Berber
1884 to Mahdi
Marewe
1885 to Mahdi
Khartoum
1885 to Mahdi
Sennar
El Obeid
MAHDI'S DOMINION
1881–98
Massawa
1885 to Italy
ERITREA
Gondar
Assab
to Italy
Obok
ETHIOPIA
Br. Somaliland
1884–85 Br. protectorate
Harar
1875–85 to Egypt
c.1881–1907
conquest under Menelik II
KABEH'S EMPIRE
ZANDE
EQUATORIA
Ubangi R.
Congo Free State
BUNYORO
BUGANDA
Lake Victoria
Equator
Witu
1885–90 to Germany
Mombasa
Pemba Is.
Zanzibar Is.
Congo R.
German East Africa
Lake Tanganyika
Brazzaville
Leopoldville
Cabinda
1886–91 to Portugal
SOUTH ATLANTIC OCEAN
Ambriz
Loanda
LUBA
LUNDA
KAZEMBE
Aldabra Is.
Angola
Benguela
Macâmedes
Lake Nyasa
Comoro Is.
R. Zambezi
LOZI
Tete
Mozambique
Portuguese East Africa
MATABELE EMPIRE
Beira
Tananarive
German South-west Africa
1884 German protectorate
Walvis Bay
TAWANA
Limpopo R.
Madagascar
1885 French protectorate
Tropic of Capricorn
SOUTH AFRICAN REPUBLIC
BECHUANA
Johannesburg
Lüderitz
1883 to Germany
Orange R.
Orange Free State
ZULULAND
B.
Natal
Durban
Cape Colony
Cape Town
INDIAN OCEAN
0 500 km
0 500 miles
N

France in North and West Africa

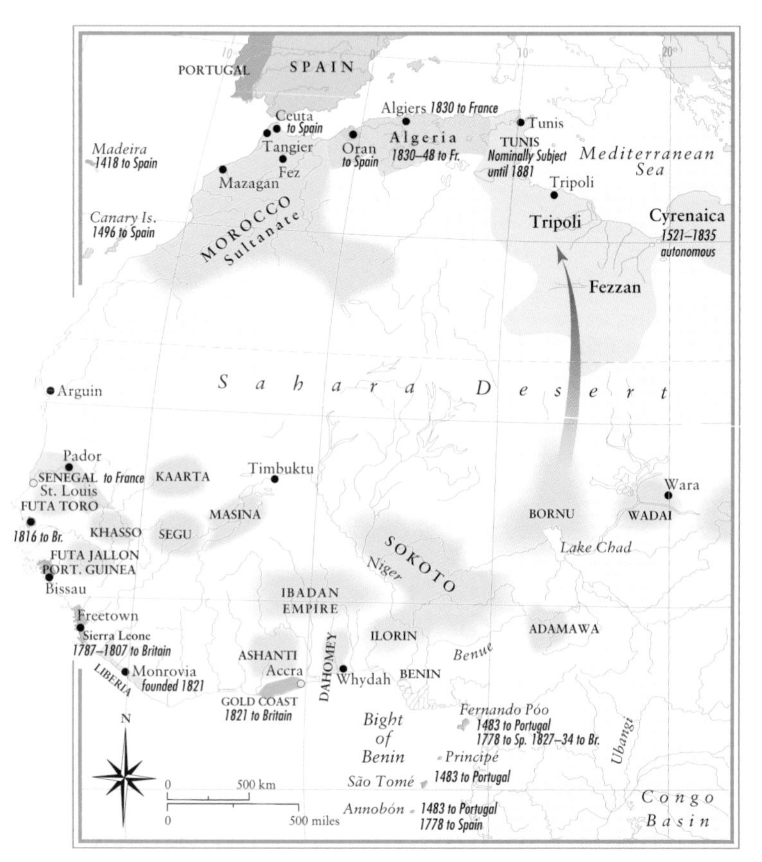

The French conquest of northwest Africa began in earnest in 1830 when the government of the restored Bourbon monarch, Charles X, supported by Marseille merchants with long-standing interests in the wool trade, invaded Algeria. While the French occupied Algiers and other coastal towns, the replacement of Ottoman power in the interior by Europeans provoked a movement of resistance by Abd al-Qadir, son of the head of the Qadiriyya, in alliance with the Sultan of Morocco. Following the defeat of the Moroccan army by General Thomas-Robert Bugeaud at the Battle of Isly in 1844 the way was opened for French colonization. Bugeaud destroyed orchards, crops, and whole villages, killing large numbers of people and leaving many thousands to starve. Vast areas of land were confiscated, with Arab and Berber clans displaced to make way for French and other European colonists. There were insurrections against the French throughout the nineteenth century culminating in a massive uprising crushed in 1871. Colonization of the productive lands of the Algerian littoral continued well into the twentieth century. By 1940 European settlers held some 2.7 million hectares, between 35 and 40 percent of the arable land, with wine (forbidden to Muslims) the dominant export.

The cultural destruction was massive. Traditional Islamic colleges were abolished or had their revenues seized, and though they were supposed to be replaced by French schools, only a small minority of Algerian Muslims benefited. Unlike the British who preferred to rule their empire through pliant surrogates, France had a policy of assimilation, and though its application was limited, it brought into being a small Francophone elite that identified with French civilization. In the 1920s and 30s a nationalist movement combining Islamic reformers grouped around Abd al-Hamid bin Badis (Ben Badis) and Arab nationalists inspired by Messali Hajj gained ground, planting the seeds for the full-grown war of independence that erupted in the late 1950s, with support from the Soviet bloc, Egypt, and other Arab countries. In 1958 a counter-movement by French colonists opposed to independence toppled the government of the Fourth Republic and brought General de Gaulle to power in France. Contrary to the colonists' expectations, however, de Gaulle conceded Algerian independence. After protracted negotiations at Evian, France recognized Algerian sovereignty in 1962. However, the economic, social, and political ties between France and Algeria remained close, with the FLN—the nationalist party that negotiated independence—replacing the French administration as a quasicolonial Francophone minority ruling over a majority of Arabic and Berber speakers. In December 1991 the army intervened to prevent the Islamic Salvation Front (FIS) from coming to power in national elections. More than 100,000 Algerians lost their lives in the ensuing civil war, which partly represented a struggle between a Francophone elite committed to Western values and the Islamists who claimed to possess a superior cultural legitimacy.

French colonial ambitions in Algeria spilled

over into neighboring Tunisia, an autonomous Ottoman province that France took over progressively after 1881. By 1945 there were some 144,000 European settlers occupying about one-fifth of the cultivable land. These settlers, however, never formed such a powerful domestic lobby as their counterparts in Algeria. After being defeated in Indo-China after the Second World War France conceded Tunisian independence in 1956. The same pattern of French economic penetration followed by administrative control and colonization occurred in Morocco, with the important difference that the country retained its status as a Muslim polity under the Sharifian dynasty (claiming descent from the Prophet) that came to power in the seventeenth century. Like the Iranian rulers of his day, the Moroccan Sultan was short of revenues from which to pay his armies. This was especially so after the production of one of his most valuable commodities, sugar, passed into European hands with the development of plantations in the Canaries and the Americas. In order to maintain his hegemony over insubordinate tribes, the sultan mortgaged his customs revenues and borrowed heavily from French banks. When this provoked a revolt among the ulama the French intervened directly, imposing a protectorate (alongside a smaller one granted to Spain) in 1912. Moroccan land was opened up to purchase by Europeans, who by 1953 controlled about 1 million hectares, or 10 percent of the crop land and 25 percent of orchards and vineyards (though Europeans formed barely 1 percent of the population). Unlike Algeria and Tunisia, however, the dynasty was able to place itself at the head of the movement for independence. In 1953 the French made Sultan Muhammad V into a hero by sending him into exile when he refused to agree to a system of dual sovereignty. After massive protests and violence the French allowed the sultan to return, conceding independence in 1956. The dynasty remains in power under Sultan Muhammad's grandson, Muhammad VI.

The pattern of colonial conquest followed by nationalist revolt was repeated less starkly in other parts of the French empire in Africa, where France had economic ambitions but little interest in colonization. Its primary economic interest was to stimulate the production of cash crops such as peanuts, timber, and palm oil. The French collected taxes in cash and used forced labor on banana, cocoa, and coffee plantations. They built railroads to transport goods from the interior to the Atlantic, destroying the time-honored camel traffic across the Sahara. African trade was undermined, with Levantine Arabs, Greeks, and South Asians taking over the retail trade in French colonies. African education was neglected, with only 3 percent of Africans in the French empire enabled to go to school. Nevertheless a small Francophone elite was fostered, which would come to power after independence. In 1958 de Gaulle offered to France's African colonies the choice between immediate independence or self-government within the French economic community. Only Guinea opted for immediate independence (a costly decision that seriously impaired its economic development). France's remaining dependencies in West Africa acquired complete independence in the course of the 1960s.

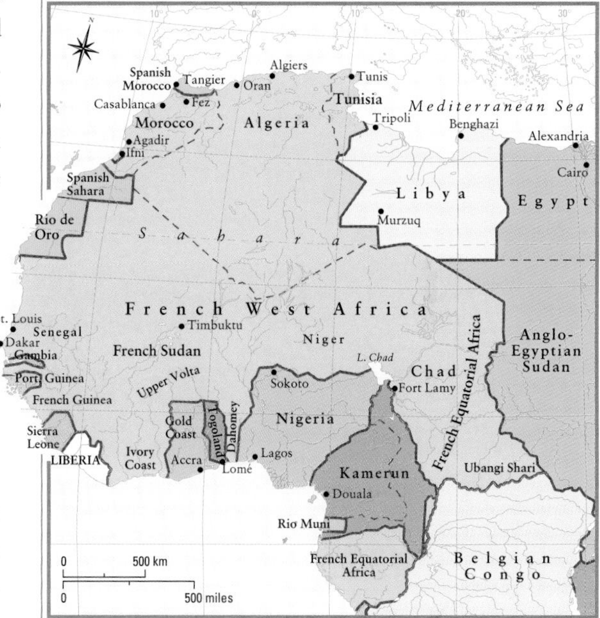

Growth of the Hajj and Other Places of Pilgrimage

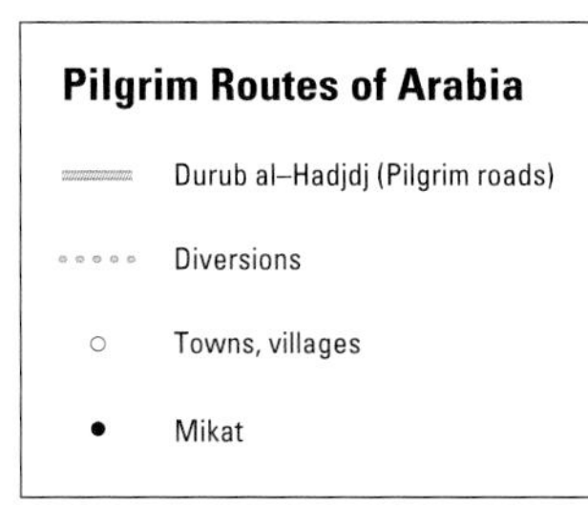

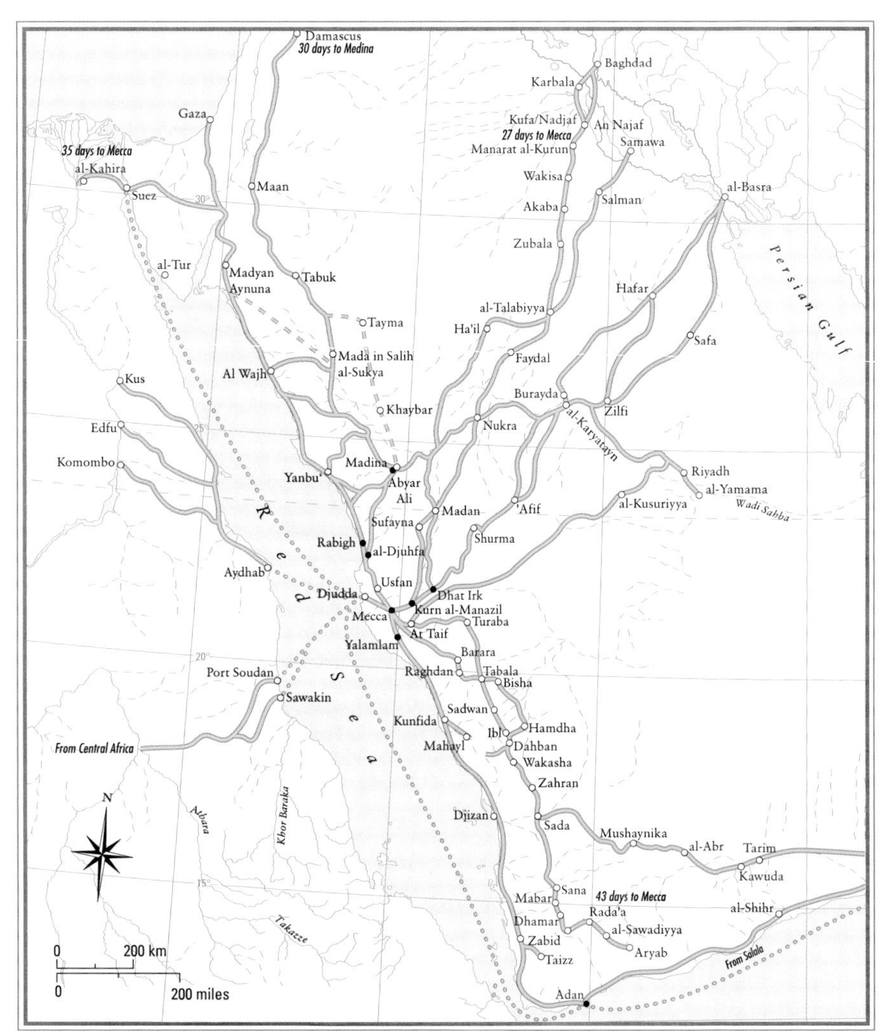

The hajj is one of the five "pillars" or religious duties that every Muslim is obliged to perform at least once in his or her lifetime. Today the duty is made comparatively easy by affordable air transportation. The hajj terminal at Jedda airport—a vast tented structure spread over several acres—accommodates more passengers at one time than any other airport terminal in the world. The hajj physically connects Muslims from all parts of the world with each other. It attracts about one million pilgrims from abroad each year, and about the same number of pilgrims from within Saudi Arabia (including Saudis and foreign residents). About 50 percent of the overseas pilgrims are from the Arab world, 35 percent from Asia, 10 percent from subsaharan Africa, and 5 percent from Europe and the Western Hemisphere.

The origins of the rites of the hajj are obscure. Shortly before his death in 632 Muhammad took the preexisting cults of Mecca and its vicinity and reformed them. Spread over several days the reformed versions include the tawaf (circumambulation) around the Kaba, the square temple at the center of the sanctuary in Mecca; the say or ritual running between the hillocks of Safa and Marwa; a day spent on the plain of Arafat; the onrush—now a massive jam of people and traffic—through Muzdalifa; the stoning of the jamarat (pillars) representing the devil at Mina. In reforming the pagan hajj Muhammad may have redirected a series of solar, rainmaking, and other rituals surrounding the Black Stone. A mysterious "heavenly rock" or a meteorite, it is set in the southeastern corner of the Kaba toward the exclusive worship of Allah as revealed to the patriarch Abraham (Ibrahim) and his son Ishmael (Ismail), the mythical ancestor of the Arabs. The final act of the hajj, the sacrifice of an animal commemorating the sheep that Allah accepted in place of Abraham's son, is celebrated throughout the Muslim world at the Id al-Adha, when Muslims kill their own animals or consume ritually slaughtered animals at home. The umra (minor pilgrimage) is limited to the sanctuary surrounding the Kaba and can be performed separately at any time of the year or in conjunction with the hajj.

In premodern times the journey could be extremely arduous, especially from distant peripheries. It could take many years of a person's life—even a whole lifetime—to complete the "fifth pillar" of Islam. Vast moving caravan cities under the command of the Amir al-Hajj set out from Syria, Egypt, and Iraq. The caravan commanders were generals in the field. In fact, their primary duty was to protect the pilgrims from the attacks of the marauding bedouin or (from the late eighteenth century) by the tribes belonging to the Wahhanbi-Saudi movement who regarded all non-Wahhanbis as infidels. Ibn Jubair, who made the pilgrimage in 1184 described the tent of the commander of the Iraqi caravan on the Plain of Arafat as resembling a "walled city" or "powerful fortress" with "four lofty gates," through which one entered a series of vestibules and narrow passageways. In the nineteenth century the arrival of steamship navigation under colonial auspices combined with the emergence of special hajj savings clubs placed the pilgrimage within reach of thousands of ordinary peasants and townsfolk from outlying regions such as Bengal, Malaya, and the Dutch East Indies who could never have hoped to fulfill the religious duty in preindustrial times.

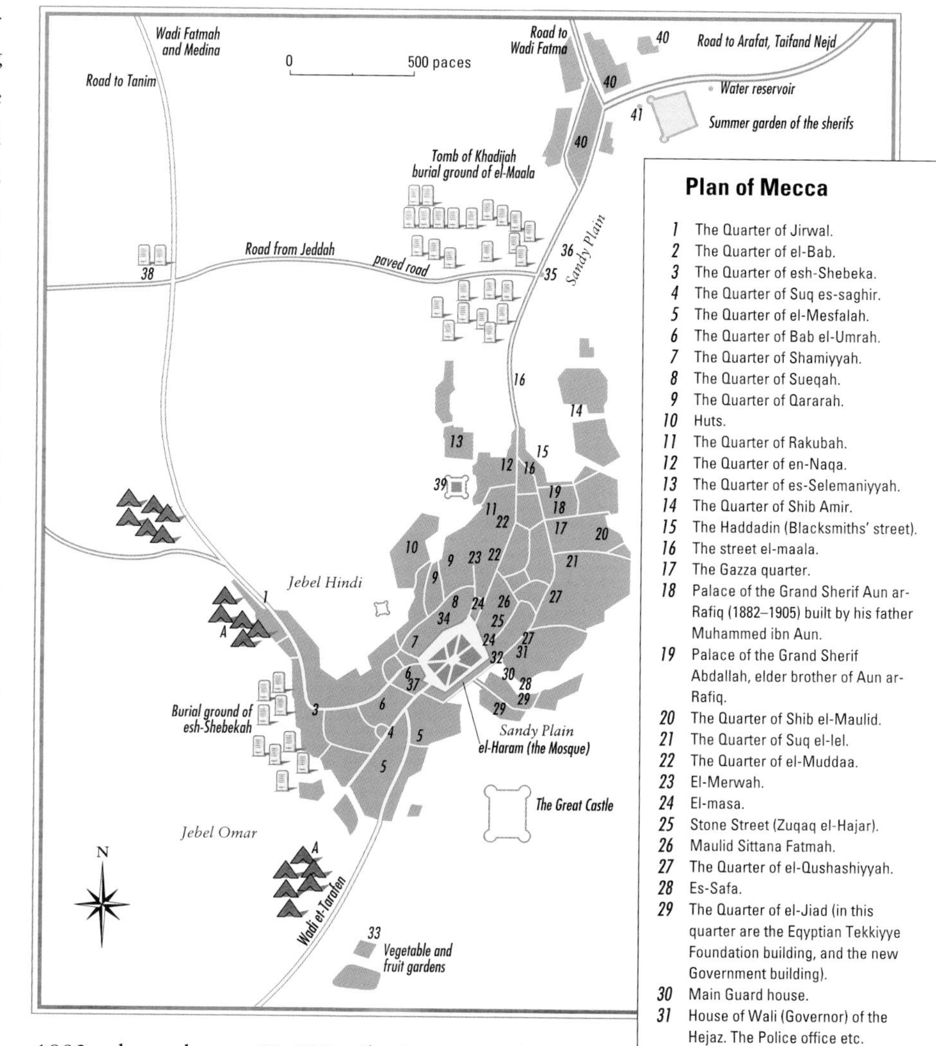

Plan of Mecca

1 The Quarter of Jirwal.
2 The Quarter of el-Bab.
3 The Quarter of esh-Shebeka.
4 The Quarter of Suq es-saghir.
5 The Quarter of el-Mesfalah.
6 The Quarter of Bab el-Umrah.
7 The Quarter of Shamiyyah.
8 The Quarter of Sueqah.
9 The Quarter of Qararah.
10 Huts.
11 The Quarter of Rakubah.
12 The Quarter of en-Naqa.
13 The Quarter of es-Selemaniyyah.
14 The Quarter of Shib Amir.
15 The Haddadin (Blacksmiths' street).
16 The street el-maala.
17 The Gazza quarter.
18 Palace of the Grand Sherif Aun ar-Rafiq (1882–1905) built by his father Muhammed ibn Aun.
19 Palace of the Grand Sherif Abdallah, elder brother of Aun ar-Rafiq.
20 The Quarter of Shib el-Maulid.
21 The Quarter of Suq el-lel.
22 The Quarter of el-Muddaa.
23 El-Merwah.
24 El-masa.
25 Stone Street (Zuqaq el-Hajar).
26 Maulid Sittana Fatmah.
27 The Quarter of el-Qushashiyyah.
28 Es-Safa.
29 The Quarter of el-Jiad (in this quarter are the Eqyptian Tekkiyye Foundation building, and the new Government building).
30 Main Guard house.
31 House of Wali (Governor) of the Hejaz. The Police office etc.
32 Madrasah, now used as office of the Committee for the Aqueduct of Zubaydah and bureau of the Reyyis (Chief of the muaddhins).
33 Birket Majin (pronounced Majid) great cistern in connection with the aquaduct.
34 Court of Justice and dwelling house of the Qadhi.
35 Tomb of Abu Talib (uncle of Muhammad).
36 Water place in connection with aquaduct.
37 Tomb of Seyyid Aqil.
38 Tomb of the Saint Shikh Mahmud.
39 Jebel Queqian.
40 The Quarter of Maabdah.
41 Reservoir of water from the aquaduct. Several such reservoirs are now in all the main streets.
A Bedouin huts.

A disastrous side effect of the consequent increase in attendance was a series of devastating cholera outbreaks. In 1865 an epidemic originating in Java and Singapore killed an estimated 15,000 out of 90,000 pilgrims before the hajj—which occurred in May—was over. By the following month the disease had spread to Alexandria, where 60,000 Egyptians died. By November the disease had spread as far as New York. Quarantine restrictions introduced by the Ottoman and colonial governments shielded Egypt and Europe from infection, but cholera continued to rage in the east and in the Hijaz, where there were eight epidemics between 1865 and 1892. The worst of all occurred in 1893 when almost 33,000 pilgrims out of a total of 200,000 perished at Jidda, Mecca, and Medina. The epidemics continued until 1912, by which time the strict quarantine regulations had finally taken hold. Compared with the horrors of the late nineteenth and early twentieth century, recent disasters to have afflicted the hajj, such as the death of more than four hundred mainly Indonesian pilgrims in the fire that broke out at Arafat in 2000, seem almost minor.

Many, if not most, pilgrims supplement the hajj with a visit to the Prophet's mosque at Medina, where Muhammad's family, wives, and prominent Companions are buried. In 1925 the puritanical Saudi-Wahhanbi movement leveled all the structures marking these graves. Ziyara (the custom of visitation or praying at them) was severely restricted. According to Wahhanbi belief, a belief not shared by other Sunni communities, ziyaras amount to saint veneration or shirk (idolatry). The restrictions are an aspect of the virulently anti-Shiite orientation of Wahhanbism, which was manifested in the Saudi–Wahhanbi attacks on the shrines of the Shiite imams, Ali and Hussein at Najaf, and Karbala in Iraq, in 1801. However, ziyaras to the tombs of the imams and their descendents are an important aspect of popular Shiism. Some of these ziyaras are performed at all times of the year, others at

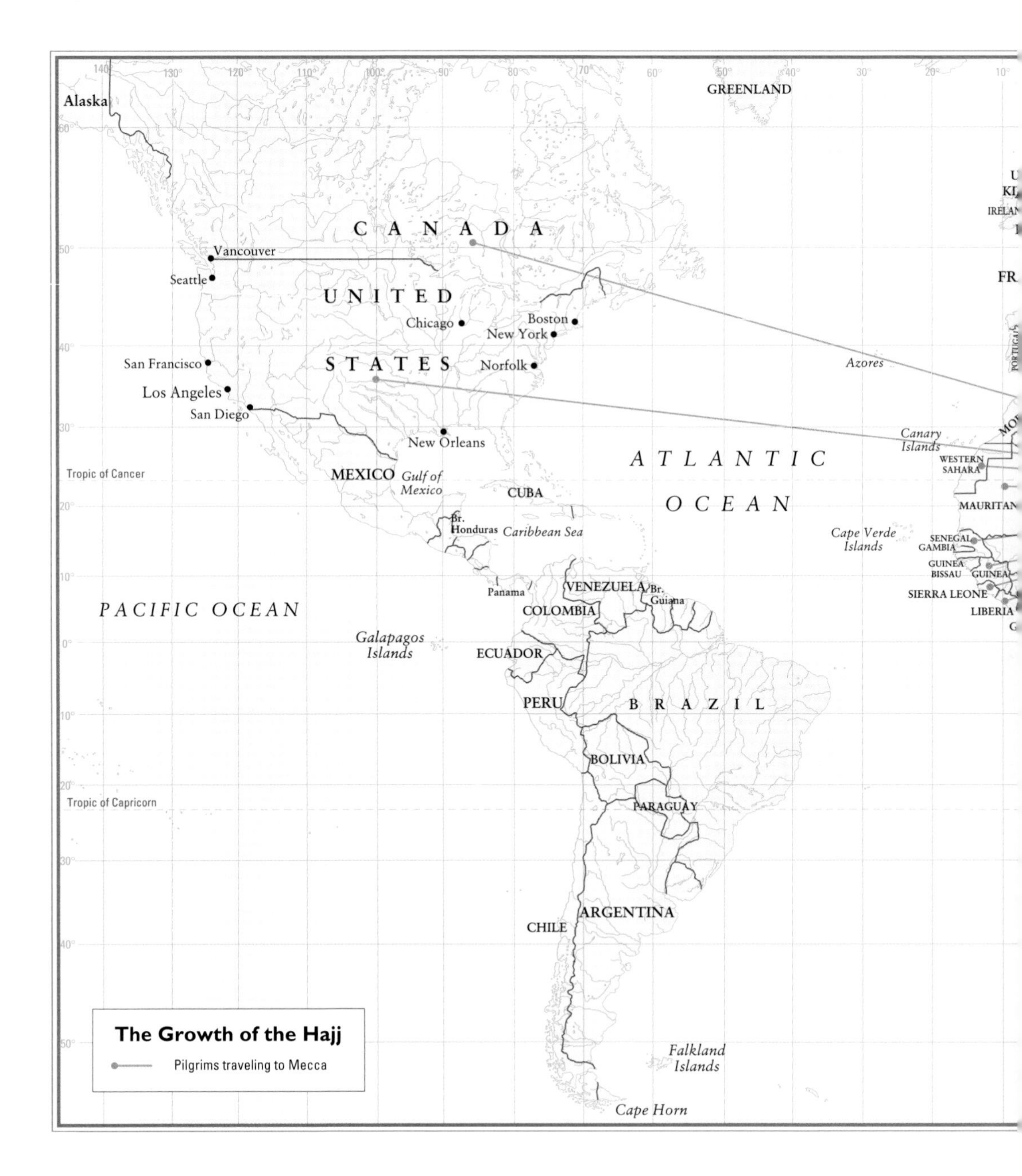

special times in the Muslim calendar. For example, the ziyara of the Imam Rida in Mashhad is recommended in the month of Dhu al-Qada. Ziyaras are popular with women, especially to the shrines of female saints such as Sayyida Zainab (daughter of the Imam Ali) in Cairo and Sayyida Ruqayya (daughter of Imam Hussein) in Damascus. The shrine of Hussein at Karbala is visited on Thursday evenings, but especially at the annual festival of Ashura (the day of his martyrdom) when thousands of Shiite pilgrims from all over the world congregate at the mosque surrounding his tomb. Other Muslim saints have shrines whose sanctity is associated with national or regional identities. Two of the most prominent are the shrines of Moulay Idris (founder of the Idrisid dynasty) at Fez in Morocco and Amadu Bamba (c. 1850–1927) in Senegal.

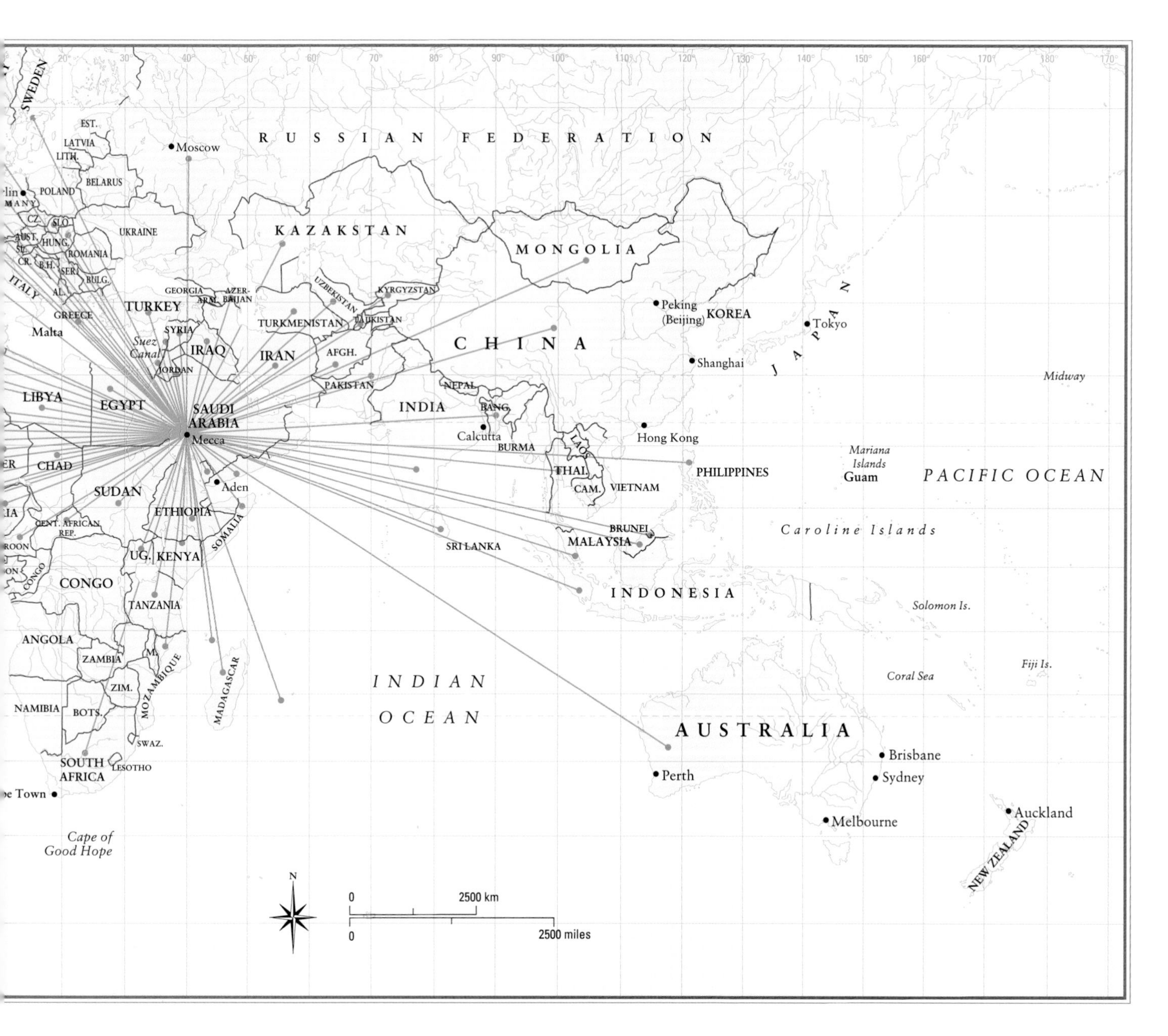

Expanding Cities

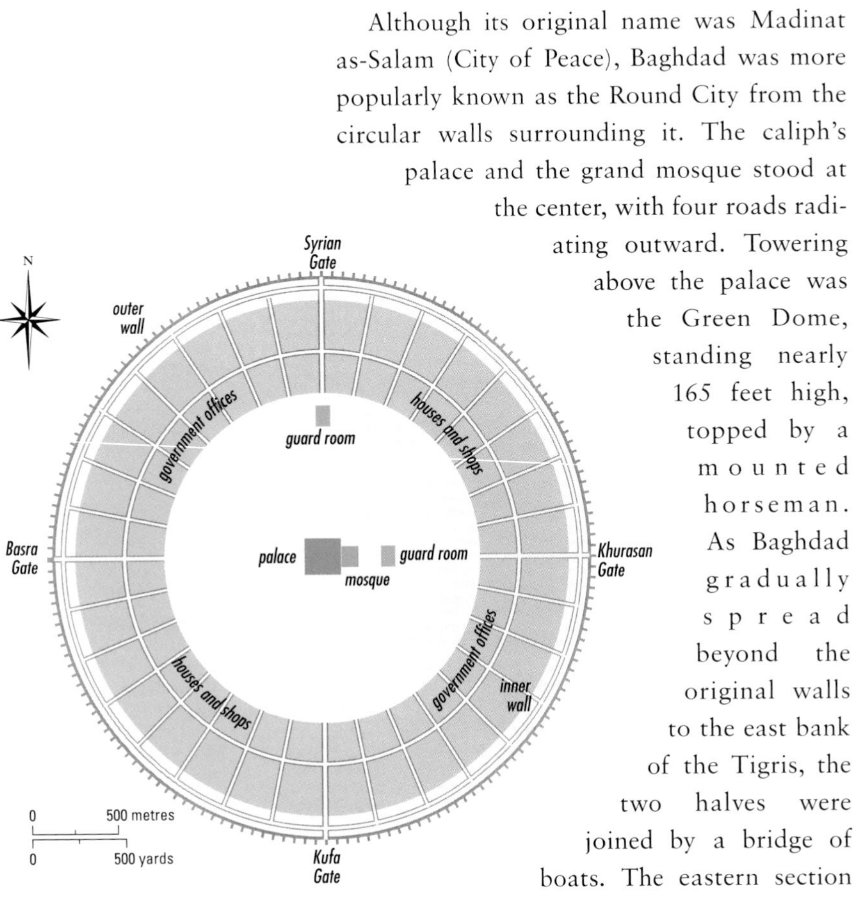

Baghdad

Founded in AD 762 by Abu Jafar al-Mansur, the second Abbasid caliph, the city of Baghdad was originally built on the west bank of the Tigris River.

Although its original name was Madinat as-Salam (City of Peace), Baghdad was more popularly known as the Round City from the circular walls surrounding it. The caliph's palace and the grand mosque stood at the center, with four roads radiating outward. Towering above the palace was the Green Dome, standing nearly 165 feet high, topped by a mounted horseman. As Baghdad gradually spread beyond the original walls to the east bank of the Tigris, the two halves were joined by a bridge of boats. The eastern section was called Rusafah.

Baghdad reached the height of its commercial prosperity and cultural power during the eighth and ninth centuries. Under the rule of the caliphs al-Mahdi and Harun al-Rashid, it stood at the nexus of the trade routes between the East and West linking Asia with Europe. Its impressive buildings and magnificent gardens gave it the reputation of the richest and most beautiful city in the world.

In the latter half of the ninth century, the Abbasid caliphs' power was weakened by internal strife leading to civil war. When the Mongols invaded Baghdad in the thirteenth century, the caliph was murdered along with thousands of his subjects. Whole quarters were destroyed by looting and fire. The irrigation system on which the city and its gardens depended was wrecked, adding dramatically to the city's decline. By the time Baghdad became part of the Ottoman Empire in 1534 it had suffered obscurity and neglect for several centuries.

Improvements were made on a modest scale at the beginning of the twentieth century with the building of schools and hospitals. The oil boom of the 1970s brought increased wealth to Baghdad and the city began to develop on a much more impressive scale, with the construction of middle-class residential areas. New sewers and water lines were laid and above ground a network of superhighways was constructed, as well as a new airport. Eleven bridges connected the two halves of the city, many of which were subsequently destroyed by US bombing in 2003. Tahrir Square, standing on the river's left bank at one end of the Jumhuriyah Bridge, is now the heart of the city from which its main streets radiate.

Under the dictatorial regime of Saddam Hussein a number of massive monuments were constructed, including the notorious "Victory Arch" a vast confection in bronze actually modeled from maquettes of Saddam Hussein's forearms. An altogether more impressive example of recent monumental art is the Shahid (Martyrs') Monument commemorating the dead of the Iran–Iraq War (1980–88). Designed by Ismail Fattah, it consists of a vast onion-dome vertically sliced into two sections and glazed with traditional blue ceramic tiles. Apart from these monuments most of the improvements to Baghdad were brought to a halt by the war with Iran in the 1980s, the Gulf War that followed Iraq's invasion of Kuwait, and the UN sanctions imposed afterward. The major exceptions to this story of renewed decline were the presidential palaces, actually vast compounds surrounded by high walls or fences, containing Saddam's lavishly decorated residential villas for visiting dignitaries set beside artificial lakes. Before the removal of the Iraqi Baathist regime by US military action in March 2003 access to these sites by UN weapons inspectors had been a major source of contention between the regime and the United Nations.

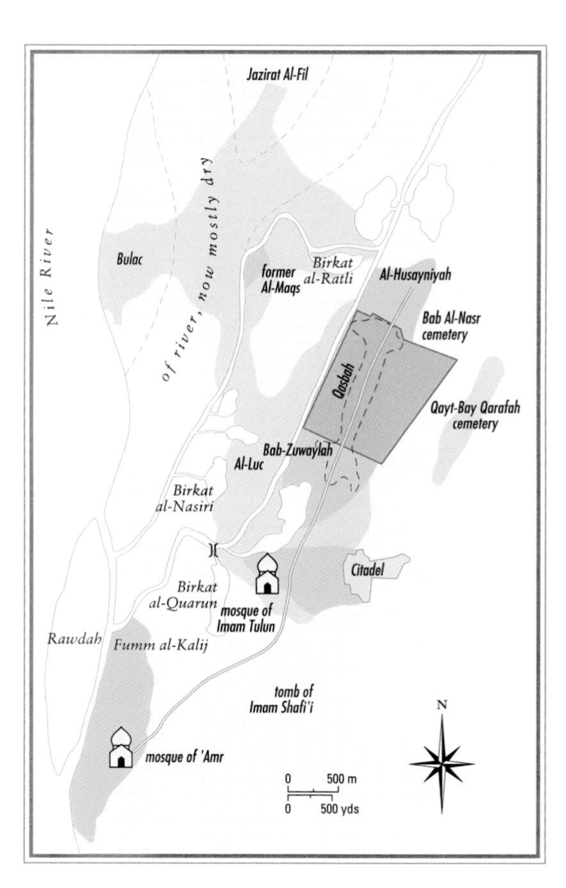

Cairo

Cairo, which comes from the Arabic word *al-Qahira,* meaning the victorious, takes its name from the city founded by a brilliant general Jawhar al-Siqilli. A slave of Sicilian, possibly Slav origin, he conquered Egypt in 969 on behalf of his master, the Fatimid Caliph al-Muizz. Like the previous conquerors he staked out a separate garrison city for his troops, north of the city, Al-Fustat, founded by the Arabs, who had conquered Egypt in 642. The Fatimid city with its palaces, schools, and mosques, includes al-Azhar, the world's oldest university. Cairo was founded by Jawhar in 970 and was embellished by the Mamluk amirs, who built hundreds of mosques, tombs, inns, hospices, hospitals, and other public buildings. Their distinctive decorative style made use of the same Muqattam limestones as the pyramids of Giza (and in some cases, using the pyramids' outer casings). Salah al-Din al-Ayyubi (Saladin) who took over after the collapse of the Fatimids, built the magnificent citadel to the south where Muhammad Ali, the nineteenth-century reforming autocrat, constructed the great Ottoman-style mosque that still commands the old city.

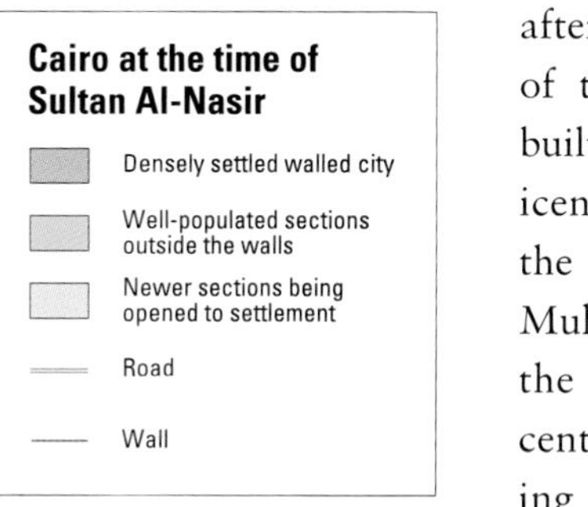

The earliest settlement in this crucial spot on the east bank of the Nile, opposite the pyra-

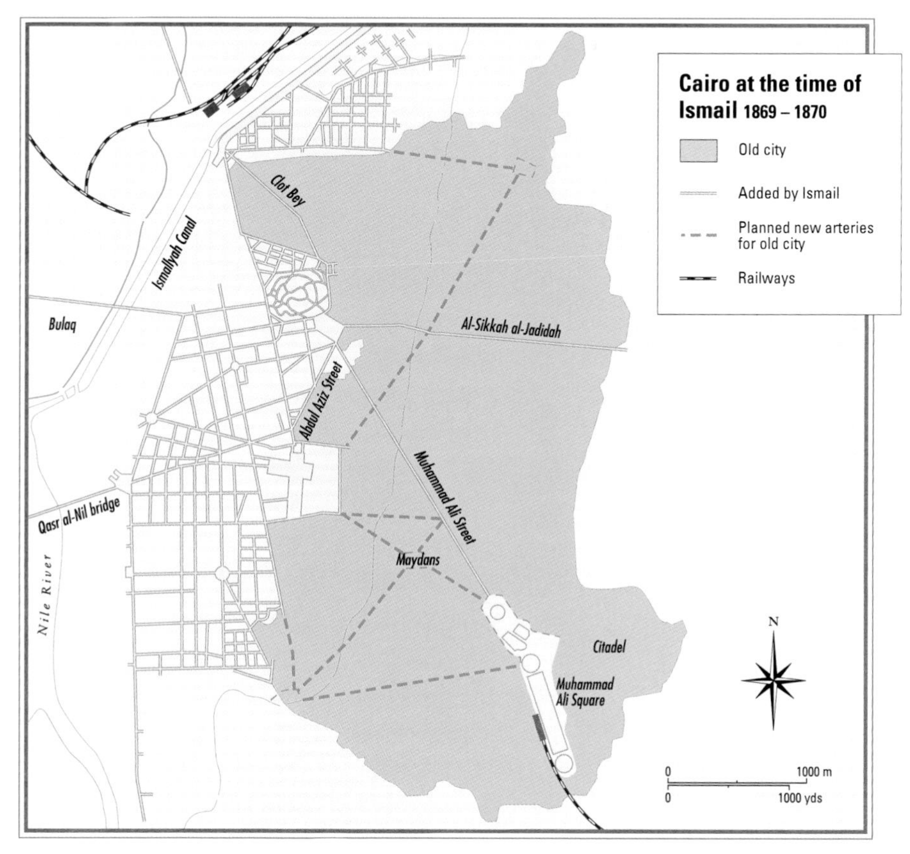

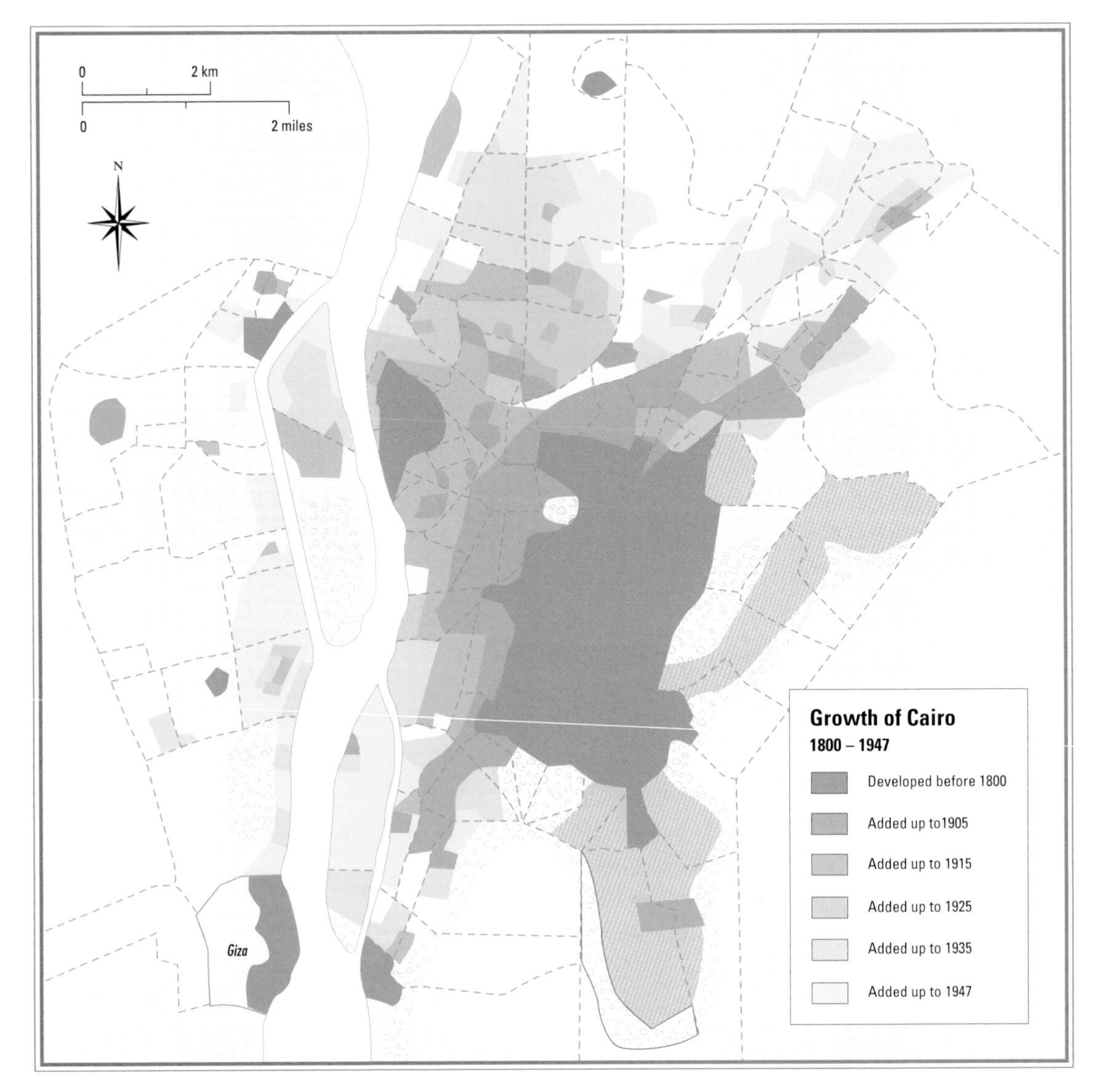

mids, was Babylon (now Misr al-Qadima), a fortress built by the invading Persians in 525 BC to guard an important crossing of the Nile. The city's steady northward migration (which continued into the twentieth century with the construction of the desert suburb of Heliopolis) was influenced by the prevailing northerly breezes, which sent the smells of ordure and burning rubbish southward. Before the nineteenth century the city's westward expansion was limited by the river's floodplains. The Mamluk amirs and Ottoman princes built fine palaces with vast palm-shaded gardens while most of the populace lived in labyrinthine streets and alleyways contained within the medievals walls of al-Qahira. The European-style city of fine boulevards and circuses was laid out in the 1860s in conscious imitation of Baron Haussmann's redesigned Paris. Improved flood control and the stabilization of the riverbanks and the two large islands of Rawdah and Gezirah allowed the city to expand across the river toward Giza and Imbaba. This makes modern Cairo (with 18–20 million people) one of the world's largest megalopolises.

Tashkent

Until the collapse of the Soviet Union in 1991 Tashkent, with a population of 2.3 million, was the fourth-largest Soviet city after Moscow,

Leningrad, and Kiev. Much of it was destroyed by an earthquake in 1966, which wrecked 95,000 homes and left 300,000 people (one-third of its population) homeless. Rebuilt as a model Soviet city, it has broad boulevards, wide public spaces with splashing fountains, and rows of concrete office and apartment buildings in the international modernist style. Though it retains traditional Uzbek motifs and arcades, and galleries with open verandas, mosaics, and paneling. The city has spacious parks and a modern underground railroad system. After Uzbekistan became independent in 1992 the Russians, who formed about half of the population, were reported to be leaving at the rate of 700 a week. However, Russian is still spoken by at least half of Tashkent's citizens.

Before the reconstruction there were two distinct cities, the old Islamic city and the modern Russian one, separated by a canal. Some of the labyrinthine streets and alleyways of Old Tashkent, with traditional homes built around pleasant vine-shaded courtyards, survived the earthquake. Tashkent is the most recent of several names given to the old city, originally an oasis settlement for nomads and traders on the Chirchik River, a tributary of the Syr Darya. When the Arabs defeated a Chinese army at the battle of Talas in 751 the settlement was known as Chach, Arabized to al-Shash. Arab writers described it as a prosperous place of vineyards, teeming with bazaars and busy craftsmen. Tashkent, meaning "stone-town" in the local Turkic languages, first appears on coins in the Mongol period. Though sacked by the Mongols, the city recovered some of its previous prosperity under Timur and his successors. Contested by successive rulers, Uzbeks, Kazakhs, Persians, Mongol Oirots, and Kalmyks, it nevertheless maintained a degree of autonomy. In the eighteenth century it was divided into four, sometimes mutually hostile, quarters sharing a common bazaar. Conquered by the Russians in 1865, its population had almost tripled (from 56,000 to 156,000) by the time the Transcaspian Railroad reached Tashkent in 1898. The Soviet period saw intensive industrialization and the expansion of residential quarters with generous parks and gardens. Mosques, madrasas, and other religious buildings were either destroyed, or converted into factories, warehouses, or printing presses. Since independence the whole city has been reasserting its Islamic character, with large brightly-domed mosques being constructed alongside modern shopping malls and arcades stocked with goods from southeast Asia.

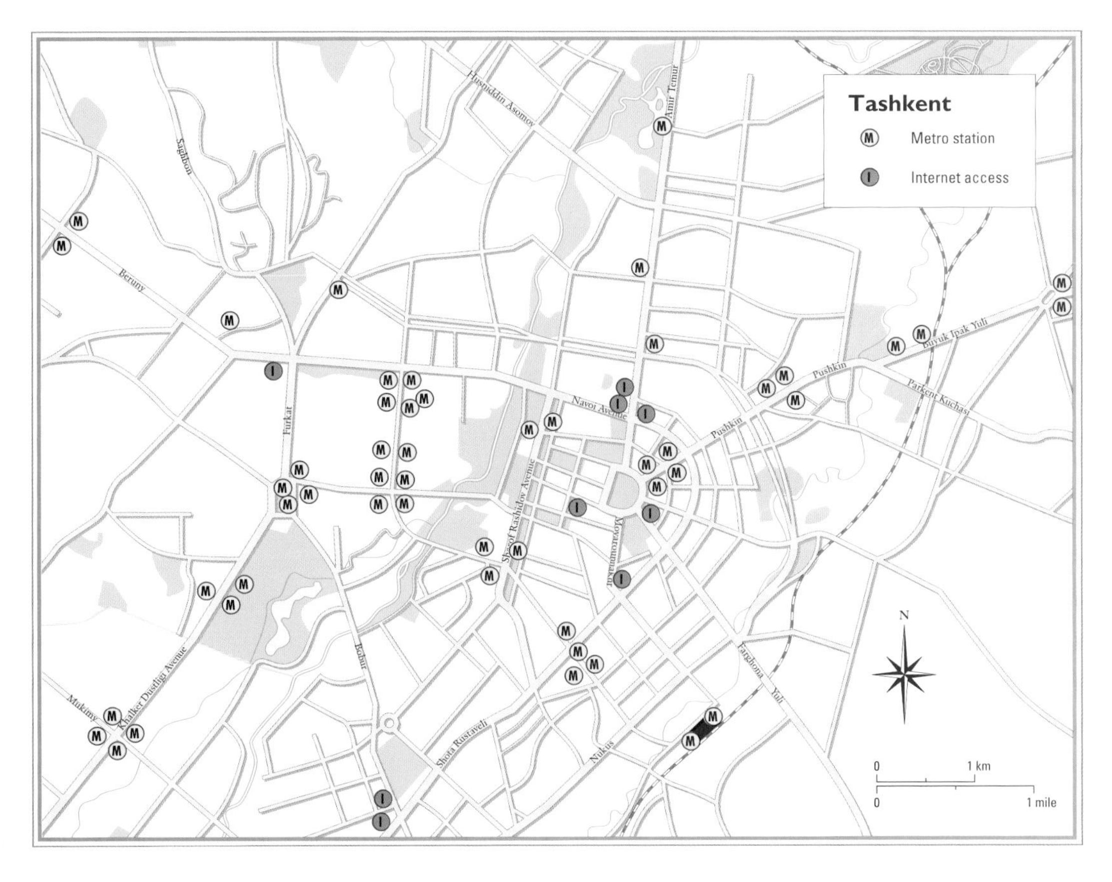

Impact of Oil in the 20th Century

The impact of oil and natural gas has been a mixed blessing for the Muslim societies of western Asia and particularly the Gulf region (including Iraq), which contains between 60 and 65 percent of the world's proven oil reserves. On the one hand it has enabled the oil-bearing countries to build impressive modern cities with high-rise buildings, shining shopping malls, six-lane highways, state-of-the-art communications systems, and other trappings of modernity. It has enabled Saudi Arabia, once one of the world's poorest and least developed countries, to provide impressive health-care and education systems for its population (including the formerly secluded female half). On the other hand, it has added to the region's instability by consolidating the power of tribal oligarchies whose control of the oil has enabled them to govern by a combination of patronage and repression.

An oil refinery plant in Saudi Arabia. Approximately 95 percent of the world's oil has been produced by about 5 percent of its oilfields, two-thirds of which are located in western Asia, Saudi Arabia being the world's largest producer.

The most conspicuous example of the disastrous effects of oil dependency was seen in Iraq, where the network of kinship controlled by Saddam Hussein extended itself through every branch of society after the nationalization of oil in 1972. The group controlled the distribution of land (confiscated from old regime landowners or political opponents) licenses for setting up businesses (including arms imports), foreign exchange, and labor relations. Its coercive power was reinforced through the ubiquitous mukhabarat (intelligence services), which acquired a fearsome reputation for torture and extra-judicial killing. Iraq was an extreme example, but the same considerations apply to most of the big oil-producing Arab states where a single ruling family exercises power through a network of patron-client relationships and is freed from the constraints exercised by elected bodies of tax-paying citizens. Oil also frees the rulers from the need to democratize their societies by placing the industries on which they depend in the hands of nonenfranchised foreign workers and administrators. The electorate for the Kuwaiti parliament, for example, is restricted to males from families resident before 1959—meaning that only 80,000 out of a potential 600,000 Kuwaiti men (not to mention the foreigners who constitute between 70 and 85 percent of the workforce) are eligible to vote. Even with such a restricted franchise the ruling family has at times found parliament unacceptably critical, dissolving it between 1976–81 and 1986–92. At the same time full Kuwaiti citizens (whose average per capita income in 1998 measured more than $22,000 per annum) are able to enjoy an extensive cradle-to-grave welfare system, with state utilities, health care, housing, telecommunications, and education all heavily subsidized by the state.

The political volatility of the Gulf region, demonstrated by three major wars since 1980 has stimulated the search for oil in other Muslim regions, notably Central Asia and the Caspian. The post-Soviet states of Azerbaijan, Turkmenistan, Uzbekistan, and Kazakhstan have promising oil reserves, but cannot export their oil without sending it through pipelines that pass through neighboring countries. The most economical route from Turkmenistan and Azerbaijan would run though Iran to the Gulf using Iran's existing network of pipelines. This route, however, has been opposed for political reasons by the US, which favors a much more expensive project running to Ceyhan on Turkey's Mediterranean coast.

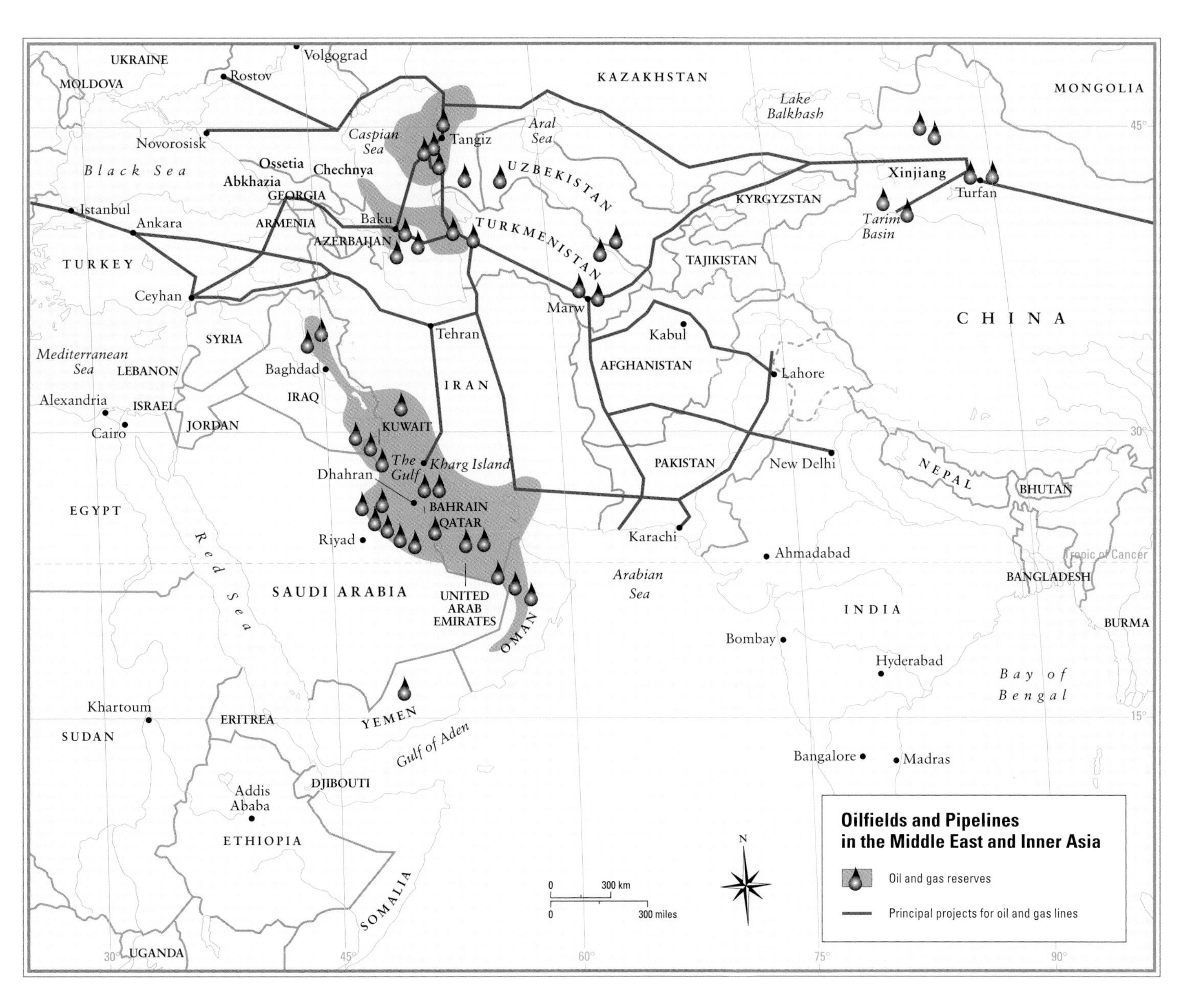

Water Resources

Water and its scarcity have had a determining impact on the core regions of the Islamic world. In ancient Egypt many centuries of human experience in ordering the flow of the Nile's annual flood through complex systems of basin irrigation lay behind the finely calibrated geometry of the pyramids. In Mesopotamia, as in Egypt, the state, with its bureaucratic structures of power and control, was the gift of the river. In Arabia the aridity of the land and the value of water is fundamental to the language of Islam. In the Koran the rare and precious rain that makes the desert bloom overnight is one of the ayat (signs or proofs) of God, a metaphor for the resurrection. "...for among His signs is this: thou seest the earth lying desolate—and lo! When We send down water upon it, it stirs and swells [with life] Verily, He who brings to life can surely give life to the dead ... for behold! He has the power to do anything!" (Koran 41:39). The root meaning of Sharia—the divine law—is the way or path to a watering place, the source of life and purity. An eighteenth-century Arabic dictionary likens the Sharia to the "descent of water" that quenches man's thirst and purifies him through fasting, prayer, pilgrimage, and marriage. Water management was fundamental to the success and failure of Islamic governments in the past. In the Upper Euphrates region the early Abbasid rulers restored and extended the system of underwater channels built by the Sasanians, bringing new lands under cultivation. Neglect of irrigation in subsequent centuries hastened the dynasty's economic and political decline.

Water management was central to the development of modern Egypt. Under the dynasty of Muhammad Ali the first barrages were built to control the Nile floods, bringing new lands under cultivation and releasing the floodplain between Cairo and Gizeh for a new European-style city of circuses with radiating boulevards. Gamal Abd al-Nasser, the charismatic nationalist leader who overthrew the monarchy in 1952 precipitated the 1956 Suez crisis by nationalizing the Suez Canal after the US refused to finance the High Dam at Aswan. Built with Soviet help, the dam at the head of Lake Nasser now controls the river by storing its floodwaters in what is now the world's largest artificial reservoir. Some experts consider the High Dam to have been a long-term ecological disaster. The dam has stopped the river from bringing the rich nutrients from the tropical regions, increasing the salinity of the soil, and reducing fish stocks in the eastern Mediterranean. Dams built by Turkey on the Euphrates have been no less contentious. The Keban (1975) and Karakaya (1987) dams, each designed to store about 30 million cubic kilometers of water to generate electricity and to regulate the river's flow, were partly financed with loans from the World Bank. However the World Bank refused to contribute to the larger Ataturk Dam, which has a storage capacity of 46 cubic kilometers, because the downstream riparians, Syria and Iraq, failed to approve the project. The dams and associated irrigation projects have reduced the flow of the Euphrates by almost half, from some 30 million to just below 16 million cubic meters per year. In defense of its action Turkey argues that the average use of the flow by Syria and Iraq has never exceeded 15 cubic kilometers per year—so neither need suffer. Turkey is also developing the Tigris through a series of projects that may lead to reductions in flow, but improvements in reliability. Iraq is the main beneficiary of the Tigris. Any shortfall affecting the Euphrates as a result of Turkish engineering could be made good by developing the Tigris waters.

Nowhere is the highly charged issue of water management more apparent than in discussions about sharing the waters of the Jordan River, central to the Arab–Israeli dispute. The peace treaty between Israel and Jordan signed in October 1994 included the provision of a phased 200 million cubic meters of water per year for Jordan, to be allocated partly from current Israeli sources and partly from joint development. During the preliminary negotiations between Israel and the Palestinians, known as Oslo (1993) and Oslo II (1995), water was included as one of five crucial issues along with territory, Jerusalem, Jewish settlements, and refugees. With the continuing intifada (uprising) and the breakdown of the so-called "road map to peace" sponsored by the US, the UN, the European Union, and Russia, the issue remains unresolved. However the very fact that the sharing of water could have been part of the negotiations illustrates an important truth: the principal water resource for the Israeli, Palestinian, Syrian, and Jordanian economies, both at present and in the future, lies outside the region in the form of "virtual water."

"Virtual water" is a concept used by economists and hydrologists to indicate the quantities of water needed to produce imported foods, such as wheat from water-rich regions like North America. Every ton of wheat or similar food commodity requires approximately one thousand times its volume in water to produce it. Judging by the rate of cereal imports into Western Asia and North Africa, the region has been "running out" of water since the 1970s. This has not, however, led to starvation. By importing wheat and other staples from regions where soil water and soil moisture are high the countries of the region have subsisted by means of the "virtual water"' embedded in the staples they import. According to this analysis, it is cheaper and much more sensible to import food measured in terms of "virtual water" than to produce it locally. For example, Saudi Arabia is using fossil water from nonrenewable aquifers to grow wheat in considerable quantities. It is now the world's sixth-largest exporter of cereals. But the cost is prohibitive. In 1989 Saudi farmers were being paid $533 per ton to produce wheat available for $120 on the world market. The global trading system in grain can deliver 40,000 million cubic meters of virtual water embedded in grain imports without visible stress. No engineering system could mobilize one-tenth of that amount with the same degree of flexibility.

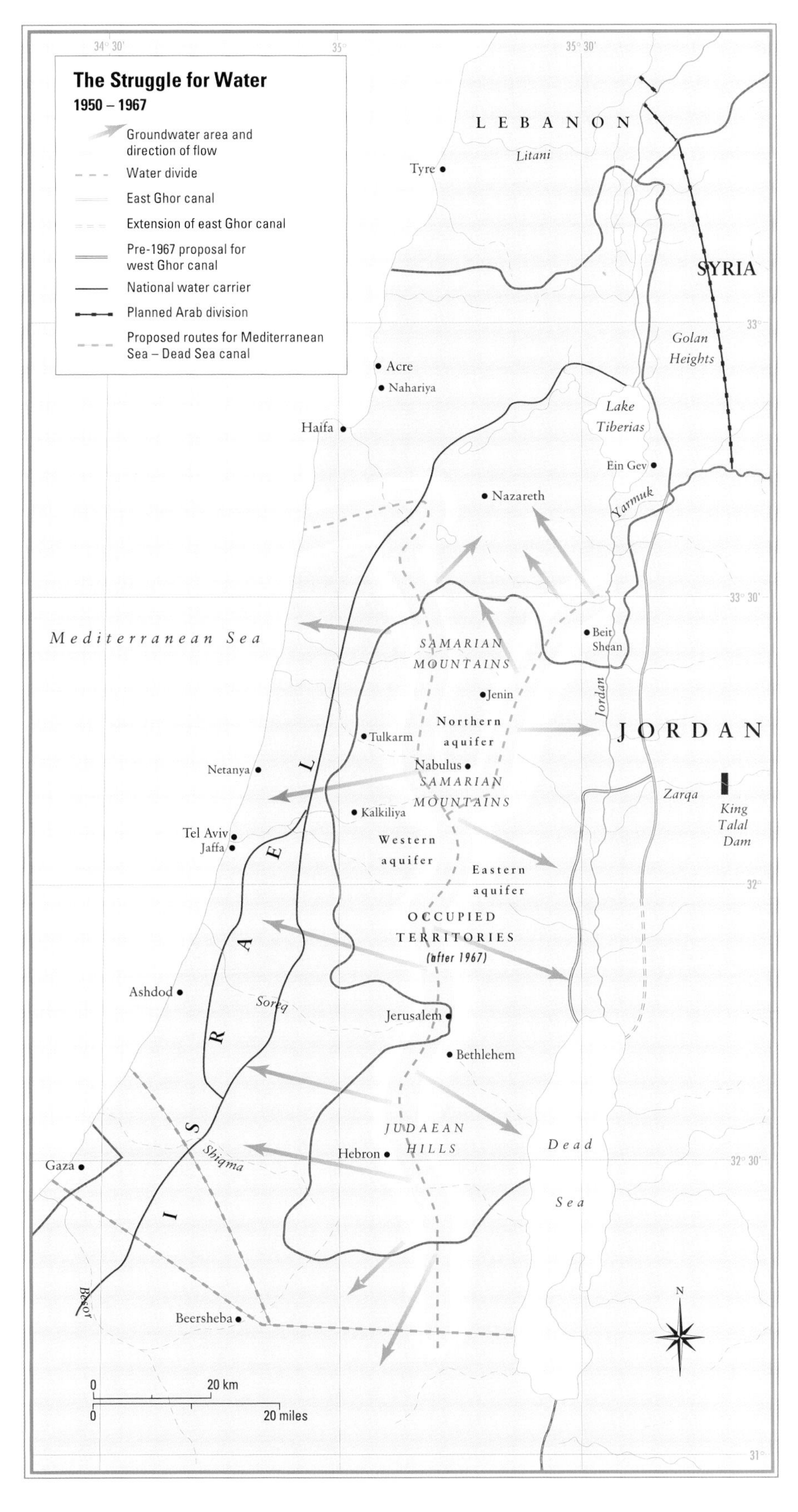

The Arms Trade

The main elements of modern armed forces are the types of weapons used, the sources of supply of weaponry, and the organization of people to use these weapons. The armed forces of states with a mostly Islamic population have few characteristics that distinguish them as Islamic.

All of these states have organized armed forces staffed by full-time personnel. They are arranged on a system of military structures developed in Europe in the eighteenth century and adapted to modern equipment including aircraft. For example, the term squadron was used historically to

Shaheen I, Pakistan's surface-to-surface missile can carry any type of warhead, including a nuclear device, up to 434 miles (700 kilometers). The picture was taken in October 2003, at a time when peace talks with India over the disputed territory of Kashmir were apparently stalled.

describe small groups of ships or cavalry and then was applied to aircraft. Uniforms too have a strongly European design. The armed forces of all states are infused with the culture that creates them and those in Islamic states are no exception. Thus Islamic traditions can be found in the styles and heraldry of units. Some states, notably the smaller states in the Gulf, make extensive use of mercenaries. However, this is an age-old cross-cultural practice still found elsewhere in, for example, the UK's units of Nepalese Ghurkhas and the French Foreign Legion. Similarly, some Islamic states have created elite units closely associated with the rulers of the country as seen in Iran's revolutionary guards (the Pasdaran Inqilab) or Royal Forces in Jordan, but this too is a cross-cultural practice.

The types of weapons systems include armored vehicles, planes, ships, missiles, and in a few cases chemical and nuclear weapons. All of these types of weapons had been developed in a form recognizable today by the industrial powers in the Second World War.

All of the Islamic states form part of the

developing world. None has an advanced industrial base, which means that all their major weapons systems have to be imported. The exceptions to this are twofold. First, rifles, pistols, their ammunition, and other small-scale weapons are produced in abundance. Second, a few states with powerful allies, notably Pakistan, Turkey, and Egypt, have been given some assistance in developing a manufacturing industry for weapons. Pakistan is thought to have obtained technical assistance for its nuclear program from China.

In common with the vast majority of states, Islamic nations from Morocco to Indonesia are nowadays mostly within the orbit of the US. Consequently such states tend to train and organize along US lines. This is continuing to replace earlier British, French, and Russian influence except in the cases of Syria and Libya where Soviet era weapons and organization are quite noticeable. Iran is perhaps exceptional in developing an independent center of military practice but this is still in a weak and early state. Some members of the Iranian government have proclaimed nuclear weapons un-Islamic. While similar sentiments are expressed in Christian states, it is hard to find them inside government.

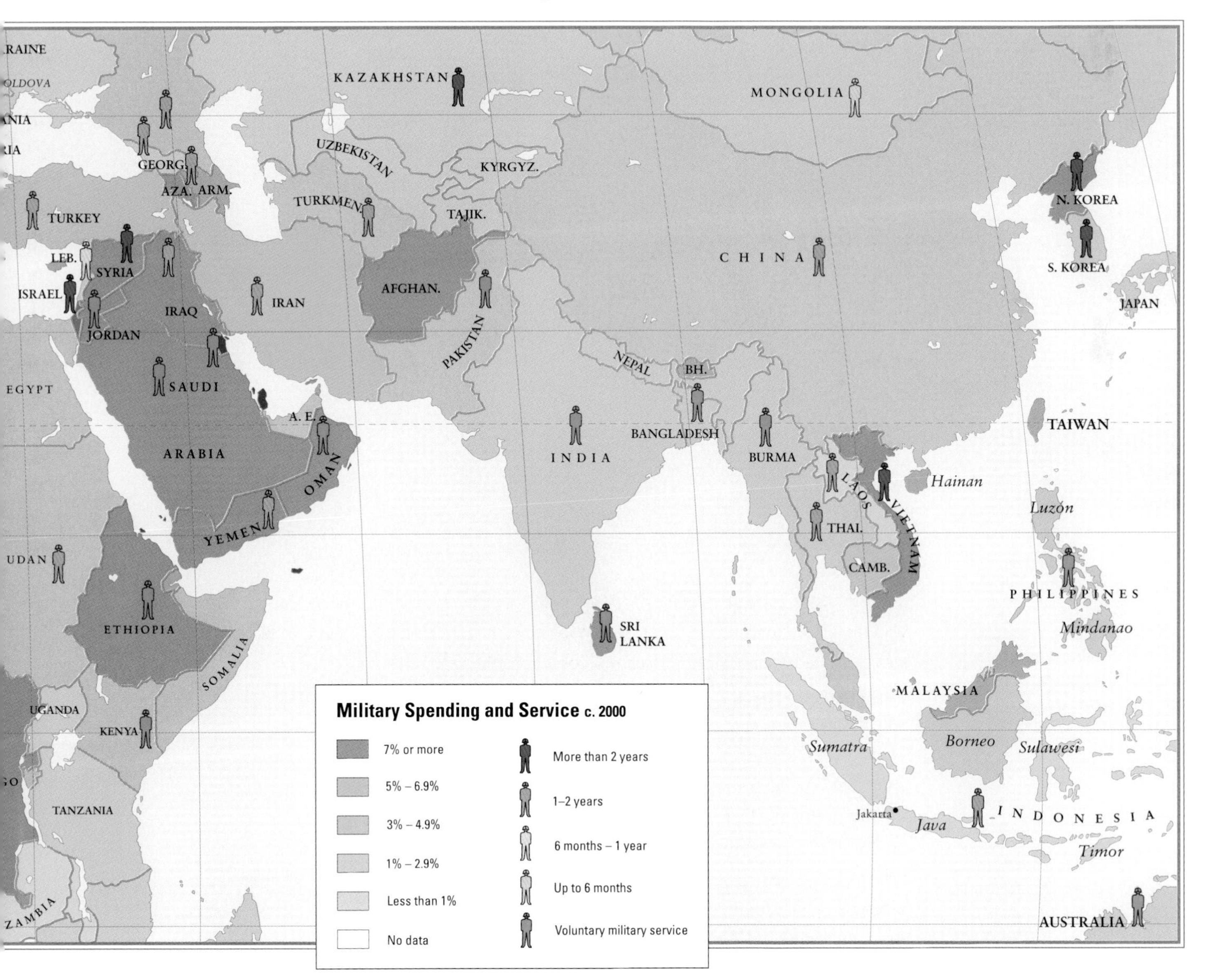

Flashpoint Southeast Asia 1950–2000

Young girls in Acheh, Indonesia, learning the Koran. Historically a center of Muslim resistance to Dutch colonial rule, Acheh is the only Indonesian province where the Sharia has been reintroduced as the basis of public law.

The late 1940s and 50s saw the emergence of a diverse set of nations in Southeast Asia. At present, the region is comprised of the Republic of Indonesia, Federation of Malaysia, and the Sultanate of Brunei, where Muslims are a majority, and the Republics of Singapore and the Philippines, Myanmar (the Socialist Republic of the Union of Burma), the Kingdom of Thailand, the Lao People's Democratic Republic (Laos), the People's Republic of Kampuchea (Cambodia), and the Socialist Republic of Vietnam, where Muslims are minorities.

Muslim involvement in the formation and development of a number of these nations over the past fifty years has been diverse. It has been punctuated, in part, by a series of flashpoints involving Muslims of different orientations and aspirations.

The formation of the Republic of Indonesia in 1949–50 saw uprisings (1948 and 1953) of many Muslims in western Java, southern Sulawesi, and Acheh (northern Sumatra), whose leaders disagreed about the decision to limit the role of Islam in the new republic. In recent years, Indonesia has seen a series of local, regional, and international conflicts involving Muslims. Between 1999 and 2000, conflicts between Muslims and Christians broke out on the eastern Indonesian islands of Maluku and South Sulawesi. In October 2002, bombs (allegedly planted by members of the international terrorist group, al-Qaeda) exploded in a nightclub on Bali, leaving 202 people dead and 300 people injured.

Malaysia gained its independence in 1957 and formed a federation between Malaya, Singapore, Sabah, and Sarawak. Singapore seceded from the federation in 1966 and espouses a multiethnic religious policy of governance. In contrast, Islam is the

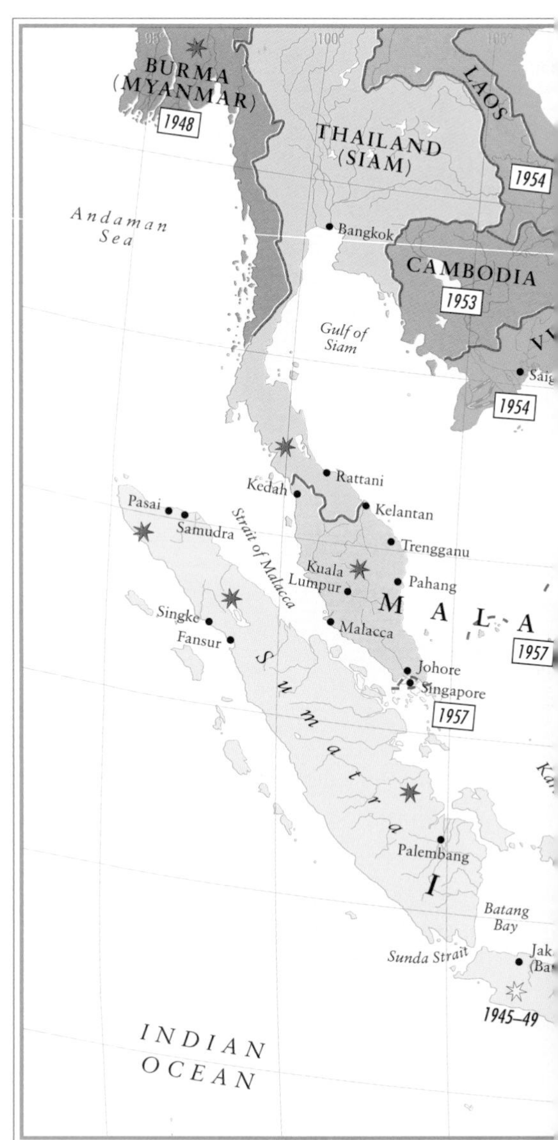

state religion of Malaysia. Since before its founding, there were recurrent tensions in Malaysia between its Chinese and Malay populations, which erupted into the race riots that took place in 1969. Insofar as Malays are Muslim and constitute a majority, such intercommunal conflicts have a religious dimension. But Malaysia is also witness to intracommunal tensions in which Muslims continue to debate the nature and extent of Islam's role in the matters of governance.

In the Philippines, Muslims (often referred to as Moros) reside mostly on Mindanao and the Sulu archipelago. The early 1970s saw Muslims calling for separation from the Philippine state and the establishment of an autonomous homeland for Philippine Muslims. Successive Philippine governments have attempted to broker settlements with Muslims in the region. Muslims in Thailand are primarily located in Satun in northwestern Thailand, and the southern provinces of Pattani, Yola, and Narithiwat, which border Malaysia. Muslim resistance to the Thai state in the form of armed struggles and separatist calls reached their climax in the 1990s. Muslims in Myanmar (Burma) mostly reside in Arakan on the Myanmar border with Bangladesh, and have been in continual conflict with Myanmar since the 1950s about their status.

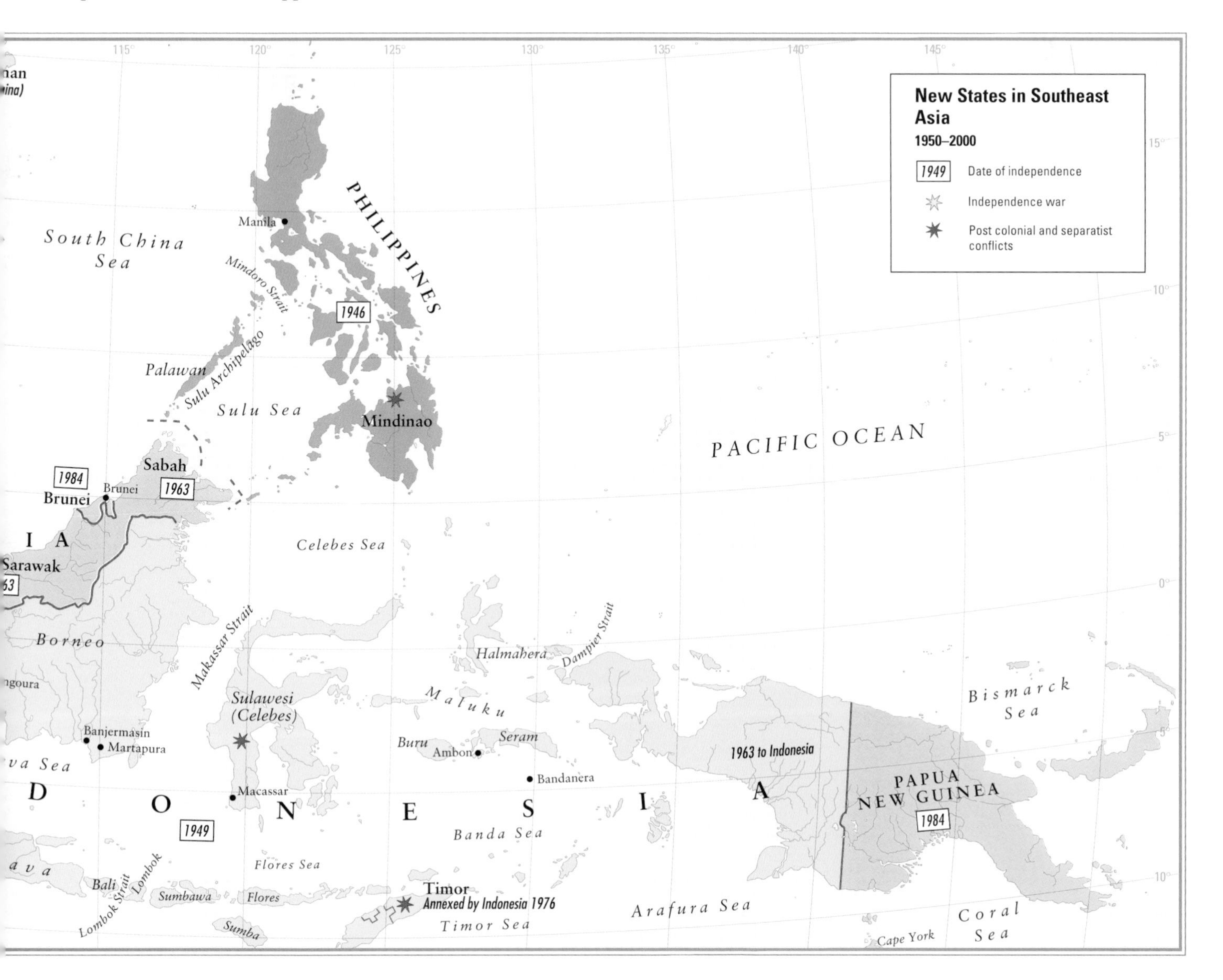

Flashpoint Iraq 1917–2003

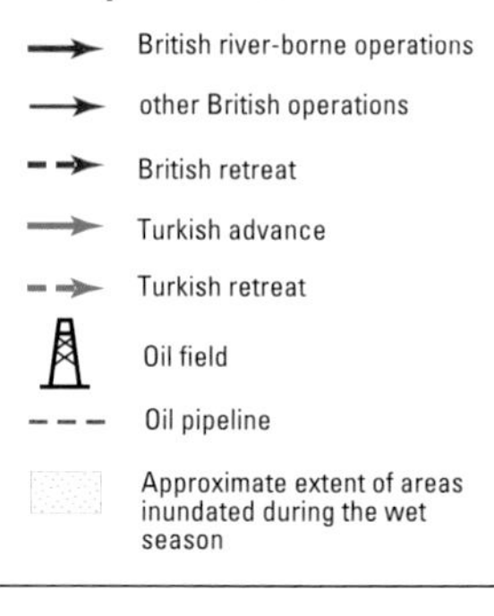

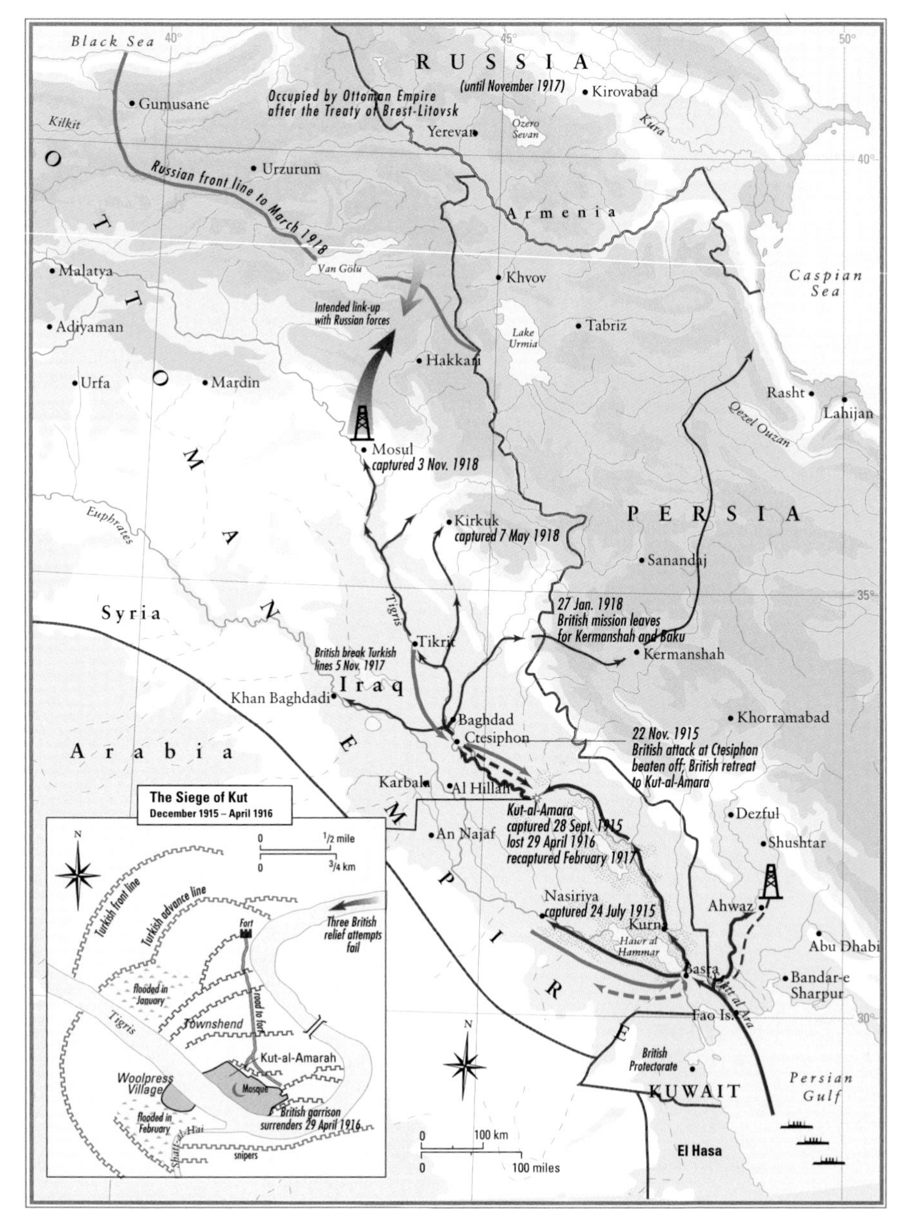

Like the majority of Arab states, Iraq became an independent state after the breakup of the Ottoman Empire at the end of the First World War. From its beginnings it faced problems in creating an integrated sense of national identity. Though ruled by Ottoman governers adhering to the Sunni tradition, the majority of the Arab population (about 60 percent) were Shias with strong religious and cultural ties to neighboring Iran, where Shiism has been the state religion since the sixteenth century. About one-quarter of the population (based mainly in the north) was Kurdish. During the last years of Ottoman rule a movement for autonomy fueled by Arab nationalist sentiment had developed among Ottoman army officers and urban notables. When Britain, which had captured Baghdad in 1917 and installed a military government based in Basra, was awarded a mandate for Iraq at the San Remo Conference in 1920, it faced a series of revolts by Ottoman officials, landowners, tribal chiefs, Sunni and Shia ulama, and army officers. The British response was to establish a constitutional monarchy under Faisal ibn Hussein, son of the Sharif of Mecca whom the French had removed from his throne in Damascus. The British mandate ended in 1932 when Iraq was admitted to the League of Nations, but Britain retained its airbases at Shuaiba and Habbaniya, and a controlling interest in the IPC (Iraqi Petroleum Company), which started exporting oil in 1934. Though the Iraqi elite was included in the government it remained divided between different factional and tribal interests, while the troubles in Palestine caused by Jewish immigration fueled nationalist sentiments and anti-British feelings. A pro-Axis *coup d'étât* by a group of nationalist officers known as the Golden Square led to a second British occupation of Baghdad and Basra in 1941.

The tensions caused by the 1956 Suez crisis and Iraq's adherence to the pro-Western Baghdad Pact (including Turkey, Iran, and Pakistan) aimed at containing Soviet power surfaced in the revolution that, with communist support, overthrew the monarchy in 1958. However the new military government was itself replaced in 1963 (and again in 1968) by officers belonging to the secular-oriented Baath (Renaissance) Party. Under Saddam Hussein al-Tikriti (vice president to General Hasan al-Bakri and the regime's effective "strong man" long before he formally assumed the presidency in 1979) the al-Bu Nasr clan from Tikrit effectively used the East European-style Baath Party apparatus to build a formidable network of power based on a combination of patronage and coercion. The regime proved remarkably durable. It took steps toward creating a sense of Iraqi national identity based on the Arab-Muslim and pre-Islamic Mesopotamian heritage, with archaeology, folklore, poetry, and the arts enlisted to enhance Iraqi distinctiveness. The Kurds were ruthlessly suppressed, with some 1,000 villages destroyed and thousands of civilians killed by chemical gas. The Shia for the most part supported the government during the disastrous war with Iran (1980–89), although there was significant opposition from the Dawa movement founded by the murdered Ayatollah Baqr al-Sadr in the 1960s. After coalition forces drove the Iraqis out of Kuwait in 1991, a Shia rebellion in a number of southern cities including Basra, Najaf, and Karbala, was ruthlessly suppressed—despite the presence of US forces in the area. In its drive to stamp out the last vestiges of opposition the government then proceeded to drain the southern marshlands inhabited by the Shia. The Kurds, however, were protected by Allied air power.

Contrary to expectations, the regime of UN sanctions imposed on Iraq after the invasion of Kuwait merely served to strengthen its purchase over Iraqi society, enriching the networks controlled by Saddam Hussein and his sons through the monopoly they obtained over illegal oil exports and the UN-approved "oil for food" program. The destruction of the regime following the Anglo-American attack on Iraq, in March 2003, was completed with the capture of Saddam Hussein in December. It was far from clear, however, if the Americans would succeed in their stated purpose of installing a democractic system of government acceptable to all sections of the Iraqi population.

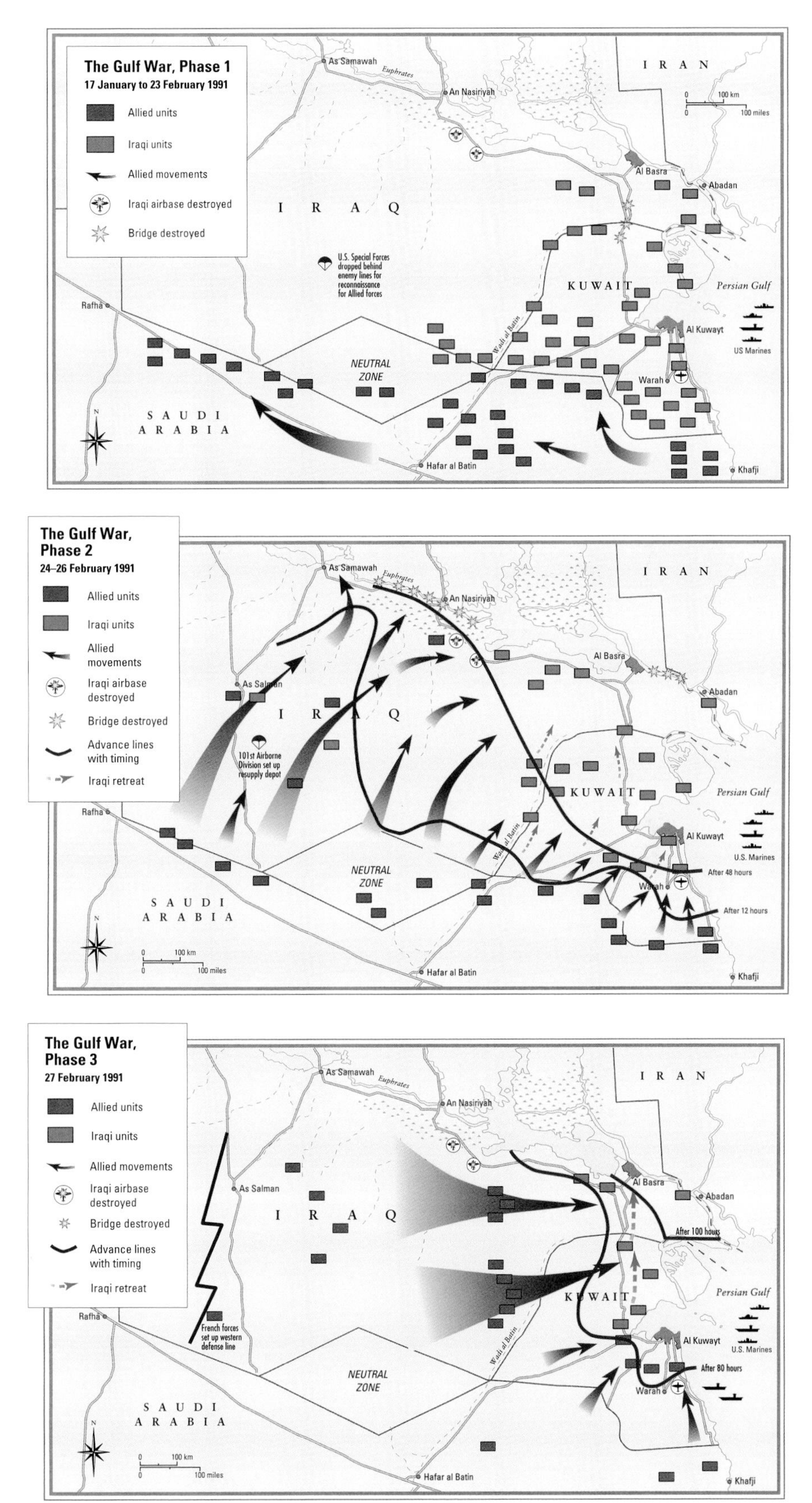

Afghanistan 1840–2002

An Afghan mujahid (warrior) carries a shell to the frontline. Later they were to receive the Stinger Surface-to-Air missile. This weapon, though light and portable, contained sophisticated target-seeking electronics. Secretly supplied to the mujahidin via the Pakistani intelligence services (ISI), it had a devastating impact on the Soviet occupation by enabling relatively untrained tribesmen to bring down helicopter gunships.

A mountainous region with deep valleys, deserts, and arid plateaus, Afghanistan has never been a single political entity although parts of it were incorporated into the Pushtun Empire founded by Ahmad Shah Durrani (r. 1747–72). The population is extremely varied, with that largest ethnolinguistic grouping, the Pushtuns, comprising about 47 percent. This group is concentrated in the southern belt of the territory that straddles the border with Pakistan, with Tajiks, the second-largest group (comprising 35 percent) living mainly in the north, along with Uzbeks, Turkmen, and Kirghiz (8 percent), and the Imami Shia Hazaras (7 percent).

The disintegration of the Durrani Empire into fratricidal strife in the nineteenth century opened the way for Russian and British penetration. Britain's concern to protect its empire from Russian encroachments prompted its two invasions of Afghanistan in 1839–42 and 1879–80. Needing a strong central government to consolidate Afghanistan as a buffer state against the Russians Britain installed the "Iron Amir," Abd al-Rahman Khan (r. 1880–1901). He consolidated his power over the country by waging jihad against the Shia and forcibly converting the indigenous non-Muslim "infidels" of Kafiristan. Departing with precedent he claimed to rule by divine right rather than tribal delegation. Non-Pushtuns were discriminated against and suffered oppressive taxation.

Elements of the modern state, however, were also introduced, with a centralized army used to repress rebellious tribes and the government organized into separate departments of state. During the reign of Abd al-Rahman's son Habibullah (r. 1901–19) the army was professionalized and modern education introduced. Habibullah's son Amanullah (r. 1919–29) pushed the process of modernization further by enacting sweeping legislative changes, including the abolition of slavery. He began to allow the education of women and brought about changes in their status including almost equal rights in marriage, divorce, and inheritance. He also introduced Western dress at court. The reforms provoked a rebellion by the conservative ulama and chieftains affiliated to the Naqshbandi order and Amanullah was forced into exile in 1929.

The Pushtun military leader Nadir Shah (r. 1929–33) took over from Amanullah and his successor, Zahir Shah (r. 1933–73), reinstated the Sharia courts. He rewarded the Pashtun tribes on which they depended by granting their leaders government posts and allowing rampant discrimination against non-Pushtuns in the allocation of resources. At the same time the program of modernization was resumed in a modified form, with the state taking the leading part in economic development. Under the combined strategic pressures of the Cold War and the regime's Pushtun-oriented nationalism (which generated tensions with neighboring Pakistan) an influential part of the Pushtun elite moved closer to Moscow. This process resulted in the ousting of Zahir Shah by his cousin and former prime minister, Muhammad Daud, with support from Saudi Arabia, Pakistan, and Iran. Daud abolished the monarchy and proclaimed himself president of the republic of Afghanistan. The Soviets responded by sponsoring a coup by the communist People's Democratic Party of Afghanistan (PDPA), a move that resulted in direct Soviet intervention in 1979 to prop up the Parcham (non-

Pushtun) faction of the PDPA under Barbak Kamal. The ensuing jihad—supported by Pakistan, Saudi Arabia, and the United States—attracted volunteers from many Muslim countries, including the wealthy Saudi Islamist Osama bin Laden. With the help of US-supplied Stinger missiles, the mujahadin forced the Soviet Union to withdraw its troops from Afghanistan in 1989. Far from generating a sense of national unity, however, the struggle against the Soviets served to intensify interethnic strife, as the central institutions of state disintegrated. The factional fighting that followed the Soviet withdrawal and the collapse of the Marxist regime of General Najiballah in 1992 opened the way for the radical Pashtun-dominated Taliban regime (supported by Saudi Arabia and Pakistan) headed by Bin Laden's close ally Mullah Muhammad Omar. After taking Kabul in 1994 the Taliban barred women from schools and other workplaces, massacred the Shia Hazaras, and brought Iran to the brink of military intervention by murdering nine of its diplomats.

After the attacks on New York and Washington in September 2001 by terrorists allegedly belonging to Bin Laden's al-Qaeda network the Americans removed the Taliban regime by a massive bombing campaign. The new Pashtun leader Ahmad Karzai, installed by the United States following an international conference in Berlin, is a cousin of Zahir Shah.

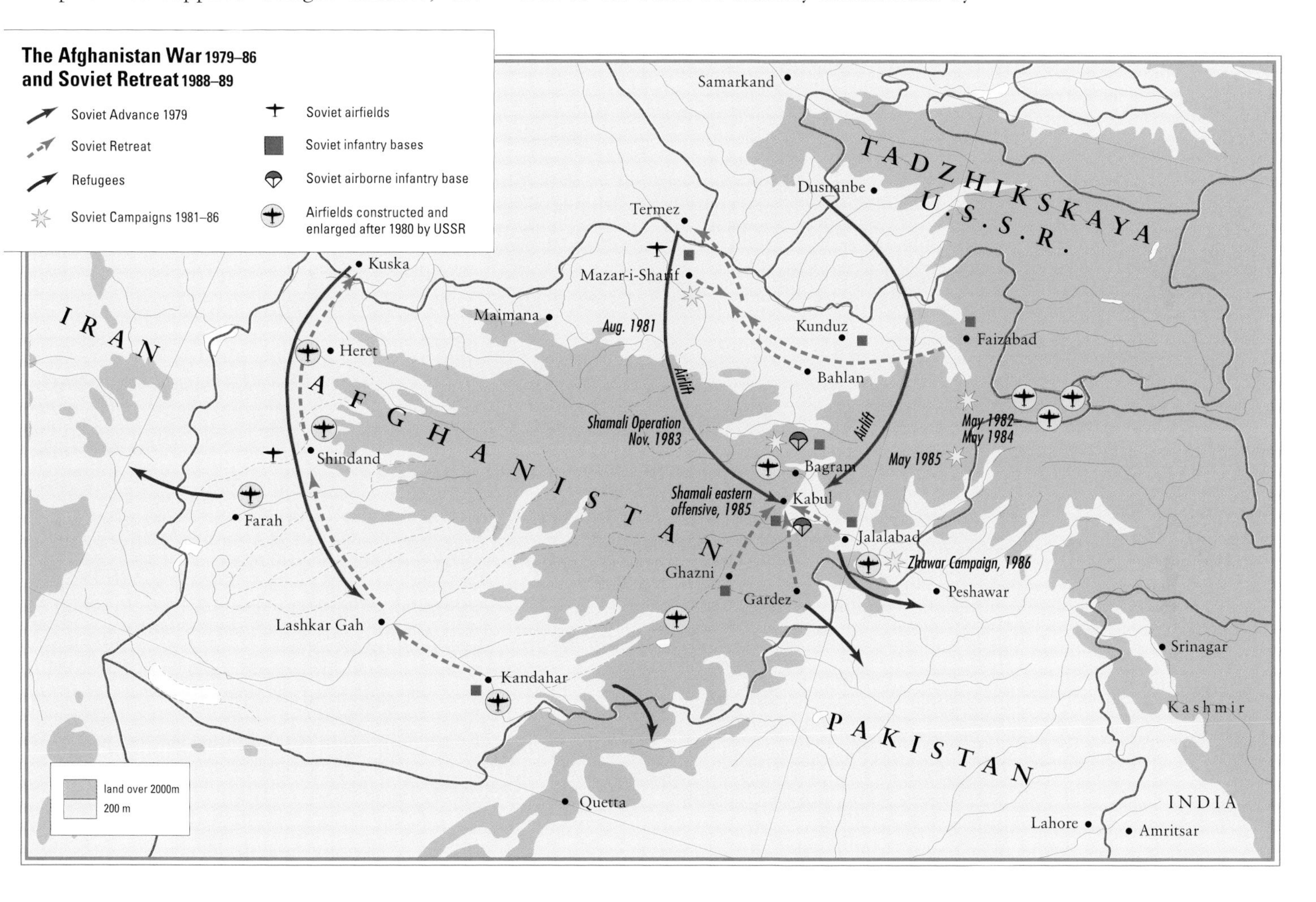

Arabia and the Gulf 1839–1950

The modern history of Arabia and the Persian Gulf is a complex pattern of interactions between the local forces on the ground and regional and global powers. The stakes are vastly increased through the presence of oil and the growing dependence of Western economies (including that of Japan) on regular affordable supplies. Until the discovery of oil the region was mostly poor (except for the pearling centers of Kuwait and Bahrain, and trading port of Muscat) and of no great interest to the outside world. Britain, however, needed to protect its Indian Empire from potential rivals or competitors, including Tsarist Russia, the Ottoman Empire, and Iran. In 1839 it captured Aden, which became a vital coaling station (and later oil refueling depot) on the route to India.

The development of Aden initiated a process whereby the whole of the South Arabian littoral and its hinterland—including the highlands of Lahej and the feuding city states of the Wadi Hadhramaut—were pacified by the British during the 1930s using Royal Air Force bombers as the ultimate sanction. The South Arabian protectorate (later renamed South Yemen, before being united with Yemen in 1991) included some twenty-three sultanates, emirates, and tribal regimes under overall British control, with the sultans dominating the cities and the hereditary class of sayyids, who claimed descent from the Prophet, holding land and serving as mediators among the clans of the interior.

Further east the Omani Albu Said dynasty under its leader Sayyid Said bin Sultan (1807–56), created an extensive Indian Ocean empire that grew wealthy on the slave trade and the export of ivory and spices from the sultan's domains in Zanzibar. Under a series of treaties between 1838 and 1856 Sayyid Said bowed to British demands to restrict slavery—providing further pretexts for British intervention. On his death in 1856 the British resolved a dispute between his sons Majid, and Thuwaini by decreeing that Zanzibar, inherited by Majid should pay Muscat, inherited by Thwaini, for the loss of revenue resulting from the division of the empire between them. British intervention in the Gulf region north of Muscat was prompted by the suppression of piracy as well as slavery. Under a series of treaties signed between 1835 and 1853 the shaikhs of Arab seafaring tribes who lived by preying on shipping (Arab as well as British) agreed to a truce suspending all piratical activity (while also agreeing to suppress the slave trade). Compliance was supervised by the British Indian Navy. The Trucial System protected pearling and also benefited Arab shipping, which had suffered most from the insecurity caused by piracy, with local merchants sending their goods via better armed and protected British ships. The Trucial States (now the United Arab Emirates) remained British protectorates until 1971, with Britain supplying officers and controlling foreign policy.

Britain expanded its influence to include Kuwait in 1896 where it established an informal protectorate to guard its client, Shaikh Mubarak, from direct occupation by Turkey. As the major power in the region Britain intervened in many local disputes, regulating contested frontiers and trying to guarantee continuity of succession. The most notable cases include the quarrel between Abu Dhabi, Oman, and Saudi Arabia over the Buraimi Oasis. This led to the expulsion of Saudi forces by the British-led Trucial Oman Scouts in 1955, and Iraq's claim to Kuwait (dating from Ottoman times when the shaikh formally acknowledged Ottoman suzerainty), which Britain resisted by sending troops to guarantee its independence in 1961.

Arabia and the Gulf c. 1900
SUBAY Major tribe
Territory under British control
Territory under Italian control
Ottoman Empire c.1900
OTTOMAN EMPIRE
Syria
Iraq
PERSIA
NEJD
Hejaz
El Hasa
Asir
Yemen
PALESTINE
Red Sea
Persian Gulf
Gulf of Oman
Arabian Sea
Rub el Khali
Pirate Coast
KUWAIT Under British Protection 1899
BAHRAIN Under British Protection 1861
QATAR Under British Protection 1916
TRUCIAL OMAN Under Brit. Prot. 1853
OMAN British Protectorate 1891
HADHRAMAUT British Protectorate 1888
ADEN British Protectorate 1903
Aden Captured by Britain 1839
ERITREA (to Italy 1899)
ANGLO-EGYPTIAN SUDAN
ABYSSINIA
(to Oman)
RUWALA
ANIZA
'ANIAARKAT
BANA SAKHR
BANA ATIYA
HUWAYTAT
SHAMMAR
DAFIR
ANIZA
UJMAN
HUTAYM
HARB
BILLI
JUHAYNA
'UTAYBA
SUBAY
AWAZIM
BANI
HARB
QAHTAN
MURRA
SUBAY
ZAHRAN
HUDHAYL
GHAMID
DAWASIR
YAM
Euphrates
Tigris
Qezel Ouzan
Wadi Sabba
Halil
Khor Baraka
Atbara
Takazze
Adana
Maras
Diyarbakir
Hakkari
Tabriz
Rasht
Lahijan
Iskenderun
Antakya
Aleppo
Mosul
Qazvin
Latakia
Kirkuk
Tehran
Hama
Sanandaj
Tripoli
Homs
Hamadan
Qumm
Beirut
Kermanshah
Kashan
Damascus
Borujerd
Haifa
Habbaniyah
Baghdad
Khorramabad
Karbala
Al Hillah
Isfahan
Gaza
Jerusalem
Amman
An Najaf
Dezful
Yaid
Ahvaz
Abu Dhabi
Basra
Abadan
Kerman
Al Jawf
Sakakah
Shiraz
Kuwait
Sirjan
Tabuk
Firuzabad
Tayma
Hail
Bandar-Abbas
Al Wajh
Buraydah
Unayzah
Al Qatif
Bandar-e Lengeh
Dhahran
Jask
Al Hufuf
Sharjar
Medina
Abu Dhabi
Riyadh
Khaburah
Yanbual Bahr
Muscat
Jiddah
Mecca
At Taif
Suakin
Abha
Kassala
Massawa
Asmara
Sana
Al Hudaydah
Zabid
Mukalla
Aduwa
Taizz
Mocha
Shuqra
N
0 100 km
0 100 miles

Rise of the Saudi State

Abd al-Aziz Ibn Saud (seated lower left) developed the Ihkwan (brethren), recruited from Bedouin tribes, living lives of extreme ascetism and total adherence to the Sharia. With this committed force, whose highest ambition was to die fighting to extend their own puritan Islamic standards, Ibn Saud built the state that became Saudi Arabia in 1932.

The establishment of the Kingdom of Saudi Arabia in the twentieth century replicates many of the features of Muhammad's original movements and the jihad movements in North Africa as analyzed by the great Arab philosopher of history Ibn Khaldun (1332–1406). The original Saudi state, founded in the eighteenth century, was built on an alliance between a religious reformer of the Hanbali school, Muhammad Ibn Abd al-Wahhab, and Muhammad al-Saud, a chief of the Aniza. After wreaking devastation in Iraq and the Hijaz, the Saud's sphere was greatly reduced by Egyptian intervention in 1818 and was briefly eliminated in the 1890s when power passed to the pro-Ottoman al-Rashid family. In reviving his ancestral state after raiding the Rashid stronghold at Riyadh in 1902, Muhammad al-Saud's descendent Abd al-Aziz (known as Ibn Saud) followed the same classical pattern of combining the military power of the tribes with the moral force of a religious revival. All who failed to adhere to the Wahhabite code were subject to persecution. Ibn Saud's warriors, known simply as Ikhwan (brethren) were organized into agricultural settlements called Hijras. These were inspired by the community founded by the prophet Muhammad at Medina in 622. Here the former nomads were given military training and indoctrinated into strict Wahhabite tenets. With the Hijra colonies located at strategic points all over the Nejd plateau, the Ikhwan could be mobilized rapidly, while Ibn Saud was spared the cost of a standing army.

Unlike the original Islamic movement, however, the Saudi state's outward momentum was blocked by the European powers that held sway on Arabia's perimeters. While Britain collaborated with Saudi expansion into al-Hasa, the Hijaz, and (with Italian connivance) Asir on the borders of Yemen, Ikhwan raids into Transjordan and Iraq were met with devastating fire from the Transjordanian Frontier Force and the British Royal Air Force, since Britain had guaranteed the integrity of the Hashemite kingdoms granted to the sons of the Sharif Hussein of Mecca, former ruler of the Hijaz.

After winning recognition from the international powers, Ibn Saud faced an internal rebellion from disaffected Ikhwan who had become resentful of Western influence and technologies. He defeated them at the battle of Sabilla in 1929.

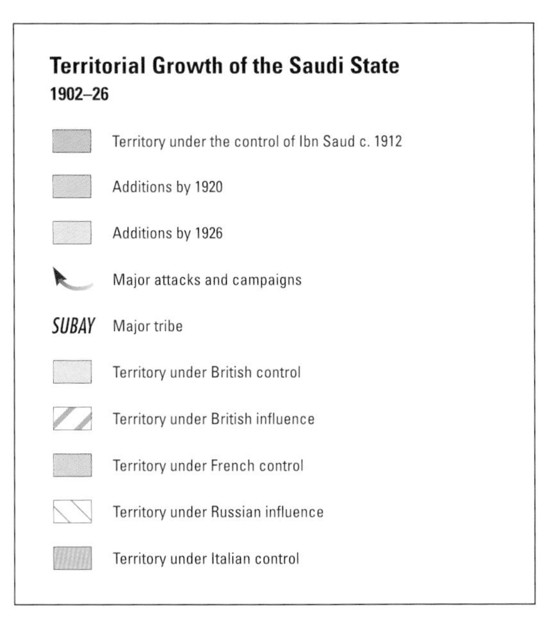

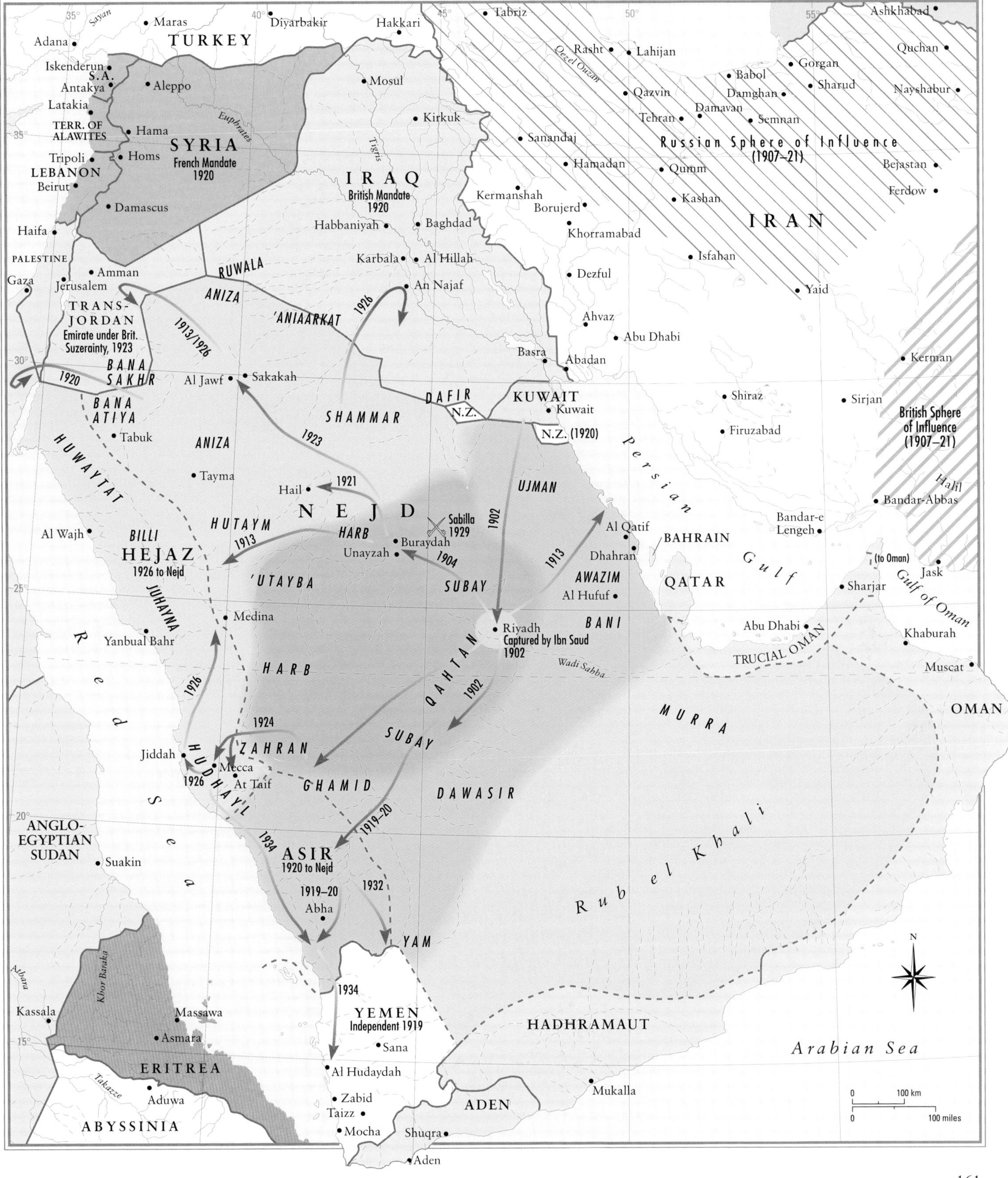
TURKEY
SYRIA
French Mandate 1920
IRAQ
British Mandate 1920
IRAN
Russian Sphere of Influence (1907–21)
British Sphere of Influence (1907–21)
LEBANON
PALESTINE
TERR. OF ALAWITES
S.A.
TRANS-JORDAN
Emirate under Brit. Suzerainty, 1923
KUWAIT
N.Z.
N.Z. (1920)
NEJD
HEJAZ
1926 to Nejd
ASIR
1920 to Nejd
YEMEN
Independent 1919
ADEN
HADHRAMAUT
OMAN
TRUCIAL OMAN
QATAR
BAHRAIN
ANGLO-EGYPTIAN SUDAN
ERITREA
ABYSSINIA
Red Sea
Persian Gulf
Gulf of Oman
Arabian Sea
Rub el Khali
Riyadh
Captured by Ibn Saud 1902
Sabilla 1929
RUWALA
ANIZA
'ANIAARKAT
SHAMMAR
DAFIR
BANA SAKHR
BANA ATIYA
HUWAYTAT
BILLI
HUTAYM
HARB
'UTAYBA
JUHAYNA
SUBAY
UJMAN
AWAZIM
BANI
QAHTAN
ZAHRAN
HUDHAYL
GHAMID
DAWASIR
MURRA
YAM
Adana
Maras
Diyarbakir
Hakkari
Tabriz
Ashkhabad
Iskenderun
Antakya
Aleppo
Latakia
Hama
Homs
Tripoli
Beirut
Damascus
Haifa
Gaza
Jerusalem
Amman
Mosul
Kirkuk
Baghdad
Habbaniyah
Karbala
Al Hillah
An Najaf
Basra
Abadan
Kuwait
Al Jawf
Sakakah
Tabuk
Tayma
Hail
Buraydah
Unayzah
Al Wajh
Medina
Yanbual Bahr
Jiddah
Mecca
At Taif
Abha
Al Qatif
Dhahran
Al Hufuf
Abu Dhabi
Sharjar
Khaburah
Muscat
Jask
Bandar-Abbas
Bandar-e Lengeh
Rasht
Lahijan
Qazvin
Tehran
Damavan
Semnan
Babol
Damghan
Gorgan
Sharud
Quchan
Nayshabur
Sanandaj
Hamadan
Qumm
Kashan
Kermanshah
Borujerd
Khorramabad
Isfahan
Dezful
Ahvaz
Yaid
Shiraz
Firuzabad
Sirjan
Kerman
Bejastan
Ferdow
Suakin
Kassala
Massawa
Asmara
Aduwa
Al Hudaydah
Sana
Zabid
Taizz
Mocha
Shuqra
Aden
Mukalla
1902
1904
1913
1913/1926
1920
1921
1923
1924
1926
1919–20
1932
1934
(to Oman)
Wadi Sabba
Euphrates
Tigris
Qezel Ouzan
Halil
Khor Baraka
Atbara
Takazze
Sayan
N
0 100 km
0 100 miles

Flashpoint Israel–Palestine

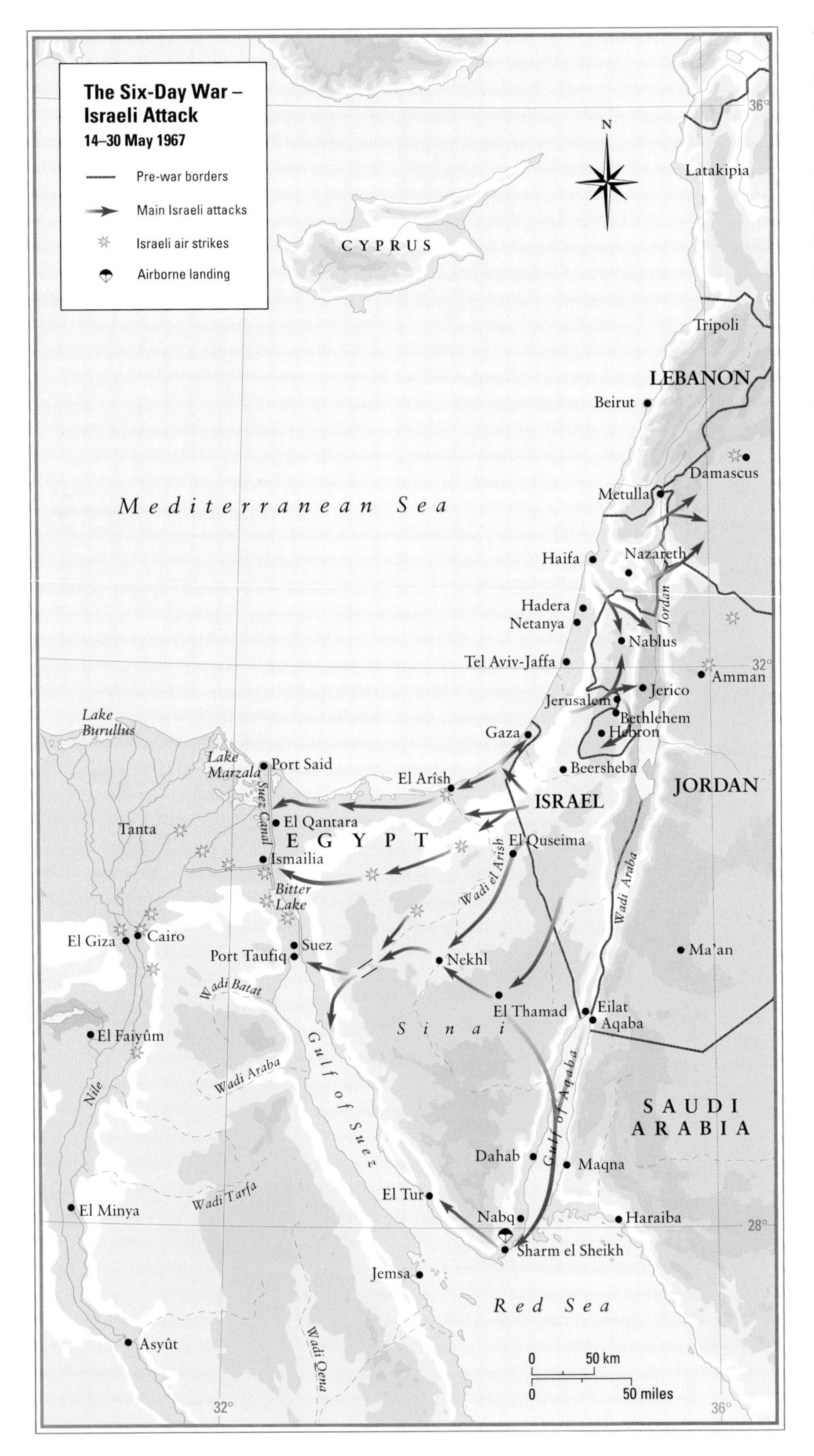

The roots of the Arab-Israeli conflict lie in the age-old yearning of Jews to return to Eretz Yisrael, the land promised by God to the Prophet Abraham. Modern Zionism built on this tradition, seeing salvation from persecution in the acquisition of land where a Jewish sovereign state could be created. In 1878, the first Jewish settlement was established at Petah Tikva. During the First World War the British made contradictory commitments to Arabs and Jews. They promised an independent state to the Sharif of Mecca, whose sons Faisal and Abdullah led the Arab Revolt against the Ottoman Turks, while allowing the establishment of a national homeland for the Jewish People in Palestine—a project that met with increasing support among Jewish communities in Europe after the Nazi accession to power in Germany. A plan for dividing Palestine into Arab and Jewish states, which followed an uprising by Palestinian Arabs beginning in 1936, was suspended on the outbreak of hostilities in 1939. After the Allied victory in the Second World War revealed the horrors of the Nazi genocide, pressure for mass Jewish immigration became overwhelming. A 1947 UN partition plan providing for Arab and Jewish states "each entwined in an inimical embrace like two fighting serpents," in the words of one official, was accepted by the Jewish leaders but rejected by the Arabs. On May 14 1948, the British withdrew and on the following day Israel's independence was recognized by the major powers. The new state survived simultaneous but poorly coordinated attacks by the armies of the surrounding Arab states, leaving it with more territory than had been awarded to it under the UN plan. Transjordan—later Jordan—gained control of a part of Palestine, including East Jerusalem, which contains shrines sacred to Jews, Christians, and Muslims. Attacks by Jewish irregulars, such as the massacre of Palestinian villagers of Deir Yassin in 1948, prompted the flight of thousands of Palestinians, creating the refugee problem which would fuel subsequent wars in 1956, 1967, 1973, and 1982.

The third Arab-Israeli war, in June 1967, left Israel in control of Sinai, Gaza, the West Bank, and the Golan Heights, with Israel subsequently annexing Arab East Jerusalem and planting Jewish settlements in the Occupied Territories. Limited military success achieved by the Egyptians in the fourth Arab-Israeli war in October 1973 emboldened the Egyptian President Anwar Sadat to make his historic visit to Jerusalem in 1977. This initiated the process that culminated in the signing of the Egyptian-Israeli peace treaty at Camp David in 1979, followed by disengagement agreements with Syria and a treaty between Israel and Jordan in 1994. The Palestinian problem, however, remains unresolved. Although the Palestine Liberation Organization, under its chairman Yasser Arafat, recognized Israel's right to exist in 1988 and achieved limited autonomy for Palestinians in Gaza, Jericho, and other parts of the West Bank under the 1993 Oslo accords, the Islamist organizations including Hamas and Islamic Jihad reject the peace process. Continuing Jewish settlements, terrorist attacks on civilians (including suicide bombings), and Israeli measures such as the creation of a Berlin-style wall between Israel and the West Bank and the targeted killings of Palestinian leaders, have made the prospects for peace increasingly difficult.

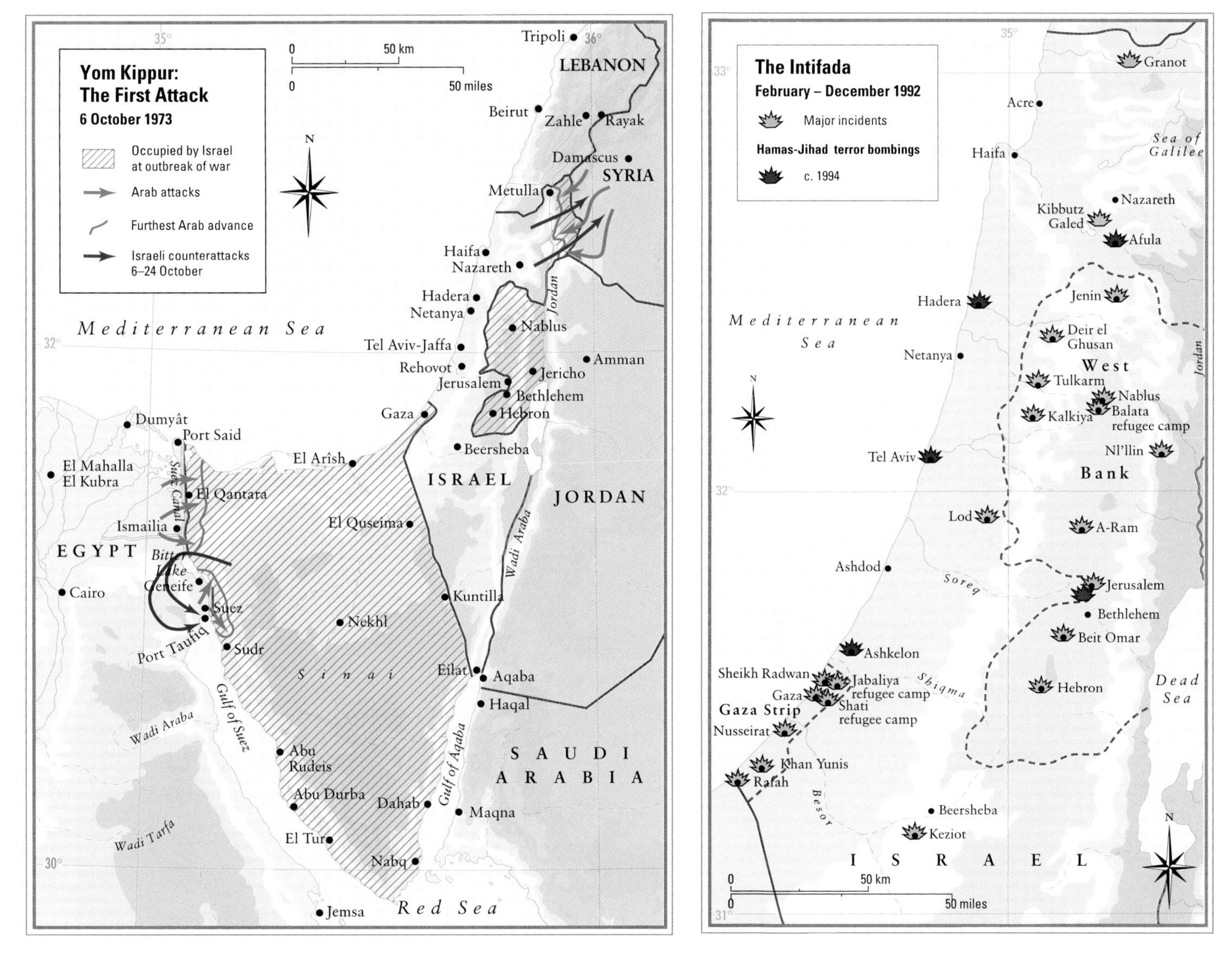

Flashpoint Gulf 1950–2003

There were several wars fought in the Gulf in the second half of the twentieth century. The three major wars were the Iran-Iraq war of 1979–89, the Iraqi invasion of and subsequent expulsion from Kuwait in 1990–91, and the war which began in 2003 with the US-led invasion of Iraq.

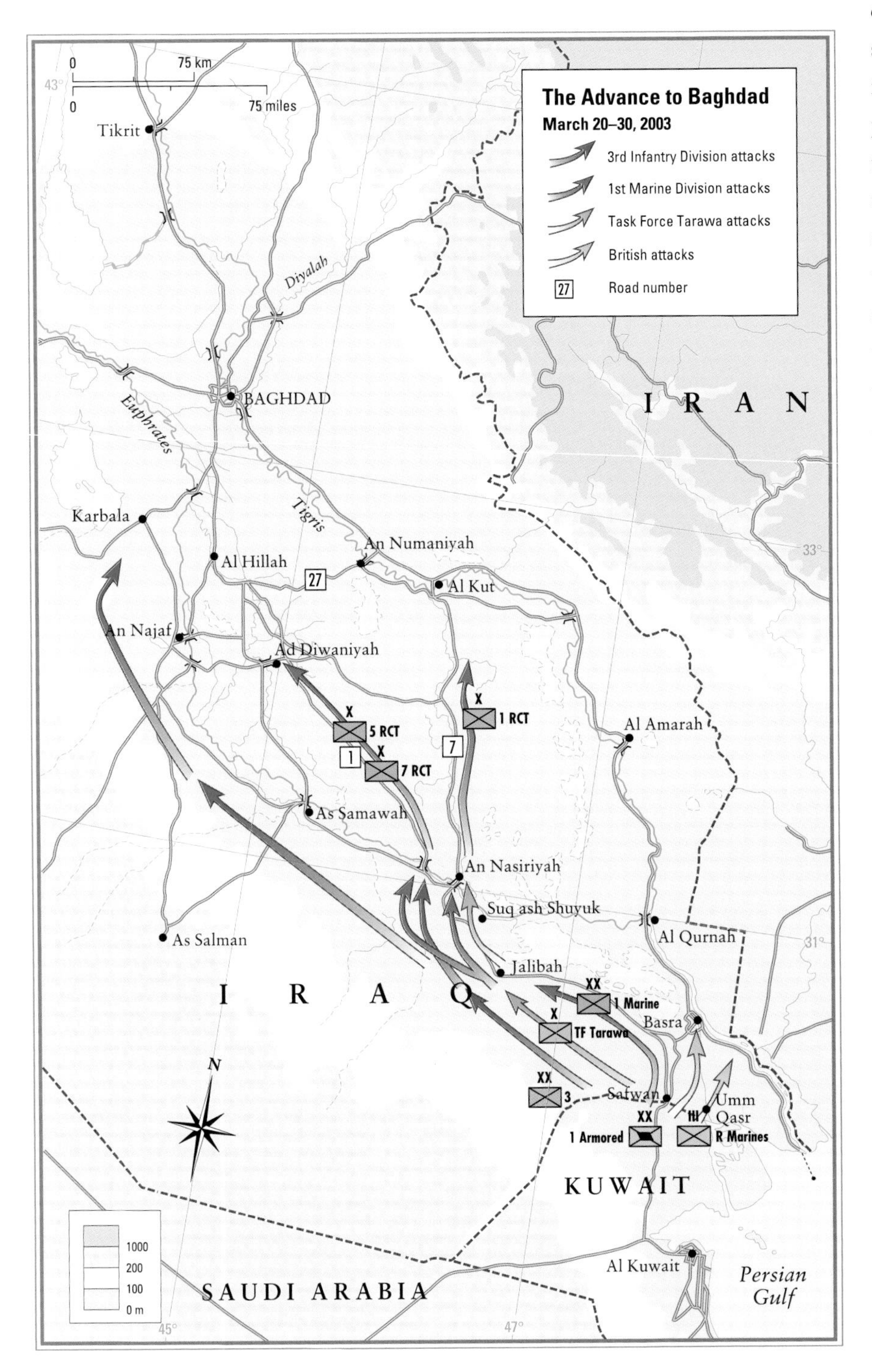

In each of these wars the motives of the combatants remain in dispute. There is considerable underlying evidence that oil was an important contributory factor. In the centuries prior to the discovery of oil the region was not the focus of major war between local states or the European powers. In contrast, the rich sugar-producing islands of the Caribbean were fought over frequently in the eighteenth and early nineteenth centuries. Oil provided the money for states in the region to acquire very large quantities of armaments in the second half of the twentieth century and these made large-scale war more possible. Saddam Hussein's exact motivation in attacking first Iran and then Kuwait a decade later may never be known. However, in both cases the prospect of a quick victory resulting in the acquisition of oil-producing areas seems to have had a part to play. Some allege that the US actively encouraged the attack on Iran as a means of curbing the recent Iranian revolution. Both states proved remarkably resilient despite the strains of war. And against Iranian expectations, Shiite citizens of Iraq put their Arab or Iraqi identity before their allegiance to their co-religionists in Iran.

The Iran-Iraq war resulted in hundreds of thousands of casualties on both sides and lasted for almost ten years. It was a war that involved all the characteristics of major industrialized warfare as it developed during the First and Second World Wars, including mass infantry attacks, trench warfare, combined arms battles involving tanks, aircraft, artillery, missiles, and poison gas. Although the Iranians protested at the illegal use by Iraq of chemical weapons the international community remained silent on the matter. This issue continues to influence Iranian attitudes to what it regards as Western double standards on weapons of mass destruction (WMD).

The Iraqi invasion of Kuwait in August 1991 was probably triggered by Iraq's poor financial condition and a misreading of the likely international reaction. Not only was the attack on a UN member state (and a member of the Arab League), it was a blatant violation of international law. If unopposed it would have left Iraq in control of a far larger proportion of the world's oil reserves than it had already. From an Iraqi perspective it is possible to argue that borders and states handed down by colonial rulers and without historical basis do not deserve to be respected. However Iraq had formally recognized Kuwait's sovereignty within its present borders in 1963. In any event the UN-backed coalition, including large army units from Egypt and Syria, expelled Iraq from Kuwait early in 1991.

In 2003, the US and UK attacked Iraq. They made claim to be implementing UN resolutions that the UN itself had failed to carry out and that Iraq presented a regional and indeed global threat from weapons of mass destruction (including nuclear, biological, and chemical weaponry). Most of the world regarded the attack as a breach of the UN's founding principle of outlawing aggressive war. The US was supported by neither Mexico nor Canada despite both nations' economic dependence on the US.

No operational weapons were found in the Iraqi armed forces and as of late 2003 no manufacturing programs of WMD were found either. The first phase of the war was completed in a few weeks as US armored forces drove to and occupied Baghdad and Iraq's other major cities. The exact nature of the battles that took place and the extent that the Iraqi regular army fought against overwhelming odds remains unclear. Despite the success of the Americans in capturing Saddam Hussein in December 2003, the coalition forces continued to be subject to sporadic guerrilla attacks.

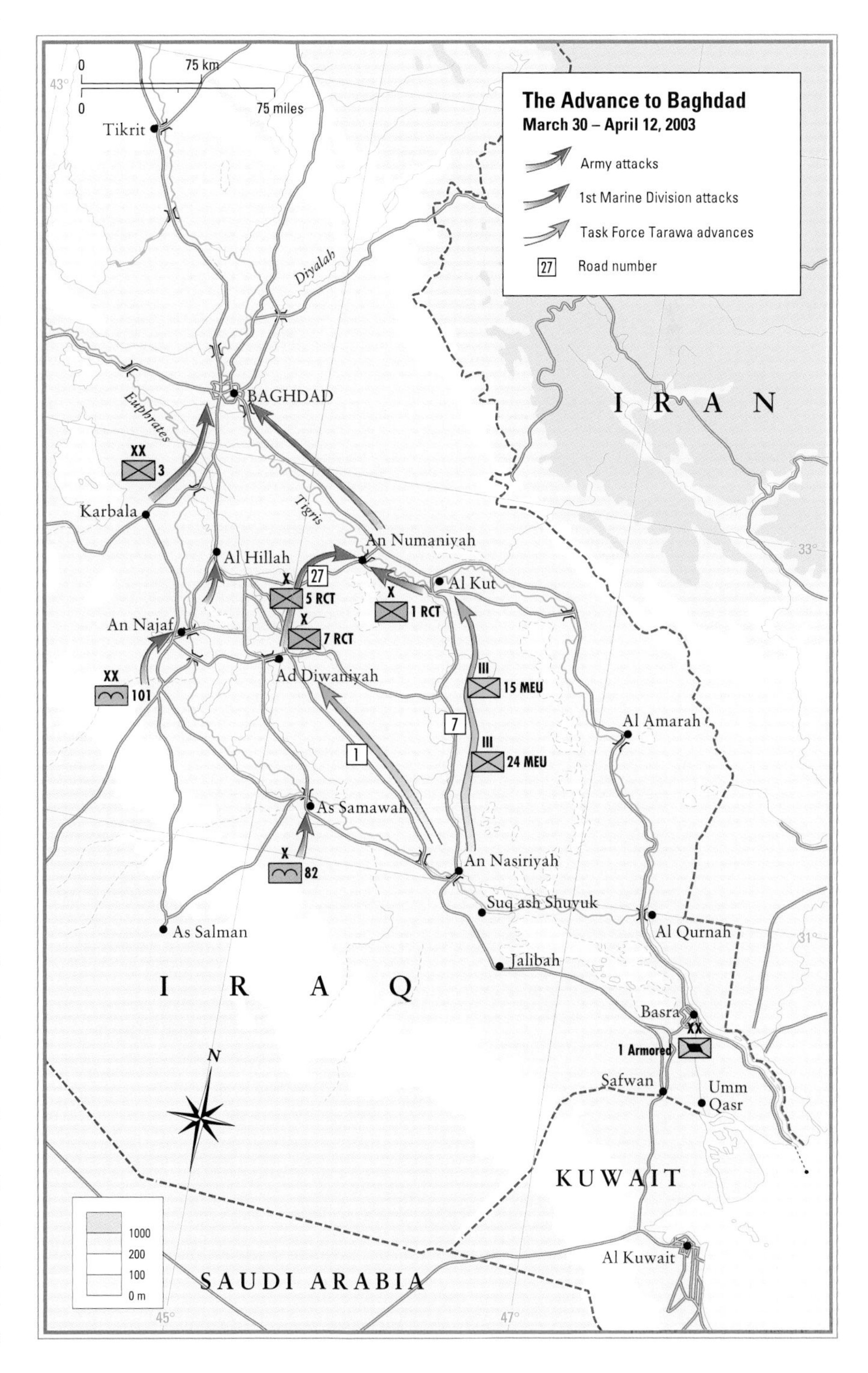

Muslims in Western Europe

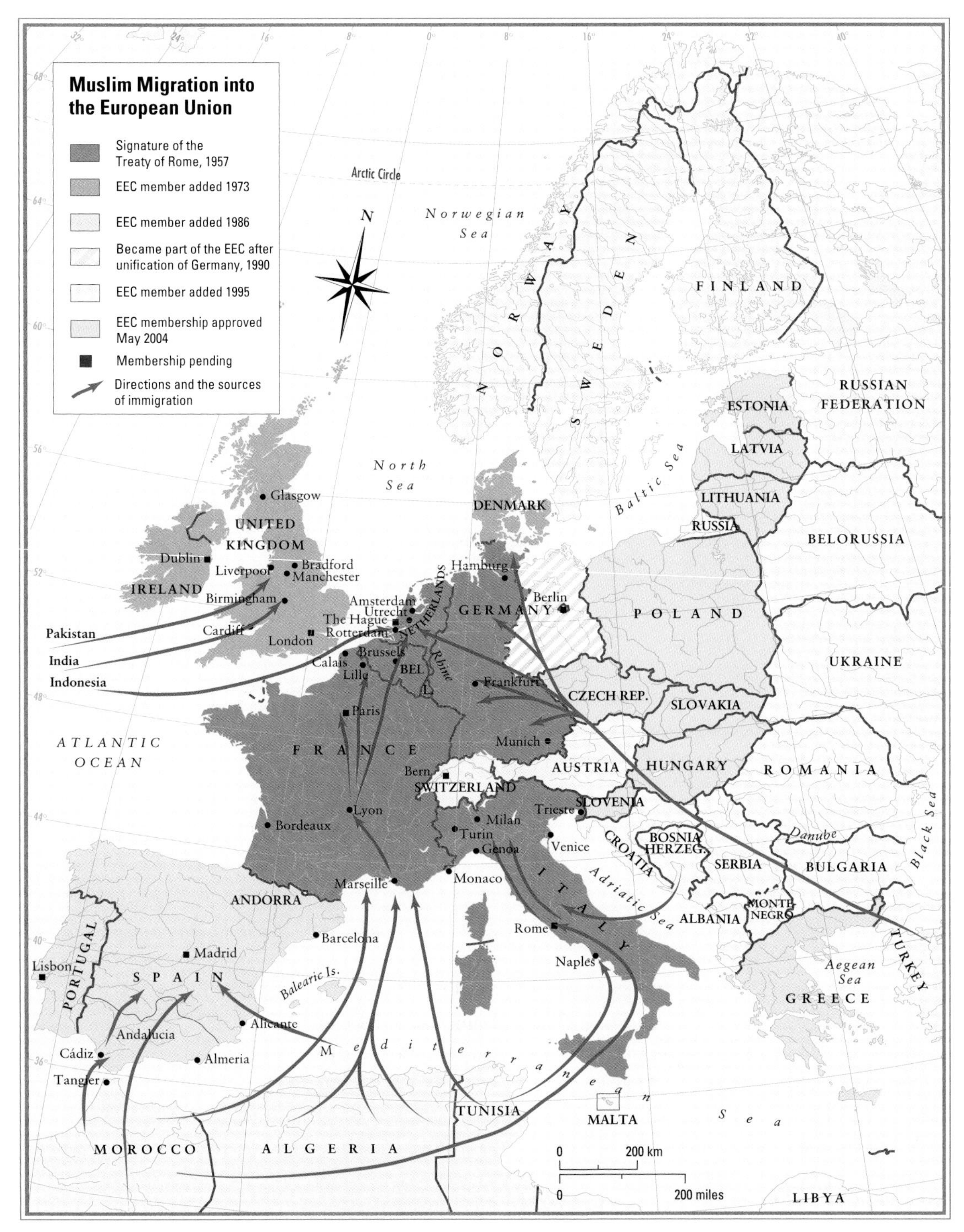

France (Paris)

The majority of migration to France from Muslim countries has been from Algeria, prior to the 1960s. Increasingly, other Moroccan and Tunisian Muslims, as well as those from western Africa, have established themselves there. Originally most migrants were male sojourners who sent remittances home, but from the 1980s the gender balance has been settled as families were established. Although there are significant communities of Muslims in Marseilles, Lyons, and Lille, Paris is the primary city of settlement. The main Paris mosque was established in 1926, but the main Muslim areas of the city were populated in the period after the 1950s. Muslims in France still tend to be focused on their countries of origin with many mosques representing this diversity. Sufi groups are particularly active in Paris, especially those from the North African traditions such as the Darqawiyya and Alawiyya. These groups attract some French converts to Islam.

Germany (Hamburg, Munich, Frankfurt)

Muslim migration to Germany is dominated by Turks. During the 1950s, Germany actively encouraged the migration of workers from Turkey. Most of the employment opportunities on offer were unskilled or semiskilled. During the 1970s, there was an increased movement of Turkish workers to Germany that led to the development of particular focused communities. During this period, families joined the original migrants. Most workers were accorded the status of "guest worker," which emphasized the official notion of the settlement being temporary. During the 1980s, the Muslim communities began to establish social and religious provision by building mosques and forming religious associations, many linked to groups based in Turkey. Likewise, Sufi groups, such as the Naqshbandiyya, have been very active and often through these groups, converts to Islam have played a significant role in the Muslim communities.

United Kingdom (London, Glasgow, Manchester, Birmingham, Bradford)

Muslim migration to the UK began from the mid-nineteenth century with settlement of Yemeni seamen in the ports of Cardiff, South Shields, Liverpool, and London, and eventually in Birmingham. However most Muslim migration to the UK has been from southern Asia (Pakistan and Bangladesh), where, during the 1950s and early 1960s, many economic migrants arrived to take up employment by invitation. During the 1960s, the arrival of families led to the establishment of various provisions of religious and cultural services, as happened in most migrant communities in Europe. London, in particular, has attracted diverse communities. This has led to a more liberal cultural and religious perspective than among other Muslim communities in the UK. Significant numbers of Arabs, as well as Pakistanis and Bangladeshis, mix with more recent Muslim refugees and overseas Muslim students. Bradford has a more homogeneous community of Pakistani origin, which has led to a less diverse religious focus. Birmingham, on the other hand, though constituting a community predominantly of Pakistani origin, has a far more diverse Muslim community that includes a significant number of converts of Afro-Caribbean origin. Increasingly, Muslim youth in the UK are rediscovering Islam as a part of their personal identity. Young Muslim women are adopting the use of hijab as a means of asserting their own identity based on self-exploration rather than accepting the religious assumptions and practices of the previous generation. As in other European contexts, Sufism plays a significant role as a religious movement, especially in attracting converts.

The Netherlands (Amsterdam, Rotterdam, The Hague, Utrecht)

The Netherlands has a diverse Muslim community made up of Turks and North Africans as well as Moluccans from the former Dutch East Indies. As the communities established themselves, there has been an increase in the number of mosques since the 1980s. Many of these mosques are linked to the countries of origin, especially those of Turkish origin, where imams are provided by Turkey. The Dutch state provides the teaching of home languages in schools, but as in other parts of Europe, religious education is provided by the mosques.

Italy (Rome, Milan, Turin)

Italy has a diverse Muslim community, predominantly made up of Moroccans and Tunisians with increasing numbers from the former Yugoslavia. During the 1980s and 90s the Moroccan community in particular established mosques and the provision of religious educational needs.

Spain

Spain, with its Muslim history, is significant as a European country developing a resurgence of engagement with Islam, especially in the south. The majority of migrant Muslims to Spain have been from North Africa, the majority from Morocco. There are also communities from sub-saharan Africa and the Middle East. There has been an increasing number of mosques established and the provision of religious education. Generally, Spanish attitudes to Islam are quite sympathetic and there is a significant convert movement of Spaniards, in particular in Andalusia. Here the assertion of regional autonomy and conversion to Islam may be experienced as the rediscovery of an identity suppressed for many centuries.

Built around 1750, the mosque in the castle garden of Schwetzingen demonstrates many Islamic architectural forms, and also includes European influences.

Muslims in North America

Muslim populations in the US originate from an early period. There is evidence to suggest that the first Muslims arrived with Spanish explorers in the sixteenth century. But the initial substantial communities resulted from immigration from Syria and Lebanon during the 1860s with further influxes in subsequent decades. The period following the Second World War saw significant numbers arriving in response to the economic and political constraints in their land of origin, including Europe, southwestern Asia, East Africa, India, and Pakistan.

The main states where Muslim communities settled were Michigan, Ohio, Indiana, Illinois, Massachusetts, Iowa, Louisiana, New York, and Pennsylvania. In Canada, Muslim communities have not been so concentrated in particular locations and are more geographically mobile. The countries of origin have also contrasted with the US with the majority of Muslim migrants to Canada originating from Arab countries, North Africa, subsaharan Africa, southeastern Europe, Turkey, Iran, Afghanistan, the Far East, and East Africa. Some originated from countries of the British Commonwealth. In both the US and Canada, conversion has been a factor in the emergence of Muslim communities. African-American converts in the US, in particular, have been very significant.

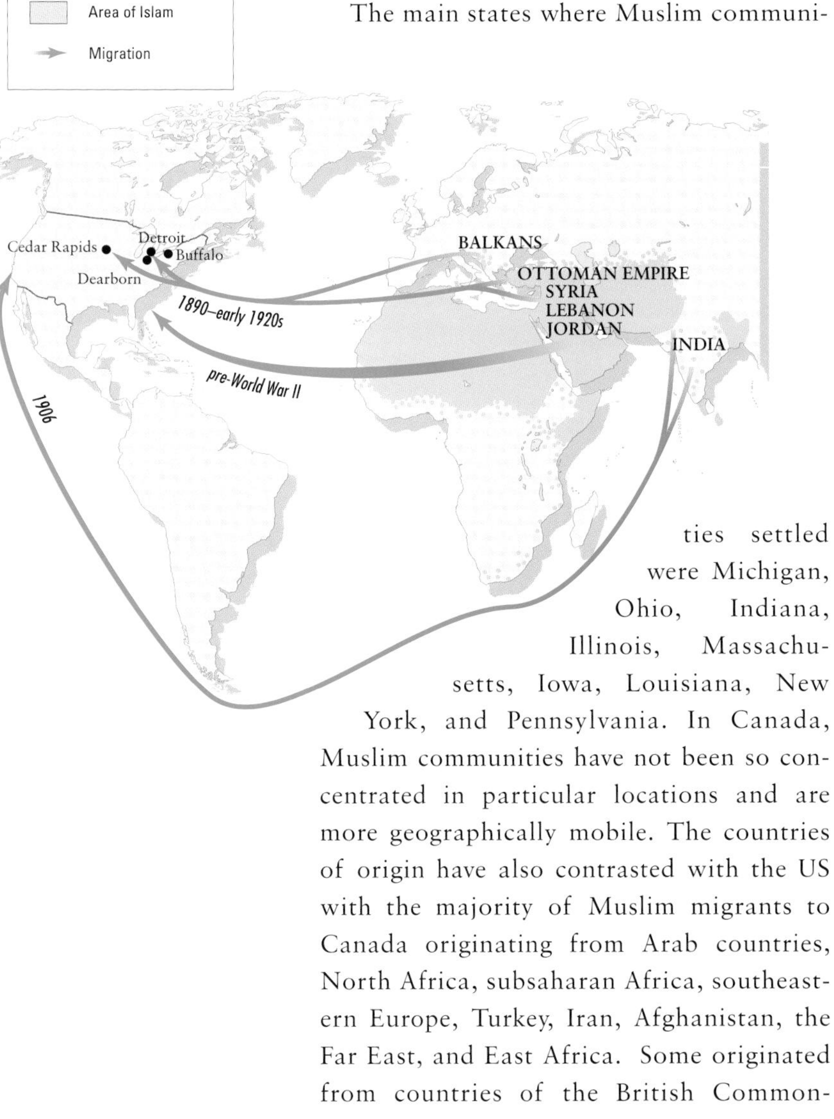

The Nation of Islam (NOI), a separatist movement among African-Americans, has not been considered part of Islam by the majority of Muslims. It remains a significant force, although since since 1976 when Warith Deen Muhammad, the son of the NOI founder, Elijah Muhammad, took over part of the movement, an increasing proportion of African-American Muslims have aligned themselves with mainstream Sunni Muslim belief and practice. African-American Muslims make up a significant proportion of the Muslim community in the US. Conversion in prison among Black inmates is particularly significant as a response to racism and institutionalized brutality, and draws on the Muslim ancestral origins of many African-Americans. White converts are not as significant in numbers, but are, nonetheless, vocal exponents of the faith, often, as in Europe, associated with Sufi movements. The early establishment of Muslims in North America has led to a period of assimilation in which, with exception of the African-American Muslims, issues of religious identity have been subsumed in cultural integration. With the arrival of overseas Muslim students and more recent migrants who were practicing Muslims, for example, from Pakistan, there has been an increase in the assertion of religious identity. There is generally a wide spectrum of religious practice in North American communities. Although many Muslim associations and mosques are ethnically based, there are also Muslim organizations that are trans-ethnic.

The Muslim Students' Association, founded in 1963 by Muslim students at the University of Illinois-Urbana, has been particularly significant in asserting a Muslim identity in contradistinction to an ethnic identity. Other umbrella organizations in the US and the Council of Muslim Communities of Canada have made significant contributions in the shift toward a collective Muslim identity. At a local level, most concentrations of Muslims in cities such as Detroit, New York, and Chicago, have provision for halal food, funerary facilities, mosques, and community halls, as well as organized educational provision for religious instruction for children. In terms of relationships with the wider community, Muslims in North America, in the US in particular, have experienced significant challenges over the last twenty-five years. After the Iranian Revolution in 1979 when Americans were held hostage in the Tehran embassy public opinion concerning Islam and Muslims began to shift in a negative direction. The events of September 11th, 2001, other attacks on Americans, and the killing of Israeli civilians (with whom Evangelical Christians as well as Jews tend to empathize strongly) have had a massive impact on Muslim communities in the West generally, but especially in the US. Community and religious leaders have had to counter the negative stereotyping of Islam as a religion of violence, while addressing the politicizing of Islam in their own communities.

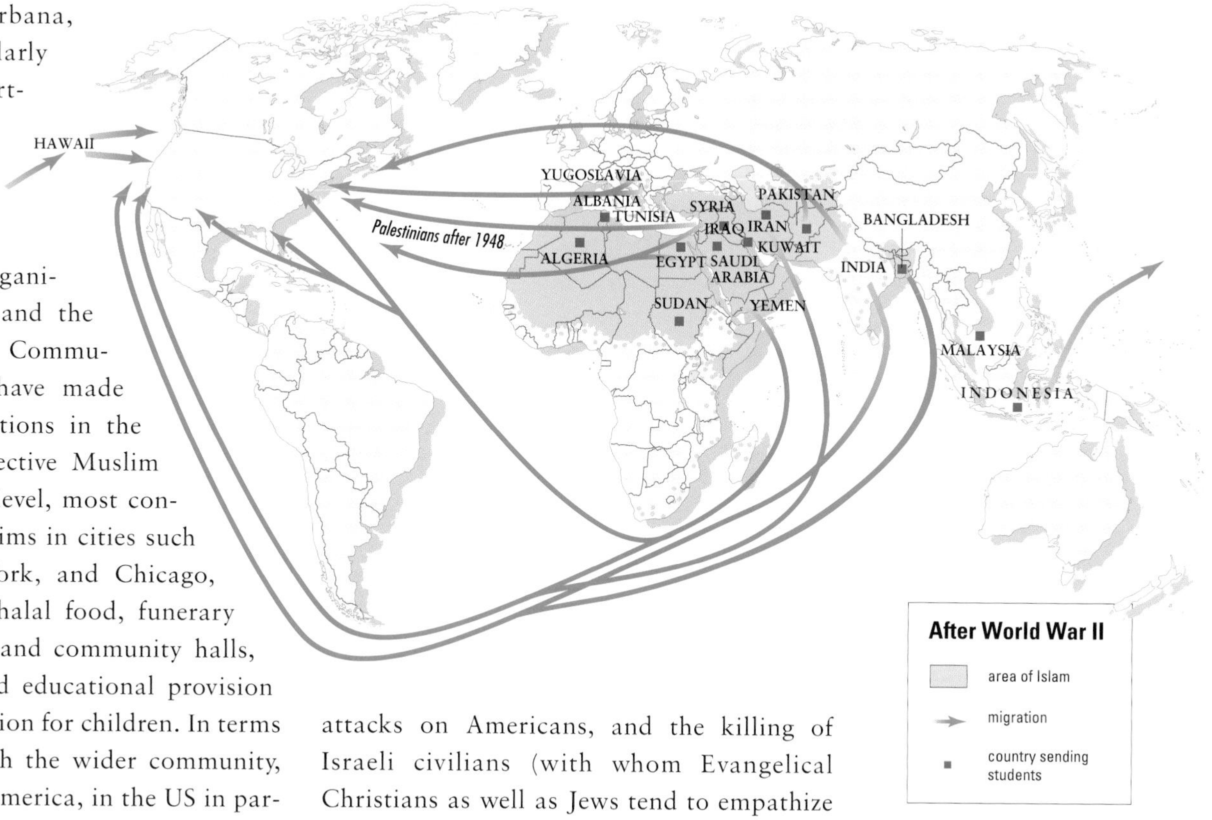

After World War II

area of Islam

migration

country sending students

The Black Muslim leader Malcolm X began his life as a petty criminal before his conversion to the separatist Nation of Islam (NOI). His pilgrimage to Mecca in 1964, however, persuaded him that separatism was wrong, and that true Islam included people of all races. Three NOI members were convicted for his murder following his assassination in February 1965.

Mosques and Places of Worship in North America

The Islamic Society of North America's Headquarters Mosque, near Indianapolis, Indiana. Designed by architects Gulzar Haider and Mukhtar Khalil, and completed in 1981, it displays a progressive, modern profile for the faith of up to 8 million Americans and Canadians. As well as a prayer hall, the building contains a library and administrative offices.

Following the establishment of communities in the US, the 1920s saw the first appearance of mosque buildings to serve the religious and social needs of Muslims. As in Europe, homes initially functioned as mosques, followed by the conversion of existing houses to serve as mosques. The construction of mosques built specifically for the purpose came at a later phase. Most mosques were originally established to serve ethnically defined communities and were not sectarian as such, the buildings being used for both social and religious purposes. Often for larger events, such as the Id prayers, public and private halls have been hired to accommodate worshippers—this has been the case in Toronto, Montreal, and Edmonton in Canada. The first African-American mosque, of the Nation of Islam, was established in Harlem in 1950.

However, up until the 1960s, there were insufficient mosques to serve the growing Muslim community who instead used private prayer rooms and spaces to fulfill religious obligations. There are now over 1,000 formal mosques in the US.

One of the largest mosques built in the US is the Detroit Islamic Center, which was erected between 1962 and 1968. The construction was paid for by the local Muslim community who formed its congregation. Grants coming from the Egyptian, Saudi Arabian, Iranian, and Lebanese governments, revealed the shift toward mosques becoming less ethnically focused in terms of congregations. In the US, the Council of Masjids has been established to facilitate the provision of mosques to serve the Muslim community. A report in 2001 showed that mosque attendance, based on ethnic analysis, included southern Asians (33 percent), African-Americans (30 percent), and Arabs (25 percent). Imams still tend to be recruited from overseas from countries including Egypt, Turkey, and Pakistan, but increasingly there are US-trained imams as more provision for imamate training is established. Some imams are also funded from overseas but most have their salaries paid for by local communities. A Council of Imams was established in 1972. Mosques are, in the main, managed by local consultative councils.

Mosques and other buildings used by Muslims in North America including Ithna Ashari Husayniyyes, Ismaili Jamat-khanas and Nation of Islam temples serve a range of functions besides being places of worship. They are used for educational purposes, such as weekend schools, children's classes, lectures, and adult education. They provide libraries, bookstores, and small publishing facilities for Islamic materials as well as providing facilities for social events, such as weddings and funerals. Crucially, they present a point of contact for non-Muslims to learn about Islam and to meet Muslims—an issue of vital importance in the aftermath of the attacks on New York and Washington in 2001. As the Muslim communities of North America evolve, mosques and other congregational centers are becoming the focal point for community initiatives.

Attendance at places of worship should not necessarily be equated with the development of the Muslim-American community in its broader aspects. A 1987 study found that only 10–20 percent of Muslim-Americans attended mosques regularly (as compared with about 40 percent church attendance for the Christian population). While some younger Muslims may be reaffirming their Islamic identities by observing religious rituals and practices, the majority of recent immigrants from South and Central Asia may be more concerned with integrating themselves into mainstream American society.

The Islamic Cultural Center, constructed in 1984 at Tempe, Arizona

Islamic Arts

A vibrant tradition of the arts flourished in Islamic lands. In contrast to other artistic traditions elsewhere, the most important arts in

Chinese porcelain was much admired in the Islamic world and its influence can clearly be seen in this Saljuq jug.

Far right: *Equally, in the portrait of Selim III, European influences can be seen in this personal representation.*

Islam are those considered "decorative," "minor," or "portable" in other traditions, such as textiles, calligraphy and the book arts, ceramics, metalwork, glassware, and the like. Most of them involved the transformation of humble materials, such as plant or animal fibers, sand, clay, or metal ores, into sublime works of art, characterized by luminous colors and intricate designs. Many of the finest objects are ultimately utilitarian pieces, such as bath buckets and serving trays, to be used in everyday life.

It is often said that Islam prohibited figural representation in its art, but that is not so. Rather, Islam discouraged depictions in all religious contexts probably out of the same fear of idolatry that other religions had grappled with in earlier times. In other contexts, particularly private and courtly settings, a lively tradition of pictorial art evolved. The walls of palaces, for example, were often painted with figural scenes; mosques were not. There, nonrepresentational decoration based on geometric, vegetal, and epigraphic ornament reigned supreme. While all figural art produced in the lands of Islam is, by definition, not religious, the converse is not necessarily true. Nonrepresentational art was appropriate and esteemed in any setting, whether secular or religious.

Textiles were the mainstay of economic life in medieval Islamic times. Made of wool, flax, silk, and cotton, they ranged from gossamer organdies and muslins (named after the towns of Urgench in Central Asia and Mosul in Iraq) to the sturdy rugs, felts, and cloths used by nomads for their tents. Cloth was not only used to dress individuals but served to define and furnish spaces in this dry land of little wood where people normally sat on carpets and leaned against bolsters. People at all levels of society used textiles. The majority were plain, but wealthy patrons, ranging from caliphs to merchants, coveted exotic, brightly colored, elaborately decorated cloths. Raw fibers were enlivened with bright dyes made from a variety of materials, which were themselves traded widely. Artisans developed an amazing range of techniques, from embroidery and tapestry to drawloom weaving and ikat dyeing, to make their fabrics beautiful.

The veneration of the word in Islam meant that books and writing were highly valued everywhere. The introduction of paper from

Central Asia in the eighth century led to an explosion of books, book-learning, and book production, with the associated arts of calligraphy, illumination, binding, and ultimately, illustration. The fanciest manuscripts were copies of the Koran, made first on parchment and later on paper. They often had superb nonfigural illumination but were never illustrated. Books with pictures, particularly copies of Persian epic and lyric poetic literature, became popular in the Persianate world from the fourteenth century, when Persian-speaking rulers in Iran, Turkey, and India established ateliers that produced some of the most magnificent books ever made anywhere.

Many of the other arts associated with the lands of Islam use fire to transform materials taken from the earth. Muslims inherited ancient traditions of pottery from the Near East but transformed them through the development of new ceramic bodies, colorful glazing techniques, and decorative repertoires. Some of these features, such as overglaze luster painting developed in ninth-century Iraq, the artificial paste (fritware) body developed in twelfth-century Egypt and Iran, and underglaze painting developed in twelfth-century Iran, erupted in a burst of creative ceramic activity unrivaled until the eighteenth century in Britain. Although the majority of production was unglazed earthenware for storing and transporting water and foodstuffs on a daily basis, fancy dishes, bowls, jugs, bottles, and ewers made in the Islamic lands were avidly collected and imitated from China to Spain. Glassblowing, a technique that had been invented in pre-Islamic Syria, remained a specialty of the Levant. Glassmakers made thousands of gilded and enameled lamps used to light the many mosques and schools erected to spread God's word.

The prophet Muhammad is said to have discouraged the use of gold and silver vessels, and Muslim craftsmen took the art of fashioning wares for daily use from copper alloys, such as brass and bronze, to new heights. Many of these trays, basins, bowls, buckets, ewers, incense-burners, lamps, candlestands,

polycandela, and the like were decorated with inlays of precious metal to enliven the surface. Those metalwares used in religious settings differed from those used in domestic settings only in their decoration, which tended to be epigraphic, geometric, and vegetal, rather than figural.

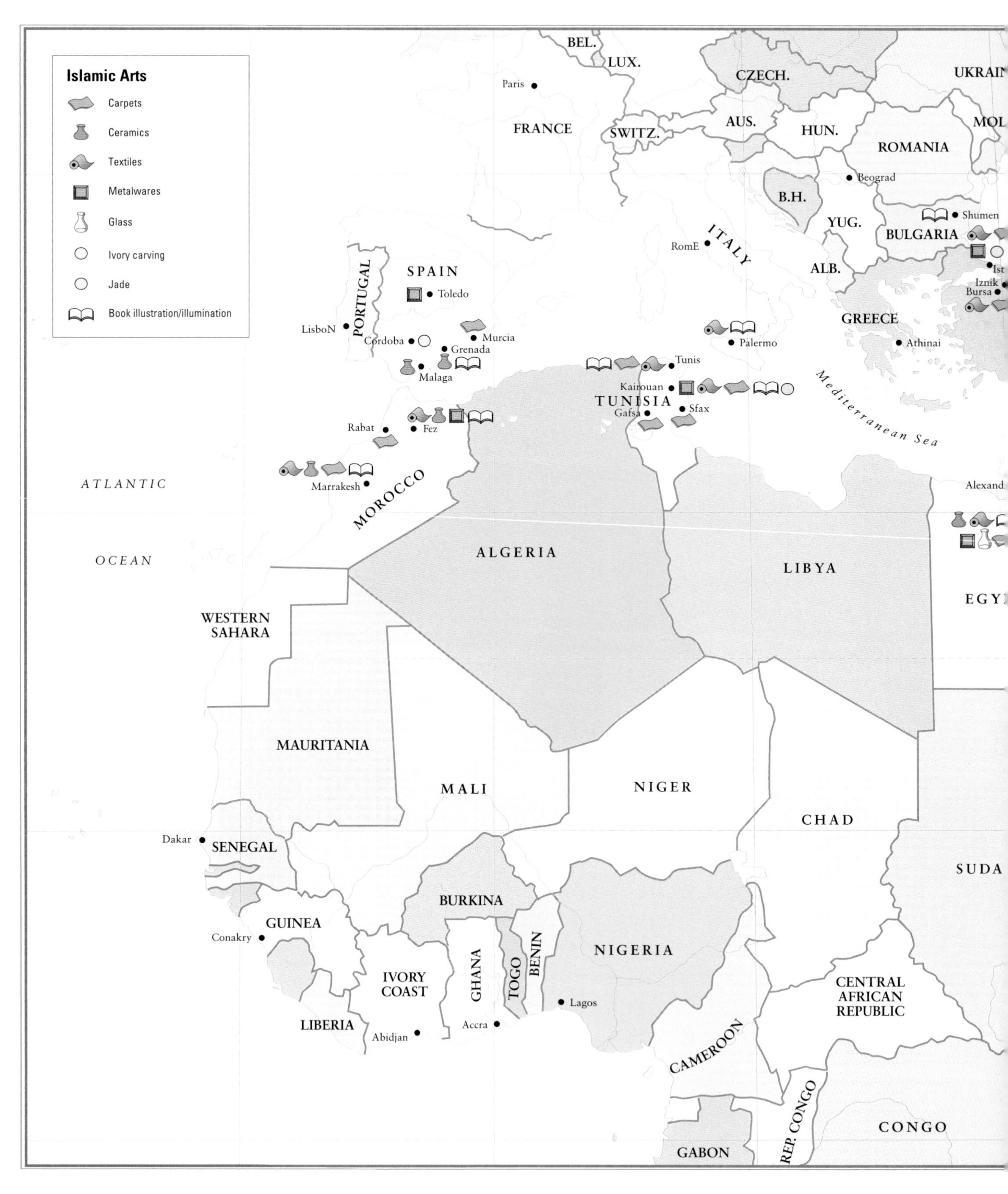
Islamic Arts
Carpets
Ceramics
Textiles
Metalwares
Glass
Ivory carving
Jade
Book illustration/illumination
BEL.
LUX.
Paris
FRANCE
SWITZ.
CZECH.
AUS.
HUN.
ROMANIA
UKRAI
MOL
Beograd
B.H.
YUG.
Shumen
BULGARIA
ITALY
RomE
ALB.
Ist
Iznik
Bursa
GREECE
Athinai
PORTUGAL
SPAIN
Toledo
LisboN
Cordoba
Murcia
Grenada
Malaga
Palermo
Tunis
Kairouan
TUNISIA
Gafsa
Sfax
Mediterranean Sea
Rabat
Fez
ATLANTIC
OCEAN
Marrakesh
MOROCCO
Alexand
ALGERIA
LIBYA
EGY
WESTERN SAHARA
MAURITANIA
MALI
NIGER
CHAD
SUDA
Dakar
SENEGAL
BURKINA
GUINEA
Conakry
NIGERIA
IVORY COAST
GHANA
TOGO
BENIN
Lagos
CENTRAL AFRICAN REPUBLIC
LIBERIA
Abidjan
Accra
CAMEROON
REP. CONGO
CONGO
GABON

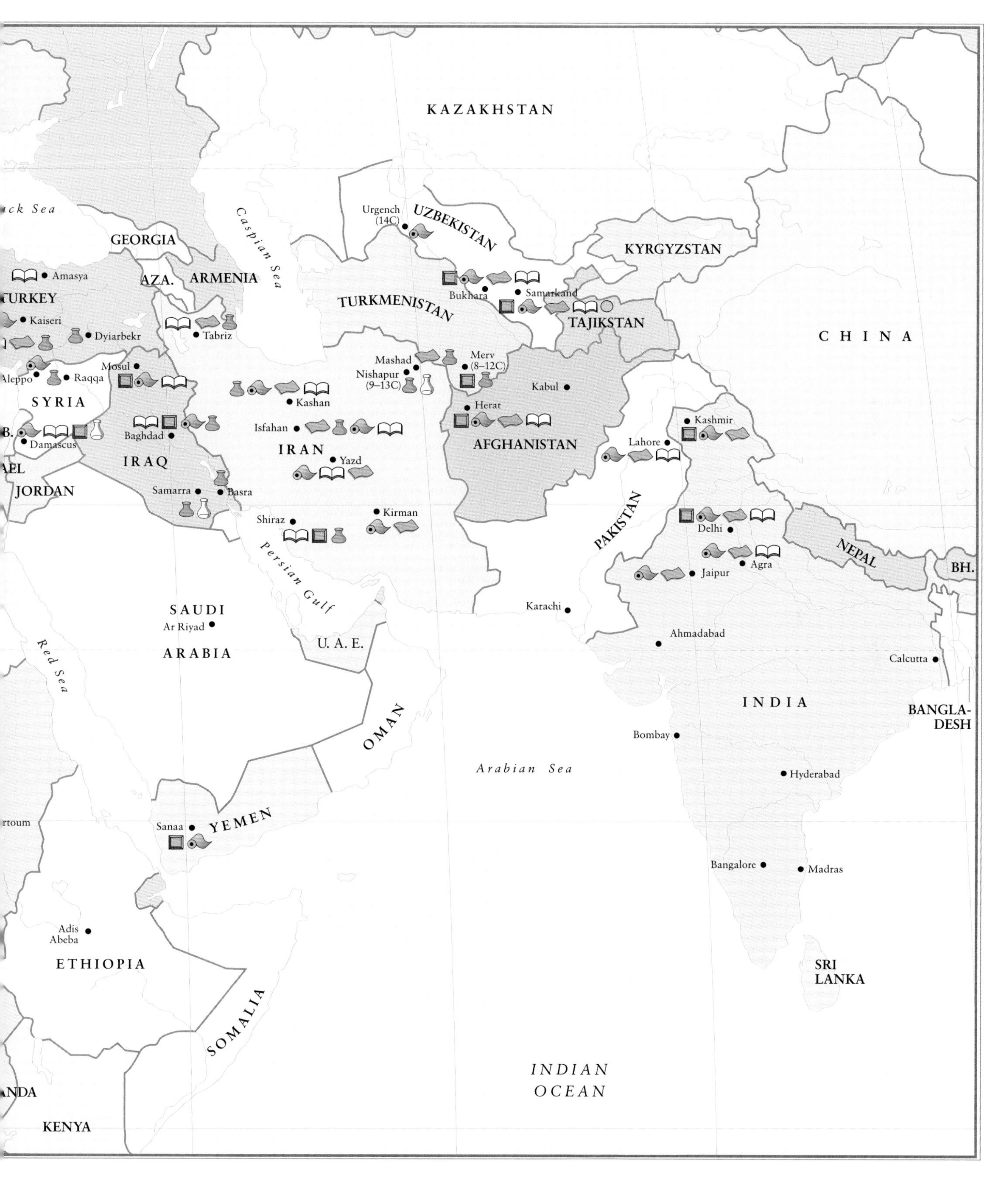
KAZAKHSTAN
Black Sea
Caspian Sea
GEORGIA
Amasya
AZA.
ARMENIA
TURKEY
Kaiseri
Tabriz
Dyiarbekr
Aleppo
Raqqa
Mosul
SYRIA
Damascus
Baghdad
IRAQ
JORDAN
Samarra
Basra
Kashan
Isfahan
IRAN
Yazd
Shiraz
Kirman
Persian Gulf
Urgench (14C)
UZBEKISTAN
Bukhara
Samarkand
TURKMENISTAN
TAJIKSTAN
KYRGYZSTAN
CHINA
Mashad
Nishapur (9–13C)
Merv (8–12C)
Kabul
Herat
AFGHANISTAN
Kashmir
Lahore
PAKISTAN
Delhi
Agra
Jaipur
NEPAL
BH.
Karachi
Ahmadabad
Calcutta
SAUDI ARABIA
Ar Riyad
Red Sea
U. A. E.
OMAN
INDIA
BANGLA-DESH
Bombay
Arabian Sea
Hyderabad
Sanaa
YEMEN
Bangalore
Madras
Adis Abeba
ETHIOPIA
SRI LANKA
SOMALIA
INDIAN OCEAN
KENYA

Major Islamic Architectural Sites

The presence of Muslims in any given area is marked by distinctive building types, most notably the congregational or Friday mosque. While the mosque can take many forms depending on local materials and building practices, it is always a structure oriented toward Mecca, large enough to accommodate the Muslim male population. Mosques were generally built of brick or stone and covered with vaults or domes. Wood was often unavailable or too expensive to use for roofing in this largely arid region, although it was used in heavily forested regions such as Anatolia and Southeast Asia. Elsewhere, fine woods were reserved for mosque furniture, such as minbars (pulpits) and reading-stands, which were often inlaid with other woods, bone, ivory, and mother-of-pearl. Mosques were elaborately decorated in glazed tile and carved stucco and strewn with pile or flat-woven carpets. These displayed vegetal, geometric, and epigraphic designs. Figural depictions were avoided in religious contexts and are found only in secular settings. Virtually all mosques have a mihrab or niche in the wall facing Mecca, and many have one or more attached minarets, towers from which the call to prayer could be given. Since mosques were normally constructed of the best quality materials available and were regularly maintained over the centuries, they are usually the best preserved buildings in any particular place.

Rulers often built lavish palaces as symbols of their wealth and authority. These have not survived as well as mosques, however, because their design and construction were more experimental. In addition, successors were often reluctant to maintain the splendid achievements of their rivals. Archaeological investigations in the Islamic lands have focused on deserted or abandoned palaces, such as Khirbat al-Mafjar, the Umayyad retreat near Jericho, and Samarra, the ninth-century Abbasid capital in Iraq. Only a few Islamic palaces have survived above ground, such as the Alhambra in Granada, Topkapi Saray in Istanbul, and the Red Fort in Delhi. Islamic palaces are normally showy but poorly-constructed buildings in which appearance and display take precedence over form and structure. Unlike Versailles or the Hermitage, Islamic palaces are typically additive structures with small pavilions arranged around internal courts and magnificent gardens.

Although the prophet Muhammad is said to have frowned on the construction of monumental tombs over the graves of the deceased, in many parts of the Islamic lands, building tombs became a major form of architectural patronage. Tombs were constructed over the graves of particularly pious individuals as well as of rulers who were anxious to preserve their memory in an uncertain world. Most tombs are domed structures, either squares, octagons, or circles, and range from the modest marabouts of North Africa to the monumental Taj Mahal. Many have a mihrab to direct the prayers of worshippers who come to venerate the deceased. Some have adjacent structures to accommodate the expected visitors and to provide public services ranging from Koran schools to soup kitchens. In this way, patrons were able to use a charitable foundation to justify the construction of a tomb.

Muslims were buried directly in the ground, wrapped only in plain white shrouds. Thus, the burial goods that archaeologists depend on for understanding other cultural traditions do not exist in the Muslim lands. The relative aridity of much of the region, particularly Egypt and Central Asia, however, has helped preserve fragile organic materials that might otherwise have been lost through burial. The most important of these are textiles, which played the central role in the medieval Islamic economy. Many of these fragments appear so unprepossessing that they are rarely displayed in the museums; paradoxically, the best-known textiles from the Islamic lands, many inscribed with Arabic blessings, were preserved in European churches, where they were used to wrap the bones of Christian saints.

Archaeological finds attest to the broad network of trade routes that crisscrossed the Islamic lands, connecting China, India, and tropical Africa with Europe. Thanks to the domestication of the camel before the rise of Islam, most trade went overland, with caravanserais often erected at 15-mile intervals to accommodate travelers, their beasts, and their wares. Some trade went by sea, following the Mediterranean coasts or the monsoon winds around the Indian Ocean. Recent advances in underwater archaeology have allowed the exploration of shipwrecks, such as the eleventh-century one found at Serçe Limani off the coast of Turkey. This site yielded a huge quantity of cullet, broken glass collected for recycling.

An enclosed courtyard of the Qansuh al-Ghuri Caravanserai in Cairo

Far Left: *A relief plaque, part of a palace built by al-Mamum, Toledo's most powerful* taifa *ruler.*

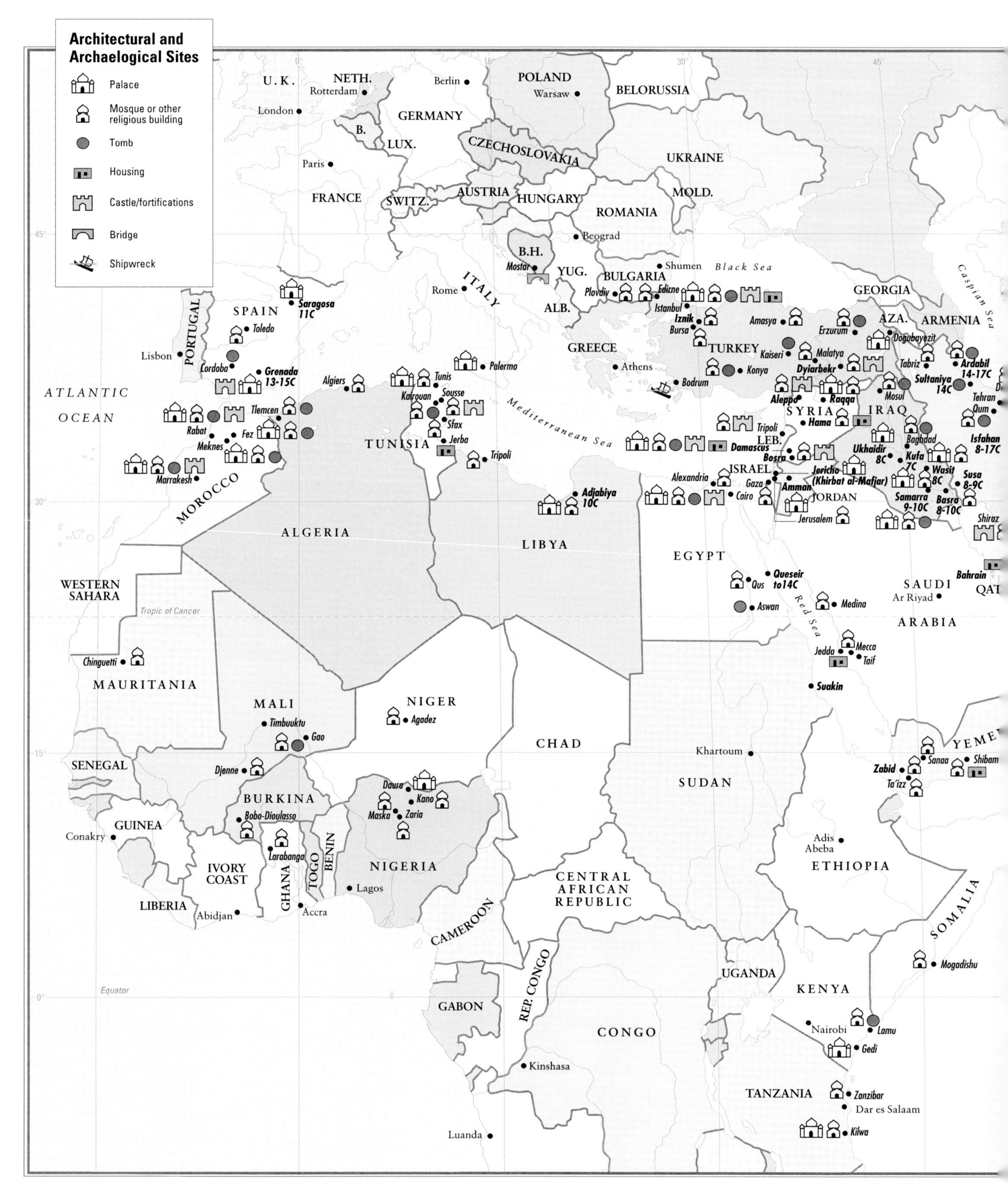
Architectural and Archaelogical Sites
Palace
Mosque or other religious building
Tomb
Housing
Castle/fortifications
Bridge
Shipwreck
U.K.
NETH.
Rotterdam
London
Berlin
POLAND
Warsaw
BELORUSSIA
GERMANY
B.
LUX.
CZECHOSLOVAKIA
UKRAINE
Paris
FRANCE
SWITZ.
AUSTRIA
HUNGARY
MOLD.
ROMANIA
Beograd
B.H.
Mostar
YUG.
Shumen
Black Sea
BULGARIA
Plovdiv
Edirne
Istanbul
GEORGIA
Caspian Sea
ITALY
Rome
ALB.
Iznik
Bursa
Amasya
Erzurum
AZA.
ARMENIA
Dogubayezit
PORTUGAL
SPAIN
Saragosa 11C
Toledo
Lisbon
Cordoba
Grenada 13-15C
GREECE
Athens
TURKEY
Kaiseri
Konya
Malatya
Dyiarbekr
Tabriz
Ardabil 14-17C
Sultaniya 14C
Bodrum
ATLANTIC OCEAN
Algiers
Tunis
Palermo
Kairouan
Sousse
Sfax
Tlemcen
Rabat
Fez
Meknes
Marrakesh
MOROCCO
TUNISIA
Jerba
Tripoli
Mediterranean Sea
Aleppo
Raqqa
Mosul
SYRIA
Hama
IRAQ
Tehran
Qum
Isfahan 8-17C
Tripoli
LEB.
Damascus
Bosra
Baghdad
Ukhaidir 8C
Kufa 7C
Wasit 8C
Susa 8-9C
ISRAEL
Alexandria
Gaza
Amman
Jericho (Khirbat al-Mafjar)
Cairo
JORDAN
Samarra 9-10C
Basra 8-10C
Jerusalem
Shiraz
Adjabiya 10C
ALGERIA
LIBYA
EGYPT
WESTERN SAHARA
Tropic of Cancer
Qus
Queseir to14C
Aswan
Red Sea
Medina
SAUDI ARABIA
Ar Riyad
Bahrain
QAT
Mecca
Jedda
Taif
Suakin
Chinguetti
MAURITANIA
MALI
Timbuuktu
Gao
NIGER
Agadez
CHAD
SENEGAL
Djenne
Khartoum
SUDAN
YEMEN
Sanaa
Shibam
Zabid
Ta'izz
BURKINA
Daura
Kano
Maska
Zaria
Bobo-Dioulasso
GUINEA
Conakry
Larabanga
IVORY COAST
GHANA
TOGO
BENIN
NIGERIA
Lagos
Adis Abeba
ETHIOPIA
LIBERIA
Abidjan
Accra
CENTRAL AFRICAN REPUBLIC
CAMEROON
SOMALIA
Mogadishu
Equator
GABON
REP. CONGO
UGANDA
KENYA
Nairobi
Lamu
Gedi
CONGO
Kinshasa
TANZANIA
Zanzibar
Dar es Salaam
Kilwa
Luanda

KAZAKHSTAN
MONGOLIA
UZBEKISTAN
KYRGYZSTAN
TAJIKSTAN
Turkestan City 14-15C
Khiva 19C
Bukhara
Samarqand
Termez 10-14C
Balkh
Merv 8-12C
Nishapur (9-13C)
Herat
Kabul
Ghazni
AFGHANISTAN
Kashmir
Lahore
Multan
PAKISTAN
Bam 9-13C
Karachi
Tatta
Delhi
Jaipur
Ajmer
Fatehpur Sikri 16C
Agra
Jaunpur
Sasaram
Ahmadabad
Mandu
NEPAL
BH.
Pandua
Calcutta
INDIA
BANGLA-DESH
BURMA
Bombay
Arabian Sea
Bijapur
Gulbarga
Hyderabad
Bangalore
Madras
SRI LANKA
INDIAN OCEAN
CHINA
Harbin
Shenyang
Beijing
Tianjin
N. KOREA
Seoul
S. KOREA
Xian
Yangzhou
Shanghai
Chengdu
Wuhan
Chongqing
Guangzhou
Taiwan
Hong Kong
Hainan
LAOS
VIETNAM
Yangon
THAILAND
Bangkok
CAMBODIA
Ho Chi Minh
Luzón
Manila
PHILIPPINES
Mindanao
MALAYSIA
Malacca
Sumatra
Borneo
Sulawesi
INDONESIA
Jakarta
Demak
Kudus
Java
Timor

World Distribution of Muslims 2000

There are approximately twelve hundred million Muslims in the world today, about one-fifth of humanity. The vast majority reside in the central belt of territories extending eastward from the Atlantic seaboard of North Africa to Indonesia. Due to the historic spread of Islam into the tropical regions of South and Southeast Asia where intensive cultivation permits high population densities, the nation with the largest number of Muslims (182 million) is Indonesia. This is a country far removed from the southwestern Asian matrix where Islam originated. Next in order of magnitude is Pakistan with 134 million, followed by India (121 million), Bangladesh (114 million), Egypt (61 million), and Nigeria (61 million). Of the top six Muslim countries containing more than half the world's Muslims, only one, namely Egypt, is Arabic-speaking and became part of the Islamic world close to the time of its origins. In one of them, India, Muslims live as a large, but still vulnerable, minority. Demographically, the "old" Islam that came into being in the course of the Arab conquests has been overtaken by the newer and younger Islam of the mainly tropical peripheries.

In terms of the legal and sectarian traditions about 85 percent of the world's Muslims belong to the Sunni mainstream and, formally if not always in practice, subscribe to one of the four Sunni madhhabs (legal schools). The Hanafi school, the official school of the Ottoman Empire, predominates in former Ottoman domains, including Anatolia and the Balkans, as well as in Transcaucasia, Afghanistan, Pakistan, India, the Central Asian republics, and China. The Maliki school predominates in the Maghreb and West Africa; the Shafis are represented in Egypt, Palestine, Jordan, the coastlands of Yemen, and among Muslims populations in Pakistan, India, and Indonesia; the Hanbali in Saudi Arabia. However different schools have long coexisted in some places, and there is considerable overlapping in countries such as Egypt where legal modernism has allowed the talfiq (piecing together) of rulings from different schools. Non-Sunni Muslims constitute about 15 percent of the total population worldwide. The Kharijis who split with the main body of Islam in 660 are represented through a modified version known as Ibadism in Oman, Zanzibar, and Tahert in southern Algeria. Shia are concentrated in Iran, southern Iraq, Kuwait, and Bahrain, with substantial minorities in Afghanistan (3.8 million or 15 percent), India (3 percent or 30 million), Lebanon (34 percent or 1.2 million), Pakistan (20 percent or 28 million), Syria (12 percent or 2 million), Turkey (20 percent or 3 million), the United Arab Emirates (16 percent or about half a million), and Yemen (40 percent or 7 million) The great majority of the Shia—about 85 percent—belong to the Imami or Ithashari (Twelver) tradition. Most of the Imami Shias adhere to one or other of the senior religious leaders or Grand Ayatullahs known as Marjas ("sources" of emulation or legal judgement) who act as the qualified interpreters of Islamic law. Other Shia communities include the Zaidis in Yemen and the Ismailis or Seveners belonging to two surviving traditions. These derive from the Fatimid caliphate: the Mustalians (known in South Asia and East Africa as Bohras) who follow the Dai Mutlaq (chief missionary) of the Imam-Caliph al-Mustali (d. 1101) and the Nizaris, who follow the guidance of the Aga Khan, a nobleman of Persian ancestry descended from Muhammad b Ismail whom they regard as their Living Imam. The Nizaris lived in small communities in Syria, Persia, Inner Asia, and northwestern India until migrations to Africa and the West, beginning in the nineteenth century.

Many active Muslims whether Sunnis or Shiites adhere to one of the legal traditions outlined above. In many countries with Muslim majorities, however, elements of Islamic law (especially laws involving personal status, such as marriage divorce and inheritance) have been incorporated into the legal systems of the state. In most Islamic countries the modern state—starting with the Ottoman Tanzimat reforms that brought Islamic institutions under progressive state control—has eroded the autonomy of the ulama who interpreted, diffused, or administered the Sharia in the past. At the same time their religious authority, based on the exclusive access to the scriptures, has been undermined by the rise of secondary education and the spread of literacy. Many of the Islamist movements are led and supported by the beneficiaries of modern technical education who have come to Islamic teachings directly through primary or secondary texts (the Koran, hadith, and the writings of modern ideologues and scholars) rather than through the mediation of traditional scholarship.

At first sight the trend toward what might be called the laicization or democratization of religious authority in Islam could lead to more orthodox or standardized versions promoted by such organizations as the Saudi-based Muslim World League. However, despite the attacks of reformers and the religious imperialism emanating from wealthy but culturally conservative oil-producing regions, the mystical traditions of Sufism have proved highly resilient and adaptive. In subsaharan Africa and many regions of Asia (including the former Soviet territories) versions of Islam mediated through charismatic leaders trained in disciplines that supplement (but do not necessarily replace) the formal religious duties of prayer, fasting, almsgiving, and pilgrimage are continuing to make headway, building on traditions that have long been communicated orally or through interpersonal relationships. The varieties of Islamic faith and practice embedded or "frozen" in texts are only a part of its rich symbolic vocabulary and repertory of meanings. As the older forms of religious authority decay or prove inadequate to address the challenges of modernity, other forms of spiritual authority and social power emerge.

Far left: *Calling the faithful to prayer, a sound that echoes across the diverse Muslim world.*

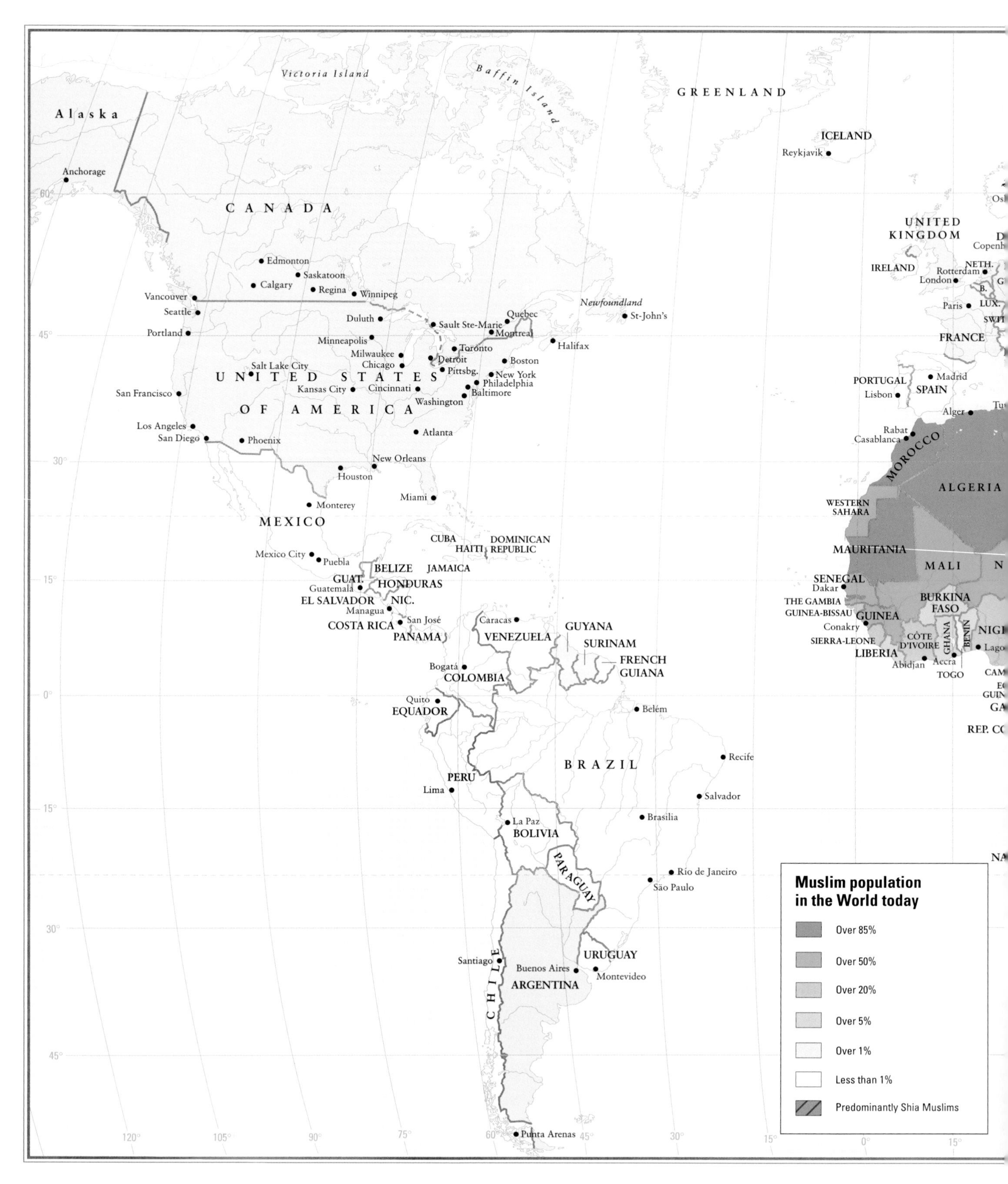

Victoria Island
Baffin Island
GREENLAND
Alaska
Anchorage
ICELAND
Reykjavik
CANADA
Edmonton
Saskatoon
Calgary
Regina
Winnipeg
Vancouver
Seattle
Portland
Duluth
Sault Ste-Marie
Quebec
Montreal
Newfoundland
St-John's
Halifax
Minneapolis
Milwaukee
Chicago
Toronto
Detroit
Pittsbg.
Boston
New York
Philadelphia
Baltimore
Washington
Salt Lake City
UNITED STATES OF AMERICA
Kansas City
Cincinnati
San Francisco
Los Angeles
San Diego
Phoenix
Atlanta
New Orleans
Houston
Miami
Monterey
MEXICO
CUBA
HAITI
DOMINICAN REPUBLIC
Mexico City
Puebla
BELIZE
JAMAICA
GUAT.
Guatemala
HONDURAS
EL SALVADOR
NIC.
Managua
San José
COSTA RICA
PANAMA
Caracas
VENEZUELA
GUYANA
SURINAM
FRENCH GUIANA
Bogatá
COLOMBIA
Quito
EQUADOR
Belém
BRAZIL
Recife
PERU
Lima
Salvador
Brasilia
La Paz
BOLIVIA
PARAGUAY
Rio de Janeiro
São Paulo
Santiago
CHILE
Buenos Aires
ARGENTINA
URUGUAY
Montevideo
Punta Arenas
UNITED KINGDOM
IRELAND
London
Rotterdam
NETH.
B.
LUX.
Paris
FRANCE
PORTUGAL
Lisbon
Madrid
SPAIN
Alger
Rabat
Casablanca
MOROCCO
ALGERIA
WESTERN SAHARA
MAURITANIA
MALI
SENEGAL
Dakar
THE GAMBIA
GUINEA-BISSAU
GUINEA
Conakry
SIERRA-LEONE
LIBERIA
BURKINA FASO
CÔTE D'IVOIRE
Abidjan
GHANA
Accra
TOGO
BENIN
Muslim population in the World today
Over 85%
Over 50%
Over 20%
Over 5%
Over 1%
Less than 1%
Predominantly Shia Muslims

Novaya Zemlya
FINLAND
RUSSIAN FEDERATION
St-Petersburg
EST.
LAT.
Nizhniy Novgorod
Perm
Yekaterinburg
Moscow
Chelyabinsk
Omsk
Novosibirsk
Minsk
BELORUSSIA
Samara
Kiev
UKRAINE
Kharkov
Volgograd
MOLDOVA
Rostov
KAZAKHSTAN
MONGOLIA
Sakhalin
ROM.
Belgrade
Harbin
BULG.
UZBEKISTAN
KYRGYZ.
Hokkaido
Istanbul
Ankara
GEORGIA
ARMENIA
AZER.
Shenyang
Beijing
Tianjin
N. KOREA
JAPAN
TURKEY
TURKMEN.
TAJIK.
Seoul
Athens
Honshu
S. KOREA
Tokyo
Pusan
Yokohama
SYRIA
Tehran
Kabul
CHINA
LEB.
Baghdad
AFGHAN.
Lahore
ISRAEL
IRAQ
IRAN
Alexandria
Cairo
JORDAN
Chengdu
Wuhan
Shanghai
PAKISTAN
KUWAIT
Delhi
NEPAL
BHUTAN
EGYPT
SAUDI ARABIA
Riyad
QATAR
U.A.E.
Karachi
Ahmadabad
Dhaka
Guangzhou
Taiwan
Calcutta
Hong Kong
INDIA
BURMA
BANGLA-DESH
LAOS
Bombay
Hainan
OMAN
VIETNAM
YEMEN
Hyderabad
Yangon
Luzon
Khartoum
ERITREA
THAI.
Manila
SUDAN
Bangkok
Bangalore
Madras
CAMB.
Addis Ababa
DJIBOUTI
Ho Chi Minh
PHILIPPINES
ETHIOPIA
SRI LANKA
Mindanao
SOMALIA
BRUNEI
MALAYSIA
UGANDA
KENYA
Nairobi
Sumatra
Borneo
Sulawesi
RWANDA
BURUNDI
INDONESIA
PAPUA NEW GUINEA
Jakarta
Java
Dar es Salaam
TANZANIA
EAST TIMOR
MALAWI
ZAMBIA
MOZAMBIQUE
MADAGASCAR
ZIMBABWE
AUSTRALIA
Maputo
SWAZILAND
Brisbane
Durban
LESOTHO
Perth
Sydney
Adelaide
Melbourne
NEW ZEALAND
45°
60°
75°
90°
105°
120°
135°
150°
165°
180°

World Terrorism 2003

Far right: *The twin towers of the World Trade Center in New York burn before collapsing on September 11th 2001, when two hijacked airliners hit the towers at the 80th and 95th floors. Most of the nearly 3000 victims, who came from more than 100 nations, were trapped on the upper floors.*

There are numerous definitions of terrorism but in general usage the term refers to illegal armed activity by "subnational groups" or "non-state actors," whether supported covertly by state sponsors or operating wholly as free-lance guerrilla organizations. It is also defined in terms of method and purpose. The US, for example, defines terrorism as "the calculated use or threat of violence to inculcate fear, intended to coerce or intimidate governments or societies." While certain kinds of activity such as assassination, kidnapping, and hijacking are associated with armed insurgents in most parts of the world, the killing of civilians by the use of explosive devices is far from being confined to nonstate actors. Although the methods of delivery used by governments and "terrorists" may differ, the results may be equally brutal. Cluster bombs dropped from the air, for example, resemble suicide bombings in the indiscriminate way they target civilians. Movements described as "terrorist" by governments typically contest the label and usually the legitimacy of the party that uses it. Rather than being a description of a type of activity, terrorism tends to be used as a term of abuse. Governments everywhere denounce armed opponents who challenge their monopoly over the use of violence as "terrorists," while insurgents and their supporters denounce as "state terrorism" methods used by governments, such as "targeted killings," detentions without trial, the use of torture, and the destruction of homes belonging to suspected insurgents or their families.

The attacks on New York and Washington on September 11 2001 by Islamist insurgents who hijacked four civilian airliners and flew two of them into the World Trade Center towers in Manhattan, causing the death of nearly three thousand people has inevitably created a climate in which terrorism and Islamic militancy are considered synonymous. The spectacular nature of the attacks—shown live on television throughout the world—placed other conflicts between governments and armed insurgents in the shade. In 2001–03, however, many of these conflicts were occurring outside the Islamic world. They included bloody campaigns against their respective governments by Maoists in Nepal, Tamils in Sri Lanka, Basques in Spain, separatists in Corsica, rebels belonging to LURD (Liberians United for Reconciliation and Democracy) in Liberia, and several other conflicts in Central Africa such as in the Congo and Rwanda, not to mention the decades-long struggle between the Colombian government and the Revolutionary Armed Forces of Colombia (FARC). However, the "war on terrorism," declared by President George W. Bush in the aftermath of 9/11, seemed to target Islamic groups particularly, along with the Muslim governments (notably Syria, Iran, and Iraq), allegedly sponsoring them. In the case of al-Qaeda, the militant Islamist network presided over by the Saudi dissident Osama bin Laden, held responsible for the 9/11 attacks, as well as the attacks on the US embassies in East Africa in 1998, and several atrocities after 9/11 (including the bombing of a discotheque in Bali, which killed more than 200 people, mostly Australian tourists), the US responded by military action aimed at "regime change" in two countries—Afghanistan and Iraq—which it accused of supporting al-Qaeda. While there was no question that the Taliban regime in Afghanistan, removed in the summer of 2002 after a massive US bombing campaign, had hosted bin Laden and his inner circle of al-Qaeda operatives, the case against the Iraqi leader, Saddam Hussein, who fell from power after the Anglo-American invasion of Iraq in March 2003, was much less certain. After the fall of the regime no evidence was produced that Iraq possessed weapons of mass destruction (the official pretext for the war), or that the regime was implicated in the attacks of 9/11 as claimed by senior members of the US administration.

Al-Qaeda is a global network with links to Islamist movements in several Muslim countries and as such has stimulated a global response by the US and its allies. Britain and several other countries including Australia, Italy, Spain, and Poland, sent military contingents to Iraq. The FBI has assisted local security agencies in numerous countries. US Special Forces and military advisors have been sent to help government forces fight Chechen insurgents in Georgia (to protect the Baku-Tbilisi-Ceyhan pipeline), and the Philippines, where Islamic separatists of the Moro Islamic Liberation Front have been waging an armed insurgency on the southern island of Mindanao (with support from the al-Qaeda-connected Abu Sayyaf group). The US is heavily involved in supporting Israel against Islamist Palestinian insurgents and has so far failed to pressure Israel into abandoning the illegal Jewish settlements in the occupied territories for fear of antagonizing influential lobbies (Jewish and Christian fundamentalist) in the US. In Uzbekistan the US has given unqualified backing to the repressive government of President Islam Karimov who has found it expedient to designate the political opposition as Islamist "terrorists." In contrast, in Sudan, where a Muslim government had faced a twenty-five year insurgency by non-Muslim southerners, the US had put its weight behind the rebels of the SPLA (Sudan People's Liberation Army) in order to pressure a Muslim government into reaching terms.

In general, Western countries led by the United States are deploying their superior military resources to support existing states, based on boundaries drawn up by the colonial powers in Africa and Asia, many of which are challenged by armed insurgencies. Since a high proportion of these challenges come from Muslim groups, the "war on terrorism" is seen by many in the Muslim world as having a distinctively anti-Muslim bias.

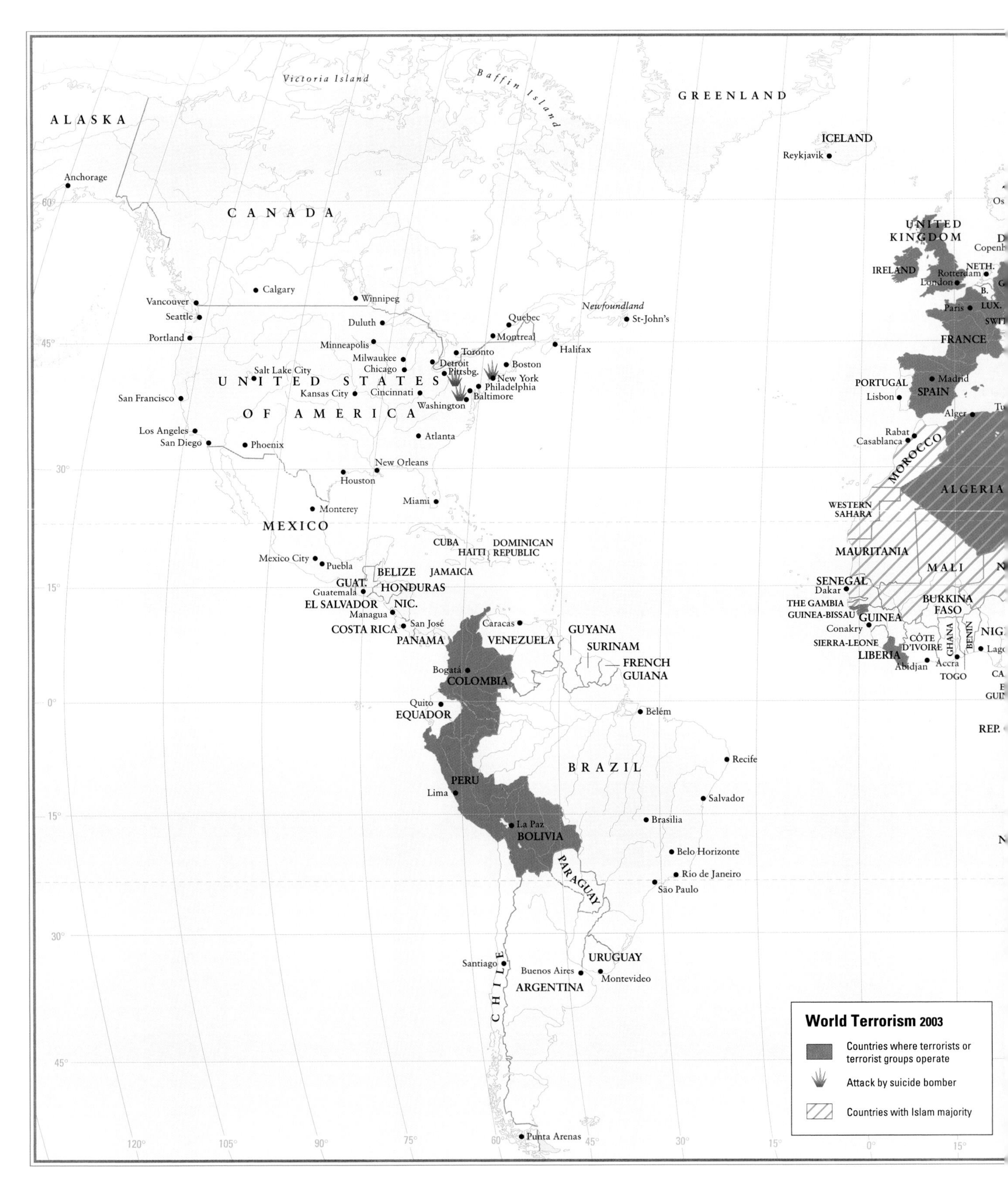
World Terrorism 2003
Countries where terrorists or terrorist groups operate
Attack by suicide bomber
Countries with Islam majority
ALASKA
CANADA
GREENLAND
ICELAND
Reykjavik
Victoria Island
Baffin Island
Anchorage
Calgary
Vancouver
Seattle
Portland
Winnipeg
Duluth
Quebec
Montreal
Newfoundland
St-John's
Halifax
Minneapolis
Milwaukee
Chicago
Toronto
Detroit
Pittsbg.
Boston
New York
Philadelphia
Baltimore
Washington
Salt Lake City
UNITED STATES OF AMERICA
Kansas City
Cincinnati
San Francisco
Los Angeles
San Diego
Phoenix
Atlanta
New Orleans
Houston
Miami
Monterey
MEXICO
Mexico City
Puebla
CUBA
HAITI
DOMINICAN REPUBLIC
BELIZE
JAMAICA
GUAT.
Guatemala
HONDURAS
EL SALVADOR
NIC.
Managua
San José
COSTA RICA
PANAMA
Caracas
VENEZUELA
GUYANA
SURINAM
FRENCH GUIANA
Bogatá
COLOMBIA
Quito
EQUADOR
Belém
BRAZIL
Recife
PERU
Lima
Salvador
Brasilia
La Paz
BOLIVIA
Belo Horizonte
PARAGUAY
Rio de Janeiro
São Paulo
Santiago
CHILE
Buenos Aires
ARGENTINA
URUGUAY
Montevideo
Punta Arenas
UNITED KINGDOM
IRELAND
London
Rotterdam
NETH.
B.
LUX.
Paris
FRANCE
PORTUGAL
Lisbon
Madrid
SPAIN
Alger
Rabat
Casablanca
MOROCCO
ALGERIA
WESTERN SAHARA
MAURITANIA
MALI
SENEGAL
Dakar
THE GAMBIA
GUINEA-BISSAU
GUINEA
Conakry
SIERRA-LEONE
LIBERIA
BURKINA FASO
CÔTE D'IVOIRE
Abidjan
GHANA
Accra
TOGO
BENIN
60°
45°
30°
15°
0°
120°
105°
90°
75°
60°
45°
30°
15°
0°
15°

RUSSIAN FEDERATION
KAZAKHSTAN
MONGOLIA
CHINA
INDIA
JAPAN
N. KOREA
S. KOREA
UZBEKISTAN
TURKMEN.
KYRGYZ.
TAJIK.
AFGHAN.
PAKISTAN
IRAN
IRAQ
SYRIA
TURKEY
SAUDI ARABIA
YEMEN
OMAN
EGYPT
SUDAN
ETHIOPIA
SOMALIA
KENYA
UGANDA
TANZANIA
MALAWI
ZAMBIA
MOZAMBIQUE
ZIMBABWE
MADAGASCAR
NEPAL
BHUTAN
BANGLA-DESH
BURMA
LAOS
VIETNAM
THAI.
CAMB.
SRI LANKA
MALAYSIA
BRUNEI
PHILIPPINES
INDONESIA
EAST TIMOR
PAPUA NEW GUINEA
AUSTRALIA
NEW ZEALAND
Moscow
St-Petersburg
Omsk
Novosibirsk
Beijing
Tokyo
Delhi
Bombay
Karachi
Tehran
Baghdad
Kabul
Jakarta
Manila
Sydney
Perth

Muslim Cinema

Motion pictures entered Muslim societies soon after its emergence in the West and was initially introduced to select audiences. Within a few months of debuting in Europe in 1896, the films of the Lumière brothers were screened in the Arab world to a predominantly elite audience. In Egypt, for example, screenings were held at

the Tousson stock exchange in Alexandria, and in Morocco at the Royal Palace in Fez. In Turkey, private showings were held at the sultan's court, the Yildiz Palace in Istanbul. In 1900, the Iranian monarch, Muaffar al-Din Shah, traveled to France to see the "cinematograph" and "the magic lantern." In the same year Mirza Ibrahim Khan, his photographer, filmed "The Flower Ceremony" in Belgium and produced the first Iranian film.

The local film industry in these states emerged from the efforts of foreigners or minority individuals. For example, it was a Romanian citizen of Polish origin, Sigmund Weinberg, who began public screenings of films at a beer hall in Galatasaray Square in Istanbul. In Iran, Ovenes Oganians, an Armenian-Iranian, began the building of public cinemas in 1905, establishing the first film school in 1929 and producing the first Iranian feature film in 1930.

Most parts of Africa and Asia were exposed to film as part of the colonial experience. Thus, the Arab world provided largely an exotic backdrop for Western films. As such, French audiences were enamored with North Africa, Palestine attracted great interest as the Holy Land, and Egypt was intriguing for its ancient history. While the colonial industry produced 200 films in North Africa, only perhaps six starred Arab actors.

The introduction of sound in vernacular languages boosted local film production, with Egyptian cinema, for example, attracting both local investors and audiences by including popular Egyptian musicians and singers such as Umm Kulthum. Egyptian cinema not only became a leading force in other Arab countries but also influenced cinema further afield, such as the film farsi genre of pre-Revolutionary Iran. In most other Arab countries, however, a native film industry failed to develop because of financial constraints and colonial pressures. Most of these countries entered the film industry after their independence (Lebanon and Syria in the 1940s, North Africa in the 1950s and early 1960s).

During the colonial period, films imported to the Arab countries were often used instrumentally to promote colonial interests. Even the Japanese, during their occupation of Indonesia (1942–45), used the burgeoning Indonesian film industry to bolster their war efforts. At the same time film assisted in the standardization of Indonesian as a national language. In the Arab world film production took on an increasingly nationalist and socialist bent after independence, with states such as Syria, Algeria, and Tunisia using the film industry to promote their national identity on screen. In Iran, Daryush Mehrjui's prize winning film *The Cow* and Massoud Kimiai's *Qeysar*, both produced in 1969, mark the beginnings of the New Wave, Iranian art cinema, after which Iranian films gained increasing international acclaim. Around the same time, in 1970, Yilmaz Guney's *Umut* (Hope), also a prize-winning film, became a turning point in Turkish cinema and marked the New Wave period of Turkish films.

In Iran, filmmakers faced an uncertain future between 1978–82 as a result of, among other things, financial instability and government's lack of interest in cinema during the transitional period. With a few exceptions, no films of any quality were produced during this time. Prior to the revolution, most of the ulama either rejected cinema or ignored it. However, after the revolution, the Islamists came to recognize its power and decided to bring it under their control. For Khomeini the adoption of cinema became an ideological weapon with which to combat the pro-Western and imperialist culture of the Pahlavi regime. By 1989 (the year of his death), films like Bayzai's *Bashu, The Little Stranger*, gained Iranian cinema international acclaim once more. By providing the space for an ongoing discourse within society, Iranian cinema has become an important medium in the discourse of change.

During the '80s, the Arab states started to withdraw from cinema production. The Algerian film industry went bankrupt while the Egyptian one faced a major economic crisis. Television and mass video production compounded this decline in filmmaking across the regions. Films in North Africa, Syria, and especially Lebanon were coproduced with the West. In 1980 the number of films produced in Turkey suddenly dropped, though it rose again toward the end of the 1980s.

Most of the states in the region maintain a firm control on the film industry, recognizing its importance as an agency for change and vehicle for protest. In Turkey, for example, this strict censorship operates at two levels: that of the screenplay and of the finished film. A similar process occurs in Indonesia, where censorship is applied both before shooting and during editing. In Iranian cinema, screening of all final products requires state approval. With few exceptions, this approval is also required at the postscript stage. In most Arab countries, film projects must first obtain a shooting license before obtaining other licenses from the Ministry of Information or other such censorship authority in order to ensure their commercial viability.

Mention should be made of Bollywood, the Indian cinema industry based in Mumbhai, not only because it was heavily imitated in many Muslim countries, especially during the initial decades, but because of the significant presence of Muslims as scriptwriters, producers, musicians, and actors. There is also a genre known as the Shahenshah (king of kings), which goes back to *Pukar* (1939), a film about the Mughal emperor, Jehangir. It is regarded as the first notable "Muslim social film." While the latter continued to surface in other films such as Mughal-e-Azam, in later productions the Muslim social presence took on a less regal character, dealing mainly with the North Indian Muslim middle class. This genre gradually declined after the 1970s. Finally, after a notable absence, with less than forty full-length films and shorts, Afghanistan rejoined the world cinema stage with *Osama* (2003), a co-production of Afghanistan, Japan, and Ireland. The first feature from post-Taliban Afghanistan, it was screened at various international film festivals including Cannes and London.

Far left: *Iranian director Samira Makhmalbaf poses for photographers after being awarded the Jury prize for the film* Panj E Asr *(Five in the Afternoon), during the closing ceremony of the 56th Cannes film festival in May 2003. The daughter of acclaimed director Mohsen Makhmalbaf made her first film,* The Apple *(1998) when she was only 18.* The Blackboard *(2000) a film about Kurdish refugees on the Iran-Iraq border, also won a Jury prize at Cannes.*

Internet Use

Before the digital age Islamic questions were often addressed locally with the ulama, the acknowledged interpreters of the tradition, acting as the primary agents of religious authority. In the Sunni world the spread of literacy and secondary education was eroding this primacy even before the appearance of the World Wide Web. The internet is accelerating this process by facilitating the individual exercise of ijtihad (independent judgment based on the primary sources of Koran and hadith). Once the exclusive preserve of qualified scholars, this development is eroding traditional hierarchies of learning.

Muslim websurfers do not have to consult Koranic concordances or weighty books of fiqh (jurisprudence) to arrive at judgments but can simply access the sources online by scanning the Koran or collections of hadith (reports of the prophet Muhammad's sayings or actions) using keywords. Alternatively they can e-mail their questions to the hundreds of websites offering social, moral, religious, and in some cases, political guidance. With many of the best funded websites based in Saudi Arabia or the Gulf the answers often have a conservative character and may not always be sensitive to the questioner's social or economic circumstances. For example, questions from young women living in North America about how to deal with abusive parents may stress the importance of filial duty over their rights as citizens.

For Shiites in the Twelver or Ithnashari tradition for whom clerics rather than texts are the primary dispensers of authority, the web provides access to rulings by living marjas (sources of imitation/emulation) such as Grand Ayatullah Sistani, the leading marja in Iraq. Web pages on this site cover contemporary concerns such as credit cards, insurance, copyright, autopsies, and organ donation, as well as advice about religious duties. Some Sufi orders maintain websites detailing the spiritual lineages of their shaikhs and transcripts of special prayer and dhikr (rituals of remembrance) practices. However since

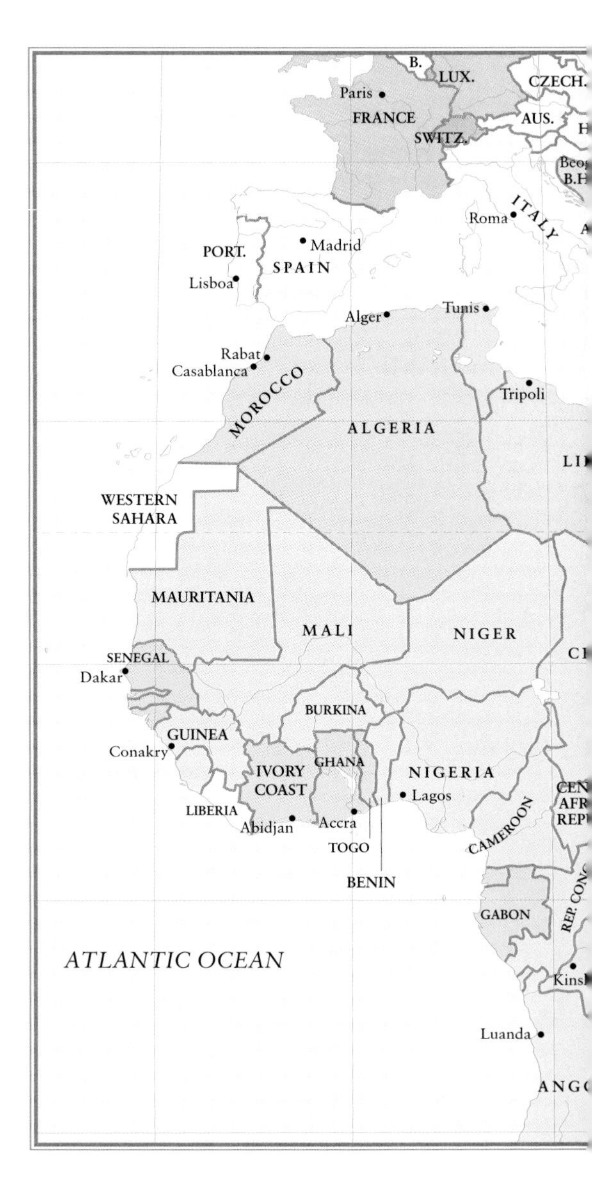

many Sufi practices are closed to outsiders, only the more orthodox orders maintain sites. Political Islam is widely represented, with most political parties, including Islamist ones, accessible through their websites. Opposition forces are also represented, although in some cases access to banned groups is restricted by governmental controls. Islamic women's groups are active in cyberspace countering patriarchal practices such as those promulgated by the former Taliban regime in Afghanistan in the name of "true" Islamic teachings. With access to the internet spreading rapidly throughout the Muslim world, the long-term effects are ambiguous. On the one hand a "universal" Islamic discourse is emerging that transcends the local traditions, including even the mainstream traditions represented by institutions such as Cairo's al-Azhar. On the other hand, the emerging discourse cannot avoid accommodating diversity and dissent, as minorities and splinter-groups are able to challenge mainstream opinion in cultures where religious and political pluralism have often been repressed.

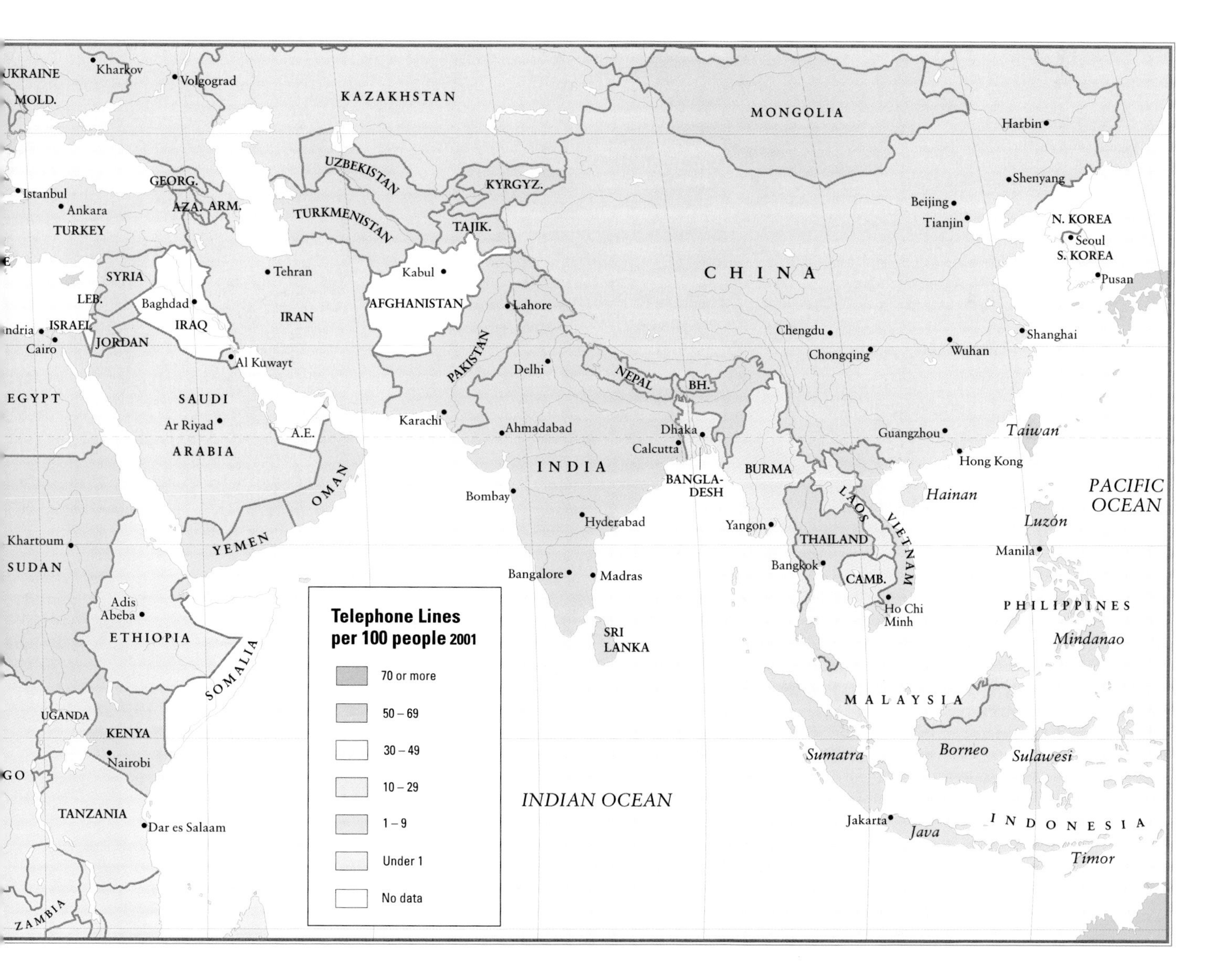

Democracy, Censorship, Human Rights, and Civil Society

Western scholars define democracy as a method for protecting the civil and political rights of the individual, providing for freedom of speech, press, faith, opinion, ownership, and assembly, as well as the right to vote, nominate and seek public office. Muslim traditions of democracy exist in the Arabian concept of shura (council based on participatory discussion), harking back to the Bedouin system where the shaikh is primus inter pares.

When the Ottoman Empire was divided into separate nation-states after the First World War, several attempts were made to introduce systems of democratic rule. Most of them were unsuccessful, discredited by rigged elections or manipulation by powerful interest groups. Multiparty systems were replaced by single party systems, by military governments, or by a combination of both. Here again, however, the revolutionary models borrowed from Eastern Europe proved no less susceptible to manipulation by vested interests or groups whose asabiyya (collective solidarity) was rooted in combinations of kinship and sectarian allegiance. In the Muslim world lying beyond the former Ottoman domains, the position is not greatly different. Of the fifty-odd Muslim-majority states belonging to the Organization of the Islamic Conference only Turkey can be described as an established democracy—although it has a history of political manipulation by the military who regard themselves as guardians of the secular tradition bequeathed by the founder of modern Turkey, Kemal Atatürk. Other countries, including Malaysia, Indonesia, and Jordan have been described as transitional or uncertain democracies, and Pakistan has enjoyed periods of democratic rule in between bouts of military government.

In the context of human rights generally the situation is broadly similar, given that two of the fundamental human rights embedded in such documents as the Universal Declaration of Human Rights and the International Covenant on Civil and Political Rights—the rights of peaceful assembly and freedom or expression—are prerequisites for all forms of democratic government.

For example, in the Index of Human Rights compiled by Charles Humana in 1991, Muslim majority countries consistently scored below the world average of 62 percent, with Iraq at 17 percent at the bottom of the world league table (a distinction it shared with Myanmar) and Sudan with 18 percent, a close second. At 65 percent Jordan alone remains above the world average, though Tunisia (with 60 percent) and Malaysia (61 percent) are close to it. Critics of Humana's system object that his methodology is culturally loaded with western liberal values, that women in Islamic countries, for example, do not require the same protection as women in western countries and that female inheritance and property rights were instituted by the Sharia more than a millennium before they were introduced in the West. Such cultural relativism, however, is often opposed by women's organizations inside Muslim countries, which campaign to eliminate discriminatory provisions in personal status codes with respect to legal status, marriage, divorce, child custody and inheritance. Women's organizations have also campaigned against the reduced sentences passed by courts in cases of "honor killings" where victims are held to have "provoked" attacks by male relatives by transgressing traditional codes of sexual conduct, and against laws that prevent them from passing on their nationalities to their children.

Freedom of speech as exemplified by a free

press is also conspicuously absent in most Muslim countries, though restrictions vary from one state to another. Opposition forces, including Islamists, protest against measures which muzzle them politically. Islamists themselves, however, have demonstrated their opposition to unrestricted freedom of speech by attacks on writers they regard as critical of Islam, including Farag Foda (assassinated in 1992), the Nobel laureate Neguib Mahfouz, Egypt's foremost novelist, physically attacked and injured by the same assassin, and Nasr Abu Zaid, an Egyptian scholar who was forced into exile for applying historical-critical methods in interpreting the Koran.

The "war on terrorism" launched by the US administration in the wake of the September 11 attacks on New York and Washington, which overthrew the governments in Afghanistan and Iraq led to a curtailment of civil liberties in the United States. There the US Patriot Act permitted the indefinite detention of terrorist suspects and the administrative detention of jihadis (some of them barely older than children) accused of fighting for the Taliban regime in Afghanistan. At the same time the neoconservatives running the administration stated that their aim was to bring to countries such as Iraq and Afghanistan Western standards of democracy, good governance, the rule of law, human rights, and women's rights. Many people in the Muslim world, however, doubted whether such standards could be instituted as a result of military action. Both in the Arab and the wider Islamic world both the incumbent regimes and their Islamist opponents would argue that the indigenous tradition of Shura, combined with that of baya (obedience to an established ruler) provided a better model for stability, whereas Western-style pluralism was a recipe for fitna (strife).

Both the ruling authorities in countries such as Saudi Arabia, Iran, and Sudan, and the Islamists who sometimes oppose them argue that safeguards enshrined in the Koran are just as valid as those protected by Western law. They hold that the public and private spheres are both subject to the law and that secularism is alien to their history. The proponents of democracy, however, who include some leading Islamist thinkers as well as the advocates of secular liberalism, believe that such arguments are simply being used as strategies for retaining power. In the aftermath of "9/11" and the wars in Afghanistan and Iraq, avenues for peaceful political change have been closed off, leaving people to choose between tolerating the status quo, exile (for those who can manage it), or violence. Critics of Western policies point out that it has tacitly accepted this pattern of repression for reasons of expediency, and in the case of the oil-bearing regions of western Asia, to protect its energy supplies.

Islamic version of democracy dates back to the concept of the shura (participatory discussions). However, the Western ideal of the popular vote by the adult population is not available in many Muslim majority states.

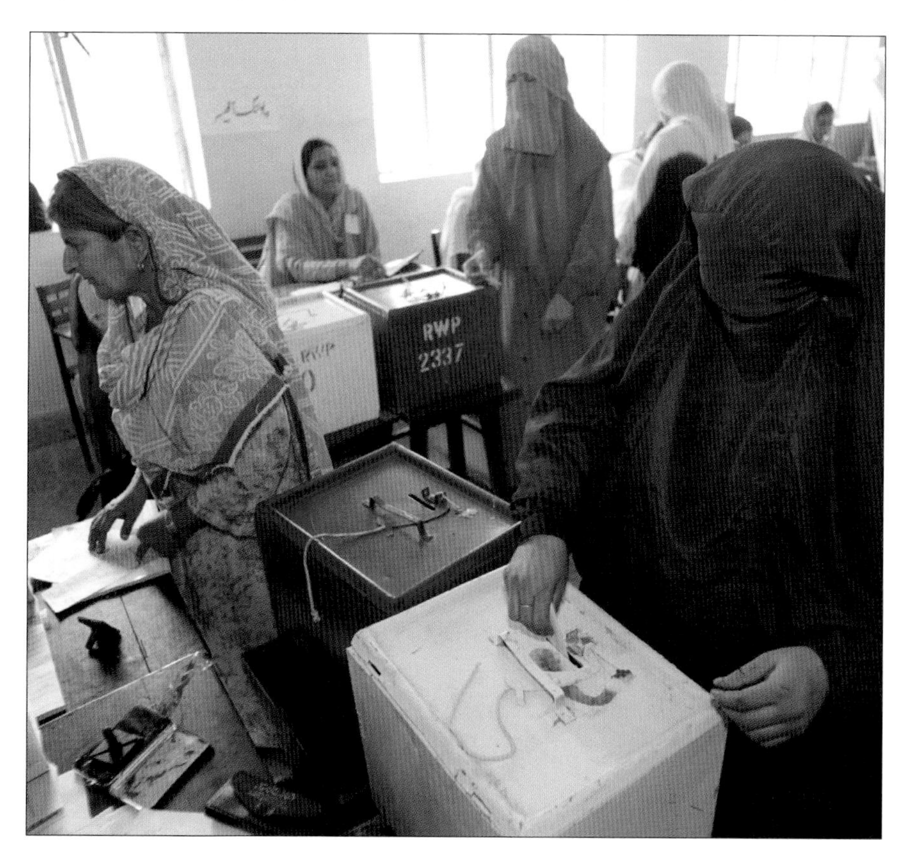

Modern Movements, Organizations, and Influences

Far right: *In this computer graphic illustration, Mamoun Sakkal has produced an image which reflects, through its lively composition, the great variety of Islamic religious ideas. In the 3-dimensional Kufic script the Islamic shahada (creed) reads, "there is no god but God and Muhammad is the messenger of God."*

The terms "Islamism" and "Islamist" have come to be used for political movements and their supporters, which aim for the establishment or restoration of Islamic states based on the rule of the Islamic Sharia law. The term "Islamists" is an English translation to the Arabic word islamiyyun—a term the movement's advocates use to distinguish themselves from muslimun—ordinary Muslim believers. All Islamists believe that Islam is the solution to contemporary problems of Muslim states. Although the numerous Islamist groups that mushroomed and spread throughout the Muslim world during the last three decades of the twentieth century differ among themselves on the details of how Islamic states should be run, nearly all are agreed that the return to God includes the rejection of the cultures of Western materialism and hedonism (exemplified by sexual permissiveness) and the duty to support fellow-Muslims in conflict with non-Muslims in places such as Palestine or Kashmir, though not all Islamists support terrorist actions.

The ground for the Islamist movements was prepared by the reformist and salafiyya movements in the eighteenth and nineteenth centuries, which had sought to purge Islamic belief and ritual from the accretions and innovations acquired over the centuries, particularly the cults surrounding the Sufi walis (saints), living and dead. An Islam pruned of its medieval accretions was better able to confront the challenge of foreign power than a local cult bounded by the intercessionary power of a particular saint or family of saints. The modern Islamist movement, however, is usually traced back to the Muslim Brotherhood, founded in 1928 by Hasan al-Banna, an Egyptian schoolteacher. The Brotherhood's original aims were moral as much as political: it sought to reform society by encouraging Islamic observance and opposing Western cultural influences, rather than by attempting to capture the state by direct political action. However during the mounting crisis over Palestine during and after the Second World War the Brotherhood became increasingly radicalized. It played a leading part in the disturbances that led to the overthrow of the monarchy in 1952 but after the revolution it came into increasing conflict with the nationalist government of Jamal Abd al-Nasser. In 1954, after an attempt on Nasser's life, the Brotherhood was suppressed, its members imprisoned, exiled, or driven underground. (Banna himself had been murdered in 1949 by the intelligence services of the old regime.) After its suppression, the Brotherhood became internationalized, with affiliated movements springing up in Jordan, Syria, Sudan, Pakistan, Indonesia, and Malaysia. The Brotherhood found refuge in Saudi Arabia, under the Amir (later King) Faisal ibn Abd al-Aziz as well as political and financial support, with funds for the Egyptian underground and salaried posts for exiled intellectuals.

A radical member of the Brotherhood, Sayyid Qutb, executed in 1966 for an alleged plot to overthrow the Egyptian government, proved to be the movement's most influential theorist, although some of his ideas were influenced by the Indian scholar and journalist, Abu al-Ala al-Maududi (1906–79). One of Maududi's doctrines, in particular, would have a major impact on Islamic political movement. He believed that the struggle for Islam was not for the restoration of an ideal past, but for a principle vital to the here and now: the vice-regency of man under God's sovereignty. The jihad was not just a defensive war for the protection of the Islamic territory. It might be waged against governments which prevented the preaching of true (i.e., the Islamist version of) Islam. Taking his cue from Maududi, Qutb likened contemporary Islamic society to the jahiliyya, the "state of ignorance" prevailing in Arabia against which the Prophet himself inveighed and fought.

In most Sunni countries the Brotherhood and its offshoots can be divided into a mainstream tendency that will work within the frame of existing governmental systems, where permitted, and is also engaged in social welfare work, and a radical or extremists tendency that seeks to achieve its aims by violence. However the lines dividing the extremists from the mainstream are not always clear. Violence is interactive and in many cases, such as the atrocities perpetrated by Islamist terrorists in India, Israel-Palestine, and Egypt it may be seen as a response to that inflicted on the Islamists by governments which themselves use violence, including torture and "targeted killings," to repress or destroy opposition. Where opportunities for political participation have been available, as in Jordan, Yemen, Kuwait, and Malaysia the level of violence has been notably less than, for example, in Israel-Palestine or Algeria. In Egypt violence by extremist factions of the Islamic Associations, including attacks on tourists, seriously alienated the mass of public opinion, not least because millions of Egyptians are dependent on tourism for their livelihoods.

There remains, however, a hard core of Islamist militants who are committed to the "liberation" of Muslim lands from "infidel" rule, regardless of circumstances. This arm of the movement, inspired by the writings of Sayyid Qutb and the fiery rhetoric of Abdullah Azam—one time mentor of the Saudi dissident Osama bin Laden—gained momentum during the American- and Pakistani-backed jihad against the Soviet occupation in Afghanistan (1979–89) when thousands of volunteers received training in methods of irregular warfare. Fired by what they see as their divinely-supported victory in Afghanistan the militants aim to "liberate" all lands that were once Islamic (including Spain) from rule by non-Muslims or by unjust "infidel" governments (by which they mean most existing Muslim states). Since they see Western financial and military support as a primary factor in the survival of "non-Islamic" regimes, they have not hesitated to take their jihad into the heart of Western power.

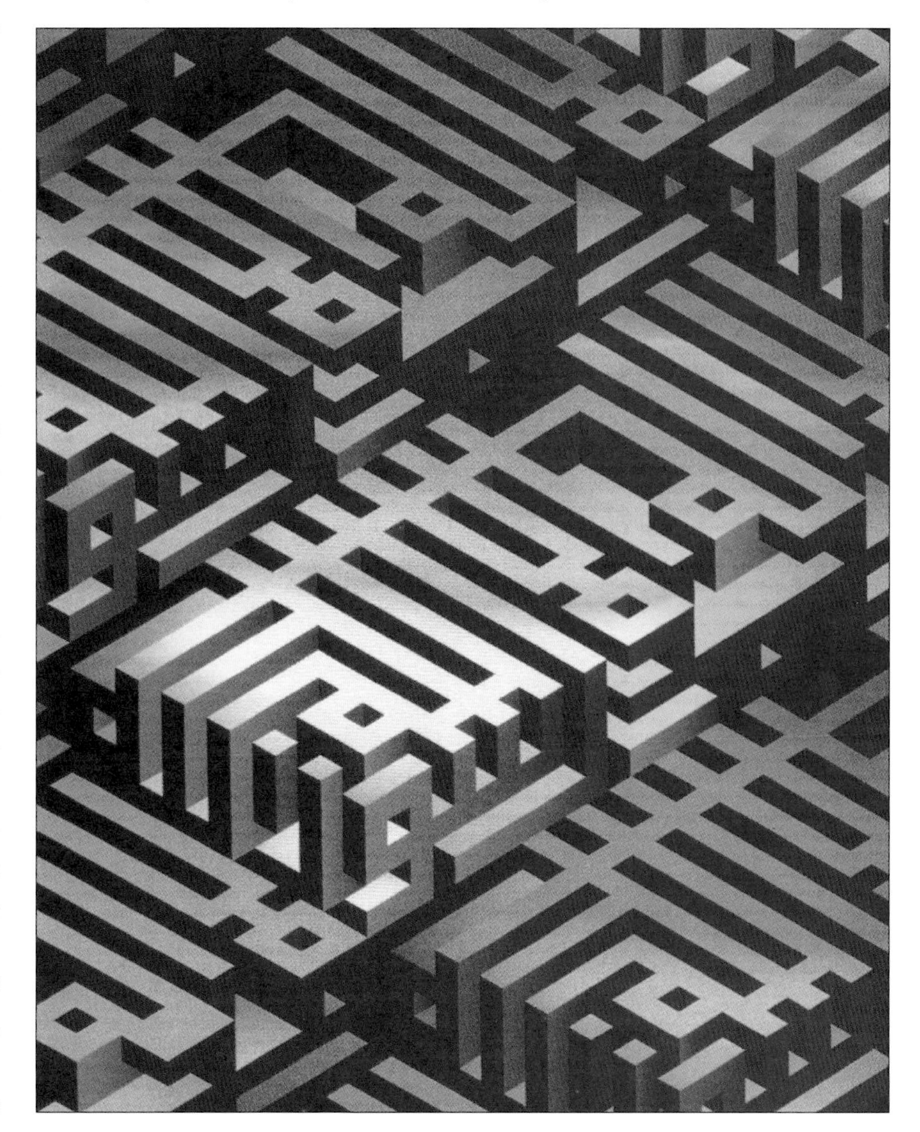

Chronology

c. 570–622	Muhammad in Mecca.
622–632	Muhammad in Medina.
632–634	Caliphate of Abu Bakr. Muslims triumph in wars of apostasy. Arabia unified.
634–644	Caliphate of Umar. Most of Fertile Crescent, Egypt, and much of Iran conquered. Expansion into North Africa.
644–656	Caliphate of Uthman. Conquests continue northward, eastward, and westward Text of the Koran collected and standardized.
656–661	First *fitna* or civil war during caliphate of Ali.
660, 668, 712	Arabs fail to capture Constantinople.
661	Murder of Ali. Establishment of Umayyad caliphate by Muawiya in Damascus.
680	Second *fitna*. Muawiya's succession by his son Yazid provokes rebellion by Hussein b. Ali. "Martyrdom" of Hussein and followers at Karbala.
685–705	Reign of Abd al-Malik, builder of the Dome of the Rock in Jerusalem.
687–691	Kharijis prevail in much of Arabia.
711	Arabs advance into Spain.
712–713	Arabs conquer Transoxiana (Bukhara and Samarkand).
728	Death of Hasan al-Basri, early Sufi master.
732	Battle of Poitiers: Charles Martel checks Arab advance into France.
744–750	Third *fitna*. Weakened by internal dissent, Umayyad dynasty overthrown by Abbasids (749).
756	Umayyad rule established in Spain.
765	Death of Jafar al-Sadiq, sixth Iman of the Shia. Movement divided between Ismailis, Ithnaashjaris ("Twelvers") and Zaidis.
767	Death of Abu Hanifa (b. 699), founder of the Hanafi legal school.
786–809	Reign of Harun al-Rashid, model caliph of Islam's "golden age."
795	Death of Malik b. Anas (b. 713), founder of the Maliki school.
801	Death of Rabia of Basra, mystic and poet.
813–833	Caliphate of al-Mamun. Ascendancy of Mutazili ("rationalist") school of theologians.
820	Death of al-Shafi (b. 767), founder of the Shafi school of law.
847–861	Caliphate of al-Mutawakkil, who reverses pro-Mutazili policy.
861–945	Break-up of Abbasid Empire as provinces become independent until caliphate government loses territorial power completely.
855	Death of Ahmad Ibn Hanbal (b. 780), founder of Hanbali school.
870	Death of al-Bukhari (b. 810), *hadith* collector.
873	Death of Muslim (*hadith* collector. "Disappearance" of 12th Imam of the Shia, Muhammad al-Muntazar (the "Awaited One").
873–940	Lesser *ghaiba* or Absence during which Imam of Twelver Shia is represented by Four *wakils* (deputies).
874	Death of Abu Yazid al-Bistami, first of the "drunken" Sufis.
909	Creation of first Ismaili Fatimid state in Ifriqiya (present-day Tunisia).
922	Execution of al-Hallaj for heresy, a martyr for later Sufis.
929–961	Umayyad ruler Abd al-Rahman III establishes Umayyad caliphate at Cordoba (Spain).
940	Beginning of the Greater *ghayba* (absence or occultation) when Twelvers lose contact with their Imam.
945	Shii Buyids take Baghdad, making caliph a virtual prisoner.
969–1171	Fatimid (Ismaili) caliphate in Egypt.
998–1030	Mahmud of Ghazna (present-day Afghanistan) invades northern India.
1037–1220	Saljuq Turks, starting in central Iran and moving westward, restore Sunni orthodoxy to the heartlands.
1056–1167	Almoravid dynasty, originating in Subsaharan Africa, halts Christian advance in Spain.
1071	Saljuqs defeat Byzantines at Battle of Manzikert, opening Anatolia to Turkish settlement.
1090–1118	Nizari Ismaili uprisings against Sunni caliphs.
1091	Saljuqs make Baghdad their capital.
1096–1291	Crusaders hold parts of Syria and Palestine.
1099	Crusaders take Jerusalem.
1111	Death of al-Ghazali (b. 1058), Sunni mystic and jurist.
1130	Death of Ibn Tumart, founder of Almohad dynasty in Spain.
1187	Saladin (Salah al-Din al-Ayyubi) expels Crusaders from Jerusalem.
1198	Death of Ibn Rushd (Averroes) (b. 1126), philosopher.
1205–87	Rise of Delhi Sultanate in India.
1220–31	Mongol raids in Transoxiana and eastern Iran cause massive destruction of cities
1225	Almohads abandon Spain. Muslim presence reduced to small kingdom of Granada (1232–1592).
1227	Death of Chingiz Khan.
1240	Death of Ibn al-Arabi (b. 1165), Sufi theosophist.
1256	Fall of Alamut, last Ismaili stronghold south of the Caspian Sea.
1258	Destruction of Baghdad by Mongols.
1260	Mamluks (military slaves) who succeed the Ayyubids in Egypt, defeat the hitherto invincible Mongols at the Battle of Ain Jalut in Syria.
c. 1300	Emergence of Ottoman (Osmanli) dynasty in Bithynia on the Byzantine frontier in western Anatolia.
1326	Ottomans capture Bursa, their first real capital.
1362	Ottomans capture Adrianople (Edirne) in Balkans.
c. 1378	Emergence of Timur Lenk (Tamerlane) a Turk who rose in the Mongol service in Transoxiana to conquer much of central and western Asia.
1389	Ottomans defeat Serbs, assisted by Albanians, Bulgarians, Bosnians, and Hungarians, at Kosovo in central Serbia.
1405	Death of Timur.
1453	Mehmed "The Conqueror" (1451–81) captures Constantinople and subdues Byzantine Empire.
1498	Vasco da Gama rounds the Cape of Good Hope, ending Muslim monopoly of Indian Ocean trade.
1501	Rise of Safavid power in Iran. Twelver Shiism becomes the state religion.

1517	Ottomans conquer Egypt and Syria.
1526	Battle of Paniput (India) enables Babur, a Timurid prince to become founder of the Mughal Empire; Battle of Mohacs makes Catholic Hungarians tributaries of Ottomans.
1529	Ottomans besiege Vienna.
1552	Kazan Khanate annexed by Moscow.
1556–1605	Reign of Akbar, third Mughal emperor, who fosters Hindu-Muslim cultural and religious rapprochement.
1682–99	Ottomans lose Hungary and Belgrade in war with Austria and Poland.
1718	Peace of Passarowitz consolidates Ottoman losses to Habsburgs.
1739	Delhi sacked by Iranian monarch Nadir Shah, ending effective Mughal power.
1757	Wahhabis take al-Hasa in eastern Arabia. British victory at Plassey opens India to British expansion.
1762	Death of Shah Wali Allah, Sufi reformer in Sirhindi tradition.
1774	Treaty of Kuchuk Kaynarji. Following defeat by Russia, Ottomans lose Crimea. Tsar recognized as protector of Orthodox Christians in Ottoman lands.
1779	Qajar dynasty established in Iran.
1789–1807	First westernizing Ottoman reforms under Selim III.
1798	Napoleon Bonaparte lands in Egypt, defeats the Mamluks at the Battle of the Pyramids, generates interest in European culture.
1805–48	Muhammad (Mehmed) Ali begins modernizing process in Egypt.
1806	Wahhabis sack Shiite shrines of Najaf and Karbala.
1815–17	Serbian revolt against Ottomans.
1818	Britain becomes paramount power in India.
1820	Muhammad Ali begins conquest of Sudan.
1821–30	Greek War of Independence.
1830	French occupation of Algeria begins. Khartoum founded as British-Egyptian outpost on the Upper Nile.
1832–48	European powers save Ottoman sultan from invasion by Egyptian Viceroy, Muhammad Ali.
c. 1839–61	Failure of Indian "Mutiny" leads to abolition of the East India Company, opening the way for incorporation of India into British Empire.
1859	Defeat of Imam Shamil in Caucasus followed by Russian annexation of Chechnya and Daghestan.
1867	Foundation of the academy of Deoband in northern India by a group of the reformers who eschew all contact with the British.
1868	Russian annexation of Kazakhstan completed. Amirate of Bukhara becomes Russian protectorate.
1869	Opening of the Suez Canal.
1875	Collapse of Egyptian finances. Suez Canal sold to British.
1876	First Ottoman constitution promulgated after palace revolution.
1876–1909	Sultan Abd al-Hamid suspends constitution, enacting major reforms in education, transportation, and communications through dictatorial rule.
1881	French protectorate in Tunisia.
1882	British occupation of Egypt.
1885	General "Chinese" Gordon killed in Khartoum during Mahdist revolt against British-backed Egyptian rule.
1889	Return of Muhammad Abduh, al-Afghani's disciple to Egypt, decides to collaborate with the British. Military students in Istanbul found first "Young Turk" revolutionary organization, Society of Union and Progress.
1897	Death of Sayyid Jamal al-Din al-Afghani (b. 1838), pan-Islamic reformer and activist.
1898	Defeat of the Mahdist movement under an Anglo-Egyptian force under General Kitchener at the Battle of Omdurman. Death of Sir Sayyid Ahmed Khan (b. 1817), Islamic modernist reformer and founder of Aligarh College (1875).
1905	Death of Muhammad Abduh (b. 1849), founder of the modern *salafiyya* reform movement.
1906	Muslim League founded in India.
1906–08	Constitutional Revolution in Iran.
1908	Young Turk revolution forces Sultan to restore constitution and reconvene parliament.
1909	Separate Muslim and Hindu provincial electorates in India.
1911–13	Italy takes Tripoli from Ottomans.
1912	French protectorate in Morocco.
1914–18	Defeat of Ottoman Empire in First World War. Egypt formally declared British Protectorate.
1916–18	British-backed Arab revolt against Turkish rule under leadership of Sharif Hussein of Mecca, his son Faisal, and T. E. Lawrence.
1917	Balfour Declaration opens the way for increased European Jewish settlement in Palestine.
1917–20	Russian Revolution and civil war leads to Soviet–Muslim conflicts in Central Asia. Muslims of Kazakhstan, Azerbaijan, and the Caucasus struggle for regional independence. Overthrow of Autonomous Republic of Turkestan by Russian forces (1918) precipitates Basmachi revolt. Bukhara and Khiva absorbed into Soviet states. Some leading Muslim *Jadidists* (renovators) join the Communist Party.
1919	San Remo Conference. League of Nations' Mandates awarded to Britain in former Ottoman territories of Palestine, Transjordan, and Iraq, and to France in Syria and Lebanon. Faisal b. Hussein expelled by French from Damascus and established on throne of Iraq. His younger brother, Abdullah, established on throne of Transjordan. Egyptian leader Saad Zaghlul leads *wafd* (delegation) demanding independence for Egypt. His deportation sparks nationalist "revolution." Ottoman suzerainty abolished in Egypt. Britain keeps control of defence, foreign policy, Sudan, and the Suez Canal.
1919–22	Turkish War of Independence: Mustafa Kemal (Ataturk) rallies nationalist forces to defeat Greek invaders and resist European dismemberment of Anatolia.

1923 Treaty of Lausanne ensures Turkey's territorial integrity.

1924 Soviet Central Asia reorganized under socialist republics of Uzbekistan, Turkmenistan, Kazakhstan, and Kirgizia.
Ottoman Caliphate abolished. Turkish Sharia courts replaced by civil courts.
Khilafat movement in India blames British for abolition. Ibn Saud conquers Hejaz, expelling the Sharif Hussein and establishing neo-Wahhabi kingdom.

1926 Lebanon enlarged and detached from Syria under French auspices.

1928 Hasan al-Banna, Egyptian school teacher, founds the Muslim Brotherhood.

1932 Iraq granted independence and admitted to League of Nations.

1935 Death of Rashid Rida (b. 1865), Islamic reformer and leader of the *salafiyya* movement.

1936 Palestinians revolt against British rule in Palestine and the increase in Jewish immigration caused by Nazi rule in Germany. Muhammad Ali Jinnah assumes leadership of Muslim League, ending Muslim backing for Congress.
New Soviet Constitution organizes Muslim Central Asia into six Union Soviet Socialist Republics (Uzbekishan, Azerbaijan, Kazakhstan, Turkmenistan, Tajikistan, and Kirgizia) and eight Autonomous Soviet Socialist Republics including Tataristan, Bashkitia, Daghestan, and other Caucasian units under Communist control.

1938 Death of Muhammad Iqbal, poet, philosopher, and progenitor of Pakistan.

1940–47 Muslim League adopts idea of separate Muslim states for Indian Muslims.

1941 British suppress pro-Axis revolt by Iraqi army officers.

1942 British force Egyptian King Farouq to replace pro-Axis prime minister with one more amenable to the Allied cause.

1943 Beginning of Zionist terror campaign against British in Palestine

1945 Arab League founded.

1946 Transjordan, Lebanon, and Syria recognized as independent. Widespread Hindu-Muslim rioting in India.

1947 Indian independence. Creation of Pakistan out of Muslim majority areas, excepting Kashmir.

1948 British end mandate in Palestine. Arab armies routed following proclamation of Israel. Palestinian exodus creates massive refugee problem. Amir Abdullah of Transjordan annexes east Jerusalem (including the Old City and the West Bank).
Egyptian prime minister Muhammad Nuqrashi assassinated.

1949 Hasan al-Banna assassinated by Egyptian security agents in retaliation for the murder of Nuqrashi.

1952 Egyptian monarchy overthrown by Arab nationalist army officers led by Gamal Abd al-Nasser with support from the Muslim Brotherhood.

1956 Nasser nationalizes the Suez Canal, provoking Anglo–French military intervention in secret collusion with Israel.

1958 Pro-British Iraqi monarchy overthrown in bloody *coup d'étât* masterminded by General Abd al-Karim Qasim.

1963 Execution in Egypt of Sayyid Qutb, writer and Muslim Brotherhood's most militant ideologist.
Iraq's President Qasim overthrown in coup by Baathist military officers under Abd al-Salam Arif.

1965 Palestinian Liberation Organization (PLO) founded.

1967 (June) The Six Day War leaves the whole of Sinai peninsula, the West Bank (including the Old City of Jerusalem), and the Syrian Golan Heights under Israeli military control.
Yassir Arafat (Abu Ammar), commander of al-Fatah, the largest guerrilla organization, becomes leader of the PLO

1968 President Abd al-Rahman Arif (brother and successor of Abd al-Salam) overthrown by General Ahmad Hassan al-Bakr. Real power held by Saddam Hussein al-Tikriti.

1969 Pro-British Sanusi monarchy in Libya overthrown in Nasser-style *coup d'étât* led by 27-year-old Colonel Muammar al-Qadhafi.
Organization of the Islamic Conference (OIC) established to promote Islamic solidarity and foster political, economic, social, and cultural cooperation among Muslim states.

1970 Hafez al-Asad, an air force general from the Alawi (Nusairi) minority takes power in Syria at the head of the Baath Party.
Civil war in Jordan between the army and Palestinian guerrillas ("Black September").
Anwar al-Sadat succeeds to the Egyptian presidency following the death of Abd al-Nasser.

1972 Bangladesh, formerly East Pakistan, wins independence with Indian army help.

1973 October (Ramadan/Yom Kippur) War. Egypt establishes a bridgehead on the East Bank of the Suez Canal—the first major success of Arab arms against Israel.
Organization of Petroleum Exporting Countries (OPEC) under the leadership of Iran and Saudi Arabia imposes a four-fold increase in the price of crude oil, leading to massive "petrodollar" surpluses for investment in industrialized economies and support for Islamic movements (as well as worldwide economic recession).

1975 Lebanese civil war provoked, in part, by presence of militant Palestinian refugees and Israeli reprisals against them.

1977 Beginning of negotiations between Egypt and Israel.
Zia ul-Haqq, Pakistani general, assumes presidency and imposes martial law. Former President Zulfiqar Ali Bhutto executed. Zia initiates Islamization program.
Death of Ali Shariati (b. 1933), Islamist philosopher, in Southampton, Britain.

1978–79 Growing unrest in Iran against dictatorship of Shah Muhammad Reza Pahlavi.

1979 Ayatollah Khomeini returns from exile in Europe to establish the Islamic Republic in Iran. Fifty-two U.S. diplomats taken hostage and held for 444 days.
Camp David peace accords between Egypt and Israel begin the peace process between Arabs and Israelis.
Death of Abu al Ala al-Mawdudi (b. 1909), Indo-Pakistani ideologue and founder of the Jamaati-i-Islami.
President Zia ul Haqq introduces Hudood ordinance, prescribing Koranic penalties for certain categories of theft, sexual misconduct, and drinking alcohol.
Soviet invasion of Afghanistan in support of ailing Communist regime. Western training and armaments for the *mujahidin* (holy warriors) creates a well-trained cadre of Islamist militants.

1980–88 Iran–Iraq war, provoked by Iraqi attack on Iran, becomes the longest-lasting international conflict of the twentieth century, leading to the loss of at least half a million lives on the Iranian side and massive economic dislocation.

1981 Assassination of Anwar al-Sadat by Islamic extremists.

1982 Israeli invasion of Lebanon and expulsion of PLO to Tunisia. Up to 10,000 people killed in government reprisals after failed Muslim Brotherhood rebellion in Syrian city of Hama.

1987 Beginning of the *intifada*—a massive, popular uprising of Palestinians against Israeli occupation, spearheaded by stone-throwing children.

1988 Shaikh Ahmad Yasin, head of the Islamic Center in Gaza and a member of the Muslim Brotherhood, founds Hamas, the Islamic Resistance Movement.
Ayatollah Khomeini, Iran's religious leader, "swallows poison" and accepts a ceasefire with Iraq.
Death of President Zia ul-Haqq of Pakistan in suspicious air crash.
Publication of *The Satanic Verses* by British Muslim author Salman Rushdie.
Muhammad Mahmud Taha, leader of the Republican Brotherhood and a reformer with Sufi leanings, hanged for "apostasy."

1989 *Fatwa* pronounced against Rushdie by Khomeini prevents detente between Iran and the West, despite the presence of pragmatists in the government.
June: Khomeini dies and is succeeded as supreme religious leader by Ali Khamenei.
In Algeria the Islamic Salvation Front (FIS) wins 55 percent of the vote in the regional elections.

1990 Invasion of Kuwait by Iraqi leader Saddam Hussein.

1991 Operation Desert Storm, led by the United States with military support from Britain, France, Italy, Saudi Arabia, Egypt, Syria, and Pakistan, expels Iraqi troops from Kuwait. Shiite revolt in Iraqi cities of Najaf and Karbala brutally suppressed.
Disbanding of Soviet Union after failed anti-Gorbachev coup leads to independence for the former Soviet Republics of Central Asia (under the leadership of ex-members of the Soviet nomenklatura). In Tajikistan rivalry between the ex-communist leadership and Islamist opposition leads to a bitter and costly civil war.
In Algeria the FIS wins 49 percent of the vote in the first round of the general elections. The army intervenes to prevent victory for the FIS in the second round, provoking an eight-year civil war said to have cost at least 100,000 lives.

1992 Farag Foda, the prominent Egyptian humanist and writer, gunned down by Islamists in Cairo.
"No-Fly Zones" established in northern and southern Iraq to prevent Iraqi attacks on Kurdish and Shiite populations. UN sanctions imposed on Iraq lead to significant hardship among vulnerable groups, especially children.

1994 Cheb Hasni, a popular *rai* singer, murdered in France. Tahar Djaout, award-winning novelist and editor, shot outside his home in Algiers.

1995 More than 7,000 Muslims massacred at Srebrenica in Bosnia after UN fails to protect enclave from Bosnian Serb attack.

1996 Taliban movement based on *madrasa*-educated students in rural Afghanistan, capture Kabul. Their program of pacification bears harshly on women and minorities.

1997 More than 60 European tourists massacred near Luxor by Islamists.
Muhammad Khatami, former minister of culture, elected President of Iran.

1998 Taliban fighters murder between two and five thousand members of the Shiite Hazara community after the capture of Mazar-el-Sharif.
Al-Qaeda attacks the U.S. Embassies in east Africa

1999 In Algeria Abd al-Aziz Bouteflika, former foreign minister, elected President on a program of reconciliation.
Pro-democracy demonstrations in Iran suppressed by police and street gangs under conservative control.
NATO bombing campaign forces Serbs to relinquish Kosovo, reversing "ethnic cleansing" of mainly Muslim Albanians.
Russia bombs Chechnya on pretext of suppressing "Islamic terrorism."

2000 (February) Russians occupy Grozni, the capital of Chechnya.
In Pakistan, General Pervez Musharraf overthrows democratically-elected government of Nawaz Sharif.

2001 (September) Suicide hijackers linked to al-Qaeda attack the World Trade Center in New York and the Pentagon in Washington, killing approximately 3,000 people.
U.S. bombs Afghanistan, removing Taliban regime.

2002 (October) Terrorist group linked to al-Qaeda kills more than 200 people, mostly Australians, in bombing of nightclub in Bali, Indonesia.

2003 (March) U.S. and U.K. attack Iraq without UN support, on pretext that Saddam Hussein is hiding weapons of mass destruction. No such weapons found.
Islamist terrorists linked to al-Qaeda kill civilians in Casablanca, Riyadh, Istanbul, and other cities.
(December) Saddam Hussein captured near his home town of Tikrit.

Glossary

Abd — "Servant" or "slave"; commonly used as a name when coupled with one of the names of Allah. *See also* Ibada.

Adhan — Call to prayer performed by muadhin (muezzin).

Ahl al-Bait — "People of the household"; specifically used on the Phophet's household.

Ahl al-Kitab — "People of the book"; originally referred to Muslims, Jews, and Christians but came to include Zoroastrians and other groups prossessing sacred texts.

Ahl al-Sunna — "People of the Sunna" (Sunnis); those who uphold customs based on the practice and authority of the Prophet and his companions, as distinct from the Shiites and Kharijis. *See also* Sunna.

Al — "Clan" or "House"; as in Al Imran (3rd Sura of Koran), Al Saud, etc. Not to be confused with al-, the definite article.

Alawi — Member of ghulu (extremist) Nusairi sect in northeastern Syria which venerates Ali.

Alid — Descendant of Ali, cousin and son-in-law of the Prophet.

Alim — *See* Ulama.

Amir — "Commander"; originally military commander but subsequently applied to rulers and members of their families. Amir al-Muminin ("Commander of the Faithful"), a title held by caliphs and some sultans.

Ansar — "Helpers" of Muhammad native to Medina, as distinct from the Muhajirun who accompanied him from Mecca.

Asabiya — Tribal or group solidarity; a term used by philosopher Ibn Khaldun in his theory on state formation in North Africa.

Ashura — The tenth of the month Muharram, when Shiite rituals are held commemorating the death of the Prophet's grandson Hussein.

Aya — "Sign" or "miracle"; used for verses of the Koran.

Baraka — "Sanctity" or "blessing" vested in, and available from, holy people, places, or objects.

Bast — "Twelver' Shiite institution of sanctuary in mosques and other holy places.

Baya — "Contract" or oath of allegiance binding members of an Islamic sect or Sufi tariqa to their spiritual guide.

Chador — Traditional Iranian garment covering women from head to foot. *See also* Hijab.

Dai — "Propagandist" or missionary, especially in Shiite Ismaili movements. *See also* Dawa.

Dar al-Harb — The "realm of war" or those lands not under Muslim rule, where, under certain circumstances, a war or jihad can be sanctioned against unbelievers.

Dar al-Islam — "Realm of Islam"; originally those lands under Muslim rule, later applying to lands where Muslim institutions were established.

Dawa — "Propaganda" or mission.

Dervish — "Mendicant"; member of a Sufi tariqa.

Dhikr — "Mentioning" or "remembering"; specifically used for Sufi rituals designed to increase consciousness of God which include the repetition of his name(s).

Dhimmi — Non-Muslim peoples afforded security of life and dhimma (property) under the Sharia on payment of a jizya (poll tax).

Din — "Religion" or "belief" as opposed to dunya (worldly existence).

Dua — Prayer (additional to salat).

Fana — The extinction of individual consciousness, and thus union with God, in Sufism.

Faqih — Exponent of fiqh.

Faqir — "Pauper"; term applied to ordinary member of Sufi tariqa.

Fatwa — Legal decision of a mufti.

Fidaiyyia — Soldiers prepared to sacrifice their lives in the cause of Islam. Now used for guerrilla fighters. (Singular: fidai.)

Fiqh — "Understanding" of Sharia, the system of jurisprudence based on the usul al-fiqh.

Fitna — "Temptation" or "trial"; the name given to the civil wars which broke out within the expanding Muslim empire during the first 200 years after Muhammad's death.

Ghaib — "Unseen" and "transcendent"; hence al-ghaiba, the "occultation" of the Hidden Imans in Shiite doctrine.

Hadith — "Tradition" or report of a saying or action of the Prophet. One of four roots of Islamic law. *See also* Sharia, Usul al-fiqh.

Hajj — The annual pilgrimage to Mecca. One of the five rukns (duties) of Islam, required of every believer once in his life if possible.

Halal — That which is "permissible", particularly foods which comply with Islamic dietary rules.

Hanafi — Referring to the Sunni legal madhhab ascribed to Abu Hanifa.

Hanbali — Referring to the Sunni legal madhhab ascribed to Abu Hanbal.

Haram — A sanctuary, "that which is forbidden" by the Sharia.

Hijab — "Screen", veil traditionally worn by Muslim women in public. Always covers the head, but not necessarily the face and hands.

Hijra — "Emigration" of Muhammad from Mecca to Medina in 622 CE, the base year of the Muslim calender.

Ibada — Religious worship.

Id al-Adha — "The festival of the sacrifice" on the last day of the Hajj.

Id al-Fitr "The festival of breaking the fast" at the end of Ramadan.

Ijima Consensus of the Muslim community or scholars as a basis for a legal decision. Shiites interpret it as a consensus of Imams.

Ijtihad Individual judgement to establish a legal ruling by creative interpretation of the existing body of law. *See also* Muijtahid.

Ikhwan The "Brothers", soldiers of Abd al-Aziz, founder of the Saudi dynasty, and adherents of the Hanbali reformer, Abd al-Wahhab.

Ikhwan al-Muslimin Muslim Brotherhood, a society founded in 1929 by Hasan al-Banna; originally aimed at reestablishing a Muslim polity in Egypt.

Ilm "Knowledge"; in particular, religious knowledge, of ulama.

Imam "One who stands in front" to lead the salat, hence the leader of the Muslim community. In Shiite tradition, Ali and those of his descendants considered to be the spiritual successors of Muhammad.

Iman "Faith" or religious conviction.

Infitah The "opening up" of the Egyptian economy to the West in 1972, in the hope of attracting foreign investment.

Islam "Self-surrender" or "submission"; reconcilliation to the will of God as revealed to Muhammad. *See also* Muslim.

Isnad "Support"; chain of authorities transmitting a hadith, thus guaranteeing its validity.

Jafari Referring to the sole Shiite madhhab ascribed to the Imam Jafar al-Sadiq.

Jahl "Ignorance", hence jahiliya (period of ignorance), or pre-Islamic times.

Jihad War against unbelievers in accordance with Sharia. Also applied to an individual's struggle against baser impulses.

Jizya Poll tax levied on dhimmis in a Muslim-ruled society.

Kaba Cubic building in Mecca containing the Black Stone, believed by Muslims to be a fragment of the original temple of Abraham. Focus of salat (prayer) and the Hajj. *See also* Qibla.

Kafir "Disbeliever" or infidel who has rejected the message of the Koran.

Khalifa Caliph, the "deputy" of God on earth. In the Koran applied to Adam, and hence to all humanity in relation to the rest of creation; specifically applied to the early successors of the Prophet as leaders of the Islamic state or khilafa, and to the successors of founders of Islamic states or Sufi tariqas.

Khaniqa Sufi hospice, mainly in areas of Persian influence.

Kharijis "Those who go out"; members of a group of puritanical Muslim sects during Umayyad and early Abbasid times. (Arabic plural: Khawarij.)

Khums "Fifth', a tax of one-fifth of all trading profits, payable to mujtahids in Shiite areas.

Khutba Sermon preached at Friday prayers.

Kiswa Black clothing or covering of the Kaba, renewed annually.

Kitab "The book", or religious scriptures.

Koran (Quran) "Discourse" or "recitation", the immutable body of revelations received by Muhammad.

Kufr "Disbelief", an ungrateful rejection of Islam. *See also* Kafir.

Kuttab School at which the Koran is taught.

Madhhab "Adopted policy", specifically applied to five recognized systems of fiqh (jurisprudence).

Madrasa "College", especially for religious studies.

Maghrib "Sunset", hence the salat (prayer) at sunset. Also Muslim "occident", i.e., northeastern Africa, Morocco, for which the French transliteration "Maghreb" is commonly used.

Mahdi "Awaited One"; a Messiah and reformist leader who aims to restore the original purity of the Islamic faith and polity. In Shiite tradition the Twelfth Imam.

Maliki Referring to the Sunni legal madhhab ascribed to Malik ibn Anas.

Maruf "Known", term used in the Koran for familiar and approved custom; hence, generally, "the good."

Mashriq "Sunrise"; Levant.

Maslaha That which is "beneficial"; term used for the principle of public interest in the Maliki madhhab, adopted by modern legal reformers.

Mawlid "Birthday"; festival celebrating the anniversary of a religious figure.

Mawali "Associates" or "clients"; status at first given to non-Arab converts to Islam. (Singular: Mawla.)

Mihrab Niche in wall of mosque indicating Qibla.

Millet Non-Muslim religious community within the Dar al-Islam.

Mufti Expert on the Sharia, qualified to give fatwas (rulings) upon questions of law.

Muhajirin Those who emigrated from Mecca to Medina with Muhammad. See also Hijra.

Mujahid Soldier fighting a holy war or jihad. (Plural: Mujadidun.)

Mujtahid Religious scholars sanctioned to make individual interpretations to determine points of law, especially among Shia.

Mukhabarat Intelligence services, security police.

Munkar "Unknown"; term used in the Koran for wrongful action as distinct from maruf: hence evil generally.

Murid — "Aspirant", or follower of a Sufi master.

Murshid — Sufi master.

Muslim — One who has submitted to God; a follower of the religion revealed to, and established by, Muhammad. *See also* Islam.

Mutazilis — "Those who stand aloof"; theologians belonging to the rationalist school which introduced speculative dogmatism into Islam.

Nisab — Minimum amount of wealth prior to assessment for zakat.

Pir — Persian Sufi master.

Qadi — Judge administering Sharia.

Qibla — Direction of the Kaba to which Muslims turn while praying, hence the recess in a mosque which shows it.

Qiyas — "Analogy"; the principle in jurisprudence used to deal with new situations not mentioned in the Koram or Sunna.

Ribat — Sufi hospice.

Risala — "Report" or "epistle". (Plural: rasail.)

Rukn — "Pillar'; one of the five religious duties prescribed for Muslims—hajj, salat, sawm, shahada, and zakat.

Sadaqa — Voluntary contribution of alms.

Salaf — "Predecessors"; appellation of the first generation of Muslims. Salafi: term describing the twentieth-century reform movement inspired by them.

Salat — Ritual worship performed five times daily, one of the rukns (five pillars) of Islam.

Sawm — Annual fast and daylight abstinence during the month of Ramadan, one of the rukns of Islam.

Sayyid — Descendent of Ali's son Hussein. Sidi (local usage in the Maghrib) is applied to members of saintly lineages.

Shahada — Profession of faith whereby a Muslim declares his acceptance of God and his Prophet; one of the rukns of Islam.

Shaikh — "Elder"; head of a tribe or Sufi master.

Sharia — "The path to a water-hole'; a name given to the sacred law of Islam which governs all aspects of a Muslim's life. It is elaborated through the discipline of fiqh.

Shia — "Party' of Ali, comprising those groups of Muslims who uphold the rights of Ali and his descendants to leadership of the Umma.

Shirk — "Association" of partners to the divinity; idolatry.

Silsila — "Chain" of baraka (inherited sanctity) or kinship connecting the leaders of Sufi orders to their founders.

Sufi — Follower of Sufism, the Islamic mystic path, from suf (wool) garments worn by early adepts. (Arabic: tasawwuf.)

Sunna — Custom sanctioned by tradition, particularly that of the Prophet enshrined in hadith.

Sunni — *See* Ahl al-Sunna.

Sura — Chapter of the Koran.

Sultan — "Authority" or "power"; actual holder of power, as distinct from the khalifa; later common term for sovereign.

Tahlil — Prayer—la ilaha illa allah (there is no deity but God)—particularly used in Sufi rituals.

Taifa — Organization of a Sufi order, as distinct from its spiritual path.

Takbir — The phrase "Allahu Akbar" (God is most great).

Tanzimat — Administrative decrees, reforms instituted by the nineteenth-century Ottoman sultans.

Taqiya — Dissimultation of one's beliefs in the face of danger, especially among Shiites.

Taqlid — "Imitation", or the basing of legal decisions on the existing judgments of the four Sunni madhhabs.

Tariqa — "Path" of mystical and spiritual guidance. A term which also came to be applied to the organization through which a tariqa extends itself in Muslim society.

Tasawwuf — *See* Sufi.

Tawaf — Ritual circumambulation of the Kaba by a pilgrim during the Hajj or Umra.

Tawhid — "Unity" of God. Central theological concept of Islam.

Tawil — Esoteric or allegorical interpretation of the Koran, predominant among Shiites.

Tekkes — Sufi centers in Turkish-speaking areas.

Ulama — "Learned men', in particular the guardians of legal and religious traditions. (Singular: alim.)

Umma — Community of believers, in particular the community of all Muslims.

Umra — Lesser pilgrimage to Mecca which can be performed at any t ime of the year.

Usul (al Fiqh) — "Roots" or foundations of jurisprudence. In the Sunni madhhabs they comprise: The Koran, the Sunna, ijma (consensus) and qiyas (analogical deduction). *See also* Fiqh.

Wali — "One who is near God"; a saint in popular Sufism.

Waqf — Pious endowment of income, originally for a charitable purpose; sometimes used as a means of circumventing the Sharia's inheritance laws.

Watan — "Homeland" or "nation", a concept borrowed from Western nationalism.

Wazir — Administrator or bureaucrat apponted by the ruler.

Zakat — "Purity", a term used for a tax of fixed proportion of income and capital (normally 2½ percent) payable annually for charitable purposes; one of the rukns of Islam.

Zawiya — "Corner"; building for Sufi activities.

Further Reading

Ahmed, Akbar S., *Living Islam – From Samarkand to Stornoway*, London, 1993.

Ahmed, Akbar and Donnan, Hastings, (eds.) *Islam, Globalization and Postmodernity*, London, 1994.

Ahmed, Leila, *Women and Gender in Islam: Historical Roots of a Modern Debate*, New Haven, CT., 1994.

Ali Addallah Yusuf, (tr.) *The Holy Quran* (with commentary), Leicester, 1979.

Al-Qaradawi, Yusuf, *The Lawful and the Prohibited in Islam*, Helbawy et.al. (tr.), Indianapolis, ID., 1985.

Arberry, A.J. *The Koran Interpreted*, Oxford, 1990.

Armstrong, Karen, *Muhammad: A Western Attempt to Understand Islam*, London, 1991.

Asad, Muhammad, *The Message of the Quran*, Gibraltar, 1980.

Beinin, Joel and Stock, Joe, (eds.) *Political Islam: Essays from Middle East Report*, London, 1997.

Bell, Richard, *Introduction to the Quran* (1953), ed. and rev. W.M. Watt, Edinburgh, 1978.

Bouhdiba, Abdalwahab, *Sexuality in Islam*, (tr.) Alan Sheridan, London, 1985.

Cook, Michael, *Muhammad*, Oxford, 1983

Coon, Carleton S., *Caravan: The Story of the Middle East*, rev. edn., New York, NY.., 1961.

Coulson, N.J., *A History of Islamic Law*, Edinburgh, 1964.

Daftary, Farhad, *A Short History of the Ismailis*, Edinburgh, 1998.

Denny, Frederick Mathewson, *An Introduction to Islam*, New York, NY., 1985

Donner, Fred, *Early Islamic Conquests*, Cambridge, MA., 1982.

Eickelman, Dale F., *The Middle East: An Anthropological Approach*, Englewood Cliffs, NJ., 1981/1989.

Edge, Ian (ed.) *Islamic Law and Legal Theory*, Aldershot, 1996.

Geertz, Clifford, *Islam Observed,* New Haven, CT., 1968.

Gibb, H.A.R., Bernard Lewis, et al., (eds.) *Encyclopaedia of Islam*, 6 vols. Leiden, 1962.

Gilsenan, Michael, *Recognizing Islam*, London, 1983.

Guillaume, A. (tr.) *The Life of Muhammad: A Translation of Ibn Ishaq's Sirat Rasul Attah*, Karachi and London, 1955.

Hodgson, Marshall G.S., *The Venture of Islam: Conscience and History in a World Civilization*, 3 vols., Chicago, IL., 1974.

Hourani, Albert, *Arabic Thought in the Liberal Age*, Oxford, 1969.

Hourani, Albert, *A History of the Arab Peoples*, 2nd ed. London, 2000.

Ibn Khaldun, *The Muqadimmah: An Introduction to History*, F. Rosenthal (tr.) 3 vols., New York, NY., 1958; ed. and abridged by N. Dawood, London, 1978.

Keddie, N.R., (ed.) *Scholars, Saints and Sufis: Muslim Religions Institutions Since 1500*, Berkeley, CA., 1973.

Lapidus, Ira, *A History of the Islamic Peoples*, 2nd ed. Cambridge, 2002.

Mayer, Ann Elizabeth, *Islam and Human Rights: Tradition and Politics*, Boulder, CO., 1991.

Mernissi, Fatima, *Women and Islam: An Historical and Theological Enquiry*, (tr.) Mary Jo Lakeland, Oxford, 1991.

Momen, Moojan, *An Introduction to Shi'i Islam*, New Haven, CT., 1985.

Peters, F.E., *Muhammad and the Origins of Islam*, Albany, NY., 1994.

Rahman, Fazlur, *Islam*, Chicago, 1979.

Richard, Yann, *Shi'ite Islam*, (tr.) Antonia Nevill. Oxford, 1995.

Rodinson, M., *Mohamed*, Harmondsworth, 1971.

Rosen, Lawrence, *The Anthropology of Justice – Law as Culture in Islamic Society*, Cambridge, 1989.

Roy, Olivier, *The Failure of Political Islam*, London, 1994.

Ruthven, Malise, *Islam: A Very Short Introduction*, Oxford, 2000.

Ruthven, Malise, *Islam in the World*, 2nd ed. London, 2000.

Ruthven, Malise, *A Fury for God: The Islamist Attack on America,* London, 2002.

Said, Edward, *Orientalism*, London, 1978.

Schacht, Joseph, *An Introduction to Islamic Law*, Oxford, 1964.

Trimingham, J.S., *The Sufi Orders in Islam*, Oxford, 1971.

Waines, David, *An Introduction to Islam*, Cambridge, 1995.

Watt, W.M., *Muhammad at Mecca*, Oxford, 1953.

Watt, W.M., *Muhammad at Medina*, Oxford, 1956.

Acknowledgments

Most of the essays accompanying the maps in this volume were written by Malise Ruthven, with editorial overview provided by Professor Azim Nanji (with contributions on pages 24–25, 66–69, 96–102), and, for Harvard University Press, Professor Nur Yalman and Kathleen McDermott. In preparing the texts and maps special mention should be made of the works of two outstanding American scholars of Islam: Marshall G.S. Hodgson's *The Venture of Islam* (3 volumes, University of Chicago Press, 1974) and Ira Lapidus's magisterial *A History of Islamic Societies* (revised ed., Cambridge University Press, 2002). Sheila Blair and Jonathan Bloom wrote the texts and kindly provided the cartographical information for pp. 172–179. The following also contributed to the text: Dr. Jonathan Meri (p. 36–37); Dr. Nader El-Bizri (p. 38-39), Farhad Daftari (p. 50–51); Dr. Zulfikar Hirji (p. 76–77, 152–153); Safaroz Niyozof (p. 94–95); Richard Gott (p. 116–117); Dan Plesch (p. 150–151, 164–165); Trevor Mostyn (p. 162–163, 192–193); Mustafa Draper (p. 166–169); Nacim Pak (p. 188–189). Dr. Abdou Filali Ansari contributed to the initial discussions concerning the choice of subjects.

The publishers would like to thank the following picture libraries for their kind permission to use their pictures and illustrations:

The Collection of Prince and Princess Sadruddin Aga Khan 10, 35, 173
Bodleian Library, Oxford 11
Werner Forman Archive 16
Hulton Getty Archive 17, 36, 44, 49, 53, 59, 62, 91, 101, 102, 111, 112, 114, 118, 132, 146, 150, 152, 156, 160, 169, 180, 185, 188, 193
Corbis 21
e.t. archive 24, 72, 82, 84
Metropolitan Museum of Art 26
Deutsches Archaiologisches Institut, Madrid 28
Aga Khan Trust for Culture, Geneva 30, 74, 80, 94, 122, 170
Bibliothèque Nationale, Paris 31, 57, 64, 177
Bildarchiv Steffens 39, 147
Cartographica Limited 40, 43, 76
Bildarchiv Preußischer Kulturbasitz 51, 172
David N. Kidd 69
Ianthe Ruthven 71
D. Dagli Orti, Paris 78, 88
Agence Rapho, Paris 87
Institute of Oriental Studies of the Russian Academy of Science 92
Images Colour Library 128
British Museum 131
Foto-Thome, Germany 167
Dr Omar Khalidi 171
Institut Amatller, Barcelona 176
Mamoun Sakkal 195

For Cartographica Limited:
Illustration: Peter A.B. Smith
Cartography: Francesca Bridges, Peter Gamble, Isabelle Lewis, Jeanne Radford, Malcolm Swanston and Jonathan Young
Typesetting: Jeanne Radford
Picture Research: Annabel Merullo and Michéle Sabèse

Map List

Index